THE TEXAS WAY

Money, Power, Politics, and Ambition at the University

WILLIAM H. CUNNINGHAM

WITH MONTY JONES

BRISCOE CENTER
FOR AMERICAN HISTORY
THE UNIVERSITY OF TEXAS AT AUSTIN

Distributed by Tower Books, an imprint of
the University of Texas Press

This book is dedicated to my family and to the outstanding staff and faculty at the University of Texas at Austin. Together, they have brought great pleasure to me for more than forty years.

Frontispiece: William H. Cunningham preparing to take office as president of the University of Texas at Austin, August 12, 1985. *UT Office of Public Affairs Records, Dolph Briscoe Center for American History, the University of Texas at Austin, e_utopa_00010.*

Contents

Preface

When Bill Cunningham approached me about publishing *The Texas Way*, his memoir of his leadership at the University of Texas, I could see that there were multiple reasons for the Briscoe Center to get the manuscript into print. The Briscoe Center's policy is to publish book projects that are based on our archival, artifact, and library collections. Not only is Bill's superb memoir significant enough to deserve publication on that basis alone, but it also has numerous connections with our holdings, which include the archives of the University of Texas at Austin and the UT System.

The Briscoe Center serves as the official repository for these historically valuable records, notably those of the Office of the President of the University of Texas, as well as the Office of the Chancellor of the University of Texas System. We hold the papers of numerous faculty members, administrators, student organizations and publications, and more. We are also the home of the Shirley Bird Perry Oral History Project, named for Bill's close friend and colleague, which includes an extensive interview with Bill and interviews with faculty, administrators, regents, and donors whose tenures overlapped his. In addition, we have the papers of Bernard Rapoport, Bill's friend and advisor who served as chairman of the UT Board of Regents, and Ann Richards, the governor of Texas during an important period of Cunningham's tenure as chancellor. As a result, the Briscoe Center has extensive documentation of Bill's career at the university as a faculty member, dean, and president, as well as his service as chancellor of the UT System.

Among his many achievements at the university, Bill also played a significant, even critical, role in the creation and development of the Briscoe Center. In 1986, during one of many times of severe stress on the university budget, he provided nearly $1 million to the center for the acquisition of the Natchez Trace Collection. This massive archival treasure trove elevated the center to a position of national leadership in the study of the cotton and slave economy of the antebellum South. In 1988, Bill persuaded Houston oilman and former university regent J. R. Parten to fund the Parten Chair in the Archives of American History, the first unrestricted endowment in the center's history. The Parten Chair made it possible for the center to significantly expand its programs and acquisitions.

Bill also played a leading role in the addition of three historically significant properties to the center's portfolio. In 1991 he directed the transfer of ownership of the Sam Rayburn Museum in Bonham to the university, where it became part of the center. In 1995 he led the way for Winedale Historical Complex in Round Top to join the center and helped establish the center as an independent organized research unit at the university, a key move in our administrative development. In 1998 Bill worked with UT President Larry Faulkner to make the John Nance Garner Museum (now the Briscoe-Garner Museum) in Uvalde a division of the center. The impact he has had on the Briscoe Center's development is just one example of the impact he has had across the Austin campus and on the University of Texas System as a whole. There are few people who can claim that same legacy.

But perhaps the most important reason for publishing this book is that it expertly fills a void in the historical record, as there are few monographs on the university's history, especially on this era. Bill and his co-author Monty Jones have exhaustively researched and meticulously prepared this book, one that will undoubtedly become a valued resource for anyone interested in the University of Texas and in higher education.

DON CARLETON, PH.D.
J. R. PARTEN CHAIR IN THE ARCHIVES
OF AMERICAN HISTORY
EXECUTIVE DIRECTOR, THE DOLPH BRISCOE
CENTER FOR AMERICAN HISTORY

Foreword

Bill Cunningham was a *wunderkind* of the academic universe and remains a gifted and multi-faceted leader and teacher today. Over the last five decades, I have been privileged to know some of the most talented and accomplished leaders in public and private life, and Bill Cunningham stands tall among those colossi.

When I first met Bill more than thirty years ago, I was immediately taken by this tall, good humored, obviously intelligent, and affable young marketing professor, brimming with a superabundance of energy and a very palpable personal presence. I thought to myself: "This guy is special." In terms of velocity and trajectory, however, I did not comprehend that I was present at the career equivalent of a Cape Canaveral rocket launch.

As Bill speedily ascended the academic ladder at the University of Texas at Austin and the UT System, I watched with admiration and awe as he intelligently and pragmatically coped with numerous and sometimes inflammatory issues, while retaining the devotion and allegiance of even those who had been his rivals for preferment. Ultimately, Bill served for seven years as president of the University of Texas at Austin and eight years as chancellor of the UT System. In terms of the academic world, that is a record rivaling the age of Methuselah.

Being *any* major university president is an exceedingly complex and achingly difficult job under any and all circumstances. One has to "wrestle" with the governing body of the institution; the faculty, many of them tenured; the alumni; the generation of donations; media attention; and a student body abrim with testosterone, estrogen, and an exuberant sense of freedom and newly invigorated self-importance.

These juggling act complexities are magnified many fold, however, in the case of a major university that is *public*. Why? Because public universities are directly involved in an ongoing political process, where all of their constituencies, official and unofficial, have access to influence the governing legislature and gubernatorial administration and, moreover, their educational institutions are constantly in competition for public funds with other governmental needs, wants, desires and predilections, including, in a large and populous state, other public universities and systems. In extreme instances, the legislature can even redefine or reshape the goals, structure, leadership and functioning of a university. By way of flavorful outré examples, one public Texas university ran afoul of the chair of the House Appropriations Committee and, as a result, the university received a total two-year appropriation of $12,000 in the initial House appropriations bill, while a newly appointed, truly delightful and jocular public university leader told me, with a big grin, that in order to retain his job his first priority had to be "beating LSU in football."

Bill Cunningham's memoirs are a fascinating, intriguing, and visceral confirmation of the diverse and often labyrinthine problems confronting a public university leader as well as an entertaining "manual," applicable in principle to leading any kind of life or institution, on astute, pragmatic problem resolution, solution and avoidance. His tongue-in-cheek asides enliven its pages as he grapples with surmounting bureaucratic obstacles to creating an Executive MBA program and a "School" of Accounting; deals with neighborhood opposition to a university land acquisition; expands the university's science curriculum to make it more contemporaneously impactful; struggles with over-enrollment problems; focuses on putting the Bass Concert Hall on a self-sustaining basis; raises a prodigious amount of private funds to both better and enlarge the offerings of the university; deals with the denouement of a seminal lawsuit; strives to increase minority student and faculty recruitment and retention; confronts "hazing" issues; handles student protests; deals with the complexities, nuances, and issues of a high-achieving athletics program; works to enhance the economic development of Austin and Texas; and deals wisely and successfully with the Texas Legislature as to the funding and programmatic needs of the university and higher education *in toto*.

Herb Kelleher and William H. Cunningham in a Graduate School of Business class-room on January 30, 2003. *Courtesy of William H. Cunningham.*

Bill's book will delight aficionados of the University of Texas and the UT System as they relive the events and personalities of his long reign, but its informational and educational ambit is far greater for those who seek to learn to excel by "doing," by accomplishment, in both demanding and sometimes tribulous circumstances. My personal witnessing and comprehension of what it requires to be an outstanding public university leader led me to recommend four former university chancellors for membership on the Southwest Airlines Board of Directors, whom I collectively and facetiously referred to as "the Dead Chancellors Society," in reference to the movie *Dead Poets Society.*

Bill Cunningham has been an insightful, wise, innovative, enjoyable, focused and collaborative board committee chairman and lead director at Southwest Airlines for many years. His contributions to Southwest's well being are immeasurable in value, and his people-

oriented personality has motivated him, on a regular basis, to address
our Management in Training Classes, a most unusual dedication and
participation by a corporate board member. Bill is also, at heart, a risk-
taking entrepreneur who has helped to start a number of new businesses and jokingly refers to himself as an "aspiring capitalist pig."

Yes, Bill Cunningham is truly a "man for all seasons," who has
led a fabulously successful and contributory life. His memoirs are not
only most enjoyable reading but tremendously instructive on how to
cope with and conquer variegated sets of problems. For those who
strive to learn from life, his memoirs should in fact, be their catechism.

I began by stating that Bill "was" a *wunderkind*. I was mistaken. In
heart, mind, and spirit Bill Cunningham will *always* be a *wunderkind*!
If you desire to be a perpetual *wunderkind* yourself, read Bill Cunningham's memoirs.

HERB KELLEHER
FOUNDER AND CHAIRMAN EMERITUS,
SOUTHWEST AIRLINES

Acknowledgments

I first conceived of this book in 2000 toward the end of my eight-year tenure as chancellor of the University of Texas System, which followed my seven years as president of UT Austin. I was aware that no UT leader had ever attempted to write a comprehensive account of the main issues and events of his administrative career, and I dared to think that my unique perspective on the period of my presidency and chancellorship would be of interest—at least to those who care deeply about the university and its history—and perhaps also to those in the wider world who are concerned about issues such as educational opportunity, the advancement of knowledge in the sciences and humanities, the role of higher education in economic development, and, yes, even less lofty topics such as intercollegiate athletics and the rough-and-tumble world of statehouse politics.

Many colleagues and friends encouraged me to pursue this book, and an opportunity to start the project arose a few years later when my eventual coauthor, Monty Jones, retired from his position in the public affairs office of the UT System. Monty had worked with me since 1990 as a liaison with the news media, a speechwriter, and a writer and editor on numerous projects. He brought to his assignments at the university a wealth of knowledge about the media and higher education, principally from his work as the higher education reporter at the *Austin American-Statesman*. Given this background, as well as our always congenial working relationship and his deep understanding of my way of thinking and my relationship with the university, I could not have hoped to find a more suitable collaborator on this book. It is certain that I could not have brought this project to a completion without his able assistance.

We were aided at every step by my longtime executive associate, Connie Saathoff, whose outstanding organizational skills and attention to detail helped keep the project manageable and on schedule. Connie kept track of our numerous drafts of chapters, organized meetings, assisted with research, and kept the many other activities of my office running smoothly. Connie also kept charge of my computerized calendar, which became rather old-fashioned in recent years but was one of the first of its kind when Darwin Klingman (a business professor and computer genius) devised it when I was serving as president. That searchable calendar facilitated our research by enabling Connie to pinpoint meetings and participants over the fifteen years that I served as president and chancellor.

I owe debts of gratitude to many people who served as sounding boards to check my memories and interpretations of events and who read and commented on various drafts of the chapters. Perhaps more than anyone else upon whom I called, I relied on Shirley Bird Perry to check my recollections against hers and to balance my perspective with her own finely nuanced understanding of the university and the complex issues it faced. The book benefits enormously from Shirley Bird's incomparable perspective on the history and contemporary events of the university.

Ed Sharpe read and commented on the entire manuscript and advised me on many instances when I needed to qualify or amplify an account of events. Herb Kelleher also read the entire manuscript and made numerous useful comments, as well as graciously consenting to write the foreword.

Mike Millsap and two of his former colleagues in the UT System office of government relations, Armando Diaz and Tom Scott, read and commented on the chapters dealing directly with state politics. They also joined Monty and me for several discussion sessions where we hashed out our varying memories of not only what happened in the offices and hallways of the legislature but also why events happened as they did. Tom also was extraordinarily generous with his time in helping research the material that makes up Chapter 31, "The Numbers Tell the Story." Jess Hay also read the chapters dealing with politics, as well as several others, and his comments proved invaluable.

Charlie Mullins read and advised me on the chapters dealing with health affairs, particularly the story of the origins of the Regional Academic Health Center in the Lower Rio Grande Valley. Tom Staley commented on several chapters, particularly the final chapter, which attempts to provide a context and perspective for the current state of higher education in Texas and what may lie in the future.

Others who read and commented on chapters in their areas of expertise included Bill Collier, a former reporter at the *Austin American-Statesman* and former head of public relations at Freeport-McMoRan Inc.; Randy Wallace, associate vice chancellor-controller and chief budget officer at the UT System; Henry Bose, professor of molecular genetics and microbiology in the UT Austin School of Biological Sciences; Mary Ann Rankin, dean of the UT Austin College of Natural Sciences from 1994 to 2011; Darcy Hardy, executive director of the UT TeleCampus from 1997 to 2010; and Butch Worley, currently deputy director of men's athletics at UT Austin and a member of the staff of athletics director DeLoss Dodds since 1987.

Francie Frederick and her staff at the Office of the Board of Regents of the UT System responded with speed and efficiency when I asked them to research a variety of details that would certainly be lost to history without their valuable records.

Two former students at UT Austin read the chapters related to student affairs and took time from their busy schedules to meet with me and Monty over breakfast at Cisco's to discuss their unique perspectives on the university. They are Howard Nirken, an undergraduate during the 1990s, and Darrick Eugene, who was active in the Black Student Alliance as an undergraduate in the 1980s. Both later graduated from the UT School of Law and are now distinguished attorneys in Austin.

Although I have benefited greatly from the comments of these readers and the book is more factually accurate and more nuanced in its interpretations because of their comments, the book remains an account of events from my perspective. I alone am responsible for the interpretation reflected in the book and for any errors that remain.

John Butler, the director of IC²—the UT Austin research center founded by my mentor, George Kozmetsky—and Robert Peterson, associate vice president for research at UT Austin, encouraged me to undertake the challenge of telling the university's story during a time of dramatic and far-reaching change, and IC² generously supported the project through a series of summer research grants.

The staff of the Research and Collections Division of the Dolph Briscoe Center for American History provided unfailing assistance in research involving the archives of UT Austin and the UT System, as well as the photography collections and other research resources at the Briscoe Center. The division's highly professional and efficient staff—led by Brenda Gunn, director of the division, and Margaret Schlankey, head of reference services—included Steve Arcieri, Catherine Best, Roy Hinojosa, Evan Hocker, Kathryn Kenefick, Stephanie Malmros, and John Wheat. Also serving on this staff was Ralph Elder, who deserves special recognition for his extraordinary knowledge of the university's history and the archival record.

Don Carleton, director of the Briscoe Center, was an early supporter of the project and provided encouragement and insightful advice at numerous times as the project progressed. His interest in having the Briscoe Center serve as publisher of the book was most gratifying. Thanks go also to Dave Hamrick, director of the University of Texas Press, for the press's involvement as the book's distributor.

Holly Taylor, editor and head of publications at the Briscoe Center, and Erin Purdy, the center's associate director for publications, ably guided the manuscript through the process of editing and design. The manuscript was improved in countless ways by copy editor Janice Pinney.

I cannot express the gratitude that I owe to my wife, Isabella, for her support and the willingness of her and our son, John, to excuse me from numerous family obligations to give me the time to pursue the project. Isabella also helped greatly to facilitate the research for the book through her faithful collection of news clippings and other materials about our careers at the university through the years. Isabella and I are grateful to our daughter-in-law, Jessica, and our grandchildren, Hudson, Isabella, and Harrison, for being part of our family and contributing so much to the quality of our lives.

Throughout this book I have acknowledged the profound impact of numerous colleagues and friends in ensuring that UT Austin and the UT System have been able to fulfill their missions on behalf of the people of Texas. I also want to acknowledge here my special debt to a select group of people who served as my personal mentors through the many years that I have been associated with the university—Sam Barshop, Alan Blake, Tom Craddick, Ed Cundiff, Peter Flawn, Jess Hay, George Kozmetsky, Wales Madden, Shirley Bird Perry, Bernard Rapoport, David Saathoff, Tom Uher, and Brook Whitaker. In addition, I have been very fortunate to have had a professional association with a number of nationally prominent business leaders. I would like to thank the following individuals from the business community who have been particularly strong mentors of mine: Shelby Carter, Herb Kelleher, Ben Love, Jim Bob Moffett, and Jere Thompson. All of these friends and colleagues contributed more than they could know to my career at the University of Texas.

WILLIAM H. CUNNINGHAM
AUSTIN, TEXAS
JULY 1, 2013

THE TEXAS WAY

From Michigan to Texas

Before focusing on the main subject of this book—my seven years as president of the University of Texas at Austin and my eight years as chancellor of the UT System—I want to offer a brief account of how I came to be in a position to have those wonderful opportunities. My rise in the academic world was both surprising and remarkably swift, and the story involves numerous mentors, a lot of hard work, and quite a bit of sheer good luck.

My parents, my high school teachers, and others who knew me when I was growing up in Michigan would never have predicted that I would become the president of a major research university and the chancellor of one of the nation's premiere public university systems. My parents were both college graduates and gave me every opportunity and encouragement to excel in school, but I was definitely a slow starter and did not really become serious about education until I went to college at Michigan State University. Until then, I certainly had many interests and passions—horses, sports, girls, and even early ventures into business—but academic achievement was not among them.

The lives of my parents, Earl W. and Anna H. Cunningham, were shaped by the Roaring Twenties and the Great Depression. They grew up within two hundred miles of one another in small towns in the coal mining, logging, and farming regions of southern Indiana and central Kentucky. Like so many thousands of others from that region in that era, they were both eventually drawn to the big city of Detroit by the economic opportunities it offered. That is where they met and fell in love, and that is where I, their only child, was born, on January 5, 1944.

Both of my parents came from families largely characterized by pragmatism, optimism, and an entrepreneurial spirit. Their families instilled in them a deep respect for education and a determination to advance in the world through schooling, hard work, and honest dealing with one's fellow man. They, in turn, taught those values to me, and they have stayed with me throughout my life.

My father was an engineer and executive with General Electric. His career took us to Schenectady, New York (when I was three), and then Shelbyville, Indiana (when I was eight), and back to the Detroit suburb of Bloomfield Hills the year I turned twelve. My mother, true to that era, was a traditional homemaker, but she also had a remarkable streak of independence and adventurousness. After graduating with a major in education from the University of Kentucky when she was only nineteen, she moved to Turkey, where she helped establish the YWCA in Istanbul—quite an undertaking at that time for a teenager from High Bridge, Kentucky.

My boyhood years in Indiana were delightful. We lived on a small farm outside Shelbyville, and we always had horses and dogs. The first horse we had was a wonderful present from my parents—starting a lifelong passion that, by the way, helped me fit right in when I moved to Texas many years later. Shelbyville was an ideal place for a boy to grow up, instilling in me an appreciation for small-town America as well as a love for animals. It is not by chance that my own family has a place in the Hill Country outside Austin, where we keep horses and a few head of longhorn cows and have lots of elbow room. I do believe that children learn a great deal from having to take care of and be responsible for animals. Dogs give people unconditional love while horses have much more complex personalities.

All through high school, I was a straight C student. My parents tried everything they could think of to motivate me to study harder, from mild punishments to modest rewards, but nothing worked very well. I am sure they were convinced that I was going to be an academic "failure." I know my academic adviser in high school, Mr. Schultz, did not have high hopes for me. He suggested to my parents that I go into the oil business—but at a rather modest level. Specifically, he thought that if they would buy me a gas station and help me learn how to operate it, then I would do just fine in life. However, despite Mr. Schultz's suggestions, it was just always assumed in our home that I would go to college.

I applied to Michigan State, and I did well enough on the exams to be admitted. My father always said I got into Michigan State entirely on my own only because he didn't have any connections there that would have been useful. About seven months before I graduated from high school I received a letter from William Finni, assistant director of admissions, informing me that my scores on the Michigan State entrance tests qualified me for admission, but that I needed to apply myself to try to bring up my high school grades. "It is clear that you have more brainpower than you are using. Why don't you start?" Finni wrote. I took that timely admonition to heart and became a more serious student from then on.

When I started college, in 1962, there was no reason to believe that I would magically transform myself into a good student. But whether by magic or just the mystery of the late bloomer, that is exactly what happened. My own example provides an excellent argument for the tradition of many public colleges and universities of taking a chance on seemingly marginal students. I am fortunate that society—as represented by Michigan State—and my parents did not give up on me. From the very beginning, I studied longer and more seriously than I had ever done in high school. Perhaps I was scared of flunking out, and I certainly did not share Mr. Schultz's dream of a career pumping gasoline and fixing flat tires.

My parents were probably more proud than I was when, in the spring before graduating from Michigan State with a bachelor's degree, I received a letter from S. E. Bryan, assistant dean of the Michigan State business school. Bryan complimented me on achieving a 4.0 grade point average not just once but in several semesters, and he invited me to continue at Michigan State as a graduate student.

Almost from the start of my undergraduate years, I majored in business administration and knew that I wanted to pursue a doctoral degree. Even as a freshman, I spent time in the library reading graduate school catalogs. However, at that point my goal was not to pursue a career in the academic community. I wanted to earn a doctoral degree and work for a consulting firm such as McKinsey or Arthur D. Little. I majored in general business as an undergraduate rather than a more specialized major such as accounting or finance, and this provided me with a broad business education as well as exposure to more courses outside the business school.

Michigan State did not permit students to rush a fraternity during the fall of their freshman year, and I have always thought that was a wise policy. Being away from home for the first time, living in new surroundings, meeting new people, and being presented with all the new responsibilities and opportunities of college life is enough of a challenge for a brand-new freshman. I did pledge Lambda Chi Alpha, my father's fraternity, in the spring, but I decided fairly quickly that fraternity life was not for me—at least as it was represented by a party at the end of rush week. There was, to put it mildly, a tremendous amount of alcohol at that party, and I unwisely partook of more than my share of it. When I sobered up the next day, I decided that Lambda Chi was not for me. I called my father that afternoon and, without going into all the details of the party, I told him I had decided that my chances of staying in college would be much improved if I did not pledge a fraternity. I think he was relieved.

I quickly learned that studying paid off. Doug Corney, a fellow freshman, and I began to meet at seven o'clock every Saturday and Sunday morning for breakfast. I often went out with friends on Friday and Saturday nights, but I tended to come home a little earlier than the others because I needed to study the next day. This enabled me to find an additional eight or nine hours of study time every weekend while most other students were still in bed, and a direct result was that my grades rose dramatically. Corney and I continued our weekend breakfast meetings throughout our undergraduate careers.

I had never had a "real" job except for mowing yards until the summer after my freshman year, when my father provided me with an introduction to the man who was in charge of all the Sears Roebuck stores in the Midwest. Looking my best in a three-piece suit, I showed up for an interview with this person along with the head of the tire, battery, and seat-cover department at Detroit's downtown store. It was quickly obvious that the tire and battery manager had never met the regional executive and didn't understand why he had been summoned to the office, but the upshot was that I was offered an entry-level position with Sears. I would not need my three-piece suit for this job, which involved changing tires, putting on seat covers, and doing oil changes and lubrications. I had a suspicion that the world was determined to send me into a career with a grease rag and a shirt embroidered "Bill" over the pocket, but I was determined to do well—and to make the most of the college experience when I returned to Michigan State in the fall.

The summer I spent at Sears was a very positive experience for me. I learned a little about tires, seat covers, and lubrications and a lot about dealing with the public and my colleagues in the garage. At the

My parents, Anna and Earl Cunningham, at our home in Bloomfield Hills, Michigan, c. 1958. *Courtesy of William H. Cunningham.*

end of August the manager, who I am sure was shocked that I lasted the entire summer, asked me if I would stay on and go to radiator school. My major attributes were that I came to work every day and did not drink on the job. I thanked him, but indicated that I wanted to return to college, and Sears and I then parted company on the best of terms. My parents were very smart. They wanted me to learn what life was like outside of Bloomfield Hills, and they wanted me to understand the importance of a college education. I got the message, and I was more than ready to go back to Michigan State after that summer.

The next summer I worked in a gas station near my home, washing cars and doing lubrications and general mechanical work. Finally, in the summer after my junior year, I got out of the garage business for good when I worked for General Electric as an accounting intern— again, a job that my father helped me obtain. Working at GE was a good experience for me, not because I learned a great deal about accounting, but because this was my first real experience with organizational structure, hierarchy, and effective leadership.

I graduated from Michigan State in 1966 with highest honors and was immediately accepted into Michigan State's MBA program. My parents were very proud of me, and Mr. Schultz was in shock. I completed my MBA in 1967 and then I continued at Michigan State in the doctoral program. I applied only to Michigan State and UCLA and was accepted by both. Michigan State offered me a scholarship and UCLA offered to help me find a job teaching at a local junior college. It was not a hard decision for me, and I have never regretted remaining at Michigan State.

Two faculty members were particularly helpful to me as a young doctoral student. They helped me understand that it was possible to be an entrepreneurial faculty member. Faculty members have so much free time that they can be involved in academic research, real world business problems, helping guide young people, serving their university in an administrative positions or on faculty committees, and even helping government solve some of its most important problems. Very few people in society ever have the luxury to be able to structure their own professional lives where they can be involved in so many diverse and interesting problems.

Dr. Bernard J. LaLonde was my initial Ph.D. advisor. He was a nationally recognized expert in marketing and logistics. LaLonde opened my eyes to the fact that teaching and consulting were not only compatible, but they were also symbiotic. Unfortunately for me and Michigan State, LaLonde accepted a chaired faculty position at Ohio State University in 1968. However, with typical Cunningham luck (which is always good) I soon found myself working for Dr. William Crissy as his teaching assistant.

Crissy was a superb teacher, active researcher, highly respected servant to Michigan State, and a very successful management consultant. Above all, he may have been the best people-person I have ever met (President Clinton is a close second). He loved to help young people. Whatever the issue, Crissy was there to help. Some students needed personal advice while others wanted help refining their doctoral thesis or obtaining funds to support their families or their research. Crissy and I became very close. We coauthored a book and talked regularly until his untimely death as a result of prostate cancer.

LaLonde and Crissy were the first of a series of individuals who were kind enough to mentor me at different points in my academic career. While I may not have realized it at the time, I actively pursued close personal relationships with senior individuals who could be of help to me. I enjoyed being with them and being publicly associated with them. However, more than anything else, I knew I had a great deal to learn from them and I was determined to do so. To my great pride and satisfaction, many of my early mentors have become life-long friends.

I met my future wife, Isabella Mantovani, when we were both graduate students. Bob May, who has been a friend of ours for more than forty years, introduced us. May was a doctoral student in accounting while I was working on my Ph.D. in marketing. Isabella had completed her law degree and was working on an MBA and soon a Ph.D. in marketing. We all shared an area with cubicle offices. May later joined the faculty at UT Austin and was chairman of the Department of Accounting during my tenure as dean of the College of Business. When I was serving as chancellor of the UT System, May was named dean of the college, serving in that position with great distinction.

As we prepared to leave graduate school, Isabella and I both were interested in pursuing careers as faculty members. LaLonde made a call at my request in the spring of 1969 to Dr. Edward Cundiff, chairman of the Department of Marketing at UT Austin, and I soon found myself presenting my research to the marketing faculty at the university. UT was the only school where I interviewed and, once again, with Cunningham luck I received a job offer in the spring of 1970 to become an assistant professor in the University of Texas College of Business. I accepted it immediately, and Crissy shepherded me through the rest of my doctoral program.

Isabella began contacting St. Edward's University, a Catholic university in South Austin, about employment there. The dean of the College of Business, Leo Osterhaus, expressed interest in Isabella and told her to contact him when she arrived in Austin. I successfully defended my doctoral dissertation at Michigan State in December 1970, and Isabella was in the process of analyzing her dissertation data. We were young, foolish, and naïve, and we had no idea what exciting opportunities lay ahead of us in Texas.

CHAPTER 1

The Austin Adventure Begins

Isabella and I were married on December 21, 1970, in a Catholic ceremony in Sao Paulo, Brazil, where most of her family lived. The ceremony was entirely in Portuguese, and I said "I do" at the wrong time, to everyone's amusement. We were also married in a civil ceremony at my parents' home in Florida on December 31 (I wanted the tax deduction), and then we drove to Texas. When we left Houston, Isabella was reading a description of Austin in an AAA road map. It said Austin was a small, pleasant college town that had distinguished itself by having lights on towers that gave the city an "artificial moon glow" at night. For a woman who was raised in the large sophisticated urban environment of Sao Paulo and who was educated in Brazil and the United States, this description of Austin made it seem like a country hamlet. It was almost more than Isabella could bear, and she cried the entire way from Houston to Austin.

Soon after we arrived in Austin, Isabella interviewed at St. Edward's University with Dr. Leo Osterhaus and President Ned Roy. It did not take long for them to recognize what a great find Isabella was, and they made her an offer, which she accepted, to join the faculty in the fall of 1971. However, we still had one serious problem that we needed to overcome before we could settle in comfortably as Texans. Isabella had been born in Italy and raised in Brazil. She came to the United States with a J-1 visa, which meant that the U.S. Agency for International Development was supporting her graduate education. To prevent the so-called "brain drain" problem that concerned other countries, U.S. law said people who entered the country with a J-1 visa must return to their home countries for at least two years after completion of their education.

Isabella and I were aware of the J-1 visa problem when we got married, and we decided we would deal with it when we arrived in

Texas. I spoke with Dean George Kozmetsky about the issue in January 1971, and he referred me to Judge William Heath, who was close to former president Lyndon B. Johnson and other Democratic political figures in Texas. Heath had been chairman of the University of Texas Board of Regents from 1963 to 1966. He suggested that I contact U.S. Rep. J. J "Jake" Pickle. I did not realize it at the time, but Pickle was not only an important member of Congress, but he also loved to take care of his constituents, and he loved the University of Texas, which he always proudly called "my university." Isabella and I fell into his sweet spot, and he went to work for us, both brand-new residents of Austin, as if he had known us all our lives. Pickle and his chief of staff, Cliff Drummond, did some quick research and concluded that the only way for Isabella to remain in the United States was for her to return to Brazil and to ask the president of Brazil to petition the president of the United States to allow her to enter the United States with a "green card."

Pickle indicated that the State Department told him that no one with a J-1 visa from Brazil had ever successfully broken the two-year barrier in this manner. The complex bureaucracies in the two countries made even compelling cases difficult, but Pickle said he would help deal with the U.S. government once we had a letter from the president of Brazil.

There was a happy ending to this story. In March 1971, Isabella returned to Brazil, where her family was sufficiently connected to several senior government officials that within six weeks President Emilio Médici of Brazil petitioned President Richard M. Nixon to permit Isabella to return at once to the United States. Isabella has always said that having a letter from the president of Brazil stating that he did not care if she left the country was not the biggest compliment she ever received. The simple truth is that Brazilians are romantic at heart, and President Médici saw nothing to be gained by keeping a young married couple apart.

Once the Brazilian petition was received, Pickle shepherded it through various federal agencies, and the White House approved Brazil's request in late spring 1971. What had been thought to be impossible was accomplished in a few months, thanks to many people of good will, both in Brazil and the United States. Pickle became a dear friend of ours for the rest of his life, not only because of what he did for us in 1971, but also because he always wanted to help his university. At his request, I gave one of the eulogies at his funeral in 2005. And, it is indeed a small world—my father later became good friends with Mavis Heath, Judge Heath's widow, when they were both living in Westminster Manor, a retirement community in Austin.

Isabella and I lost no time getting immersed in all the normal duties of assistant professors—teaching a full round of undergraduate courses, publishing articles in academic journals, and devoting as much energy to faculty governance and professional activities as was allowed by time and opportunity. I found all of this fulfilling and soon felt right at home. Isabella's career took off much faster than mine. After serving as an assistant professor at St. Edward's for one year she was named acting dean of the College of Business when Osterhaus went on sabbatical. When Osterhaus returned to St. Edward's in the fall of 1973, Isabella became a visiting assistant professor of marketing at UT Austin, where she worked closely with Kozmetsky on multiple teaching and research projects.

Isabella and I found the UT College of Business under Kozmetsky's leadership to be very paternalistic and family-oriented. We regularly attended college-wide parties, and Ronya Kozmetsky hosted teas for faculty wives at her home several times a semester. I am sure that many of the young faculty members resented this system and attended as few events as possible, but Isabella and I embraced it. It gave us a chance to interact on a social basis with many senior faculty members and their wives from across the college, such as Glenn Welsch, Ray Sommerfeld, Floyd Brandt, Gaylord Jentz, Ernie Walker, and Abe Charnes. I did not look on these events as political occasions, but they clearly gave me an opportunity to develop friendships with important people from across the college that lasted for many years. Kozmetsky was very smart and was often well ahead of his time. While the term "bonding" was not yet in vogue, he understood the idea that everyone associated with the college would work better together at many different levels if the faculty got to know each other in a social setting. This was the first lesson among many from Kozmetsky that played an important part in my management philosophy throughout my career. At the department level, Ed and Peggy Cundiff did a wonderful job of making the young marketing department faculty members feel welcome and part of a caring organization.

By the spring of 1974, Isabella decided she needed to expand her academic and professional horizons, and she made an appointment

Isabella Cunningham in her office in the College of Communications in 1978. *UT Office of Public Affairs Records, e_utopa_00004.*

to meet with Dr. Peter Flawn, who was then the president of UT San Antonio. UT San Antonio was particularly interested in recruiting faculty members who could speak Spanish. Isabella's résumé indicated that she spoke Spanish, French, Italian, Portuguese, and English. During the interview, Flawn switched to Spanish, and Isabella responded in Spanish. Faculty members who spoke French, Portuguese, and Italian also just happened to drop by when Isabella was meeting with Flawn, so Isabella was given an opportunity to display her excellent linguistics skills. At the end of the interview Flawn told Isabella that he would be very pleased for her to join the faculty. However, he predicted this would never happen because UT Austin would never let her get away. Flawn was right, as usual. For a while we thought Isabella might be offered a permanent position on the marketing faculty, but I think some people were worried about having two Cunninghams in the same department, and that job offer never materialized. However, less than four weeks after Isabella met with Flawn, she was offered a permanent position in the UT Austin Department of Advertising, which is part of the College of Communication.

My initial career was far less interesting and exciting than Isabella's. One early success came in 1973 when I was elected to the Faculty Senate, a relatively new faculty governing entity. This was an extremely interesting opportunity for me because I was able to interact with some of the senior faculty and administrators at the university, as well as listen to discussions on important university issues. I was indeed fortunate to be able to learn by watching the first two chairmen of the Faculty Senate in action—Charles Alan Wright and William Livingston, two of the university's most distinguished faculty members and both highly accomplished speakers and parliamentarians.

My career took another turn when I decided against becoming active in the university's chapter of the American Association of University Professors (AAUP). Dr. Forest Hill of the Department of Economics was also a member of the Faculty Senate when I was first elected and was active in AAUP. He approached me in the fall of 1973 and said he thought I would be able to move up in that organization if I wanted to and even become president of the campus chapter. While I had a lot of respect for Hill, I had some concerns about AAUP's divisive "pro-labor" positions on a variety of faculty issues.

Hill organized a meeting between Frank Erwin and faculty members interested in the work of the AAUP in order to discuss university governance and the role of the board of regents. Erwin was a member of the board and a close political ally of President Johnson's, and he was the power behind the throne in most Democratic political decisions in Texas. Erwin was an excellent lawyer who enjoyed participating in confrontational debates that focused on the future of the university and the role that faculty members should play in university governance. He was never shy about discussing his views with the faculty, and he accepted Hill's invitation to explain his point of view and listen to faculty members. We met in a classroom at 7:00 p.m., and there were only six faculty members in attendance. Erwin strode in, larger than life, and looked around and sat down. His opening comment was, "If this is all you can get to meet with Frank Erwin, you ought to be embarrassed." I said to myself that Erwin was right—we should be embarrassed. From the turnout at that meeting it was clear to me that Hill was taking a knife to a gunfight. The faculty was not interested in the AAUP, and there were other things that I should be involved in, such as teaching and research and figuring out how I could end up on Erwin's side of the equation. The next day I told Hill that while I appreciated his offer very much, I was going to pass. To the extent that university affairs can be viewed as a contest between management and labor, I decided that day that my future would be with management.

Before that meeting, I met Erwin at Love Field in Dallas. I noticed him in a bar talking with several people, and I went up in what must have seemed a rather bold manner and stood near him until I got his attention. He turned to me and said, "Who are you?" I said, "Mr. Erwin, I work for you. My name is Bill Cunningham, and I am an assistant professor in the College of Business at the university." I was very proud of my position. In his most convivial manner, he responded, "Dr. Cunningham, have a drink!" I did, and he was very cordial and gracious to me while we waited for our plane.

I made a strategic career decision immediately after I arrived at UT Austin. While I recognized that research and publication would be critical to my long-term success at the university, I also realized that I could very quickly become recognized as an important and valuable faculty member by the senior faculty and the dean if I did an excellent job in the classroom. Fortunately, I found that teaching came relatively easy to me. I enjoyed teaching Marketing 337, which was a large (five hundred students) undergraduate lecture class. Most faculty members did not want to teach 337. In contrast, I liked "performing" before large numbers of students, and the large class gave me exposure with students from all across the campus, not just from the Business School.

I was lucky enough, in 1973, to win the Jack G. Taylor Award, the college's oldest and most prestigious award for teaching excellence, and it was presented by Mr. Taylor, a distinguished alumnus of the university, at spring graduation, along with a check for $1,000. The award was always announced as a surprise and was a really big deal for the recipient. When my name was called, I was very proud and I knew that my chances of being promoted to associate professor with tenure had increased dramatically. One thousand dollars was a lot of money to the Cunninghams in 1973. Our total income that year was less than $25,000. I won six additional teaching awards from 1972 to 1982, when I was a very active teacher in the college.

I did understand as soon as I came to UT Austin that excellence in teaching and service would not be sufficient for me to gain tenure. I also needed to do research. The two leading academic journals in my field were the *Journal of Marketing* (*JM*) and the *Journal of Marketing Research* (*JMR*). I published an article from my dissertation in *JMR*, and I remember how proud I was when I received the acceptance letter. I published five additional articles in *JM* over the next six years and eighteen articles in other important academic journals during the same period.

When I came to the university in 1971, clearly one of my most important goals was to be promoted from assistant professor to associate professor, which would mean I would have tenure. Assistant professors are very competitive about these promotions among their colleagues, but I am pleased to report that the group of young faculty members with whom I started at the university always remained friends even though we were a very competitive group—people such as Bob Peterson, Mark Alpert, Bob Witt, Eli Cox, and Bob Green. The good news is that under Cundiff's and Kozmetsky's leadership, we never felt that all of us could not succeed and, in fact, we all did succeed at UT.

I was promoted to associate professor three and a half years after I arrived at the university, and only three years after that, in 1977, the Department of Marketing recommended me for promotion to full professor. I knew it was too early for such a promotion, but I believe the department felt the recommendation would encourage me to stay at the university. I was turned down by President Lorene Rogers, and I believe rightfully so. The next year the department again recommended me for promotion, and this time I felt that I was ready. Kozmetsky let me know that I was to be the number-one ranked person in the college when promotion recommendations were sent to Rogers, and this gave me confidence that if any faculty members were promoted that year, I would be among them. By this time I was a senior member of the college's administration, I had done a substantial amount of published research, and I had an excellent teaching record—and I had done all this rather quickly. Most people take ten or twelve years at a minimum from starting as an assistant professor to being promoted to full professor, so I had been on a fast track. However, Rogers again decided not to promote me to full professor. I do not know why she did this. I was aware of a long-running rumor on campus that Rogers and Kozmetsky did not get along well (a rumor that was true, to a large extent). They had very different personalities, and many people felt that Rogers resented Kozmetsky's close relationship with several

William H. Cunningham lecturing before a large Principles of Marketing class in Jester Center, c. 1972. *UT Office of Public Affairs Records, e_utopa_00002.*

powerful regents, including former governor Allan Shivers. I felt I might be a pawn in a campus political power struggle. However, promotions are always subjective judgments, and it may simply be that Rogers felt I was not ready to be a full professor.

Kozmetsky knew that I would be very unhappy about the decision. He gave me the news at the office and then I went home. Later that day he came out to our house and sat with me and Isabella for about an hour and talked about how confident he was that I would be promoted the next year and how important I was to him and the college. The fact that Kozmetsky thought enough of me to come to our house and ask me to stay at the university sealed the deal. I loved UT, and I enjoyed working with Kozmetsky. The university had been good to me, and down deep in my heart I did not want to leave. However, I was hurt by Rogers's decision, and without Kozmetsky's show of interest and affection, I probably would have left the university. I was promoted to full professor the next year, and all was forgiven.

My big break as a scholar came in 1981 when I was appointed editor of the *Journal of Marketing*. I was only thirty-seven years old. This was usually a responsibility that was given to a much more senior scholar. In applying for the position, I made a presentation to

the publications board of the American Marketing Association that
focused on a new management approach to operating the journal. I
told the selection committee that I would appoint section editors from
around the country who would coordinate all of the initial reviews
for the papers and make recommendations to me. I also said I wanted
to have at least one special issue each year that helped focus the discipline on a particular topic.

Serving as editor of the *Journal of Marketing* was my first real
management responsibility where I was largely responsible for the
success or failure of an entity. I found that I was comfortable with
delegating significant responsibility to the highly competent section
editors whom I selected. Delegation turned out to be the central ingre-
dient in every management job I ever had at the university or in the
private sector. I realized early in my career that I could get much
more accomplished by working with other people than by trying to
do everything myself. Carla Williams joined me as executive assistant
to the editor of *JM*. She put together a computer system that helped
manage the manuscripts and keep track of all the publications. Fortunately, Williams worked with me throughout my three years as editor
and played a major role in our success with the journal.

My first major administrative assignment at the university came
just after I was promoted to associate professor. Kozmetsky asked me
in 1975 to chair the college's Enrollment Controls Committee. I was
excited about this assignment because it had come from Kozemtsky
and because the committee was dealing with one of the biggest problems the college had ever faced. It was equally clear that decisions by
the college on limiting its enrollment would have significant campus-
wide implications.

The enrollment problem in the college had begun in the early
1970s, and it occupied much of the university's attention well into
the 1980s. Enrollment in the college was 3,966 in 1968, but by 1977
it had swollen to 10,580, which endangered the college's ability to
maintain a high-quality educational program. One of the roots of
the problem was that freshmen who met the campus-wide admission requirements could enroll in any undergraduate college of their
choice. Unfortunately, the business program was so popular that the
very quality that was attracting so many students was put in jeopardy
by the burdens of overcrowding.

The committee consisted of five senior professors in the college and me. Lanier Cox, a professor of business law and education, guided me through a lot of the process of running the committee. I had a great deal of respect for Cox. He was substantially older than I was and he was a highly regarded teacher, having joined the faculty at the tender age of twenty-one. He had also held numerous important administrative posts since the early 1950s, including serving as a vice president of UT Austin and vice chancellor of the UT System. Cox was a mentor to me, and we remained close after I became president. He always had a very special twinkle in his eye whenever we met. He let me know he was very proud of the progress I had made at the university.

Between 1976 and 1985 the committee made five separate proposals to the University Council, the campus-wide legislative body, and to the administration concerning enrollment management. The rhetoric at the University Council was very strong and at times quite diverse. Robert King, dean of the College of Liberal Arts, argued at a spring 1980 University Council meeting that our proposal would have serious repercussions in other colleges. "People who don't get in the business college will come to my college to build up their GPA," King said, adding that he thought the problem in the business school would solve itself, and that we should not try to solve a temporary problem with a permanent change in the rules. I responded that our method of enrollment control could be changed anytime the situation changes. I also stated that without further changes in the admission procedures the College of Business could have as many as 20,000 students in an unaccredited undergraduate program by 1988.

In the early spring of 1981, President Flawn approved a series of emergency temporary enrollment control measures for the business college, to take effect the following fall. Elements of the plan included scheduling preferences for graduating seniors, restricting the number of transfer students, and eliminating all out-of-state student admissions to the college for the 1981–1982 academic year. Flawn also approved our plan to limit entrance to upper-division business courses to students holding a minimum grade point average of 2.50. Without this forceful action on the part of Flawn, I am confident the college would have lost its accreditation the following year and the college's enrollment problem would have spun out of control.

During the April 1981 University Council meeting, our plan to limit entrance to upper-division business courses to students holding a GPA of at least 2.50 was approved. William Sutherland, a professor of English and chairman of the university's Educational Policy Committee, said the business college's plan to "weed out" students from business programs based on GPA requirements would lead to a dislocation of students and would cause a flight of students to other UT colleges, unless a coordinated campus-wide enrollment plan was adopted. Sutherland's committee recommended that the GPA not be the sole criterion for limiting enrollment, but this idea drew unified opposition from the business college and was defeated by a voice vote. The college finally had a plan in place that would permit it to manage its enrollments for the foreseeable future.

The opportunity that Kozmetsky gave me to chair the college's Enrollment Controls Committee was my first big responsibility, and, as it turned out, my big break at the university. This role clearly vaulted me to a position where I was among the leaders of the college, and I was regularly interacting in that capacity with the business faculty, the dean, the Provost's Office, and the University Council. I found myself as a young associate professor debating point-by-point with distinguished campus leaders such as the dean of the College of Liberal Arts on the campus-wide stage of the University Council, and I enjoyed it. I liked the intellectual challenge, I felt I was doing the right thing, I felt I was representing the college properly, and I felt I was doing what was in the best interest of the university as a whole. My role in this debate also gave people like Flawn the chance to see me in action, and they apparently recognized that I was someone with whom they could work.

The college went on to prepare one more round of enrollment control legislation, which resulted in the basic structure of the enrollment management program that we have today. Most of the revised proposals were drafted when I was dean in 1983 and turned down when they were submitted to Flawn. After I succeeded Flawn as president in 1985, I named Robert E. Witt to serve as acting dean and later appointed him as dean; he promptly resubmitted the enrollment proposals to the President's Office, and I quickly approved them.

The new plan permitted the college to have higher admission standards for both freshman and transfer students than did the university as a whole. It resulted in a dramatic reduction in business enrollments, and one of the innovations that made it work was the development of the Business Foundations Program, which permits students from across the university to obtain a "minor" in the business school.

Above: Isabella Cunningham and John Cunningham on a family vacation in Beaver Creek, Colorado, summer 1987. *Courtesy of William H. Cunningham.*

Left: William H. Cunningham and his son, John, c. 1986. A rare quiet moment at home. *Courtesy of William H. Cunningham.*

Witt deserves a great deal of credit for that innovation and for making the new enrollment system work. I do believe what was ultimately approved by me as dean and then as president was in the university's best interest, not merely the college's best interest.

I learned a great deal as a very young faculty member. I wanted to make my mark as a scholar and a teacher. I also wanted to be a part of management, not labor, and I became comfortable delegating responsibility and at the same time listening to experts and mentors. My focus was always on the college, but I also considered what was in the university's best interest. These fundamental principles served me well throughout my career at the university.

A few comments about family life during these early years at UT, and in subsequent years, are in order here. On August 11, 1977, Isabella and I were blessed when John Earl Cunningham came into our life. John was born at 2 a.m. at Seton Hospital—healthy, handsome, and everything a parent could want. We had planned for his care, and Teresa Zambrano Yepes (whom we have always called Chata) joined our household that year and took over John's day care. John grew up bilingual. He attended Good Shepherd's School from age three and then St. Andrew's Elementary School and St. Michael's Academy.

In 1985, when I became president of UT Austin, John was almost eight years old. He was already a very social and extroverted young man. John started to join Isabella and me on some of the university alumni trips and thoroughly enjoyed the privilege of meeting many new friends. Shirley Bird Perry took John under her wing. Her tutelage was invaluable, and John was very fond of her. On one alumni fund-raising trip, John bid on a silent auction item, a boot flask, which he proudly gave to Shirley Bird as a present.

Chata became a UT employee in 1985 and continued to live with us. Later that year, her sister Eduviges Zambrano Yepes (known as Kena) also joined the university and became a member of our household. They stayed with us until I resigned from my chancellor's duties, having followed us from the president's home to Bauer House. Their help and dedication were invaluable through all those years. They were always there for us, attending to the home, helping other staff during our social duties, and making sure that John, Isabella and I were cared for. Chata and Kena both retired from the university a few years ago. Chata, however, continues to help us as she has for the past thirty-six years.

The Zambrano sisters, Chata, Kena, and Lola (not pictured), have been loyal and dedicated to the Cunningham family and the university for many years. *Courtesy of William H. Cunningham.*

Chata, Kena, and their sister Lola (Maria Dolores Zambrano Yepes) have been members of our extended family all these years. While Lola never worked for us, she was an employee of UT until her retirement. Over the years, the Zambrano sisters, as we refer to them, have been an integral part of UT and our lives. We could not have found anyone more loyal and dedicated to us and to the university, and I am deeply grateful to them.

CHAPTER 2

Life with George—and Beyond

In the spring of 1976, George Kozmetsky named Conrad Doenges, who had been associate dean for graduate programs in the Graduate School of Business, chairman of the Department of Finance. Kozmetsky tried to recruit Robert E. Witt, who was chairman of the Department of Marketing, to succeed Doenges as associate dean. I do not know exactly what took place, but I know it ended poorly, and Kozmetsky never forgave Witt for turning down the job.[1]

Kozmetsky approached me in July to determine if I would consider becoming the associate dean for graduate programs. I may have been his only real choice at that point. Most faculty members are not interested in administrative assignments. They enjoy the ability to manage their own professional lives—something largely given up with an administrative position. To complicate matters even more, Kozmetsky was considered a tough taskmaster, and many of the faculty simply did not want to work directly for him.

When Kozmetsky asked me to become associate dean, I immediately accepted. I never considered turning down his offer, nor did I negotiate anything, such as my salary or responsibilities. On August 3, 1976, Kozmetsky issued a memo to the faculty announcing my appointment. My duties were to include "administering MBA programs, coordinating the college's Ph.D. academic program requirements, chairing the dean's basic research support committee, as well as administering visiting foreign faculty exchange programs."[2]

While all of those sounded like interesting assignments, it was clear that the administration of the MBA program was to be my primary responsibility. Kozmetsky always felt that the Dean's Office should have more involvement in the Ph.D. programs, but in reality they were operated by the departmental faculty under the supervision of the university's graduate dean. I understood this power-sharing rela-

George Kozmetsky at the blackboard in his office in the Graduate School of Business. *Prints and Photographs Collection, Dolph Briscoe Center for American History, the University of Texas at Austin, di_08378.*

tionship, and I had no interest in trying to take over the departments' doctoral programs.

The most exciting part of becoming associate dean was the opportunity to work closely with Kozmetsky. The very aspect of the job that caused other faculty members to turn down the job had great appeal for me. Our relationship was very positive, and it grew closer over the period in which I served as associate dean. Working with Kozmetsky gave me an opportunity to see a real professional in action. He was a big-time national player on numerous issues. I learned more about leadership and administration when I was Kozmetsky's associate dean than I did at any other stage in my career.

As hard as I tried, I was never able to beat Kozmetsky to the office. He was always the first one in the office every morning. He was famous for arriving by 4:30 a.m., and he regularly called meetings of his staff for 8:00 a.m. I never had a problem with early morning meetings and long days, which were perfectly consistent with my own work ethic. Despite keeping such long hours, Kozmetsky had a balanced view of the importance of both family and work. He often spoke fondly of his children and his wife, Ronya, and he also looked upon the business school faculty and staff as part of his family. In this sense, Kozmetsky was quite paternalistic.

Kozmetsky worked on big issues—the kind of issues that would affect the United States and the world. He regularly worked on projects with University of Texas superstars such as Walt Rostow, Elspeth Rostow, and Ray Marshall. The blackboard in his office was always filled with national and international problems such as how to reorganize the World Bank, how to bring capitalism to the developing world, or how to solve the nation's energy problems. His long-term executive assistant, Ophelia Mallory, was frequently summoned to take a Polaroid picture of the blackboard before Kozmetsky erased it in preparation for a new wave of ideas.

Kozmetsky's drive for excellence was astonishing. For example, we were careful never to send a document to the President's Office until it was perfect. We would go through many drafts of letters, budgets, or proposals for new academic programs. This was in an era before word processing, desktop computers, and ink-jet printers, and Mallory had to type draft after draft of important materials. Kozmetsky would frequently say not to worry about the schedule or the deadline; the most important thing was to have it right.

Few people could carry out as many responsibilities as Kozmetsky. He may have been the original multitasker. Kozmetsky not only fulfilled his administrative responsibilities as dean, he also taught a graduate course, did research, wrote and edited books, was active in fund-raising, and was a director of several major corporations including Teledyne, Gulf Oil, La Quinta, and Dell. He also served the University of Texas Board of Regents as its executive associate for economic affairs—a position tailored specifically to take advantage of his insights and wise counsel. Kozmetsky was very proud of his relationship with the board. While his main focus at the regents' meetings was on investments, there is no question that his advice was sought for many years on a host of other issues.

The height of his influence with the regents was when former governor Allan Shivers was chairman, from 1975 to 1979. Kozmetsky had a much closer relationship with Shivers than did President Rogers, and this must have been a matter of great concern for her. Kozmetsky had come to UT from California with graduate degrees from Harvard, and he was the cofounder of Teledyne, which he helped grow into a major defense contractor. He was very wealthy, and he was a national figure in business, technology, and education, and the power structure in Texas—including the university board of regents—recognized and embraced these facts.

Kozmetsky let me manage much of the college's day-to-day operations, a task that he was not particularly interested in, as long as the college was being administered properly. While my initial responsibilities were focused on the MBA program, it didn't take very long before Kozmetsky began to delegate to me more and more assignments. I would regularly visit with him to discuss the central priorities for the college and how he wanted me to proceed. He was the dean and it was his vision that as associate dean I was trying to execute.

Sy Schwartz was our assistant dean for administration and served in the role of a chief financial officer. Schwartz and I always got along very well. He was very close to Kozmetsky, but he was also very supportive of me, and Kozmetsky must have realized that Schwartz would keep me from making any serious mistakes. Tom Loomis was the assistant dean for development and Reuben McDaniel was the associate dean for undergraduate programs. McDaniel and I worked well together as we administered the college's academic programs. There could have easily been problems between McDaniel and me. We were both young, inexperienced, and highly ambitious. However, we never had any problems and have remained close friends over the years. This may have been because we both respected Kozmetsky but also because we respected each other, and we both wanted to do what was in the best interest of the university.

I quickly learned that if I tried to visit with Kozmetsky after 9:00 a.m., it would be difficult to get his attention on details of running the college. While Kozmetsky knew that my issues were important, he did not have a great deal of interest in them and knew they would be properly taken care of so he would be free to work on things of greater interest to him. In this sense, Kozmetsky was a good executive. He was perfectly capable of delegating important functions to people in whom he had confidence. This lesson was not lost on me.

I found that if I would see Kozmetsky before 7:00 a.m. I could have his complete attention. No one would interrupt, and I could ask him very specific questions and find out exactly how he wanted me to

Reuben McDaniel (associate dean for undergraduate programs). *UT Office of Public Affairs Records, e_utopa_00008.*

proceed on issues. As a result, I regularly met with him unannounced between 5:00 and 7:00 a.m. I would ask Mallory if the dean was going to be in the next day. If he was, I would take in my list of issues and questions, and we would go over them in a timely and professional manner, and I would be able to leave his office by seven o'clock and let him return to the types of issues that he was most interested in, while I tried to manage the affairs of the college.

One of my responsibilities was to deal with the American Assembly of Collegiate Schools of Business, the business school's accrediting body. Because of its large enrollment, the school had been a problem for the AACSB for several years. The organization based accreditation largely on a number of quantitative standards such as the student-faculty ratio, the percentage of full-time faculty, and the percentage of doctoral qualified faculty. If a college did not meet these standards, it was in danger of losing its accreditation.

I will never forget a meeting in the spring of 1981 when the accrediting committee visited UT Austin. The committee was composed of deans of schools that were not in the top tier, or what we might today call directional schools, and this was their opportunity to visit the University of Texas at Austin and to meet with the great Dean George Kozmetsky, who was recognized as a legend among the nation's business school deans.

The AACSB is a very important part of the life of the deans of many of these mid-level schools. They regularly attend all AACSB meetings and invest a lot of time and energy in the organization's activities. Kozmetsky rarely, if ever, attended the AACSB annual meeting. When his other options were to attend a meeting at the World Bank, the White House, the board of Gulf Oil, or the university board of regents, it was easy to see how Kozmetsky would pass on the AACSB meeting and send me instead.

I had been wining and dining the visiting deans and making arrangements for them to visit with students and faculty, showing them all our physical facilities, and providing stacks of data, and then the time came for their meeting with Kozmetsky. On most campuses, the AACSB Accreditation Committee would be meeting with the dean throughout its visit, but everyone knew that Kozmetsky was far too important to meet with them more than once. When the time came for the meeting with Kozmetsky, we sat around his magnificent marble conference table and he welcomed everyone, as he always did as a true gentleman, and then he said something like, "I'm very pleased to have you all here today, representing the ACBSC." I remember the look of pain and consternation that went around the table as it became clear to everyone that Kozmetsky did not even know the initials of the organization.

Kozmetsky recovered quite well and began as he usually did—in the middle of a paragraph—and by the time the committee members left they had forgotten about our ratios and were mesmerized by Kozmetsky's intelligence and his knowledge of world events. When it was all said and done, Kozmetsky played his part beautifully.

Soon after I became associate dean, I found myself in meetings with members of the Chamber of Commerce and senior executives of some of Austin's largest companies who were urging me to create an MBA program for business executives. The drumbeat for this type of program became stronger as Austin became more cosmopolitan and as it began to attract companies like IBM, Motorola, and Data General, all of which indicated they wanted some opportunity for advanced business education for their employees.

The university's response had always been that UT Austin was not a university merely for Austin, but was created to serve all the people of Texas. Other universities, such as UT Dallas or UT San Antonio, had their origins in service to a local or regional community, but UT Austin kept its focus on a statewide mission. Thus, for many years there was little interest on the campus in developing academic programs that would be tailored to the needs of local residents who could not interrupt their careers to go to school full time. This was a rather arrogant and self-centered position, but after all we were "The University." Most discussions of starting alternative MBA programs ended when the observation was made that we did not have sufficient resources to take care of the demand for our traditional MBA students—which was quite true.

I asked Kozmetsky in the spring of 1979 for permission to investigate the possibility of offering an executive MBA program at UT Austin. Students would go to school on Friday one week and Saturday the next week. The idea was that the student's employer would give up one day of their workweek and the employee would give up one day of his or her weekend. The employees would be sponsored by their companies, which would pay the tuition and fees. Kozmetsky liked the idea and told me to create a committee, which I would chair, to review existing programs and try to determine if there was substantial demand for one offered by UT Austin. Our committee fairly quickly reviewed the issue and gauged the local demand, and we recommended to Kozmetsky and ultimately the faculty that we start such a program, for which, by the way, we could charge substantially more tuition than for the regular MBA program. The faculty's main concern was that the college would end up offering a watered-down degree, but our response was that the courses would be taught by the same faculty who teach the regular MBA courses, and to the same academic standards.

Once the program was approved by the faculty, I went from being chairman of the committee to sales manager for the program. The only problem was, I had no sales force. Therefore, I began calling on CEOs in Austin to ask them to nominate one or more employees for our first class. My initial target was Frank McBee, who was one of the most highly respected business leaders in the city. He was CEO of Tracor, a Fortune 500 electronics company that traced its origins to laboratories at the University of Texas. McBee was an easy target.

He was always supportive of whatever initiatives the university was undertaking. He immediately agreed to sponsor one student a year in the program, and I had my first sale. I also got IBM to sign on early, and that was very important in establishing the reputation of the program. It did not take long before we had more than thirty applicants. From this group we selected twenty-two people for our first class. Paul Nelson, who directed our noncredit executive education programs and who worked for me, was given the responsibility of managing the day-to-day operations of the Executive MBA Program.

In July 1980, the state's higher education bureaucracy struck. We received word from the Texas Higher Education Coordinating Board that we could not proceed. Norma Foreman, who was head of the division of senior colleges and universities at the coordinating board, said the executive MBA program was "distinctly different" from the approved MBA program, and as a result the new program would need approval of the coordinating board before it could begin. Foreman also said that state law did not authorize us to charge more than standard tuition. This was a significant problem not only because we did not have enough money to begin the program, but also because Kozmetsky and I felt that ultimately an executive MBA program would be quite profitable for the college.

I tried to solve that problem by meeting with Lloyd Doggett, who at that time represented Austin in the Texas Senate. I asked him about the possibility of passing legislation that would permit an executive MBA program to charge higher fees and tuition than regular MBA programs. Doggett told me he thought this new program would benefit only big business, so he would not support a change in the tuition law. With that, we had no choice but to cancel the program for September 1980.

I met with Vice President Gerry Fonken in the fall of 1980 about the program as we began to think about our alternatives. It became painfully obvious that getting a tuition bill passed that would give us the ability to charge higher tuition was not within the realm of possibility, and we had to deal with the coordinating board's view that this program was so different from the current MBA program that we needed to go through the time-consuming process of seeking the board's authority to offer it, knowing that their final approval would not be guaranteed. Fonken's long experience in dealing with higher education bureaucracies paid off when he hit upon the idea of calling the program simply "a scheduling option," or Option II, as we began referring to it. The point was that we were offering the same degree with the same faculty and it was just a scheduling option, as it was going to be offered during the Fridays and Saturdays every other weekend, rather than in the traditional format. Getting a bureaucracy to do what you want is often a matter of hitting upon the right phrase or formula. This was not the first initiative to be rescued from bureaucratic obstinacy simply by moving it from one pigeonhole to another.

We dealt with the problem of the higher tuition by deciding to market the program as costing the regular tuition, but with an additional fee for books, supplies, and two summer enrichment programs. We made it clear to all the applicants that if they did not attend the summer enrichment programs it would be very difficult for them to succeed in the program. We gambled and won. No students pushed back and said they wanted to be admitted but would not attend the optional summer program.

In the spring of 1981, as we were gearing up again to begin the program, I received a call from Jim Colvin, vice president for business affairs. He had a concern that the college was going to be making money on this program, so I was invited over to his palatial office to discuss the numbers. I did not know Colvin well, but I knew he was very powerful, so I worked on my report very carefully. I put together a pro forma income statement that showed us actually losing money in the first year. I did this by putting in every expense for the program for two years, but the revenue for just one year. I showed my estimates to Colvin and talked him through all of it, explaining that the revenue estimates might be conservative, but we hadn't enrolled anyone at this stage so, as a result, we *wanted* to be conservative. I explained to him that the numbers indicated we expected a loss of $1,000, but I assured him that the college would not be asking the central administration to offset our loss. At that point, he grinned and told me to "get out of [his] office." I believe he was genuinely impressed with my mastery of governmental accounting.

I am very proud of what we accomplished in the Option II program. It has been the model of executive MBA programs that are now offered by the University of Texas McCombs School of Business in Dallas–Fort Worth, Houston, and Mexico City, as well as a night MBA program in Austin.[3]

I believe one of the most important contributions I made as associate dean was to support the ongoing effort to develop a Master's in Professional Accounting program—an effort that was ultimately successful in 1984. The origins of the MPA program can be traced to a proposal that Edward L. Summers, then chairman of the Department of Accounting, brought to Kozmetsky in February 1980—a proposal that the accounting program be reorganized as a free-standing school of accounting within the UT Austin administrative structure. It may be that no dean ever gave away control of an academic program without a fight, but even without the traditional desire to defend one's turf, Kozmetsky was not disposed to approve the secessionist ambitions of the Department of Accounting. Since his first days as dean he had never gotten along well with this large and independent-minded department, which included many forceful faculty personalities.

When Bob May succeeded Summers as chairman of the department in September 1980, he came to me to ask my advice on how to deal with Kozmetsky regarding the proposal and related governance and program issues. Relatively quickly, May and I reached the conclusion that separating accounting from the business school was not necessary and was probably not desirable, since outstanding professional accountants could not possibly be educated in isolation from a broad background in business. May's new approach was to develop an integrated BBA/MPA curriculum that would be a five-year professional program that would be administered by a new school of accounting within the business school. Administration of the new program would thus be analogous to the Graduate School of Business, which was within the purview of the business dean rather than being a freestanding unit. I thought the new curriculum and administrative structure were a good compromise, keeping the accounting program within the business school but giving it an innovative focus that would continue to attract outstanding students and help satisfy the ambitions of the senior accounting faculty. I was very pleased to serve as an "honest broker" between the Department of Accounting and Kozmetsky. My focus was on the goal of strengthening an already distinguished accounting program within the oversight of the business school.

During the development of the compromise, I also introduced May to William H. Livingston, who as vice president and dean of graduate studies made major contributions toward developing an academic program that would be free of any fatal bureaucratic flaws. With

Livingston's guidance, the proposal worked its way through the UT Austin and UT System bureaucracies and eventually won approval by the board of regents in October 1982. The creation of a new school of accounting within the business school would need approval by the Higher Education Coordinating Board, but gaining that approval became problematic after several other universities also proposed new administrative structures for their accounting programs. Livingston and I kept working for months on trying to explain our plan to the coordinating board, but in the end we decided simply to implement the new BBA/MPA curriculum without trying to create a new administrative entity. The good news is that an excellent new five-year professional accounting program was established, and it has remained one of the McCombs School's premier academic and professional programs.

In May 1982, my life took a sudden turn when Kozmetsky told me, "I have decided to relinquish the deanship. Pete and I would like you to become acting dean." I immediately said, yes sir, and he said good, and showed me a press release scheduled to be released in about an hour announcing my appointment effective September 1.

Kozmetsky then told me that Flawn "wanted to see me." I think this was a slight exaggeration. I called his office and his staff made an appointment for me one week later. Flawn was very gracious. He told me he had a great deal of confidence in me and that he was not worried about the college. He suggested that I meet with Fonken since all the deans were expected to have a close working relationship with the vice president for academic affairs and research. Fonken and I had always gotten along very well, and I understood that Flawn wanted routine matters to be handled by his office.

I decided that I would consider myself to be "dean for a year" rather than "acting dean" because, as I told the chairmen of the academic departments, the college had a lot to accomplish during the academic year and I wanted us to proceed at full speed, rather than just wait for a new permanent dean to take over. I also felt this was the best way for me to position myself as the logical heir to Kozmetsky.

The transition between Kozmetsky and me was almost immediate and seamless. The only problem we had was that I told him that I wanted to appoint Bob Witt as my associate dean. He told me this would be a big mistake. I recognized that I had the power to make this appointment, but I also knew it would make Kozmetsky very unhappy. In these circumstances, I found it easier to do both jobs, that of the dean and the associate dean, than to appoint Witt.

Kozmetsky always left the campus after graduation and did not return until late August. While I talked to George at least once a week in the summer, I was already accustomed to being acting dean during the summer. Once George walked out of the building in June 1982, he did not enter it again until after I was named dean in 1983. He was busy with his other interests, including work at IC², the UT think tank that he had created in 1977 to research the relationships among business, government, and education, but it was also clear that he wanted to give me a chance to run the college without feeling that he was looking over my shoulder.

I had always been a problem solver, and this may have been one of the reasons that Flawn wanted me to serve as acting dean. I had dealt successfully with a wide variety of issues concerning faculty, students, and alumni, and I had gained quite a bit of experience, and my instincts had served me well. On my first day as acting dean I demonstrated not only an ability to think on my feet but also to think on the floor. I was in my *Journal of Marketing* office when I received a call from Flawn at 7:00 a.m. He said, "Bill, this is Peter Flawn, and I am very upset." With that, I literally fell out of my chair and landed on the floor, but I kept talking, even though I was sitting on the floor for the rest of the conversation. I said, "Dr. Flawn, I will solve the problem if you will tell me what it is." He told me about it, and I solved it.

I was an ambitious person, and I wanted to be named dean. However, I made up my mind that I would not try to play politics to get the permanent appointment. John Thompson, a UT alumnus who was chairman of the Southland Corporation (7-Eleven), was chair of the search committee to recommend candidates to Flawn, and Ray Sommerfeld was the senior faculty member on the committee. I never had any private conversations with Thompson, Sommerfeld, or any other member of the committee, and I did not try to use any of my connections to influence the committee's work. My feeling was that the committee knew who I was, and if the committee was interested in me they would call me. I have since given this advice to many people who have been in similar positions. Most of the time they have not taken my advice, and most of the time their political maneuvering has hurt them in their efforts to obtain a position.

In May 1983, after receiving the advice of the search committee,

Flawn appointed me to the position of dean, without the "acting" qualifier. I had been named as the only internal candidate for the job, but I had no idea about what Flawn had decided until the Friday before the Saturday graduation ceremonies, when he summoned me from a meeting of the Business Advisory Council. I was, of course, gratified that my year as acting dean and my earlier experience as Kozmetsky's associate dean had led Flawn to conclude I was ready for the job.

On Monday morning I told my immediate staff that Flawn would announce my appointment that afternoon. Schwartz, who had been very supportive of me, congratulated me with all the enthusiasm of an uncle who had seen his nephew succeed. My only disappointment of the day was that Schwartz told me he would be retiring at the end of the summer. He made it clear he was proud of me and would do anything he could to support me. He said, however, that it was time for him to follow Kozmetsky's lead and to retire from the Dean's Office. Schwartz gave me one final piece of excellent advice. He said I should call for an audit of the college's finances. He told me he was confident that everything was in excellent shape but that an audit would protect me as I went forward in my new role as dean. This may have been the only time in the university's history that a dean asked the institution to audit his books. The good news was that everything was in excellent shape, as I knew it would be with Schwartz in command.

The only good news that came out of Schwartz's announcement was that I was able to hire Lewis Wright to become assistant dean for finance. Wright, like Schwartz, was a retired U.S. Army colonel, and he was in the Ph.D. program in accounting. Sommerfeld recommended him to me as someone who could replace Schwartz and lead the college's efforts to computerize all of its accounting systems. Wright not only did a great job for the college, but he went with me to both the President's Office and the Chancellor's Office. He was the first African American to serve as an executive officer of UT Austin or the UT System. He was among the most loyal and dedicated public servants that I have ever known.

It was clear that the focus of my work was going to shift immediately, and that I would become increasingly involved in efforts to raise private-sector donations for endowments in the business school. For this reason, it was going to be absolutely necessary that I have an associate dean who was qualified to oversee many of the internal

Robert Witt (acting dean), in 1985. *UT Office of Public Affairs Records, e_utopa_00006.*

affairs of the college and in whom I had complete confidence—just as Kozmetsky had had confidence in me. Bob Witt was my first and only choice for this position, and his willingness to accept my offer contributed greatly to our success on many fronts during the two years that I served as dean. I recognized when I made this appointment that

Kozmetsky would not like it, but I did not talk with Kozmetsky about this or any other appointment.

Flawn told me that the college could benefit from a long-range strategic plan—a document that would lay out a vision for the college and guidelines for how to achieve that vision through specific goals. I agreed with him at once, although I had never developed a strategic plan and had no firsthand knowledge of how to go about producing one. Witt agreed to chair a committee that would draft the plan, and we developed both a strategic plan and an operational plan for how we expected to achieve our goals. It was my first strategic plan, and I made it a practice to continue to develop such plans throughout the rest of my years as an administrator. Such planning is one important starting point for the effective management of an organization, although I agree with President Dwight D. Eisenhower's famous statement that "plans are useless but planning is indispensable."

A second decision that I made was that I wanted to work closely with the senior faculty of the college in a more collaborative manner than they had been used to. While Kozmetsky was highly respected by the faculty, he was also feared by them. I knew this would not fit my style, and I probably could not have pulled it off even if I had tried. I was too young and inexperienced, and I did not have Kozmetsky's connections to the state's power structure. To demonstrate that I wanted faculty participation in the affairs of the college, I introduced the concept of faculty retreats. The first one was held at The Woodlands north of Houston in May 1984. I invited the departmental chairmen, the associate and assistant deans, and selected senior faculty, as well as the chairman of the Business Advisory Council. I continued similar retreats throughout my administrative career.

My move to the Dean's Office coincided with the university's Centennial Endowed Teachers and Scholars Program, which raised some $160 million for endowed positions across the campus, under the leadership of Flawn and Shirley Bird Perry, who was an assistant to the president and coordinator of the university's centennial observance before being named by Flawn to the post of vice president for development and external relations. Flawn had persuaded the regents to use money from the Available University Fund to match private donations as a way of celebrating the centennial, and this became a very useful selling point to potential donors, who could see the impact of their gift doubled. The deans had a major role to play in this campaign, of course. In the beginning, I had no idea what the potential might be for contributions to the business school, but I soon found out.

Kozmetsky had set a goal of raising $3 million in new endowments, which would yield a total of $6 million with the matching money. I had not really had a chance to think about that goal when I found myself in my first meeting in the fall of 1983 as dean with the Business School Foundation. I was waiting for my turn to speak when Sam Barshop, the chairman of the foundation's endowment committee, turned to me and asked about my fund-raising goals. On the spur of the moment, I decided to double Kozmetsky's goal, which would be $6 million in donations for a total of $12 million after the matching. There was no science behind those numbers. My only thought was that I was determined to raise more money than Kozmetsky had felt was possible.

Fortunately, Tom Loomis, as assistant dean for development, had already done a great deal of staff work for the fund-raising campaign by the time I became dean, and we built on his excellent preparation. Barshop loved the business school, and he loved to raise money. Barshop, Loomis, and I began a pattern of activity that we continued throughout the time I was dean. Loomis would do the staff research and identify targets of opportunity. Barshop, Loomis, and I would then rendezvous at the airport in Dallas or Houston and make two to four calls per day in those cities.

It was a great time to raise money. The Texas economy was booming between 1983 and 1985; we had matching money to encourage our donors; and Loomis had done excellent spade work. While Kozmetsky was a great dean, he had not been a particularly active fund-raiser. One of his problems was that he had more money than most of the people he was asking to make a donation, and as a result, he may have been reluctant to ask for donations. I certainly did not have that problem, and Barshop and I were ready, willing, and able to ask people to help the college with their money.

As it turned out, I was far too conservative when I told the foundation that I would double Kozmetsky's goal. During the two years that I was dean, we raised an average of $1 million a month in gifts and matches for endowed faculty positions in the business school. That $24 million was worth more than $54 million when I retired from administrative work in 2000, and had paid out an additional $20 million in support of academic programs. I am very proud of what we accomplished because I know the money has been spent wisely to support the college's students and faculty.

Not all of the money that we raised was matched with funds for the business school. Flawn and Perry had been concerned about the colleges and schools, such as liberal arts and fine arts, that did not have as many well-heeled alumni as the largest professional schools—business, law, and engineering. Flawn developed a plan through which the donor to one college could specify that the matching funds should benefit a different college. The success of Flawn's new matching program depended heavily on the cooperation of the professional school deans, who might or might not be interested in advising their donors about this new possibility of the matching funds going to a different college.

I was a team player, and Flawn, the captain of the team, had a new game plan. My natural inclination was to support it. It was never my position that the business school did not need the matching funds, but instead that colleges and schools all across the university were in need, and the College of Business and I as its new dean had a chance to do something to support the entire university. Gift and endowment records from that fund-raising era indicate that the other deans who had access to a relatively large list of wealthy donors were somewhat less enthusiastic about giving up some of their matching money. My estimate is that the business school lost about 25 percent of its matching funds as donors decided to help other colleges. However, as a result of this fund-raising technique, I believe I acquired a reputation as a young dean who understood the importance of supporting the entire university.

In this connection, I responded to an unusual request from Frank Erwin. Perry conveyed to me Erwin's desire that I raise money for an endowed chair for Dr. Marshall Rosenbluth in the Department of Physics. Rosenbluth, who was a pioneer in the nuclear program at Los Alamos and one of the world's leading theoretical physicists, had come to UT in 1980 to do fusion energy research, and Erwin had promised him an endowed chair to support his work. I was shocked that Erwin even knew I was dean, and even more shocked that he actually wanted my help. The fact that my last experience with physics was in high school, when I barely squeaked out a C, did not help matters appreciably. Fortunately, understanding Einstein's theory of relativity is not a prerequisite for figuring out how to raise money for a chair in physics.

Loomis, Barshop, and I strategized and came up with the idea that we would approach Walter Fondren. He was a graduate of the university's geology program and he had been a successful investor and businessman. He was the son of one of the founders of Humble Oil & Refining Company and a leader of one of our state's greatest philanthropic families. The three of us visited Fondren in his office in downtown Houston, and I explained that we would like the Fondren Foundation to donate $500,000 for a chair in the business school, and that we would like his permission for the regents to match the gift with a $500,000 chair in physics, to be held by Rosenbluth. We explained, as best we could, what Rosenbluth was working on. He said to let him think about it, and in the business of fund-raising that's a great answer—simply because it is not a "no."

As we left Fondren's office, Loomis, ever the optimist, reminded Barshop and me that Edgar A. Smith's office was only two floors down in the same building. Smith was a UT graduate and the CEO of Alamo Barge Lines, and he was a good friend of mine. He held a beautiful party for me in his Houston home after I become dean, and he had helped the university raise a number of important gifts. We walked into Smith's office unannounced, and after a few moments of small talk I asked him if he would contribute a professorship in the business school with a match in physics. He said, "Physics, you have to be kidding, I have no interest in physics." Smith later funded a number of endowments at UT Austin, including a chair and a professorship in the business school, as well as fellowships in nursing and the Edgar A. Smith Building in the university's art museum complex.

Fondren called me back in about three weeks and told me he had thought it over and decided not to do what I had asked. I was about to thank him for considering our proposal and wish him well when he went on to tell me what he *had* decided: He wanted to create endowed chairs in geology, law, physics, and business. I was, to say the least, surprised, but I was also tremendously pleased and grateful when I realized that while we had asked him for a $500,000 gift, he was giving us $1,000,000, which when matched would create a total of four endowed chairs. I wasted no time in calling Perry with the news. She said I might have a future in this fund-raising business.

As dean, I served as a bridge between the Kozmetsky era and the new world that the college had to face without Kozmetsky at the helm. Kozmetsky was without question a political and economic force whose personality dominated the college throughout the sixteen years that he served as dean. However, we all knew that a time would come when Kozmetsky would have to give up the reins, and a big part of my job in the post-Kozmetsky era was to help guide the business school through that perilous period.

When I left the deanship in September 1985 to begin serving as president, we were still the largest business school in the country. Being the biggest was never important, but maintaining high academic standards was, and it was important to me that our peers across the country recognized the strengths of the business school, such as in a 1984 survey that ranked the school as a whole as fifth in the country and the accounting program as second. As I left the deanship, the college was also in extraordinarily solid financial shape, and it had an outstanding administrative team in place to continue the task of meeting the academic and financial challenges of the late-twentieth century. Such accomplishments are the work of hundreds of faculty members, students, administrators, alumni, and donors over many years of hard work, dedication, and perseverance, and I was fortunate to provide for a brief period the leadership for all who love the business school. I believe my short tenure as leader of the college marked a successful transition period that consolidated the gains of the Kozmetsky years and helped refocus the college on the challenges that lay in the future. I am grateful to everyone who helped realize these achievements.

CHAPTER 3

Appointment as President and First Steps

When Peter Flawn announced in December 1984 that he planned to step down from the presidency at the end of the summer, I never dreamed I would be considered as a possible replacement for him. I had been dean for only seven months and I was only forty years old. The regents would not only be looking for a successor to one of the most successful leaders in the history of the university, but would also be in need of a president who could steer the institution through one of its periods of greatest crisis, as a result of the state's continuing budget problems and its perennially uncertain commitment to higher education. If anyone had asked me if I felt I should be considered to become the next president of UT Austin, I would have said I was too young, too inexperienced, and had not yet proved I would be a successful dean.

So it was with some surprise that I learned in the spring of 1985 that I was being considered with a large group of other finalists for the job of president. Earlier, I had been notified by Wales Madden, a member of a special search committee of regents, faculty, staff, students, and alumni, that I had been nominated, and he asked whether I was willing to let my name go forward in the process of reviewing all those who had been nominated or had applied. I had responded only that I would consider the matter, but the truth is, I just did not feel it was appropriate to let my name go forward. Later on, at five minutes to five on the very last day that the committee was considering candidates for the presidency, Madden called me again and advised me that if I had any interest at all in the job I needed to tell him, otherwise my name would be taken out of consideration. Still without any thought that I would be considered a serious candidate, I told him it was fine with me to let my name go forward.

The public learned in May that a total of 141 people had either

applied or been nominated for the job. In those days, the list of applicants and nominees was publicly available under the state's open
records law, while any list of finalists was officially confidential—just
the opposite of the way things are now. The Texas Legislature changed
the law to the current procedure not long after I became president,
and I think one reason for the change was that the list of 141 had
been such a large group of names that it did not provide any useful
information to the public. It also may have led to some false conclu-
sions about who were the viable candidates, and there is always a
possibility that making public such a list will lead to embarrassment
for some candidates. The entire list, as published by the Austin newspaper, included fifty university presidents from around the country
(including seven from Texas institutions), a dozen or more UT deans,
vice presidents, and other administrators, the secretary of the Navy, a
former secretary of defense, a former U.N. ambassador, at least three
Aggies, and the governor of Arizona.[1]

During that spring, I met with the search committee, as well as
with several of the regents individually, and Isabella and I had dinner
with regents Robert Baldwin and Shannon Ratliff and their wives.
These meetings were quite pleasant and informative and I knew that
if I were appointed president, both of our lives would change dramatically. Isabella gave me her complete support and encouragement.

As a result of the law as it then stood, there was no official public
list of finalists, but by the end of the spring Gerry Fonken and I were
widely mentioned within the university community as being on that
list, along with three outside candidates. The university never officially made public a list of finalists, but the Austin newspaper identified them as myself; Fonken; Lattie F. Coor, president of the University of Vermont; Morton W. Weir, a vice president in the University of
Illinois System; and James G. Freedman, president of the University
of Iowa.[2]

Fonken had been, since 1979, a very strong and effective vice president for academic affairs and research, a position equivalent to that of
provost at many universities. Although the deans reported to Flawn,
they resolved most of their day-to-day issues with Fonken, and he had
proved himself an able, tough, and resourceful administrator with a
commanding knowledge of the university.

Fonken and I had no conversations about the presidency until a
week before the board of regents was to make the decision. He called

me and suggested we ought to talk about the presidential search, and I went to his office for a forty-five-minute conversation. It was a very positive conversation, mostly about our mutual interest in seeing that the regents' decision, whatever it turned out to be, would work out to the benefit of the university. I still did not think that I had a serious chance of becoming president. If the regents had asked for my opinion I would have told them that I was honored to be considered, but that they should select Fonken. He had forgotten more about the university than I knew, and he was a proven successful administrator. Selecting him would have involved very little risk. I made up my mind that if Fonken was named president, Isabella and I would host a dinner that night and invite the entire university leadership community—with lobsters flown in from Maine and champagne—as a way of showing everyone our confidence in Fonken's leadership and our wish to be part of his team.

The regents met on Thursday, August 8, and discussed the presidential decision at length in executive session, and they were scheduled to vote the next day. Meanwhile, on Thursday night, there was a large farewell dinner for Flawn at the Erwin Center, with all the regents in attendance, as well as, it seemed, just about everyone else connected with the university. The hot topic of conversation, of course, was the regents' decision the next day. My guess is that almost everyone, except the regents themselves, were as much in the dark about the decision as I was, but that didn't stop the speculation.

When I got home I had a call from Jon Newton, who had been chairman of the regents until his term on the board had ended earlier that year. He told me he thought I was going to be named president the next day and he wanted to be the first to congratulate me. I thanked him profusely, but I did not know whether he had inside information or was just making an informed guess. A little later that evening, I got a call from Jess Hay, who had succeeded Newton as chairman. Hay told me that I was going to be named president, and he asked me to meet him for breakfast at 7:30 on Friday at his suite in the Driskill Hotel, just two blocks from the UT System offices, where the regents meet. Of course I accepted.

Hay would have been one of nine people with firsthand knowledge of what was likely to happen on Friday, but technically no decision had been made by then, since the regents were prohibited by law from taking a vote in executive session. Still, they probably had gone

Newly appointed University of Texas President William H. Cunningham with former president Peter T. Flawn and Provost Gerhard Fonken, August 9, 1985. *UT Office of Public Affairs Records, e_utopa_00009.*

around the table and each of them could have expressed his or her opinion about the matter, so if one candidate had at least five supporters the outcome on Friday would have been clear—barring any last-minute changes of heart.

I was not sure what Hay might want to talk about when I headed over to the hotel Friday morning, and even less sure when on my way into the suite I met Fonken on his way out. It was a slightly awkward moment for both of us. For all I knew, a different deal had been struck overnight, and I was not going to be selected after all. When Hay and I were alone, he told me the board was going to vote to make me president later that day. He then suggested that my first act as president should be to name Fonken my second-in-command, with the new title of executive vice president and provost. I said, "Jess, great idea."

I had two reasons for this reaction. First, Hay had "suggested" it, and I was not the dumbest man in America. And second, it genuinely seemed like a great idea to me. I certainly had no illusions about being able to run the university on my own. Fonken knew the good guys from the bad guys, he understood the university's priorities and what had to be done to advance the institution in its quest for world-class status, and he had earned the respect and confidence of faculty and administrators all across the campus. I will always be grateful to Fonken for accepting this important new position and for being willing to work with me and give me the benefit of his counsel. I am also very grateful to Hay for giving me his "suggestion."

Later that morning the regents did indeed select me as president, and we announced at the same time that I was naming Fonken to his new position. As with all University of Texas presidential selections that I am familiar with, mine was unanimous when the public vote was taken. But the fact was that the sentiment on the board in the executive session was at first only five-to-four in my favor, with the minority favoring Fonken. A split like that behind closed doors is not at all unusual in such decisions and usually does not reflect any deep division in ideology or policy, but is simply a reflection of the fact that more than one strong candidate has emerged. Much more important than the initial sentiments is the willingness of the board to unite behind the candidate who has the majority's support, and I have always been grateful that some of my strongest supporters on the board during my presidency included those four for whom I was initially their second choice.

I think that as the board weighed my candidacy some members had doubts about appointing someone who was only forty-one years old, who had been a dean less than two years, and whose academic credentials were formed in a professional school rather than one of the older "arts and sciences" disciplines. In my favor were my success as an administrator in the business school, my achievements as a fund-raiser, my record of concern for the university as a whole rather than only my own college, and my perceived people skills.

Some people in 1985 interpreted our new jobs to mean that the regents had decided I would focus on fund-raising, politics, and other "external" tasks, while Fonken would handle all the "internal" business of the university. This feeling may also have been reinforced by the fact that our appointments were announced at the same time. A number of variations on that theme were stated by members of the board and others at the university, and that spin on my selection as president even found its way as far as Boston, where John Silber, president of Boston University and a former administrator at UT Austin, said that I would be the "outside" man and Fonken would run the campus.[3]

There was a small element of truth in that, but our jobs were never divided in such a rigid manner. We never labored under any illusion of a division of power along the lines of "inside" vs. "outside." Fonken's primary responsibility as provost was to serve as my chief academic officer, and it was clear that Hay and others on the board of regents gained a great sense of comfort from knowing that Fonken would be applying his experience and wisdom to the internal academic affairs of the university. Still, I felt on that first day that it was important for me to make it very clear that I was the president, responsible for the internal as well as the external affairs of the university. We developed a very effective working relationship that benefited the university—even if that relationship could not be summarized as simply as some wanted.

When we got back to the campus on Friday afternoon, I had a large stack of phone messages from reporters. My first request of Shirley Bird Perry was that she look through the messages and advise me about which calls I should return and in what order, in case I ran out of time. She quickly determined that the first thing I needed to do was to return a call from Monty Jones, then the higher education reporter at the *Austin American-Statesman*. That afternoon he asked me one of those questions one is never fully prepared for—how would I assess my main strengths for this new job? The story the next morning quoted me exactly: "I work awfully hard and always have. I enjoy people, and I enjoy having a role in trying to solve problems." I also said I would strive to build on Flawn's accomplishments so that UT would become "truly a world-class university." "That is not as complex as you may think," I said. "You work to recruit outstanding faculty and students, and you work to increase the resources of the university."[4]

Jones talked to many other people that afternoon, and I was gratified to see that they had good things to say about me. In addition to Flawn, he quoted Elspeth Rostow, former dean of the LBJ School of Public Affairs; Kermit Larson, an accounting professor; John Watson, a UT alumnus and Austin developer; and Jack Taylor, a UT alumnus and member of the advisory council of the business school. All of them expressed confidence in my leadership abilities and my commitment to the broad mission of the university. Reading that article was certainly a good way to begin my first full day as president-elect.

Shirley Bird and Bill Livingston invited Isabella and me to join them and their spouses for dinner the night I was selected. The Perrys and Livingstons were loyal and steadfast friends of ours and it was a real pleasure to celebrate with them. We had a good time talking about our hopes and dreams for the university and the things we could all do together. Isabella and I were delighted to have their expressions of support from the beginning of my presidency, and I knew I was going to be relying on their judgment and experience throughout my tenure in this new job.

I would not officially become president until September 1, but Flawn moved out of his office almost at once. He and I met at the office for about two hours on Saturday morning and talked about the university and its challenges and his perspective on a wide range of issues. At the end of our conversation, I asked him if there was anything that I could do for him. He told me that he would be officially retiring from the university at the end of August and had made arrangements with Bill Fisher, chairman of the Department of Geology, to have an office in the Geology Building. He asked me if he could have Helen Oelrich assigned to him as an executive assistant. I was pleased to accommodate him, first because he was Pete Flawn, and also because I thought that one day I could be in that same position myself. When I left my position as chancellor in 2000 and returned to faculty duties at UT Austin, I mentioned to Don Evans, chairman of the board of regents, that the one thing he could do for me was to assign Connie Saathoff, my longtime executive assistant, to me. What Flawn understood, and I later came to understand, is that many people see the university through the eyes of the president or chancellor that they knew, and that former presidents and chancellors are called upon regularly for a wide variety of advice concerning higher education issues in Texas and fund-raising for the UT System and in my case UT Austin. Having an executive assistant to help manage such issues is an excellent use of university resources.

I did laugh, at least to myself, a number of times when as chancellor I was helping the regents hire a new president for one of the system's campuses. I often heard that they would require as long as six months to execute their transition. I had from August 9 to August 31 to complete my own transition and by Monday, August 12, Flawn had turned over the office to me. He returned several times, but only for a few minutes. If any major crises had arisen, he would have taken command, but as it happened we had a relatively quiet August, which gave me time to get organized and make some plans. I was spending a couple of hours a day in the business school and the rest of the time in the President's Office. It took me a couple of weeks to get over the odd feeling I had when I entered the office and realized it was now *my* office. I made that adjustment, and I also found out about my new parking arrangements, but not before I had to ask Vice President for Business Affairs G. Charles Franklin to "fix" a parking ticket that the university police had placed on my car when I parked by the Main Building.

The day after I was selected I called each of the vice presidents and asked them to remain in their current capacities in my administration. I learned later that several of them thought I was going to ask them to resign so that I could bring in other people that I was closer to, possibly from the business school. My real concern was that they were going to quit. The simple truth was that I was smart enough to realize that I had only twenty-two days to make the transition to one of the most complex jobs in Texas, and Flawn had left me a very competent team. There was no reason to even think about making personnel changes at the time. I later learned from talking with several vice presidents that they were pleased that I had called them on Friday afternoon. This eliminated any concern that they might have had over the weekend that they would not be part of the new administration.

My second step was to invite each of the deans to come to the President's Office to meet with me to discuss the future of their college or school. This was one of the very few times that I met with a dean without Fonken in attendance. However, I was well aware of the talk that I was Mr. Outside and Fonken was Mr. Inside. I wanted to send two messages. First, I was in charge of the university, and second, I wanted to learn from them what their main goals were for their colleges and schools, and how I could help them achieve those goals. These meetings were very easy. I was one of them. The deans met regularly for a private lunch before the monthly meeting with the president, so I knew each of the deans moderately well, and I enjoyed working with them. All of us knew there would be occasions when I would veto a dean's initiative, and we knew that it would be rare for any dean to get everything he wanted, but I wanted them to know

University of Texas vice presidents, April 29, 1987. Seated, Shirley Bird Perry and Gerhard Fonken. Standing, from left, Ronald Brown, William S. Livingston, G. Charles Franklin, and Edwin Sharpe. *Prints and Photographs Collection, di_08393.*

that because I had confidence in them, my natural inclination would be to support their initiatives.

The only exception to the meetings in the President's Office was my session with Robert D. King, dean of the College of Liberal Arts. I asked to meet with King in *his* office. This may not have been as momentous as Nixon going to China, but I wanted to make the gesture of going to see him because I knew that a number of critics would be apprehensive about a business dean taking over as president, although King himself never had that kind of simplistic view. More than twenty-five years later, it does not seem strange for the dean of a business school to step up to the presidency of one of the nation's major universities, but back then there were still a lot of people who somehow felt threatened by such developments.

I knew I needed to make a special effort to persuade people that I had a vision for the university that encompassed its entire mission, including of course its pursuit of excellence in the liberal arts and natural sciences. I knew that much more would be required than merely meeting with the dean of liberal arts, but I wanted to start with that, and I wanted it known that I had gone to see him. This was my chance to reach out in a symbolic way to demonstrate that I knew the important role the liberal arts played in the university community.

Bob King was too smart to let me out of his office with just a symbolic visit. Near the end of our hour-long discussion that focused on the academic and programmatic needs of the college, I asked him if he needed any immediate help from the President's Office. He said he needed $50,000 in matching funds to support a scholarship initiative in the Plan II Honors Program. I told him at once that I would approve the request, which may have startled him. King probably felt that he had not asked for enough money, while I had no idea at the time where the $50,000 would come from.

By the way, the strongest criticism along the lines that a business dean would not have the broad background needed to run a diverse university came not from within the College of Liberal Arts or any other part of the campus, but from the news media, and in particular an article published by *Texas Monthly* in May 1986. That article, "The Quest that Fizzled" by Peter Elkind, took as its premise the idea that the University of Texas Board of Regents had had high hopes for finding a dynamic and visionary leader to follow the very successful presidency of Peter Flawn, but that these hopes had been dashed when the regents settled on me. Elkind seemed to take it as a given that any business school dean was unqualified to be president of a university that aspired to greatness. An uninformed reader would probably conclude from the article that the liberal arts, in particular, were doomed with me at the helm.

I don't know from firsthand experience what else the article said, because I stopped reading about a third of the way through. It was poorly written and extremely biased, and I was having no fun reading it. I decided just to let other people wade through the rest of it. I was pleased to see that a number of knowledgeable friends of the university wrote letters to *Texas Monthly* to take issue with Elkind's warped perspective. These included Wales Madden, a regent from 1959 to 1966 and a person with as much knowledge about the university as anyone in the state; Charles Alan Wright, the world-renowned expert on constitutional law at UT Austin; Shannon Ratliff, an Austin attorney who was a regent from 1985 to 1991; Sam Barshop, chairman of La Quinta Motor Inns and a regent from 1987 to 1993; John Fainter, an Austin attorney who had been very active in alumni affairs at UT Austin; and Bob King.

From left, William H. Cunningham, Hans Mark, Isabella Cunningham, and Marion Mark at a September 22, 1985, brunch at Bauer House in honor of the Presidential Search Committee that recommended Cunningham as president of UT Austin. *Photo by Bill Malone, copy courtesy of William H. Cunningham.*

King's letter read, in part: "As for Bill Cunningham as president, I will say this. I like him, I respect him, and he has shown me to date a commitment to liberal arts (and, more importantly, a *sensitivity* to the complexity of liberal arts needs) that belies all the meanness of that article about his selection. And his support of liberal arts has been *tangible*—I'm talking about money—as well as symbolic."[5]

The magazine published parts of a few of the letters they received. Several of the letter-writers sent me a copy of a brief response they had received from Mike Levy, publisher of the magazine. Levy attached comments from Elkind that he had solicited after receiving the letters complaining about the article. Elkind had written to Levy that he thought his article was "eminently fair" to me and that he was tired of all the "whining" by UT.[6] After reading that, I realized there was not going to be much hope for getting a fair hearing from *Texas*

Monthly, and the magazine persisted with a generally negative tone about the university for many years.

I hoped that my early meetings with the deans in September 1985 would help earn me their confidence, and in my first few weeks as president I held dozens of other meetings on and off the campus with a similar goal in mind. A university like UT Austin has more constituencies than can conveniently be counted, and I endeavored to meet with as many of them as I could. I quickly scheduled meetings with various faculty groups, both within and across the colleges and schools, and I held more than a dozen meetings with student groups, as well as hosting student dinners and receptions at our home and holding a series of campus-wide open forums for students. Then there were all the external groups, some of them a good deal less "external" than we might think—the Development Board, the Ex-Students' Association, the advisory councils of the college and school foundations, the Dads' Association, the Retired Faculty and Staff Association, and members of the Centennial Commission.

Beyond the university community, I met with members of the Governor's Office, the Texas Higher Education Coordinating Board, key members of the House and Senate, and others with whom I would have close working relationships during sessions of the state legislature. In addition, in the first six months of my presidency, I visited with no fewer than twenty-two alumni clubs—everywhere from Dallas and Beaumont and Lufkin to New York City and Monterrey, Mexico. These were only initial meetings, of course. Being a successful university president requires regular and consistent relationships with all these groups and many others like them.

I brought Connie Saathoff over from the business school as my executive assistant, and her presence in the President's Office proved to be invaluable in smoothing the transition. She knew how I worked and my expectations, and I was always glad that she was just outside the door to my office. She had been my junior staff person in the Dean's Office, but it was clear to me that she was doing the majority of work in the office. Saathoff later went with me to the UT System offices when I became chancellor, and she has come back to the campus with me to help me as a faculty member. I have told her on several occasions that I do not understand why she has dedicated so much of her life to me, but that I deeply appreciate her loyalty and dedication to me and to the university.

William H. Cunningham and Connie Saathoff, c. 2000. Connie has worked for me since I was dean of the business school. *Courtesy of William H. Cunningham.*

I am also grateful that Joyce Moos, who had managed the President's Office under Lorene Rogers and Peter Flawn, and Mary Kaszynski, who handled the President's Office correspondence, stayed on to work with me. While Saathoff knew my personal ways of working, Moos and Kaszynski knew everything about the President's Office and how it functioned, so I think together we made a good team. I was also fortunate that Moos and Kaszynski went with me when I became chancellor.

From the beginning of my service as president I relied heavily on the judgment and experience of Shirley Bird Perry. She was much more than the university's chief development officer, and I found using her long experience with the university and its many constituencies to be invaluable at almost every turn in my presidency. I was also fortunate to inherit from Flawn a group of other executive officers who made up one of the finest administrative teams in American higher education and I was smart enough not to make any sudden changes in this team. Early on, I realized that Ed Sharpe would be central to what I was trying to accomplish as president. Sharpe had been vice president for administration under Flawn, and I think one of my best decisions was to ask him to continue in that role. This was a varied role that included problem-solving and trouble-shooting, carrying out some mundane as well as some highly critical (and high-profile) assignments, serving as a diplomat, and sometimes figuring out how to coax the bureaucracy of the university into working as it should.

I spent a fair amount of time in the first days and weeks after my appointment communicating with the news media about the aspirations and challenges of the university, and most of the news coverage was quite positive. On my first official day as president, September 1, the *Dallas Morning News* focused on my fundamental goals, and I emphasized recruiting high-quality faculty and students and developing the kind of facilities, either through renovation or new construction, necessary to support them. I also talked about options for trying to keep enrollment from going over 48,000—such as higher admission standards across the university, higher standards for certain colleges, and limiting the number of transfer students and out-of-state students.[7]

These goals, as well as the need to strengthen research and the university's role in economic development, were also included in stories in the *Dallas Morning News* and the *Houston Chronicle* in October, after I had been on the job a few weeks. The *Chronicle* story included some very complimentary comments about me by King, to the effect that a president with a business background can be good for a university through enhanced fund-raising and in other ways. "Traditionally, big multi-purpose public universities don't go to their professional schools for the presidents," King said. "I anticipated on the part of my faculty some objections. . . . I haven't heard any."[8]

Parts of the *Morning News* article continued this theme: "The new president is seen as a scholar and a manager—a needed mix for dealing both with the rigors of the real world and the requirements of academe." The article also referred to me as the university's "top salesman," but I preferred not to use that term. "I like to think that I'm not in the process of selling," I told the newspaper. "What I think I am is in the process of communicating to a whole variety of constituencies about the university, whether it be alumni groups, people out in the community, members of the legislature or senior elected officials of the state."

I also tried to take that opportunity to explain the broad mission of the university: "I don't really believe the citizens of this state understand what this university does for them. We are perceived by most people simply as a place where you send your eighteen-year-old children, and when they graduate, they become twenty-two-year-old adults ready to face society. I think we do provide a place where young people get a very fine basic education, and I think if that's all we did, we would deserve support from the state. But I believe we do a lot more than that," including basic research, graduate education, and making contributions to economic development.[9]

The transition was now complete. In twenty-two days I had assembled my team, met with many of the university's internal and external constituents, and we were ready to go. These early news articles dealt with many of the themes that would preoccupy me and my administrative team during the seven years that I served as president. I began my presidency with my characteristic confidence and optimism, traits that never really left me despite a number of very trying and demanding issues that awaited me and my team.

CHAPTER 4

Hazing

Hazing was a major issue from the very beginning of my presidency. It had been a problem for decades at UT Austin and other universities across the country, but I was determined to try to do something about it. I regret that, despite all our efforts to end this barbaric practice, two students died as a result of hazing while I was president, a dozen or more were sent to the hospital with hazing-related injuries, and countless others suffered physical or psychological injuries.

I was never antifraternity, as some people charged when I launched a campaign against hazing during my first weeks as president. It is true that during my own undergraduate days I had never joined a fraternity. However, I did serve for a year as a "house mother" at the Delta Upsilon house at Michigan State, and I have a silver cup from the fraternity, inscribed "Mom," to prove it. I had been in my last year as a doctoral student, and I needed a job close to campus. For a year I lived in the fraternity house, supervised the activities of the members, took care of the St. Bernard dog, Otto, cooked breakfast on Saturday, and generally tried to keep the place from burning down. I was initiated into the chapter (without any hazing) during my second semester in the house, so I am officially a fraternity man.

I received a quick education about hazing when I became president. Early in my first semester in office I began receiving anonymous letters from mothers of fraternity members who were trying to protect their sons by drawing my attention to what they said was a pervasive problem of hazing among UT fraternities. I didn't pay much attention at first, but as the letters began to mount I realized the problem might be much greater than I had thought. One of the earliest letters that I have a record of was from a Dallas attorney who was a 1971 graduate of the university. "From reliable sources, it has come to my attention," he wrote to me in October 1985, "that two of the most prestigious honorary service organizations at the University of Texas—the Texas Cowboys and the Silver Spurs—continue to engage in what I consider to be severe hazing. That hazing consists of paddling and 'rides.' The amount of hazing is even greater today than it was in the late 1960's and early 1970's."[1]

About two weeks later, an anonymous letter warned that the Texas Cowboys had been hazing their pledges since the beginning of the semester, and that on September 18 all the "new men" had been paddled sixty times each, causing internal and external bleeding, and resulting in students being unable to attend classes. The letter went on to describe an incident on September 20, when, the writer said, the "new men" were ordered to gather in the parking lot at Disch-Falk Field and were put in the trunks of cars and driven to a site southwest of Austin. The students were blindfolded and hit with a cattle prod "several hundred times," the letter said.[2] Three days after that letter, another anonymous letter was sent to Assistant Dean of Students Glenn Maloney. This letter, from a former member of either the Cowboys or the Spurs, said that pledges from both groups had been beaten with paddles and cattle prods and then were forced to run, apparently to intensify the pain and swelling from the beatings.[3]

While university officials were attempting to investigate these anonymous reports and I was considering what action the university might take, an incident involving members of the Longhorn Band came to light. The band director, Glenn Richter, discovered in early October that members of two groups—the Longhorn Band Students Association and Kappa Kappa Psi, a service fraternity of band members—had "branded" male and female freshmen with dry ice during an initiation ceremony in Memorial Stadium. Richter suspended ten students from marching in the band for two weeks, and he contacted the Dean of Students' Office, which investigated and, in early December, suspended the two organizations for varying periods, to be followed by probation. In addition, ten students were disciplined individually. The incident took place before I had announced in November that students would face automatic suspension from the university if they participated in hazing, so the punishments in this case were consistent with the university's prior practice. I was personally relieved that this sequence of events excused me from possibly having to suspend the entire band for the rest of the football season. This would have been a real test of my resolve to deal with hazing—especially for a president who had been on the job less than three months.

While this investigation was underway, I decided on a course of action for a broader, long-term campaign against hazing. I concluded that a vigorous antihazing effort would be one of the themes that I wanted my presidency to be known for. It was a sad fact that many colleges and universities had been less than diligent in opposing hazing. Many higher education officials were in denial about this problem, and some silently and secretly tolerated it, if their light punishments were any indication. I wanted UT to be known as a national leader in fighting hazing, and my primary motive was to protect our students from getting hurt.[4]

Others on the campus were also beginning to get active in efforts to stop hazing, and I was happy to support them. Thanks to the work of enlightened student leaders such as Janey Perelman, vice president of the Students' Association; Chris Collins, president of the Interfraternity Council; and John Smith, another participant in the Students' Association, the university invited national antihazing campaigner Eileen Stevens to the campus in October 1985 for a seminar on the subject. Stevens had lost her own son to a hazing incident and was one of the nation's most effective advocates for hazing-free campuses. I was pleased that the President's Office was able to support this student-led seminar financially, and I encouraged all fraternity officers to attend.

After consulting with various campus officials, including the leading student affairs officials (Ron Brown, vice president for student affairs; Sharon Justice, dean of students; and Glenn Maloney, the assistant dean of students who supervised fraternal organizations), I decided to begin a major effort to end hazing by sending a letter that October to the presidents of fifty-five UT student organizations that had a pledge system for membership. The letter would make clear the university's policy against hazing and would require that an organization's president and pledge trainer sign a promise against the practice and then meet with me in my office. As I wrote: "I feel so strongly about hazing that I want to discuss this matter with you personally. . . . I want to sit down face-to-face with you and the pledge trainer of your organization to talk about hazing and its consequences. Let me give you my personal assurance that, as President, I will lead The University's charge against you and your organization if there is evidence

Hazing: Illegal and Immoral

Definition:

According to the University General Information Bulletin, hazing is defined as follows:
A willful act done for the purpose of humiliating a student or causing indignity, either physical or mental. This includes threatening or seriously offering to do such physical or mental violence.

Specific Examples:

1. Forced calisthenics
2. Total or partial nudity
3. Paddle swats
4. Throwing any unwanted or dangerous substance on a pledge
5. Interrogation of a pledge
6. Forcing pledges to drink alcoholic beverages
7. Transportation and abandonment of pledges or actives (rides, walks)
8. Any type of personal servitude for actives
9. Embarassing apparel of any kind worn in public
10. Calling pledges demeaning names
11. Yelling and screaming at pledges

[Not intended to represent all forms of hazing.]

Penalty:

1. Fine of between $25 and $250
2. Jail term of no less than 10 days or more than 3 months
3. Disciplinary procedures initiated by the dean, ranging from warning probation to expulsion
4. An organization found guilty of hazing can be put on probation or have its registration cancelled

"The practice of hazing is a serious violation of the laws of the State of Texas, the Rules and Regulations of The University of Texas System, and the rules of common decency. It is an antiquated and thoroughly unacceptable ritual which has no place in today's universities. I am committed to the total elimination of hazing at The University of Texas at Austin."

Dr. William Cunningham
President, The University of Texas at Austin

Sponsored by the Students' Association with partial funding from the Office of the Vice President of Student Affairs.

"Hazing—Illegal and Immoral" leaflet distributed through the *Daily Texan*, September 5, 1986. UT *Office of Public Affairs Records, e_utopa_00014.*

that you are engaged in hazing. If you are hazing, stop. If you are not, help others to stop."[5] I got the idea for these signed promises from my father. As an executive of General Electric, he had been among hundreds of employees who had been required by the company after a price-fixing scandal to write an annual letter to the chairman of the board of directors stating that he understood that price-fixing was illegal and that he would be fired if he participated in such activities. My father also encouraged me to take a strong stand against hazing at the university. "You've got to do something about this," he said after I told him about the anonymous letters the university had been receiving. "I wielded a mean paddle when I was in college," he confessed, providing further evidence to me that we were dealing with a problem that had been around for decades throughout the country.

That fall I met with all the leaders in small groups, and we made sure that everyone signed the promise not to engage in hazing. Events would prove these steps to be inadequate, but they were a significant start and they got a lot of people's attention. These letters and related educational efforts became a standard feature of my administration, as the leaders of student organizations were required every semester to renew their signed promise against hazing.

In February 1986, it was discovered that at least two Alpha Tau Omega (ATO) pledges and another student were hospitalized with infections after they had been pelted with raw eggs. One student was in the hospital nine days. The hazing had also involved sleep deprivation and other cruelties over a period of days. After a quick investigation, the Dean of Students' Office barred ATO from participating in campus activities for a minimum of three years and suspended four members for two years each. These suspensions probably had the effect of expulsions, since UT specified that it would not accept credit for any classes taken at other institutions during the suspension. The president of ATO, Matthew Zander, made two comments to the press—first, that the penalties were too harsh, and, second, that the university was simply trying to make an example out of his group. At least he got the second part right.

The four students who were suspended wrote letters of "contrition" to me suggesting that the university ought to lift the suspension. The letters were identical, down to the typographical errors. I upheld the suspensions, wondering how much the students or parents had paid a lawyer for those poorly written letters.[6]

The ATO case prompted an outpouring of letters and newspaper editorials in support of the university's efforts to end hazing. Letters commending the university arrived from parents, faculty members, state officials, regents and former regents, and business and community leaders. I was particularly pleased to have the support of W. A. "Tex" Moncrief Jr., the Fort Worth oilman, whom I did not know well at the time but who later became a very effective member of the board of regents and one of my close friends and trusted advisers. He wrote to me on February 19, 1986: "I want to commend you on your disciplining the Alpha Tau Omega fraternity for its recent infraction of the hazing regulations. This sort of juvenile delinquency needs to be stopped. I was a pledge in Alpha Tau Omega in 1937 at the University. After 'hell week' was finished I refused to accept my pin because of the same type of immaturity shown by a majority of the members of the fraternity."[7] Tex was on point, as usual.

Many other alumni have told me about the culture of hazing that prevailed at UT for decades, and how generation after generation accepted it as if it were normal behavior. Parents would send their sons to the university with full knowledge that they would undergo hazing, just as they themselves had when they had been students. Fathers often encouraged their sons to pledge the same fraternity they belonged to and told them what to expect for their initiation. Members of the older generations who had been in the Cowboys proudly displayed the "T" brands on their chests to teenagers who were about to graduate from high school and leave home for the university. Fortunately, some of the more enlightened alumni showed their brands not with pride but as a warning about how change was needed. I will never forget U.S. Senator Lloyd Bentsen showing me the "T" that had been branded on his chest when he was initiated into the Cowboys as an undergraduate in the late 1930s. Bentsen strongly encouraged me to continue my efforts to eliminate hazing on the Forty Acres. He understood very well that it was time to stop tolerating this kind of behavior.

If we felt that we had been making some major progress against the hazing problem through the spring of 1986, the next September brought everyone back to reality. On September 18, 1986, Mark Seeberger, a UT student and a pledge of Phi Kappa Psi fraternity, was found dead of alcohol poisoning in his off-campus dormitory on Guadalupe Street. After a long and difficult investigation by UT and local law enforcement officials, and after numerous attempts by some fraternity members to frustrate the investigation, it was determined that Seeberger, an eighteen-year-old freshman from Richardson, and two other pledges had been taken on a "ride" by fraternity members the night that he died.

The hazing death of Mark Seeberger was without doubt the most personally troubling event of my presidency, a heart-breaking tragedy that left me saddened, frustrated, and very angry. The investigation concluded that his hazing was not an isolated incident but part of an established pattern of physical and mental abuse of pledges by the fraternity. It was also learned that three weeks before he died, Seeberger and other pledges had been required to participate in another hazing ritual, wrestling in a mud pit at the fraternity house. A few days before those events were taking place at the Phi Kappa Psi house, I was quoted in a story about hazing in the *Daily Texan*: "The practice of hazing is a serious violation of the laws of the State of Texas, the Rules and Regulations of the University of Texas System, and the rules of common decency. It is an antiquated and thoroughly unacceptable ritual which has no place in today's universities. I am committed to the total elimination of hazing at the University of Texas Austin."[8]

I was in Galveston the day Mark Seeberger died. Ron Brown, vice president of student affairs, made the call to the family in Richardson on behalf of the university. I would have done it if Ron had been able to find me, but he called and talked to Mark's father even before I knew about the death. I know this was one of the hardest calls that Ron ever made, but he was a real professional who understood what needed to be done, and he was a person of great compassion and understanding.

Isabella and I went to the funeral home to visit with Joan and Jeffrey Seeberger. Of course they were simply devastated. Mr. Seeberger took me by the arm and said, "Let me show you my beautiful boy." The full tragedy that hazing can produce certainly hit me during that visit. I wish every fraternity member at UT could have met Mark's parents that day and could have seen Mark lying in his coffin.

A few days later, Isabella and I went by the fraternity house to talk to the students and many of their parents, at their invitation. We were on our way to a black-tie event, and for about an hour I sat on a couch in my tuxedo and told the fraternity members that we were determined to find out everything that had happened and that they

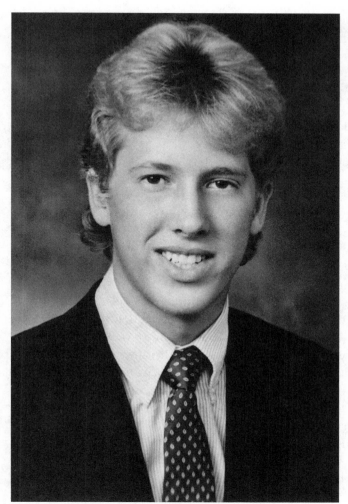

Hazing victim
Mark Seeberger.
*UT Office of
Public Affairs
Records, e_
utopa_00013.*

should not lie about it or take part in a cover-up. I tried to emphasize to them that some of them at that moment might not be in trouble, but they would certainly find themselves in trouble if they participated in a cover-up. Subsequent events would show that some of the people there that evening did in fact try to cover up the events that led to Seeberger's death. Some of them even slandered the memory of Mark Seeberger in a futile attempt to protect themselves and their organization. I was told that the attorney for one of the students involved in the "ride" had developed a strategy of blaming the victim and trying to make Mark look like the guilty party.

A Travis County grand jury investigated Mark's death for the next two and a half months but in late December declined to indict anyone, concluding that the state law against hazing was not applicable because it could not be established that Mark had been "coerced" into participating. In April 1987, the Texas Alcoholic Beverage Commission concluded their own investigation without being able to establish a "pattern" of alcohol violations by the fraternity. This is still difficult for me to comprehend. My father told me stories about hazing and alcohol at fraternity events that he attended in the 1920s. What does it take to establish a pattern? The university, however, was able to pursue disciplinary action against the fraternity as a group as well as against individual students, and some of the strongest penalties ever assessed in a hazing case at the University of Texas were handed down by Dean of Students Sharon Justice in January 1987. Phi Kappa Psi was suspended from campus activities for a minimum of four years, and eight students who were found to be directly involved in the incident were assessed penalties ranging from reprimands to expulsion.

As president, I heard the final appeals of students and organizations that had been disciplined. The Dean of Students' Office made it clear to students and their parents and attorneys that they should consider an appeal carefully, since the president had the widest latitude in making the final decision. One female student involved in the Seeberger incident appealed her punishment as assessed by Justice. She had been suspended for two semesters, with the provision that if she took courses at another university, the credits could be transferred back to UT. Her attorney pleaded with me in a letter to hear the appeal in person, expressing the hope that I would drop the suspension. I met with her and heard her plea, and my decision was to uphold the suspension, but with the added provision that credit for courses taken elsewhere during the suspension would *not* be transferable to UT. And when the fraternity appealed its four-year suspension, I decided in August 1987 to uphold the punishment and emphasized that this was a minimum suspension and that reinstatement would by no means be automatic. Perhaps if the students involved had displayed any remorse or accepted any responsibility for what they had done, I might have been more lenient.

I was amazed at the letters I received from some parents—even after Seeberger had died—urging me to be lenient with people involved in that or other hazing cases. The perpetrators were usually described as "fine, clean-cut, responsible young men" deserving of "a second chance." Some parents of Phi Kappa Psi members even wrote to me claiming the real problem was that the news media had "sensationalized" the death. How could the media "sensationalize" the death of this eighteen-year-old student? I could understand a parent wanting to protect his child, but not at the expense of minimizing the value of the life of another child. These letters from parents left me thinking it was no wonder that their children had so little sense of personal responsibility.

The Seeberger case helped mobilize support for a tough new antihazing law sponsored by State Senator Gonzalo Barrientos of Austin. The new law clarified and broadened the definition of hazing, steeply increased the fines and jail sentences for a conviction, made it easier to pursue criminal charges against organizations that condone hazing, made it a crime to fail to report a hazing incident, and required colleges and universities to inform students about the law. This law, which went into effect in September 1987, proved to be a powerful new tool for law enforcement as well as for universities, as it became easier to gain the cooperation of those with information.

One might have expected that the death of a student, harsh penalties assessed against organizations and individuals, and the publicity surrounding a tough new antihazing law would have brought at least a temporary end to hazing. But reports of incidents continued to come in. And in September of 1988, we had new reason to doubt the effectiveness of our antihazing measures when another UT student died in a hazing incident. This time it involved the Delta Tau Delta fraternity, and the victim was a member, not a pledge. Gregg Scott Phillips, a student from Austin, fell to his death from a 125-foot cliff west of Austin while being chased by two pledges as part of a fraternity ritual. The new antihazing law helped tremendously in pursuing this investigation. The following April, the fraternity pleaded no contest to a criminal charge under the antihazing law and agreed to perform 2,000 hours of community service as part of a plea bargain with the Travis County District Attorney's Office. The university placed the fraternity on probation for two years and required that future members meet a higher academic standard than usual for the next two years.

Soon after the death of Mark Seeberger, I formed a committee to study the campus's Greek-letter organizations and similarly exclusive groups, and to make recommendations for how the university could

better relate to them. This Commission on the Role of Fraternal Organizations was chaired by John T. (Jack) Ratliff, a member of the law
faculty, and included twenty-two other members—faculty, students,
staff, alumni, and community leaders from across Texas. I asked the
commission to examine the issues of hazing, alcohol abuse, the relationship between the organizations and their alumni advisers, and the
role of the university in regulating the groups. To my knowledge, this
was the first comprehensive study of its type at a university in some
twenty years, and I believe the commission made an important contribution not only to the UT community but to institutions across the
country wrestling with the same problems.

The commission presented to me, in October 1987, a thorough
report with twenty-one recommendations for action, all of which I
approved and began implementing. Among these were the hiring of a
full-time staff member to work with and advise Greek-letter fraternities and similar groups; a closer working relationship with all such
groups, including efforts to bring sororities back onto the campus
as official student organizations;[9] expanded educational programs
related to hazing and alcohol awareness; and a stricter approach to
giving student organizations the privilege of representing the university at official events.[10]

Perhaps as important as the commission's recommendations was
its vivid description of the realities of hazing, as revealed through
dozens of interviews. The report provided details of behavior that had
been accepted by too many people for too long, including the truly
barbaric activities of the Texas Cowboys and Silver Spurs. For many
years, it had been known that these groups administered severe beatings to their pledges, including the use of paddles, cattle prods, and
brands, and that they practiced other forms of hazing such as forced
consumption of food and alcohol, forced calisthenics, and sleep
deprivation. Initiates were often unable to sleep on their backs for
weeks after the beatings, and it was common to seek medical treatment outside of Austin because local hospitals would cooperate with
UT officials. This kind of behavior had been going on for years, even
as the groups officially represented the university, the Texas Cowboys
being in charge of the cannon at football games and the Silver Spurs
being responsible for Bevo, the longhorn steer mascot.

The presidents of the Cowboys and the Spurs said in the fall of
1987 that they had discontinued the hazing of new members and the

Presidential Commission on Fraternal Organizations—from left, John Ratliff, Betty Sue Flowers, and Donald Foss, October 20, 1987. *UT Texas Student Publications Photograph Collection, Dolph Briscoe Center for American History, the University of Texas at Austin, e_uttsp_00001.*

commission's report was no longer up to date. I tended to believe those two students, but stamping out hazing during one semester does not mean it has been ended forever, and there is always a possibility that old traditions will be brought back as the leadership of a group changes. So while I was impressed with the leaders of the Cowboys and Spurs in the fall of 1987, I had no illusions that we had solved the problem once and for all. In fact, I have no doubt that my successors in the administration continue to receive anonymous letters about hazing, just as I did more than twenty-five years ago.

CHAPTER 5

Enrollment Management

nrollment management was the greatest student crisis I faced as president of UT Austin. It manifested itself in two interconnected ways. First was the question of whether the university was going to be able to control its overall enrollment. Second, once students arrived on campus could the university structure its registration process so that students would be able to obtain the classes they needed to graduate in a reasonable and predictable period of time? If we could not answer both of these questions affirmatively, then the legitimacy of the university's entire mission would be in question.

Growing demand for higher education within Texas placed tremendous pressure on the enrollment of UT Austin in the 1980s and 1990s. The university tried to balance two competing enrollment priorities, which I outlined in a report to the board of regents in July 1987.

- To serve as broad a cross-section of Texas students as possible, including a growing number of minority students who had historically been denied full educational opportunity.
- To provide undergraduate, graduate, and professional academic programs competitive with the best in the nation, thereby serving students of superior ability, not only from Texas but from other states and around the world as well.[1]

The first of these priorities was derived both from a desire to do what was morally right and from a recognition that the university drew its support from a traditionally populist and egalitarian state. The second priority reflected the aspirations of the university from its very beginning, when the leaders of Texas in the nineteenth century set forth an elitist vision of "a university of the first class." This vision had always contained something of the state's frontier bravado, but in the latter part of the twentieth century it was reinforced by an understanding that the state's economic and social health required the creation of a world-class university.

If both priorities could be realized, UT Austin would be not only the biggest public university in the nation, but also the best. Few, if any, other universities have ever tried to reach both of these goals, and even now in the twenty-first century it remains to be seen whether UT Austin can do it. For several years at the end of the twentieth century, we did succeed at being the biggest, and we made significant progress toward being the best.

As the Texas population burgeoned, the number of high school graduates continued to grow, and it was anticipated that a larger and larger proportion of those graduates would pursue higher education. It was projected in the mid-1980s that the number of students graduating from Texas high schools would increase from about 160,000 in 1985 to more than 200,000 a year by the end of the century.[2] It was clear that UT Austin and other universities in Texas were facing the prospect of significant and sustained enrollment growth.

Most of the state's universities were eager for this growth, but UT Austin was about as large as it could be and still provide the quality of services that students and their parents expected. This meant we needed to take serious steps to control admissions.

The university became officially aware of the limits of growth in 1958, when the Committee of Seventy-Five, which commemorated the institution's seventy-fifth anniversary, observed that, "although sheer size is not necessarily an enemy of quality, either the faculty and facilities would need to keep pace with student enrollment or the enrollment would need to be controlled in accordance with available resources." By the time of the report of the Centennial Commission in 1983, it was clear that "unrestrained growth of the student body has stretched existing resources, personnel, and facilities beyond appropriate limits."[3] The strategic plan for the university released in November 1985 after I had been president only two months reflected this long-running theme when it said that enrollment should be stabilized at 48,000, "a level that is consistent with the capacities of the university's programs and that will not produce intolerable congestion or failures in providing counseling, advising, recreational and other support services."[4] Very simply, I felt the university lacked the budget, the space, and the faculty to serve more than 48,000 students.

The admissions policy that had gone into effect in fall 1982 provided that students who had taken specified courses in a Texas high school would be admitted if they were in the top quarter of their high school class. Even students in the bottom three-quarters of their high school class could be admitted if they had acceptable grades and scores on standardized achievement tests. For applicants who still could not meet these requirements, the university offered the Provisional Admissions Program, which allowed students a chance to prove that they could meet the academic challenge of the university by enrolling in the summer and achieving a 1.5 GPA in the summer and an overall 2.0 GPA at the end of the fall semester.

The provisional program, which began in the late 1960s, was first envisioned as an affirmative action program for minority students who did not meet regular admission requirements but might nevertheless be able to demonstrate that they could succeed at UT Austin if given a chance. The program proved popular among Anglo students and was only marginally successful in recruiting minority students. There were two major advantages of the program. First, there were a few students who had not done well in high school and who "saw the light" once they arrived at the university. These individuals became successful academic participants in the life of the university. Unfortunately, the focus was on few. Most students who had not done well in high school did not have a magical experience that transformed them into brilliant college students sometime between May 20 and June 10 of their senior year in high school.

The second advantage of the program was that when politicians or important donors put pressure on me to admit a marginal student I could easily say that while the individual they were interested in had not done well in high school, UT would let him or her attend in the summer and all they had to do was earn a 1.5 GPA in the summer and an overall 2.0 GPA by the end of the fall. Most people saw this as an attractive compromise. We never gave in on the GPA provisional admission requirements. We felt these were minimums and there were no exceptions.

Four major concerns led us to revise these admissions policies in 1987, effective with the freshman class in fall 1989. First, the 1982 policy had brought overall enrollment down below 48,000, but growth pressures were returning. By late spring in 1987, undergraduate applications for the fall were up 5 percent and admissions were up 11 percent, and enrollment in 1987 was 47,743, up from 46,140 the previous year. The university was rapidly moving back up to an enrollment level at which economies of scale no longer continued to add value.

Second, the admissions policies had produced a situation in which the campus actually had two freshman classes, one highly competitive and well-prepared academically, the other only marginally prepared for the challenge presented by UT's academic programs.

Third, there was a growing concern that the SAT was being given too much weight in admissions decisions. Average SAT scores among incoming freshmen had increased from 1025 in 1977 to 1067 in 1986. At the extremes of very high and very low scores, the SAT proved to be a good predictor of academic success at UT Austin. For students in the middle, however, the test was not a very effective indicator of academic success or failure.

Fourth, in keeping with its comprehensive mission as a major graduate research institution, the university had been placing increasing emphasis on its graduate programs for more than twenty-five years, and we expected to see further growth in the number of these students in most fields. Graduate and law students made up 23.5 percent of the student population in 1985, and their share of the total enrollment increased to 26 percent by 1992. Enrollment policies needed to be consistent with the need to strike a balance between resources employed in graduate and undergraduate programs.

These concerns were reflected in various ways in the overhaul of admissions policies approved by the board of regents in October 1987 after extensive campus discussion. The new policy was not implemented until the admissions cycle for fall 1989. That would give high school students, parents, and counselors ample time to adjust to the new rules.

In the new policy, the automatic admission category was changed from students in the top 25 percent of a high school class to the top 15 percent, and students scoring at least 1250 on the SAT or 30 on the ACT were automatically admitted regardless of class rank. Based on the availability of space, other applicants would be admitted as a function of a combination of class ranks and test scores. The Provisional Admissions Program was kept in place, as were a broad range of other affirmative action programs for African American and Hispanic students. Ethnicity was always one of numerous factors but was never the sole determinant in offering admission to a student.

The great advantage of the new policy was the increased flexibility it gave the admissions office, so that better decisions could be made. The most critical decisions focused on applicants whose scores and high school rankings were close to the borderline for automatic admission. Students in this group would have their applications reviewed by a committee that would consider writing samples, letters of recommendation, extracurricular activities in high school, the academic quality of the student's high school, the student's intended major given the enrollment needs of UT colleges and schools, and the student's ethnicity. We hoped that these admission procedures would help lower the undergraduate attrition rate and lead to more productive and fulfilling campus experiences for the students who were admitted.

In fall 1987, enrollment increased almost 1,600 over the previous fall. Then in fall 1988, the last cycle under the old policy, the total soared to 50,107. The next year (1989), when the changes that had been approved in 1987 began to show their effect, the total grew slightly, to 50,245. The fact that the increase was so slight was an indication that the new policy was beginning to work.

Even before freshmen began arriving on the campus in the fall of 1989, we knew from the number of applications and admissions for that cycle that the 1987 enrollment management plan would need to be revisited and, as a result, we increased the academic requirements in the Provisional Admissions Program for summer 1989. Instead of simply making a 1.5 GPA in the four required summer courses, now a provisional student would have to make no grade lower than a C and would have to make at least one grade of B or higher.[5] It had become very clear that students from around the state understood that if they were not regularly admitted to UT, the back door was wide open. The provisional program made it impossible for UT to control its admissions and the number of marginal students who were seeking admission through the program had increased dramatically. It was apparent that it would not be long before more than 20 percent of the freshman class would be admitted via the provisional program.

We also implemented a system-wide admissions referral program allowing applicants who had been turned down by UT Austin to be automatically admitted to other UT System schools. This program was designed to help students who were not admitted to UT Austin to stay within the UT System. Unfortunately, it was not successful.

William H. Cunningham speaks to students and media about registration problems, September 12, 1989. *UT Texas Student Publications Photograph Collection, e_utt-sp_00005.*

Recent high school graduates who wanted to go to UT Austin generally had little interest in other UT System institutions.

The second shoe in the enrollment management problem fell in dramatic fashion in September 1989 when thousands of students found it difficult or impossible to register for courses, including, in many cases, courses needed for timely progress toward graduation. The crisis was one of the clearest signals up to that time that the university's enrollment and the quality of services provided to students were intimately connected.[6]

When I became president we were using a standardized computer registration program that had been in place for many years. Students would fill out a scantron form indicating what classes they wanted, and they were given an opportunity to select one or two options if any of their first choices were not available. A computer then took everybody's needs and wants and tried to find schedules that would accommodate as many people as possible.

In the late 1970s and early 1980s, this system worked quite well. Unfortunately, by the mid-1980s, and increasingly thereafter, the university's enrollment had grown so much that the majority of students often found it difficult to register for the classes they needed during the computerized stage of registration. This meant that tens of thousands of students were forced to go through the infamous "adds and drops"—a process of revising and completing one's schedule by dealing in person with registration advisers.

Although the computerized registration system was out of date, the real problem was the inability to provide enough sections of the basic undergraduate classes to meet the demands of our growing student population. This was a function of a rapidly growing undergraduate enrollment that the university could not control, a shortage of financial resources to hire faculty and staff, and a failure on the part of several colleges to allocate the available resources in a way that would best meet undergraduate needs. Well before the crisis of 1989, students knew that the system was beginning to fail. Students began to talk about the fact that if you went to UT Austin you might not get the courses you needed to graduate "on time." The problem began with freshman English courses and ran all the way through senior-level courses in journalism, English, history, and other departments. Most of the complaints seemed to be in the colleges of liberal arts and communications, but the problem was campus-wide at the undergraduate level.

A year before the crisis of 1989, Ron Brown, vice president for student affairs, had recommended at an executive officers' meeting that we consider a new type of registration system. He maintained that the university needed some type of automated registration system, in which students would use the telephone to log on to the computer and register for their classes and then be able to complete the process in a timely and efficient manner, in most cases in one session on the computer. Although such a process would involve computers and telephones, it would have the merits of the old-fashioned registration systems when students visited Gregory Gymnasium and went from table to table to sign up for classes. You might not get your first choice of classes or class times, but you could stay in the room and move among the tables until you succeeded in putting together a complete schedule. Most students did not have to go through the adds and drops process.

Brown's idea was to develop a system in which the university's computer would take the place of Gregory Gymnasium. The only serious problem with his idea was that there was no off-the-shelf software available to handle an institution the size of UT Austin. As a result, the university would have to undertake a project to design its own customized program. We put together a task force and made a commitment to spend the money necessary to create the new registration system and make it work. Unfortunately, we had not acted in time to head off the crisis in the fall of 1989, although thanks to that earlier planning the new telephone system was ready for operation the following fall.[7]

To deal with the class availability issues, I went to work with the Provost's Office and the deans of the colleges and schools to find out what had gone wrong in the fall of 1989. This meant addressing issues of allocation of resources, assignment of faculty members to high-demand classes, and monitoring class sizes. Those are not the kind of micromanagement details that the president or the provost usually deals with at an institution the size of UT Austin, but the fall of 1989 was not a usual time.

The *Daily Texan* covered the class availability crisis in detail. One editorial argued that the problems students were encountering were not the fault of the colleges and schools, but that the fault lay on the fourth floor of the Main Building—in the President's Office. The editorial urged students to call my office or my home and complain, and the paper published both telephone numbers. We received some 160 telephone calls from students at my office, although relatively few called me at home. I was grateful that most students, even during their times of greatest frustration, were courteous about not calling me at home.[8]

I returned every call of every student who telephoned me and left a number. It was clear that many students felt no one cared, no one was communicating, and no one was on their side, so I believe the positive approach that we took to the phone calls helped to deal with this aspect of the crisis. I assured the students that I recognized that we had a problem that needed to be solved, and that I would solve it.

I explained that one of the reasons for the problems they were experiencing was a shortage of financial resources, but I emphasized

that our goal was that every student who came to the university would
be able to take the courses necessary to make timely progress toward
completing a degree. I made a personal commitment to every student
I talked to that their dean's office would advise them on what courses
to take during the current semester that would permit them to continue on their path toward graduation. In some cases this would mean
that academic degree requirements would be changed so that students
would be permitted to take another course toward their graduation
that usually would not have been part of their degree plan.

Students seemed very pleased that I called them back. Most, in
fact, apologized for having called me in the first place. They were
very pleasant on the phone, and I got the impression that they were
appreciative that I cared about the problem and was working on it.
In my own experience in dealing with bureaucracies about a problem, the greatest frustration has never been the problem itself, but the
sense that no one cares and that no one even recognizes that there is a
problem. I was determined that the university bureaucracy would not
make those mistakes. I always arrived at my office by 7:15 a.m., and
Connie Saathoff and Joyce Moos were usually already at their posts
by then. I started returning the students' calls by 7:30. I did discover
that most of our students were not taking 8:00 a.m. classes. In addition, I returned a call to one irate philosophy faculty member at 9:30
a.m. who had called me the previous day complaining that the university was not adequately staffing its undergraduate courses. I woke
him up. My first reaction was that if you would get out of bed and go
to work, we might not have such a significant staffing problem. However, I did attend the Shirley Bird Perry school for politically correct
comments. As a result, I held my sarcasm.

To begin dealing with the substance of the problem, I asked Provost Gerry Fonken and Vice Provost Steve Monti to examine the issue
of class availability and to bring recommendations to me as soon
as possible—meaning a matter of days if not, indeed, hours. They
concluded that while there was a serious problem of overcrowding
throughout the institution, most of the registration problems focused
on thirty-two high-demand undergraduate courses, each of which, of
course, was offered in multiple sections each semester. The good news
was that if we could solve the problem in those thirty-two courses, we
could resolve most of the issues. I felt we had to deal with this prob-

lem effectively in the spring 1990 class schedule. We had to avoid at all costs a spring registration disaster.

Most of the deans were very cooperative. Fonken and Monti pointed out that a number of classes in the College of Communication had five or six graduate students each, while the college was unable to provide the faculty necessary to offer enough sections of basic undergraduate speech courses to meet student needs.

I asked Dean Robert Jeffrey to come to my office in October 1989 to try to resolve the matter, and he pushed back very hard on Fonken's position that the college needed to reallocate its faculty resources for the spring to deal with the undergraduate problem. After about twenty minutes, I looked at him squarely and without any emotion and said that I understood his position and he did not have to worry about it in the future because starting in the spring the provost and I would schedule all classes of the College of Communication in *my* office.

Jeffrey got the message and he immediately became much more flexible. I have no doubt that he was very upset with me at the time, but he went downstairs to the Provost's Office and in a very short time they resolved all the scheduling issues. Several faculty members who were teaching very small graduate courses were pulled out of those courses and were assigned to teach sections of the high-demand undergraduate speech courses.

I knew that this kind of action could be only an immediate and short-term solution, since the strength of the university lies in upholding and enhancing both its undergraduate and graduate school missions. For the longer term, we would have to have additional financial support in order to expand the size of the faculty, and would have to further control the size of the student population, in order to maintain the health of both undergraduate and graduate education. But in the fall of 1989, the most serious immediate problem was not the vitality of any particular graduate seminar but the ability of the university to meet its most fundamental obligations to its undergraduates. It was absolutely essential that we focus on that problem and solve it quickly and by any means necessary.

Our next steps to head off another explosive situation in spring 1990 were to find the money to add as many faculty and course sections as we could for spring registration (which takes place in the fall) and then for the Provost's Office to take over the adds and drops process in January 1990 to make sure student needs were met.

Fonken and members of his staff went to adds and drops in January 1990, with my full authority, and sat there for three days and made decisions on class size for the thirty-two courses that had been identified as the core of the problem. When a college proposed class sizes that were judged to be unreasonably low, Fonken would simply override the deans and would make the final decisions about how many students would be in each class. The result of these decisions, as well as decisions about reallocation of resources, was that we succeeded in adding some 8,800 class seats in the spring of 1990, compared with the previous spring semester.

I had some complaints from deans about Fonken "meddling" in the affairs of their colleges, but I backed up his decisions. From one perspective, it *was* meddling. But from a more important perspective, it was problem-solving. We had no choice but to take such actions as an emergency matter. I know that increasing class sizes may have involved some damage to pedagogy in some courses. Nevertheless, the class availability problem had to be solved, one way or another. When Dean Standish Meacham called me to complain about Fonken's "micromanagement" as it affected the College of Liberal Arts, my response was, "Standish, you broke the code. We are going to manage (or micromanage) our way out of this crisis this semester."

While the university was fighting its way through the immediate class availability problem, I had not lost track of the fundamental enrollment management issue—our ability to control the number of undergraduates who were matriculating to UT.

In the spring of 1990 I shared with the UT System and the UT Board of Regents a series of additional requirements, beyond the enrollment management measures already approved by the board or undertaken by the campus, in order to achieve the goal of 48,000 students by 1994. These included:

- asking the board for new restrictions on the admission of transfer students
- developing new internal policies to increase the number of graduate students while decreasing the total enrollment (an approach that had a positive financial impact because the state formulas generated more money for a graduate student than an undergraduate)

- revising the rules under which students could transfer from one college to another or gain entry to upper-level courses in professional programs
- seeking resources to augment formula-driven appropriations for new faculty and staff positions
- continuing to monitor application patterns, availability of resources, and a variety of indicators of quality so that recommendations for further changes in admission policies could be brought to the board with sufficient lead time.[9]

In August 1990, the board of regents approved my recommendation to further tighten the rules for admission of transfer students, those who had started their college careers elsewhere but wanted to finish their undergraduate degrees at UT Austin. The next major change came in August 1992, when the regents approved further restrictions, to be effective with the 1994 admissions cycle. These changes continued the trend of increasing admissions standards, reducing the number of students gaining automatic admission, and increasing the number whose applications were reviewed individually. We kept in place an affirmative action measure that provided for an individual review of every African American or Hispanic applicant in the top half of their high school classes.

The great news was that the new telephone registration system (it was called TEX) worked as advertised. I went to the computing center with James Vick, who had succeeded Ron Brown as vice president for student affairs, on Sunday night, April 22, 1990, when it was officially turned on for fall 1990 registration.

I wanted to be there because I knew this new technology was going to be central to the success of the university. If it had failed, we did not have a Plan B, except to return to the old and clearly inadequate system of having students entering desired classes on a computerized sheet and submitting it with the hope for an eventual computer match. If we had been forced to go back to that, I would not have been surprised to see riots on the campus. Fortunately, the new computer system worked. With the flick of a switch, students anywhere in the world, so long as they had a touch-tone telephone, were now able to sign up for classes, change their classes, and operate with all the flexibility of being in a large room in the old days, with none of the long lines. While the telephone registration system did not, in itself,

UT students registering by phone through "TEX." *UT Office of Public Affairs Records, e_utopa_00015.*

add any class seats, it did alleviate logistical nightmares for students, so it made a dramatic improvement in the university experience. The phone system also added a new twist to the long and distinguished administrative career of William S. Livingston, vice president and dean of graduate studies, whose personable and memorable speaking style helped him become "the voice of TEX," always signing off with this congenial wish for students: "Goodbye and good luck."

The campus registration crisis of fall 1989 helped prompt a campus-wide review of undergraduate education in all its aspects. I appointed a special thirty-six-member Committee on the Undergraduate Experience, chaired by Frank Bean, professor of sociology, to examine all aspects of the undergraduate program and make recommendations on how to enhance and enrich the experience for our students. In the fall of 1991 I accepted this committee's comprehensive recommendations, which I believe significantly strengthened the quality of education for undergraduates at the university. One of the major recommendations was for the creation of a new administrative position with oversight for all aspects of the undergraduate program, and I was pleased to appoint Dr. George Wright to this new position of vice provost. Wright, one of the university's most distinguished teachers, had earlier been appointed by Dean Robert D. King to lead the African American studies center, and he continued to excel in his leadership role over the undergraduate program. It is a measure of Wright's extraordinary abilities that he went from those early administrative roles to serve with distinction as provost at UT Arlington and then president of Prairie View A&M University.

I am very pleased that during my tenure as president of UT Austin we were able to solve the institution's admissions, registration, and class availability problems. In addition, our admission system was changed eight times. All of these changes were by necessity incremental in nature. I do not believe that the university could have survived politically if we had tried to make all the changes at once.

William Livingston, the voice of TEX, c. fall 1990. *Prints and Photographs Collection, di_06021.*

CHAPTER 6

Apartheid and Divestment Protests

Students at many universities across the country participated in the 1970s and 1980s in a movement to put pressure on the government of South Africa to change its system of racial discrimination known as apartheid. One focus of this movement was the effort to get U.S. universities to sell their investments in companies that did business in South Africa. At UT Austin, the movement was represented mainly by a group of African American students who, along with their allies from other ethnic groups, formed several organizations and put forward an agenda for changes in the investment policies set by the board of regents. As president during some of the most active years of this movement, I was often directly involved with these students and came to admire their dedication, seriousness, and persistence. I disagreed with their position on divestment, but I believe many of them saw the antiapartheid and divestment movements as an opportunity for their generation to engage in social and political issues comparable to the U.S. civil rights movement in which their parents and grandparents had participated. They espoused the same nonviolent principles, and they challenged the status quo with the same kind of forceful dedication.

Opinion was often sharply divided over the idea of divestment. Proponents, including many black leaders within South Africa, argued that divestment would put economic pressure on the South African government to change. Many other people felt that divestment would do more harm than good for South Africa's black population by leading to a loss of jobs and other economic hardships.

There was also considerable debate about what effect divestment might have on the value of university investments, as well as over the principle of whether university endowment funds ought to be tools for the furtherance of *any* political or social agenda. The University of Texas Board of Regents was legally bound by the "prudent person rule," which required the regents to invest university resources with the same care that would be shown by a theoretical "prudent person," and it was often argued that this rule might be violated by an increased exposure to risk that divestment might bring.

The fine points of these issues were addressed on several occasions by the board of regents. Students had requested that the board divest its South African–related investments as early as 1978, but the first full-scale review of the issue by the board came in December 1984. By the time I became president, the regents had already decided against divestment.

When the regents revisited the question in February 1986, they voted against divestment on the grounds that it could cost the UT System more than $30 million a year in investment income, according to estimates of the asset management staff. The regents also reaffirmed their position that university investment decisions should be made only on the basis of sound financial analysis and not political views. At that meeting the regents also endorsed a set of business guidelines known as the Sullivan Principles, which set forth rules for how companies could operate on a limited basis in South Africa and still take responsible actions supporting the black majority.[1] The Office of Asset Management was charged with monitoring companies for compliance with the Sullivan Principles. At the same time, the regents adopted a largely symbolic policy prohibiting any investment in government-owned companies in South Africa or in securities issued by the government.

The subtleties of the divestment debate were obscured in the spring of 1986, when UT Austin experienced its first large student demonstrations in several years. Like most such events, these demonstrations were designed less for reasoned debate and more for the expression of emotion through slogans and chants. They also became, for a time, confrontational challenges to the university's regulations for public meetings. Free speech quickly became a central focus of that spring's demonstrations.

The turbulence of the 1960s was in the minds of many UT administrators in April 1986, and one reason for that was recent violent protests at Columbia, Berkeley, and other campuses over the divestment issue. Large antiapartheid demonstrations had been a feature of the Berkeley campus for many years, but a series of incidents there beginning on March 30 seemed to echo the turmoil of an earlier era. After several days of demonstrations, confrontations, and arrests over a "shanty town" erected by students as a symbolic protest, a full-scale riot occurred on the Berkeley campus on April 3, 1986. At least ninety-one people were arrested and twenty-nine people (including eighteen police officers) were reported injured.[2]

Our student affairs staff were concerned that something like the Berkeley riot might occur at UT, and we anticipated that a few students were excited about that same possibility. One reason we were apprehensive was a racial incident that had occurred in March at the Pi Kappa Alpha fraternity, which had staged what it called a "porter party," advertised with pictures of African Americans in stereotypical roles of servants. Several dozen students organized a protest and marched from the Texas Union to the fraternity house, where they lined up across the street with their signs. The police arrived to try to keep the groups apart, but before long some of the fraternity members hurled empty beer cans, a weapon of which they probably had an endless supply, at the protesters. A brief fight ensued, and at least one fraternity member was arrested.

After that incident, fraternity parties and investment policies were blurred together in some people's minds, and I believe the Pi Kappa Alpha incident was one reason the April protests over divestment were as difficult as they were. Until April 11, campus demonstrations over divestment had been peaceful and orderly. Several student groups, including the Black Student Alliance and the Steve Biko Committee,[3] had held demonstrations and had spoken at regents meetings, and the Students' Association had sponsored a referendum calling for divestment. And, as at Berkeley and many other campuses, students had erected a shanty at UT as a symbol of the plight of South African blacks.

Several hundred students and others filled the West Mall a little before noon on April 11. Although the topic of the rally was apartheid and divestment, the subject quickly changed to the university's "free speech rules" when some members of the crowd did not disperse after 1:00 p.m., the time designated for public demonstrations at that location to come to an end. A little after 3:00 p.m., UT police began arresting demonstrators who refused to end their rally. Because of the size of the crowd, the UT police had asked for help from the Austin Police Department, and a group of Austin officers had lined up at the

Apartheid protestors in front of the Main Building, September 27, 1987. *UT Texas Student Publications Photograph Collection, e_uttsp_00002.*

base of the west steps of the Main Building to help preserve order. By the end of the afternoon, forty-two protesters had been arrested, mostly without incident. Most of those who were removed from the West Mall were white, and they included a few staff and faculty, as well as some people not affiliated with the university.

By continuing their West Mall rally past 1:00 p.m., the protesters were challenging the university's regulations for maintaining order on the campus. The U.S. Supreme Court has ruled consistently that campuses have the right to regulate the "time, place, and manner" of public meetings, and the university was still operating under regulations that it had devised for antiwar protests in the late 1960s and early 1970s. Our regulations for outdoor meetings designated two campus areas—the Texas Union Patio and the East Mall Fountain—

as "free speech areas," meaning that rallies and meetings could be held there at any time. Other locations—including the highly popular West Mall—could be used for meetings only by permit, and the Dean of Students' Office regularly issued permits (including permission for the use of amplified sound) for the West Mall from noon to one o'clock. We sought to have West Mall meetings end by 1:00 p.m. so as not to interfere with classes in nearby buildings.

Groups sponsoring another antiapartheid demonstration obtained the noon-hour reservation for the West Mall again the next Friday—April 18—and we fully expected a repeat of the April 11 violations. An even larger crowd showed up, and they were clearly at least as interested in another confrontation over the meeting regulations as they were in apartheid and divestment. This time 182 people were arrested.

County Attorney Ken Oden had made it clear to UT officials that he was not interested in prosecuting demonstrators on a charge such as disruptive behavior (a misdemeanor), so we had to reconsider the logic of arresting people when there was no likelihood of prosecution. At first it seemed to me that Oden was taking a simplistic view of the law, but he said he didn't think it was a criminal offence for students merely to be disruptive and disobedient to their elders. It was clear he wanted the university to deal with nonviolent protests through its own disciplinary procedures rather than the criminal justice system. When I stood back and tried to look at the events objectively, Oden seemed to be making a lot of sense. The main question was how to maintain a safe and orderly educational environment. Oden was saying, in effect, that that was *my* job and not *his,* at least unless someone committed an assault or destroyed property, and I accepted that position.

I also recognized that what we had been trying was not working. We had fallen into the hands of the demonstrators and were actually doing what their leaders had been hoping for, making the situation more and more dramatic and helping to create sympathy for the protesters. In insisting that the old rules be enforced and that violators be arrested, I was allowing myself to be influenced too much by the other administrators. As I gained more experience, I realized that an important part of my job was to push back and challenge the advice that I was being given. I think I learned a lot during my presidency about picking the battles that were worth fighting and avoiding the others. The events of the spring of 1986 helped me learn that lesson.

So toward the end of April I decided to try a new approach—to see what would happen if we did not challenge the protesters and we would not arrest them. It took several hours on April 25, but eventually the crowd wore itself out with shouting and chanting. At the end, the demonstration had dwindled to perhaps two dozen people chanting at a TV news camera, and soon after the camera crew left, the last of the protesters did, too. Some people in the crowd probably didn't know if they had won a victory that afternoon or had been outsmarted.

The success of our strategy depended heavily on the university calendar. Ron Brown, vice president of student affairs, was fond of quoting T. S. Eliot's line that "April is the cruelest month," not in the way Eliot meant it but because the usually fine weather of April always seemed to bring out large numbers of student demonstrators who presented problems for administrators. But Ron also counseled that if we could just get through the middle of April everything would be okay because then students would have to begin studying for finals. That proved to be the case in 1986, and May was much quieter than April. Nothing can change the course of a student revolution as quickly as final exam week or an impending summer vacation.

I believe I also helped change the course of this particular "revolution" when I decided not to arrest student protesters on April 25 and announced on May 7 that I was appointing a committee of students, faculty, and staff to take a fresh look at campus "free speech" rules, particularly the rules for the West Mall. I was fortunate in being able to call on Mark Yudof, dean of the School of Law and a nationally prominent expert on the First Amendment, to chair this committee. And I was doubly fortunate that Professor Charles Alan Wright of the law school, a leading authority on constitutional law, also joined the committee. Wright had helped design the campus regulations in the earlier period of student protest, and the university benefited from his judgment on how to adapt them to this new era. Other members of this committee were Clemith J. Houston, assistant director for personnel services and employee relations; and two students, David Quan (law) and Melissa Mueller (business). I also announced that we would postpone any disciplinary action against students who had violated the rules that spring until the committee gave me its recommendations.

The committee turned out to be an ideal vehicle for getting ourselves out of the trap we had created. The truth was that very few

people really cared about whether there was a demonstration on the
West Mall at any hour, and once we got past the hurdle of defending
the rules as they were and became willing to reexamine them, that
fact became obvious. The possibility was only minimal that classes or
other university business would be disrupted by a rally on the West
Mall, so I couldn't see letting the campus be brought to a halt over
this issue.

The West Mall rules dated to the time of Frank Erwin, and the
way the university was defending them in early April certainly fit his
style. Some people in the administration thought of the West Mall as
the heart of the university and were convinced that it needed to be
protected from excessive noise, and others believed the rules needed
to be defended just because they were the rules. The breakthrough
in our executive officers' meetings came when we began to question
what was so sacred about these particular rules. My argument was
that we had upheld our obligations and had tried defending the rules,
and in the process we had discovered that they were indefensible. The
alternative was not retreat and anarchy, as some continued to fear,
but a new set of rules.

I had asked the committee to complete its work by the end of the
summer so we could begin the coming school year on a new footing.
They worked at an almost unheard-of pace for a university committee and delivered their recommendations to me on July 2, and two
weeks later I announced a number of changes in line with the recommendations. The new policy made the West Mall one of the official
"free speech areas," in which demonstrations would be allowed at
any time without a permit. Sound amplification was to be allowed for
two hours at midday and again in the early evening. At the East Mall
Fountain sound amplification would be allowed at any time.

I also announced that all disciplinary proceedings against students
in the spring protests would be dropped and the university would not
pursue criminal charges. I wanted a fresh start in September, with
rules of our own making rather than a system that we had inherited, and this "amnesty" seemed like a good way to allow the entire
campus community to start over.[4]

During the weeks that the committee was conducting its review of
the regulations, students who had been active in the divestment campaign long before the April demonstrations asked to meet again with
the board of regents. Representatives of the Black Student Alliance

From left, Art Dilly, William H. Cunningham, and Lowell Lebermann at a UT System retirement reception in 1998. *Photo by Bette Mayfield Photography, copy courtesy of William H. Cunningham.*

and the Steve Biko Committee spoke at a June meeting of the board at Balcones Research Center (now the Pickle Research Campus) and made a very professional presentation, but they did not persuade the regents to change. Jess Hay recommended to the students a report by Alan Pifer, president emeritus of the Carnegie Corporation, titled "Beyond Divestment: The Moral University," which challenged the view that divestment was a morally correct action and argued against making investments with public money based on political viewpoints.[5] Throughout the students' numerous meetings with the regents on the divestment issue, the UT System and the students were well served by the efficient and professional work of Art Dilly, executive secretary to the board of regents from 1981 to 1998. Dilly was the system's liaison for members of the public who wished to speak to the board, and he always made these arrangements with great skill, courtesy, and respect for the visitors, regardless of their status. I believe his ability to communicate with the students in such a professional manner went a long way toward establishing good relations between the board and the students, despite their strong disagreements on the divestment issue.

When the new academic year began, the student demonstrations resumed, but most students who were concerned about the issues seemed to like the new rules for use of the West Mall, and the emphasis of the rallies was on divestment and apartheid rather than free speech. This atmosphere was fouled on October 3, when someone set fire to the antiapartheid shanty that a student group called Democracy in Academia had set up at the center of the mall. The group rebuilt the shanty and tried to guard it, but incidents of vandalism continued from time to time for as long as it stood on the West Mall. The shanty served other purposes than standing as a revered symbol of the need for political change. One day when my son, John, who was nine years old at the time, and I were looking out across the West Mall from the fourth-floor terrace of the President's Office, we saw two students inside the shanty kissing. John asked me what they were doing, and I told him. He was appalled.

While most students continued to express their views on apartheid and divestment peacefully, a small number decided to go beyond discussion and debate to publicize their views about apartheid. I was delayed getting to work on the morning of October 20 by a flat tire, so I wasn't in the office[6] when sixteen people entered, announced they were taking over the area, and barricaded the doors with desks and locked them with a heavy chain. They ripped out the telephone wires, but Joyce Moos discreetly pressed a silent alarm, notifying the UT police that there was trouble. In addition to Joyce, Ed Sharpe and Connie Saathoff (who was pregnant with Kiersten) were already at work, and all of them refused to abandon the offices to the protesters.

As Isabella was driving me to work, I heard over the police radio that there were "problems in 99's office." That was the code at the time for my office, so I used the radio to call in and find out what was going on. I was told there had been a takeover of my office, and I instructed the dispatcher to get as many officers to the building as soon as possible, but not to take any action until I arrived. As I got off the elevator, I found the fourth-floor landing full of officers, with Captain Harry Eastman of the UT Police Department in charge.

Through the glass doors, I could see Sharpe, Moos, and Saathoff, and it was clear they were unharmed.

Eastman asked what I wanted him to do, and I said "get them out of my office." I never entertained for an instant the idea of talking to them about their motives or negotiating with them. As a matter of principle, I knew it would be wrong to negotiate with people who were breaking the law. I was also aware of other occasions when a university president's office was taken over by students, and it seemed that a fundamental mistake was letting the incidents drag on through prolonged negotiations. Just two years earlier, Michigan State had experienced a very difficult office takeover that had lasted more than a week, and the president eventually lost his job in part because of the way that incident had been handled. And in 1975, during the tenure of President Lorene Rogers, the same offices that I occupied had been taken over for most of a day by ten protesters demanding changes in the university's minority-related programs. In that incident, Gonzalo Barrientos, then a member of the Texas House of Representatives, was brought in to help negotiate with the protesters while about a thousand people on the West Mall chanted their support for the students inside. Watching that episode from my faculty office at the business school, I thought the university had made a serious mistake in allowing the episode to last so long and to be manipulated by others for political purposes, and now as president I was determined not to make that same mistake.

Within minutes, a group of UT police officers, led by Eastman, had climbed up the outside wall of the building on the east side and broken through the windows of the Stark Library to gain entrance to the suite of offices. I watched from the landing as the police chased the surprised protesters through the suite toward my own office on the west side. Some protesters resisted, and I saw the police use just enough force to overcome whatever resistance was offered. Some protesters lay down on the floor and the police pulled them upright by their ears and handcuffed them. I noticed that people rose straight up off the floor when they were grabbed by the ears. The goal was to arrest all the protestors, and that goal was achieved efficiently and professionally by the UT police. Some of the protesters cried "police brutality," and charged that the police had beaten them. That was not true. I watched it all from the other side of the glass, and the fact is that the police used a minimum of force and acted very professionally throughout the episode. No one ever filed a formal complaint about the actions of the police.

We found that thirteen of the protesters were UT students, one was a former student, and two were not affiliated with the university. All were charged with "disruptive activity," a misdemeanor, a charge that some people considered much too lenient. Two other students were also charged that day with disruptive activity for defacing the outside of the Main Building with paint.

The university pursued disciplinary action against the students who were involved, but the outcome of that action was complicated by the criminal cases. In late October, the Dean of Students' Office notified those involved that a penalty of suspension for one year from the date of the takeover (October 20) would be assessed against each of them. The students, however, exercised their right to have their cases heard by a hearing officer, and those proceedings were eventually postponed by an injunction issued by State District Judge Harley Clark. Judge Clark ruled that the disciplinary hearing would have to wait until after disposition of the criminal cases in order to protect the students' right against self-incrimination on the criminal charges. (Judge Clark introduced the "Hook 'em Horns" hand signal to UT in 1955 when he was a Longhorn cheerleader.) The final appeals on the criminal cases were not concluded until 1990, so some of the students graduated or left UT for other reasons well before any disciplinary action could be carried out.

It was always important to separate the actions of those who took over my office from students who continued to advocate divestment peacefully and legally. I met with some students who were strong advocates of divestment, as well as students with other viewpoints, at an open forum for students on October 21, the day after the takeover. This meeting had been scheduled for weeks. Some staff members questioned whether I should go ahead with this forum, but I felt very strongly that I should not appear to be hiding from students. The only time I was a bit nervous was when I walked into the meeting and saw ten UT police officers dressed in full riot gear carefully hidden out of sight of the audience. They were there to protect me, and I appreciated that a great deal. Of course, I received a lot of questions about divestment, apartheid, the takeover, and what might happen to those who had been arrested. The meeting went quite well.

The next day, I agreed to another meeting with students over these issues, this time with about eighteen students who had been very active in the antiapartheid and divestment protests. We met for an hour and twenty minutes in the Stark Library. We did not admit the news media because we wanted it to be a conversation with students and not a press conference, but I discussed the meeting with the media later. I talked with the students about everything from the police tactics that ended the takeover to details of the UT System's investment policy. The students were convinced that they could put together an investment portfolio that would not include any companies involved in South Africa and would still generate returns equal to what we were earning. They wanted me to promise them that I would recommend divestment to the regents if they could "prove" to me that such a portfolio was feasible, and we had a lively discussion about the ins and outs of that. They also accused the UT police of using excessive force two days earlier, but I told them I was not going to investigate those allegations because I was there, I saw what happened, and I had no doubt whatsoever that the police had acted properly. Like the students the day before, many were surprised that I had witnessed the end of the episode and was able to counter their charges of "police brutality" with the evidence from my own eyes.[7]

I did not attend the main trial of members of the "UT 16," as the *Daily Texan* and other newspapers called the protesters, even though there were only eleven defendants present for the trial, which took place in September 1987 before County Court-at-Law Judge Leslie Taylor. Saathoff and Moos testified about what had happened. They were very effective witnesses for the prosecution. One defendant was convicted in a separate trial earlier that year, and arrest warrants were issued for the remaining four, who never showed up for their trial although one of those was later arrested and pleaded guilty. A jury found the eleven guilty, and they were sentenced to jail time ranging from ninety days to five months, as well as given fines. Their final appeals were rejected by the Texas Court of Criminal Appeals in 1990. The jail sentences were a surprise to me, especially since I had been consulted by Oden regarding the punishment, and I had suggested that restitution for the damage to the office and some time of community service would be appropriate. That was what Oden had recommended to the court, but Judge Taylor was not in a lenient mood, especially after the defendants had shown disrespect for the court during the trial.

As far as I know, no one has ever offered a reasoned explanation for how this office takeover might have led to a change in investment policy by the regents, or even how it might have mobilized public opinion in support of a change in policy. At the trial almost two years later, one of the protestors offered the bizarre explanation that they had acted because they were "frustrated" and thought the takeover would persuade the regents to take them seriously and stop treating them "like schoolkids."[8]

After the office takeover, the campus was relatively calm, although the campaign for divestment continued. From August 1986 to June 1989, the amount of UT endowment funds invested in companies that did business in South Africa declined more than 50 percent, from $871 million to $410 million. Michael Patrick, executive vice chancellor for asset management, said in a report to the regents that the fact that more than ninety publicly traded companies withdrew from South Africa in that time span was responsible for a substantial part of the decline.[9]

The divestment issue abated significantly on U.S. campuses after February 1990, when the president of South Africa, F. W. de Klerk, announced the freeing of Nelson Mandela and stated that he favored an end to apartheid and the establishment of a democratic government. Although democratic elections would not be held until April 1994, when Mandela was elected president, the divestment movement certainly declined in intensity when the process toward these elections had gotten underway.

One more detail related to the aftermath of the office takeover: In those days, we had only rudimentary security procedures, mostly designed to react to a problem rather than to prevent one. After the takeover, we began stationing a UT police officer on the fourth floor when rallies or demonstrations were in progress outside the building, and occasionally we kept the main door to the offices locked. That procedure explains why, in September 1991, Officer Don Marquez was on the fourth floor when a young man who had just dropped out of school entered the office at about noon with a .357-caliber pistol, pointed the gun at my administrative assistants Connie Saathoff and Brenda Flores, and threatened to keep them hostage until I returned from lunch. If there had not been a student rally underway outside, totally unrelated to the person with the gun, Marquez would not have been present, and who knows what would have happened. As it

Officer Pascual "Don" Marquez, May 1, 1992. *UT Texas Student Publications Photograph Collection, e_utt-sp_00004.*

turned out, Marquez quickly subdued the former student, although the gun was fired during the struggle, and a bullet hit the ceiling. Marquez suffered some hearing loss from the gunshot, but fortunately no one else was injured.

Once again, the UT police came to our rescue. Officer Marquez was a highly trained professional who risked his life to protect the staff members in the President's Office. I created an award for service well beyond the call of duty and named it after Chief Don Cannon. The award was accompanied by a check for $3,000. Officer Marquez was the first recipient of the Cannon Medal. And also as a result of the incident, we established a much more elaborate security system, and the days when anyone could just take the elevator up to the fourth floor and walk into the President's Office were gone forever.

CHAPTER 7

Minority Student and Faculty Recruitment and Retention

[E]fforts to achieve greater ethnic diversity within the student and faculty population had been a priority of UT Austin since the 1970s. Administrations before mine had created dozens of programs designed to increase the participation of African American and Hispanic students and faculty in the life of the university. We expanded many of these programs and introduced a significant number of new ones. Progress was slow and difficult to achieve, and along the way some individuals may have given up on the university because of these difficulties. I always reminded our critics that we were engaged in a marathon, not a hundred-yard dash, and I was determined to make significant progress in recruiting and retaining more minority students and faculty during my presidency. On every day of my presidency—literally, every day—one aspect or another of these issues was part of my agenda.

The lessons of respect and fairness for all people that I received from my parents predisposed me to take seriously the issues of racial justice and to want to make a contribution to solving the problems that the university had inherited from the days of overt and official discrimination. Dealing with these problems as president gave me a renewed appreciation for the urgent need for society to address inequality and injustice, as well as a greater understanding of just how formidable this challenge was. I also learned a great deal from the interactions that I had with minority students as we tackled the problems, and in retrospect I believe it is fair to say that my administration worked in significant ways in partnership with the minority students who were active in dealing with these issues. We did not always agree, and as the chief representative of the university I was sometimes the target of some fairly intense rhetoric from students, but I do believe we were working toward the same goals.

I always felt that higher education was the key to freeing people from their historical bonds. While I recognize that there are a few people such as Michael Dell and Bill Gates who have been very successful in their professional and philanthropic lives without a college degree, most people who have made major contributions to society have benefitted from having a degree. I also recognized that the demographic changes that were sweeping Texas demanded success in educating all our citizens, lest the state suffer from an inadequately prepared and uncompetitive workforce. In addition, if the university was not successful in attracting significant numbers of minority students and faculty it would face major political problems from the state legislature since Texas was on a march to becoming a minority-majority state.

By the time I became president, the university had instituted a broad range of affirmative action programs designed to encourage and assist minority students. The challenges that the university faced in making these programs succeed were complicated by the long legacy of segregation and the fact that change had begun only recently. In 1985, two-thirds of the university's history (from 1883 to 1950) had occurred under officially sanctioned segregation. In contrast, only thirty-five years had elapsed since the 1950 decision of the U.S. Supreme Court in *Sweatt v. Painter*, which outlawed segregation in UT law and graduate programs, and the really serious efforts by the university to desegregate had begun only in the 1970s. Resistance to these efforts by many whites was probably inevitable, just as was the profound anger, mistrust, and alienation within the black community that university officials continued to encounter. The university had only a handful of black alumni by the 1970s, and any UT president could name just about every black graduate who was a friend of the institution. This historical context had real and serious effects on efforts to change.

In the mid-1980s, affirmative action was still a relatively new tool in efforts to expand educational opportunity. The federal government had first enforced affirmative action policies only twenty years earlier, in September 1965, when President Lyndon B. Johnson signed an executive order related to hiring and employment practices by gov-

ernment contractors.[1] Affirmative action had many critics, and part of
my job as president was to deflect this criticism and make a reasoned
case for the institution's many minority outreach programs. I was
sensitive to those who complained that affirmative action had kept
their children or grandchildren from being admitted to the university.
I would always listen to their concerns and then tell them that we
"need affirmative action today so that we would not need it tomorrow." I tried to make the point that affirmative action was a necessary
but ultimately temporary way of dealing with the continuing effects
of years of discrimination. This, along with the fact that we had the
Provisional Admissions Program, which allowed any Texan who had
graduated from an accredited high school to enter the university on
probation, permitted most thoughtful people with whom I dealt to
accept affirmative action.

Members of our student affairs team and I were reminded every
year of the importance of recruiting minority students when we
attended the annual banquets that Dr. Mario Ramirez sponsored to
recognize high school honor students in the Lower Rio Grande Valley.
We could not have had a better or more highly respected friend in the
valley than Dr. Ramirez. He was known as the Doctor of the Valley.
Dr. Ramirez often saw more than forty patients a day in his clinic in
Roma. Many of these people could not pay. Dr. Ramirez never cared,
he was there to serve the people of the valley and they received excellent medical care.

The first year I attended, in May 1986, Ramirez held the banquet
outdoors at his Vista Roma Ranch near the tiny border town of Roma,
and students from Starr, Zapata, Jim Hogg, and Hidalgo counties
were the guests of honor. These were four of the poorest counties in
the nation by economic measures, but judging by the enthusiasm and
commitment displayed at the honors banquet they were rich indeed.
Ramirez was always the driving force behind the banquets, increasingly aided as time went on by UT alumni clubs in the region, business
groups, and other community leaders. Ramirez, who had been named
a Distinguished Alumnus of the university in 1975, later applied his
passion and commitment to helping young people during a term on
the UT System Board of Regents (1989–1995) and as vice president
for South Texas programs at the UT Health Science Center in San
Antonio (1996–2007).

Others who joined me on the UT airplane for that trip included

Regent Mario Ramirez with William H. Cunningham. *UT Office of Public Affairs Records, e_utopa_00017.*

Shirley Bird Perry; Shirley Binder, director of admissions; Augustine Garza, deputy director of admissions; Roy Vaughan, director of the Ex-Students' Association; and Isabella and John. We were delighted that Monty Jones, then a reporter at the *Austin American-Statesman*, also made the trip with us to cover the event, with the newspaper paying for his seat on the state plane. Isabella made a hit with the audience with remarks in Spanish paying tribute to students from the valley who had excelled in the statewide University Interscholastic League contests, and I gave a speech that was divided between bragging about UT Austin and some words of encouragement to the students to continue their education after high school.[2]

As an example of the opportunities available at UT Austin, we announced that the university had awarded almost $800,000 in scholarships for the next fall to minority students from the six counties in the Lower Rio Grande Valley. Most of the students, almost all of whom were Hispanic, could not have attended UT Austin without such financial support. These scholarships represented about 20 percent of the $3.9 million in minority scholarships that the university awarded annually. Throughout the years I was president and chancellor, this annual event in the valley was a high priority, and my schedule was always arranged to accommodate it.

One of the first things I did as president was to appoint a Presidential Standing Committee on Recruitment and Retention of minority students. It included students, faculty, and administrators and was charged with evaluating the university's activities in this area and making recommendations to me for new approaches to recruiting and retaining more minority students. This committee made a major contribution toward sharpening our focus and guiding our efforts to introduce new programs. To give the committee an understanding of what UT was already doing, I asked Ron Brown to give me a comprehensive description of the university's recruitment and retention activities for minority students. In addition to providing a guide to where we were and how we could improve, I was confident that this inventory would prove useful in conveying to the regents, legislators, community leaders, prospective students and faculty, and the news media the breadth and depth of the university's commitment.

The inventory, prepared by Associate Vice President Shannon Janes, showed that we had at least 129 minority recruitment and retention programs.[3] During the 1985–1986 academic year, we spent $1.17 million on minority recruitment programs. In addition, we delivered $22.5 million in financial aid to minority students. The total included grants of $5.57 million, scholarships of $6.65 million, loans of $6.27 million, and employment valued at $4 million. Financial aid came from the federal and state governments, private donations, and the university's own budget. It included $3.9 million in scholarships dedicated to African American and Hispanic students, using money allocated by the board of regents from the Available University Fund. This scholarship program was the largest of its kind in the nation as well as the largest single allocation of resources from the AUF. It had been in place since 1974, starting with $1 million per year.

Other undergraduate recruitment activities in 1985–1986 included an outreach program through which UT admissions counselors visited five hundred high schools a year, most of them with predominantly minority enrollments; a program through which current minority students advised prospective students; and regional receptions for minority students and their parents.

Undergraduate retention activities included a "bridge program" that brought freshman minority students in engineering to the campus for a seven-week summer program that gave them a strong start on their first year at UT; a program matching minority upperclassmen with freshmen to personalize the transition to university life; sponsorship of special student organizations that served as support networks; early-warning grade reporting that enabled us to intervene with students who were having academic difficulty; and tutoring and other services offered through the Learning Skills Center. Similar recruitment and retention efforts were in place in graduate and professional programs. The Graduate School of Business had an extensive series of coordinated programs to attract students, both from among the ranks of UT graduates and around the country, efforts that were strengthened through the loan of an executive from IBM to help work in this area. At various times IBM also paid the salaries of its employees or retirees who worked on minority programs in the colleges of education, engineering, and natural sciences.[4] Herb Miller was one IBM executive who was "loaned" to the College of Business. The program and Miller were so successful that we later stole him away from IBM. He performed a number of important administrative functions in the college, including serving as assistant dean, and has been a very successful faculty member in the Department of Marketing.

Universities always labor under myths and misperceptions, and one that was particularly troublesome to UT Austin within the minority community was the view that the low minority numbers meant the university was not concerned about the issue or trying to correct the problem. Even more difficult for me to accept was that "institutional racism" existed at the university. This was a charge that was not only unfair, but was also difficult to define and, therefore, difficult to respond to. Many people who claimed that institutional racism existed did not have the nerve to state that I was a racist or that any other specific administrator or faculty member was a racist, but they still wanted to charge the university with racism. My standard response to this charge was how could the university be racist when it had the largest number and percentage of African American and Hispanic students of any nonminority university in the nation, the largest undergraduate university scholarship program for minority students in the nation, and a very active retention program for minority students. In addition, the university had created a Target of Opportunity Program to recruit minority faculty members. I never accepted any aspect of this charge and I pushed back energetically every time I heard it. To illustrate how difficult the rhetoric became, at a meeting in April 1986 a member of the Black Student Alliance said that having me as a judge of whether this university is racist is like having a slave owner say "my slaves are happy." Another student, Rudy Malveaux, said that my defense of the university was "insensitive" because I did not attend the university as a black student.[5]

It was clear to me that the university needed to deal with its serious image problem within minority communities. This is one reason I looked for opportunities to attend events focused on minority issues and support minority student initiatives. I always tried to attend the university's programs in honor of Dr. Martin Luther King Jr. on his birthday, not only because it was right for the university to commemorate this day but also because it was an excellent opportunity to demonstrate the commitment of the institution, and my personal commitment, to equal opportunity. Sometimes, however, groups of students and others made it clear at these events that they considered my presence suspect. I was one of the scheduled speakers on the program in 1990, when three thousand people, mainly from off campus, filled the Bass Concert Hall. They had not come to hear me but the featured speaker, Angela Davis, the noted left-wing activist from the 1960s and 1970s who had been a longtime faculty member at the University of California at Los Angeles.

I met Davis, who was then a member of the Communist Party USA,[6] in the green room before the event. Although we had nothing in common politically, I always tried to be a gracious host to all guests of the university, and we had a very pleasant conversation. After we and others on the program went on stage and I began my brief opening remarks, which focused on the continuing importance of King's life and work, the audience went wild. At first I thought they loved me, but then I realized they were booing me. There were three thousand people booing at me. The only exceptions that I saw were Joe Bill and DeDe Watkins. They were sitting right in the middle of the first row, and they were applauding enthusiastically. This was a true test of friendship. I realized that no one, with the exception of the Watkinses, was paying attention to my comments so I stopped my speech in midsentence, said "thank you very much," and sat down. My seat was next to Linda Brodkey, a faculty member in the English Department who had been a strong and vocal critic of mine for years and had been advocating a multicultural course to replace the department's tradi-

William H. Cunningham being confronted by black students over racial incidents on the UT campus, April 13, 1990. *UT Office of Public Affairs Records, e_utopa_00016.*

tional instruction in writing. As I sat down, she leaned over to me and said, "Dr. Cunningham, you have a tough job." I realized at the time how pitiful I must have looked if Brodkey was trying to comfort me.[7]

Several student organizations worked throughout these years to contribute to the solution of the problems of minority recruitment and retention. One was the Black Student Alliance, which came up with several ideas that were adopted by my administration. I did not agree with everything the BSA proposed, and sometimes I found their rhetoric less than helpful, but the organization was an important member of the university community and I believe it served as a valuable focus for the development of leadership skills among African American students.

One of the best ideas put forward by the BSA, in conjunction with the Friar Society, the university's oldest honor society, was to support cultural awareness and discussion of minority issues through establishment of the Heman Sweatt Symposium on Civil Rights, which

quickly became one of the university's most prestigious academic
meetings. The symposium series—named in honor of the man who
filed the historic lawsuit, known as *Sweatt v. Painter,* that resulted
in integration of UT graduate and professional programs in 1950—
was first proposed in the spring of 1985 as a memorial to Sweatt
that "would help counteract Black high school students' lingering
perception of UT as a racist school."[8] The next fall, a group of students—Brett Campbell and Darrick Eugene, representing the Friars,
and Kevin Williams and Barron Wallace, representing the BSA—presented to me and Ed Sharpe a brief proposal for such a symposium,
and I encouraged them to develop their idea in more detail and bring
it back to me. They did so, and in April 1986 I approved their plans
for the symposium and committed $5,000 from the President's Office
to help get planning under way for the first year's program, which
was to be held the following spring. The students had envisioned
the symposium as "an annual event wherein prominent scholars and
knowledgeable public figures would discuss the challenges involved in
ensuring that all Americans receive the civil rights to which they are
entitled by the Constitution."

The committee organizing the symposium, ably and energetically
led by Dr. George Wright, the newly appointed director of the Center
for African and African American Studies, attracted as a keynote
speaker a great jurist and civil rights pioneer, Judge A. Leon Higginbotham Jr. of the U.S. Court of Appeals for the Third Circuit. Among
the others on the program for the first Heman Sweatt Symposium
when it convened on April 9, 1987, were James S. Meredith, the first
African American student at the University of Mississippi; Lyman T.
Johnson, the first black student at the University of Kentucky; John S.
Chase of Houston, whose degree in architecture was one of the earliest graduate degrees earned by a black student at UT Austin; Norcell
Haywood of San Antonio, another early African American recipient
of an architecture degree at UT Austin; Linda Brown Smith, who as
a child was a plaintiff in *Brown v. Board of Education*; and William
Raspberry, the syndicated newspaper columnist. Such a distinguished
group of speakers for the inaugural program represented a great tri-
umph for the students and others who had worked so hard on this
initiative. The symposium has continued to bring outstanding African
American leaders to the campus year in and year out, and it has had
a lasting impact on the academic and cultural life of the university.

William H. Cunningham announcing that George Wright has been given the Jean Holloway Award for Teaching Excellence, May 1988. *UT Office of Public Affairs Records, e_utopa_00022.*

Another good idea from the BSA was the naming of the historic Little Campus for Heman Sweatt. The Little Campus is a collection of nineteenth-century buildings on the southeastern side of the campus, and for many it served as sort of a gateway to the university. Still another idea that students put forward to help with minority recruitment and retention was a summer program for new freshmen to help give them a head start on their first year at the university. The BSA and several other student groups advocated such a program based on their own experience in adjusting to university life, and in early 1986 I decided to try it as a pilot program, beginning with fifty students that summer.[9] The idea was to bring students who had received one of our minority scholarships to the campus six weeks before the fall semester of their freshman year so they could get accustomed to the university before the big crowds arrived. They took a course in learning and study skills as well as one of the standard freshman courses in English, math, or another field, and the university paid their room and board for the six weeks. The program cost the university $50,000 the first summer, and the results indicated it was worth instituting as a regular part of our retention activities.

It was apparent to Vice President for Administration Ed Sharpe and me that the university was, at best, treading water with respect to the minority community and particularly the African American community. Sharpe had gotten to know John Hargis through his volunteer work with the Ex-Students' Association and his involvement in the Association's Black Alumni Task Force. Hargis was one of the university's earliest African Americans to receive a bachelor's degree (in chemical engineering) and he had a distinguished business career. Sharpe had a great deal of confidence in Hargis, and I had a great deal of confidence in Sharpe. Sharpe felt that Hargis would make an excellent addition to the President's Office staff. He introduced me to Hargis and shortly thereafter he accepted my offer in late 1986 to become a special assistant to the president.

I was confident that with Hargis's help, the university was positioned to make major progress with the African American community both on campus and off campus. Unfortunately, tragedy struck when Hargis died of a heart attack only two weeks after he accepted my offer. It was a major loss for the university and for me personally. In February 1987 we named one of the buildings on the Sweatt Little Campus for Hargis—John Hargis Hall, the building on the southeast corner of Red River Street and Martin Luther King Boulevard. It was the only way I knew that UT could reach out to the Hargis family and publicly thank them for what John did and what he wanted to do to serve his university.

I felt more than ever that the President's Office had to make both a symbolic as well as a real effort to reach out to the African American community. Black students on campus did not trust the all-white central administration and the few African American alumni we had did not know us very well. I introduced Sharpe to Lewis Wright, whom I had hired when I was dean to be the assistant dean for financial management in the College of Business. Sharpe agreed with me that Wright could make a major contribution to the President's Office.

I felt very strongly that the university should not appoint a minority czar. I did not want the deans and department chairmen to feel that they could escape their responsibilities of hiring faculty and helping create programs that would encourage minority students to attend and succeed at UT. However, I also felt that the university was not succeeding and that we had to try something different. I felt the appointment of a highly respected African American would send a clear signal to all of the interested communities that I was serious about trying to deal with the problem of recruitment and retention of both minority faculty and students, and I was confident Wright would help develop new programs and generally energize our efforts in the area.

I wanted to make very clear that Wright was going to be a senior member of the university administration. His title was assistant vice president for administration (I promoted him to associate vice president in 1991) and he was the first African American executive officer at UT. I told him I wanted his initial primary focus to be on minority student and faculty issues, as well as the university's interaction with the African American community. While Wright's portfolio of responsibilities grew while he was in the President's Office, he played an active role in every major initiative that was undertaken by the central administration involving these critical issues from 1987 to 1993.

Frank Vandiver, president of Texas A&M, and I initiated a collaborative program between UT Austin and Texas A&M that involved the creation of five minority recruitment outreach centers. The initiative was originally Vandiver's idea, but I endorsed it as soon as I heard about it. Vandiver was a graduate of UT, and he had been the provost at Rice. While he was a strong Aggie, he was always willing to cooperate with UT to do what was best for the people of Texas. I asked Vandiver if we could partner with A&M in the outreach program that he had proposed. It took us about ten minutes to figure out how to design the program, and we joined the forces of our two great universities to make it work better than either could have done alone. The idea was to establish outreach centers staffed by university personnel and providing students as early as middle school with counseling and other services to help them start planning and preparing for college.[10]

The centers—in Dallas, Houston, Austin, San Antonio, Corpus Christi, and McAllen—would provide information about financial aid, applying to college, study skills, tutoring, and many other services. A key component of the services was information about what courses students should be taking in middle school and high school so that they would be ready for college. Officials at both UT and A&M came to realize that we needed to start reaching students earlier to really have an impact. The centers were located in neighborhoods with large numbers of minority students, and they quickly became popular places for students to gather after school. At the centers, students could find a quiet place to study as well as the other services, and each center had programs to involve parents in helping their children get on a path toward college and stay on it.

Our outreach efforts also included visits that I made every year to Texas high schools. In most years I visited at least two dozen high schools across the state, concentrating mostly on those with high numbers of Hispanic and African American students. Accompanied by officials from our admissions or financial aid offices, I would visit classrooms or speak to assemblies of selected students, and whenever possible we also met with counselors, parents, and community groups. My consistent messages to students was that it was important for them to begin preparing early for higher education, that the extensive programs of financial assistance meant a college education was within the economic reach of everyone, and that a college education would not only make them more employable but would also help them contribute to their society and bring them a more fulfilling life. I was primarily selling the idea of education but also encouraging the students to consider opportunities available at UT Austin. We tried to provide as much practical information as possible, and in some cases we were able to invite groups of students to take a bus ride to Austin, at the university's expense, to visit the campus and see firsthand what it offered.

Part of our difficulty in recruiting minority students was a result of a perception among high school counselors that UT did not provide a welcoming environment. I sought to counter this perception by going every year to all the major population centers in Texas and inviting counselors to have lunch with me. I did as many as ten lunches a year, often with fifty to a hundred counselors. Their questions were highly revealing. It was clear they were concerned about how their students could get into UT, but they were also very concerned about what would happen to them after they arrived. They wanted to know how we helped minority students deal with the social pressures of attending a large, predominantly Anglo university.[11] It was also clear to me that high school counselors were not accustomed to being invited out to lunch. The attention that we showed them was very well received and I believe paid off in our efforts to deliver the message that UT cared about their students.

Another important public relations impact of our meeting with both students and counselors was that local television, radio stations,

William H. Cunningham with minority high school students in Rio Grande City, February 1990. *UT Office of Public Affairs Records, e_utopa_00018.*

and newspapers frequently covered our visits. All of our comments were on the record. It was not unusual at all for one trip to the Rio Grande Valley to generate multiple TV and radio stories, plus front-page above-the-fold newspaper articles. Not even UT could afford to buy all of this good publicity.

We desperately needed this kind of good publicity because of the very real legacy of discrimination and even open hostility with which many minority students had been greeted in past years. Even into the 1980s and 1990s, minority students often expressed their view that UT provided an unwelcoming environment and that attitudes had not changed as much as we in the administration liked to think. The perception that minority students were unwelcome was exacerbated from time to time by racially charged incidents, often involving fraternities. One of the most disturbing traditions had to do with insulting and inflammatory words and images related to race and sex on fraternity floats during the annual spring Roundup parade down Guadalupe Street. For years people tried to ignore this behavior, but in 1990 the parade drew outrage and protests by hundreds of students. Vice President for Student Affairs James Vick and Dean of Students Sharon Justice took disciplinary action against the fraternities involved, and I leaned on the Ex-Students' Association to sever its ties to the annual parade, which Vick and I decided would no longer be recognized as a university event. Despite all the actions we took, however, serious damage to the university had already been done by the fraternities, and the institution could never fully recover.

As president and chancellor, I learned that damage to the university's reputation in racial matters could come from almost any quarter—even from a distinguished member of the faculty. In September 1997, for example, UT Austin and the UT System faced a firestorm of outrage from legislators and countless ordinary citizens after Professor Lino A. Graglia of the law school made incendiary comments that were reported in the *Daily Texan* and then picked up by the news media across the country. Graglia, something of a national hero among ultraconservative opponents of affirmative action, had disparaged the academic abilities of African American and Hispanic students and said they were unprepared to compete at UT because they came from cultures that tolerated academic failure. Graglia was well known as one of the law school's most conservative faculty members, as well as one of the most outspoken. Three years earlier, he had been selected by President Reagan for a seat on a federal appeals court, but Reagan withdrew the nomination after reports that Graglia had made derogatory comments in his classroom about African Americans.

Within twenty-four hours of his new comments, minority members of the Texas Legislature were demanding that Graglia be fired. Interim President Peter Flawn and I faced the challenge of explaining to lawmakers, regents, alumni, and others that a professor's inflammatory comments were not sufficient cause for revoking his tenure and firing him, while we also disavowed Graglia's comments in the strongest language possible and repeatedly emphasized that he spoke only for himself.

I issued a news release on Thursday, September 11 (the day Graglia's comments were first reported), in which I stated: "I strongly disagree with the comments of Professor Lino Graglia. His comments that African-American and Hispanic students cannot compete academically with whites and that they come from cultures in which academic failure is not looked on with disgrace are an insult to thousands of minority students and alumni associated with the University of Texas System.

"While his comments particularly demean minority students, they are also an affront to the entire university community. His views do not represent the University of Texas System or the Board of Regents."

Flawn and I agreed that something more was needed—that somehow we needed to impress on Graglia the seriousness of his behavior and the great damage he had done the university. We summoned him to meet us in Flawn's office on September 15, and he showed up with his attorney. I am certain that he expected to be fired, but if we fired him we knew he would almost certainly sue the university and that we would lose. I began the meeting by telling him we weren't going to fire him, and I think he was relieved. But then I made it as clear to him as I could that his stupid remarks had harmed the university, that he had exercised his academic freedom in a seriously irresponsible manner, and that I hoped I would never hear another word out of him. Graglia's response was to ask me to join him at a press conference to publicly reaffirm his rights as a faculty member. I leaned across the table and said, "Lino, you don't understand. I don't want to be seen with you. I don't want to be associated with you." I had no interest in providing Graglia any political cover.

A major expansion of our minority recruitment and retention programs began in 1989 when I approved key recommendations of the Standing Committee on Student Recruitment and Retention, chaired that year by Augustine Garza, deputy director of admissions. Garza was a key staff member who always got the job done, and a major part of the progress that the university made in expanding educational opportunity was a result of his perseverance and hard work. I had a great deal of confidence in him and, as a result, I was very pleased to receive and implement his committee report. We expanded the summer Preview Program as well as a program of "supplementary instruction" in the most difficult lower-division courses and another program of special support in math and science courses. Another recommendation was for a new freshman course that would teach academic, personal, and social coping skills necessary to function in a large university.

The value of all these efforts was reflected in a small but steady increase in minority enrollment. From 1985 to 1992, the seven years I was president, African American students grew from 3.4 percent to

3.7 percent, and in the mid-1990s they rose as high as 4.0 percent before falling back to 3.2 percent in 2000. We were grateful for every fraction of a percentage point in growth, but one can readily see that as a percentage of the total enrollment the representation of African Americans among the student population did not change significantly. During my term as president, the percentage of Hispanic students increased from 8.9 percent to 11.7 percent, and this growth pattern continued during the period I served as chancellor. Our student affairs specialists often attributed this greater degree of success with Hispanics to several factors: the greater increases in the state's Hispanic population as a whole, its greater college-age population, and a strong education ethic among Hispanics. In addition, while I am confident that at times Hispanic students were not always welcomed into all university extracurricular activities, Hispanic students had been enrolled at the university beginning with its first class in 1884. As a result, we had a significant number of Hispanics who were proud graduates of the university and they were often happy to recommend that their children and grandchildren follow in their footsteps.

Given such factors, it was not surprising that graduation rates among African American students were lower than for whites. In the mid-1980s, about 60 percent of Anglo students graduated from UT within six years after they entered as freshmen. For Hispanics, the rate was about 47 percent, and for African Americans, it was approximately 45 percent. Even for white students the rates were too low; it was clear the university needed to work harder to help more students from all ethnic groups succeed at a higher rate.

While UT Austin's student affairs and admissions staff were striving to increase minority enrollment, the university's academic officers were working just as hard to hire and keep minority faculty. This was in many ways a very different problem. While those dealing with minority student enrollment focused mainly on getting more young people from Texas high schools into higher education institutions, the effort to attract minority faculty was nationwide in scope and was heavily impacted by the dramatic lack of supply of minorities with doctoral degrees to meet the ever-increasing demand. Each year's relatively small number of new minority graduates with doctoral degrees were recruited not only by higher education institutions but also by the private sector and by government at all levels. In addition, every campus in the country faced a constant struggle to retain the minority faculty that it had succeeded in hiring, as other institutions kept trying to hire them away.

At the same time that we were trying to solve our local minority issues we had to show that UT Austin could somehow overcome the national supply and demand problem. As president, I occasionally heard advocates say that the low supply of minority candidates for any given faculty position was no excuse and that UT Austin was so wealthy that it could out-compete all the other corporations and government agencies if it really wanted to. That was certainly easier said than done. The supply problem was real and, unfortunately for the university, it was not as wealthy as some people felt.

Throughout the last quarter of the twentieth century, the number of African American and Hispanic students earning doctoral degrees remained woefully low. The National Research Council tracked the numbers annually, and for 1984 it reported, for example, that among the 31,253 doctoral degrees awarded in the United States, African Americans earned 1,049 (3.4 percent). To illustrate this problem, in 1984 only four African Americans received a Ph.D. in mathematics and three African Americans received a Ph.D. in computer science and geological science. One African American was awarded a doctoral degree in classics. The number of Hispanics receiving doctoral degrees in 1984 was equally pathetic. The problem was even more difficult because 48.5 percent of the African Americans and about half of the Hispanics earned their doctorates in education. While colleges of education were doing a relatively good job of producing minority Ph.D.'s, these graduates were not finding jobs in the colleges of liberal arts, natural sciences, engineering, or business.

At UT Austin, we were required to measure our progress in the context of two separate multiyear federally approved affirmative action plans for increasing the number of women and members of ethnic minority groups on the faculty. One plan was overseen by the U.S. Department of Labor and the other by the U.S. Department of Education, and they used different sets of national labor market data, involved different ethnic categories,[12] and employed different methods of setting goals for hiring. The Provost's Office, the academic deans, and the department chairmen devoted considerable labor not only to trying to meet the goals of these plans but also to trying to keep all the paperwork in order. In general, the goals of the two plans were to reduce or eliminate the disparities between our faculty profile and the available national labor pool.[13]

Progress was slow and uneven. In the fall of 1986, after my first year as president, the university actually had two fewer African American faculty members (in all ranks) than it had in the fall of 1982 (thirty compared to thirty-two) and only one more Hispanic (sixty-four compared to sixty-three). The lack of progress and the reversals were disconcerting, particularly in light of all the hard work that university officials had applied to the problem for many years.

In 1987 the administration put in place a new action plan that the Provost's Office and Lewis Wright designed with the hope of getting better results. I announced to the academic deans that it was necessary for the university to "reemphasize its commitment to achieve success in recruiting and retaining a faculty reflecting the full range of ethnic and cultural diversity."

While I made it clear that the responsibility of the search and hiring processes of minority faculty lay with the deans of each college, I was also making it very clear that the central administration was going to increase the monitoring of the progress that the colleges were making on this important initiative and that I would personally hold the deans responsible for helping the university recruit and retain additional minority faculty as a part of this process. I required the deans to submit reports each June to assess the progress in their colleges and schools, not simply reporting on the numbers but also evaluating the effectiveness of programs. The reports were to give special attention to new faculty mentoring programs. "I expect rigorous implementation of other initiatives and school or college unique processes that will effectively advance the institution toward achievement of minority faculty recruitment and retention goals," I told the deans.[14]

I also announced the new Target of Opportunity hiring program. The university would reserve a minimum of ten visiting or regular faculty positions to support competitive minority recruitment efforts and to better respond to unexpected recruitment opportunities. This meant, in effect, that a department could get the money to hire additional faculty if it was hiring an African American or a Hispanic. I did make it clear that if a department had open positions it would have to clearly show why these positions should not be used first to hire minority faculty members. Lewis Wright and the Provost's Office monitored and approved every hiring decision that was made through this program when I was president.

Finally, to help oversee this effort and provide assistance in nation-wide searches for qualified candidates, I established a Minority Faculty Recruitment and Retention Committee, consisting of senior faculty and staff from across the campus. The committee's charge was open-ended. I was interested in learning as much as I could from any group that would address this critical issue. Lewis Wright was my contact with the committee.

Most of the public attention was focused on the commitment to fund at least ten new positions if they could be filled with minority candidates. I tried to emphasize that there was nothing magic about that number. "We may well not hire all ten, but we will try," I told the *Dallas Morning News.* "We will continue to emphasize this program if it is successful. If it is not, we will try something else."[15]

We made some gratifying progress as a result of these policy changes, including the hiring of eighteen new minority faculty (eight African Americans and ten Hispanics) for tenured or tenure-track positions for the 1988–1989 school year (the first recruitment cycle after the changes took effect), and I decided that this remarkable level of progress justified setting aside an additional $300,000 to continue the incentive program for 1989–1990. For that second year of the program, we added three more African Americans and seven more Hispanics to the tenured or tenure-track faculty.

By the 1991–1992 academic year, we had seen gains in the number of African Americans and Hispanics in all faculty ranks, compared with six years earlier. The number of African Americans had risen from thirty to fifty-two and the number of Hispanics had risen from sixty-four to eighty-two. These still represented very small percentages, given that the campus had a total of 2,341 faculty members in all ranks, but we had made more progress than most people would have predicted. We had shown that progress in minority hiring was possible, and while continuing to maintain the university's competitive standards.

Many of the minority faculty who came to UT during those years were hired away from other institutions, so our aggressive recruitment efforts were not helping to solve the overall national shortage of minority candidates. The key to tackling that problem was to encourage more minority students to go to graduate school, and then to encourage them to enter academia after they received their terminal degrees. While I recognize that this was a very important national problem that required a national focus, the issue that was immediately on my desk was improving UT Austin numbers of qualified minority faculty.

I believe it is clear that UT Austin was doing its share to solve that problem, although we certainly kept trying to do more. Year after year, the university was among the nation's leaders in the production of African Americans and Hispanics with graduate degrees. In 1989–1990, for example, we ranked seventh in the nation in doctoral degrees among all minority students, as well as first in the nation in awarding doctoral degrees to Hispanics. In any year and by any measure, we were working hard to be part of the solution, not the problem.

Striking in any review of enrollment during this period is the surge in the number and percentage of Asian American students. During my term as president and chancellor, Asian American enrollment rose from 3.6 percent in 1985 to 12.5 percent in 2000. The number of Asian Americans first surpassed the number of African Americans in 1985. We made no attempt to declare victory in our minority recruitment efforts by celebrating our success with Asian American students. The university is very pleased to have a significant Asian American presence on the campus. They are not only hard working, dedicated students, but their very presence enriches the culture of the university. However, it was clear to me from the beginning of my service in administration that the Asian American students did not need any form of affirmative action or extra support to succeed. My focus was clearly on African Americans and Hispanics.

In hindsight, I was probably more insightful than I realized in 1985 when I said recruiting more African American and Hispanics to the campus was a marathon, not a hundred-yard dash. I do believe my administration attacked the problem very aggressively and very seriously and we did our best to "push the ball down the court." I also know that we did not make as much tangible progress as I would have liked, or as I expected to make during my tenure in administration. I believe we did, however, make significant progress in improving the quality of life for minority students on the campus, so that they came to see themselves as full members of the university community. My goal throughout my tenure as president and chancellor was to make as much progress as possible, quantitatively and qualitatively, and to help set the stage so that future administrations could be even more successful than we had been. It is indeed a marathon, not a sprint.

CHAPTER 8

The Blackland Neighborhood

When I became president of UT Austin I inherited a four-year-old dispute with the Blackland Neighborhood, a predominantly residential area east of campus, across Interstate 35. The dispute arose when UT sought to acquire land east of the highway for campus expansion. From my first briefing on this issue by Ed Sharpe, vice president for administration, and Charlie Franklin, vice president for business affairs, early in the fall of 1985, I could tell this was going to be a difficult matter to resolve. I never imagined, however, that the dispute, which was a classic example of the often-troubled interface between a large and growing urban university and its neighbors, would continue for almost my entire tenure as president.

For UT, the dispute offered a number of critically important lessons in community relations, and it introduced me to several unusual aspects of city and state politics.[1] I believe the university always acted in good faith, although not always with the best judgment. Even when relations with the neighborhood were at their lowest point, I was determined to keep communications open and to keep working to find a solution that would satisfy everyone. The challenge, as I saw it, was how to be a good neighbor and still provide the space and facilities the university needed in order to meet its long-term obligations to the people of Texas.

This long episode began in December 1981 when the board of regents authorized a plan for purchase of a thirty-two-block area east of I–35 for long-term campus expansion. A decision was made that eastward expansion was the only feasible choice, since state office buildings barred the way to the south, and going west would be prohibitively expensive and would also disrupt established student residential neighborhoods as well as intensively developed commercial areas serving the campus community. On the north side of campus, there were two seminaries, a private university, and a hospital—all very difficult to displace. The Blackland Neighborhood took its name from the color of its loamy soil and was mostly modest, single-family houses occupied largely by African Americans.

By the time I became president, much of the original thirty-two-block area had been purchased. This had been done at first through a real estate agency acting as a third party, with the identity of the ultimate purchaser remaining secret. This tactic may have helped the university keep speculators from driving up prices, but it proved disastrous for our relationship with the neighborhood once the university's involvement became known.

By the fall of 1985 the goal was to purchase land east of Comal Street, both north and south of Manor Road. North of Manor Road there was a sliver of land that was quickly acquired, partly through eminent domain proceedings, and was developed as a physical plant facility for the university. The real controversy arose over plans for the area south of Manor Road, where the goal was to acquire the westernmost sixteen blocks of the Blackland Neighborhood, that is, all the land from Comal Street to Chicon Street. It was envisioned that some parts of this tract might not be developed until well into the twenty-first century, but the goal was to acquire the land before it was further developed by someone else.

Critics would say throughout the ensuing dispute that the university's expansion was at the expense of our most vulnerable and least powerful neighbors, and some charged that this was an example of insensitivity or indifference to minority populations, an attitude they said had been characteristic of UT throughout its history. Such charges were always part of the context in which the dispute was played out. It was easy to understand how some residents felt that they were always in the way of someone else's plans, and that "someone else," when it did not consist of city and federal urban planners or state highway engineers, seemed to be the University of Texas.

President Flawn, Franklin, and other UT officials had met regularly since 1982 with the city and the neighborhood to foster cooperation and communication. One result of these meetings was an agreement in 1983 under which the city would buy and relocate houses that UT had acquired in the neighborhood. This was the first of several plans in which UT participated in efforts to promote low-cost housing, although none of the plans ever produced any dramatic results.

Another outcome of the early discussions was a program under which the university and the city paid social work interns to help residents obtain social services. Residents were also allowed to use vacant lots owned by UT as community gardens.

The Blackland Neighborhood Association had opposed the expansion from the beginning, and further opposition came from the Blackland Community Development Corporation, established in 1983 to promote housing for low- and moderate-income households. Leaders of the corporation had assured UT that they did not intend to use their government grants (mostly federal money, administered by the city) to block UT expansion and that if they bought any lots in the area that UT intended to acquire, they would be willing to negotiate an exchange of property outside that area. However, on August 27, 1985, just a few days before I became president, the university learned that the corporation had purchased a lot on Concho Street just one block east of campus and well within the area we were planning to acquire. About a month later we were told that the corporation, despite its earlier assurances, was not willing to trade this lot for another outside the sixteen-block area.[2]

These actions were an open challenge to a 1984 agreement for "peaceful coexistence" between the neighborhood association and the university as the sixteen-block area underwent a transition to "a mix of residential and university campus usage." UT had always stated that its eventual goal was to acquire the entire area, but that the acquisitions would probably be a slow process as lots came on the market. The neighborhood apparently interpreted the 1984 agreement to mean the mixed use would last "forever." The different interpretations remained a point of contention for as long as the Blackland dispute continued.

It was obvious to me when I became president that the Blackland issue, which had been on simmer for a long time, was about to boil over. I found that the neighborhood was not quite as helpless and defenseless as was often claimed. The neighborhood association and the community development corporation were always led by articulate and resourceful people who had a sophisticated understanding of the mechanics of city government, the politics of the Austin City Council and the Texas Legislature, and the ways of the news media. It was not difficult for a small group of inner-city residents, many of whom had lived in their modest homes for decades, to gain a sympa-

Ed Sharpe. *UT Office of Public Affairs Records, e_utopa_000125.*

Lewis Wright. *UT Office of Public Affairs Records, e_utopa_00026.*

thetic ear in their battle against the huge university. The conflict was portrayed as a David-and-Goliath story, and we know who won *that* contest.

One of the most prominent neighborhood leaders was Katherine Poole. During October 1985, she and I exchanged a series of letters in which each of us explained and defended our positions at some length, both about the meaning of the 1984 agreement and the dimensions of the ongoing dispute. Poole was a passionate and determined advocate, as well as a lively correspondent. At one point she observed to me that, given the history of the university's eastward march, the only thing to keep UT "from eventually possessing everything between the Tower and the Louisiana State Line is the willingness of the Texas Legislature to continue financing your speculations."[3]

As our efforts proceeded, I began to rely more and more on Sharpe and Lewis Wright, assistant vice president for administration, as the university's chief liaisons with the neighborhood. They attended many of the neighborhood association meetings, as well as other ses-

sions with leaders of the neighborhood and the city, and they helped
explain the university's position and tried to listen with sympathy to
the concerns of the neighborhood. On more than one occasion, they
helped to hold together the fragile relationship between the university
and the neighborhood, when, if they had not been there, it might
have fallen apart altogether. Beginning in 1987 we gradually changed
from treating the Blackland acquisitions as a real estate challenge and
began looking at it as a community relations issue. This change eventually produced momentous positive results.

From the fall of 1985 to the fall of 1988, the university continued
to buy parcels from willing sellers, and the neighborhood continued to
protest our "encroachment." These years also witnessed a continua-
tion of discussions about how UT could participate in efforts to provide low-cost housing, which clearly was not part of UT's core mission.

Under the 1983 agreement, the city purchased six houses from UT
for $1 per square foot and relocated and renovated them for housing
for low-income residents. Additional purchases would have been possible if the city had been interested. By early 1986, the neighborhood
development corporation had become interested in leasing houses
from UT, bringing them up to city code, and renting them to low-
income families. We evaluated a proposal from the corporation and
decided after discussions with city officials to submit a proposal of
our own. That proposal, submitted to the city in July 1986, would
have given the city the right to rehabilitate, lease, and manage any
houses acquired thereafter by UT in the sixteen-block area, with the
leases to run for five years and with the possibility of annual extensions depending on the university's needs for the property. This proposal represented a major shift in our policy, since up to that point we
had not been interested in maintaining houses on the land that we had
bought, always advocating instead that houses be moved if anyone
wanted them or, failing that, that they be demolished. We did not hear
back from the city on our proposal for over two years.[4]

After more housing proposals were explored by all the parties
without success from 1986 through 1987, I decided to undertake
a broad re-evaluation of our policy in 1988, a pivotal year for the
Blackland dispute. The re-evaluation led to a major new proposal by
UT to the city in July and then, in December, an elaboration on that
proposal that eventually proved to be the key to resolving the dispute
with the neighborhood.

It was ironic that while UT was formulating a new policy for the sixteen-block area, the inflammatory rhetoric from the neighborhood association was reaching new levels of intensity. The association's May 1988 newsletter warned that UT was working "furiously" with city and state politicians to "oil the waters" for "total annexation of west Blackland." The newsletter accused UT of trying to subvert the authority of the neighborhood association and pressuring homeowners to sell their property, and it promised that at an upcoming meeting the association would "discuss new ways to escalate the struggle."[5] None of this rhetoric was helpful in resolving the dispute, but, as is not unusual with such organizations, leaders of the neighborhood association were often more cordial and cooperative in private than when they were playing to their various audiences in public.

The newsletter's reference to UT's efforts to "oil the waters" with politicians refers to an April 4 meeting in my office. At my invitation, Mayor Frank Cooksey, City Council Member Sally Shipman, Acting City Manager John Ware, and Paula Philips, director of the city's Housing and Community Services Department, met in my office late that afternoon with me, Sharpe, Franklin, and Wright. My outline for the discussion at that meeting could not have provided a stronger contrast with the neighborhood association's portrayal of UT as an evil and sinister force. I began the meeting by informing our guests that the recent proposal from the mayor and the neighborhood association had been a catalyst for a review of the Blackland issue, and that I wanted to share my current thinking with them and get their reactions. I then discussed briefly our four basic working assumptions: "We continue to need the land and want to acquire it over a period of time. We are concerned about the owner-residents in the area and the transition of the neighborhood. We want to be a working partner with the current residents during the transition. We are concerned about the availability of affordable housing in Austin, but UT could not be in the affordable housing business over the long run."[6]

Then I revealed that we had been thinking about dividing the sixteen-block area into two sections, one that UT would expect to develop in the near term (perhaps one to three years) and another that we would not develop for perhaps ten years or even much longer. We wanted to explore the possibilities for treating these sections in different ways, and we wanted to talk directly with owner-residents in both sections to discuss options that would make it easier for them to sell their property and be satisfied with the outcome.

For the section that we would expect to use in the near term, I presented these options:

- A purchase agreement that would give the owner a *no-cost* lease for one to three years, with annual extensions of a lease until UT needed the land.
- An offer for UT to buy a house and then move it to a site outside the sixteen-block area, with the cost of the new lot and moving expenses paid by UT.
- An arrangement through which a seller could live in a house in the long-term section, either through a purchase agreement that would give the owner a five-year guaranteed lease with possible annual extensions, or an agreement to eventually move a house outside the area as described above.

We looked on these options as potentially very attractive business deals for the property owners. We weren't aware of any other real estate transaction in the country that would be so advantageous to the seller. Yet it seemed that these were the kinds of opportunities that the neighborhood association insisted on describing as "pressuring individual property owners to sell." It was increasingly clear that some neighborhood leaders would always try to make UT look like the villain in an old-fashioned melodrama.

My presentation was cordially received, but I am afraid it was received with less enthusiasm and excitement than it was presented. I was thinking of it as a creative breakthrough that would demonstrate once and for all the university's intention to be a good neighbor. Meanwhile, we proceeded to draft a formal response to the most recent proposal from the neighborhood, from December 1987, for low-cost housing. I wrote to Mayor Cooksey on April 13, 1988, that UT was prepared to go forward at once with identification of university-owned houses that would be suitable for interim use as affordable housing. The city's Department of Housing and Community Services was evaluating thirty-five properties for potential leasing, but we still had no definitive agreement about how the various parties would work together.

Our efforts to develop a new approach were largely rebuffed by the president of the neighborhood association, Veon McReynolds, who wrote to me on June 1 commending me for my interest in the afford-able housing issue but "taking marked exception" to what he called our efforts to "pressure" residents into selling to the university. "We have met with your representatives on several occasions," McReynolds wrote, "and now believe that, unless there are fundamental and substantial changes in the policies of your institution, we have no other options than to enter into a bitter and protracted era of hostility."

McReynolds went on to criticize just about everything UT had done as well as the way it had done it. He found UT to have been "abusive" in the way it had approached residents with offers to purchase their property, in violation of zoning regulations in the way it had used property adjacent to residential areas, and in opposition to the 1984 agreement for mixed use of land. He concluded: "Your destruction of the Blackland Neighborhood has not only been insensitive and artless, but is unnecessary. You do not need the land. Unless you respond immediately to address the above listed abuses by your organization, we have no choice but to launch a bitter and protracted struggle to bring public pressure to correct your misuse of state powers and resources."[7]

I chose not to respond to this. My guess is that in the distant past, one of the surest ways to produce a "bitter and protracted struggle" with UT was to threaten university officials with one. I was determined not to let that happen. As a UT official I tried not to allow myself to be driven off course through my responses to other people's threats. It was good that I ignored this latest blast of rhetoric because during the next few weeks we were actually able to make progress toward a solution.

In early June, I and a number of other campus and UT System officials again met with city officials, and we discussed our evolving ideas for the Blackland Neighborhood at some length. By this time we had refined the plan to divide the neighborhood into two sections, and I presented the latest version to City Council members. We also shared the new plan with neighborhood leaders, and the *American-Statesman* carried a detailed news story about it. The plan separated the neighborhood into western and eastern sections, roughly divided by Leona Street. We had not changed our long-term goal of acquiring the entire sixteen blocks, but the eastern section would be off limits to development by UT for at least ten years, during which time the city could use any UT property in that section for low-cost housing.

We also outlined again a full range of options to help owner-residents in either section relocate if they chose to sell to UT. We thought of this plan as a reasonable and humane response to the concerns of residents and the neighborhood as a whole.

McReynolds's response was more positive than before. After telling the newspaper that the new flexible approach was "a far cry better than what they were doing," he added: "I think the university is trying to make amends for some of the evil that they have done. They're a little late, but I would hope that we could still move toward peaceful coexistence rather than have an adversarial relationship."[8]

On June 22, the city housing department informed us that they had identified nineteen houses, from among forty-five owned by UT in the neighborhood, that it wanted to use for the affordable housing program. The others were deemed too dilapidated for renovation or otherwise unsuitable, so we expected to demolish them in the coming weeks.

Meanwhile, we shared our newly developed approach to the Blackland problem with residents and others, and on July 1, I wrote to Mayor Lee Cooke (who had been elected in May) and presented to him a formal summary of our long process of review of UT policy in response to the affordable housing proposal the previous December from the Blackland Neighborhood Development Corporation and Mayor Cooksey. I outlined again a four-part initiative that UT was prepared to undertake, based on the east-west division of the neighborhood:

- Leasing houses in the eastern section to the city for housing for at least ten years.
- Selling (for $1) any houses in the western section if the city would move them.
- Generous incentives to owner-residents to assist in the transition to university use.
- Removal of any remaining structures owned by UT.

Cooke responded on July 17 that the city was in general agreement with this initiative and said we should work with the city legal and housing offices to formalize an agreement. In the midst of these positive discussions, a group of homeless people and advocates for the homeless, along with their pet goose, Homer, staged an "occupation" of several boarded-up houses owned by UT in the neighborhood. This action was advertised as part of a nationwide series of demonstrations in support of a federal affordable housing act that Congress was considering. I asked the UT police to watch the protesters discreetly, but I emphasized that we wanted to avoid a confrontation. The protesters made their point and most left peacefully. At least three people, however, were charged with criminal trespass after spending the night in a boarded-up building and refusing to leave.

On July 19, Franklin sent a letter to Blackland residents informing them of the plan to use some houses for affordable housing and to move or demolish houses that the city did not want. On July 25, UT began razing most of the structures that the city said it could not use. We had not demolished any houses in the neighborhood for more than two years, since the 1986 discussions with the city about affordable housing possibilities, and some of the houses that were knocked down in July 1988 had been boarded up for that entire time. Many were of such insubstantial construction that the demolition was accomplished in a matter of minutes.

We had received comments from many residents that the boarded-up houses were a safety hazard and unsightly, and after the city found them unusable our demolition of them was welcomed by some in the neighborhood. We anticipated, however, that others might protest the demolition, so we quietly moved the demolition equipment to a nearby area the night before and got an early start on July 25. Many people in Austin had vivid memories of Frank Erwin personally commandeering a bulldozer in 1969 and challenging students who had perched in trees along Waller Creek in an effort to keep them from being uprooted for a project to expand the football stadium. More than two dozen people had been arrested that day. I had no intention of climbing up into the seat of a bulldozer, and I didn't want anybody to be arrested, so I told Franklin to have his people get there early in the morning and knock over all the houses as quickly as possible, and then come back during the next several days to haul away the debris. A small group of protesters did arrive at about 9:00 a.m. One of them climbed onto a roof and vowed to defend that house from destruction—the sort of action we had feared. He stayed up there most of that hot July day, and late in the afternoon he was informed that he was on top of a house that UT did not own.

My phone had started ringing that morning as soon as word spread that we were demolishing houses. City Council members were calling to ask me to postpone the demolition—even though the city had said it could not use the houses and city officials had known for weeks that we would demolish houses the city didn't want. We were carrying out a plan that everyone at the city had agreed on, but some of them had second thoughts. I told Franklin I wanted the bulldozer to destroy every house by noon, at which point I would return calls from council members.

Some people attacked the demolitions as a travesty, especially while there were homeless people in Austin, even though we demolished only houses that were uninhabitable and unsuitable for renovation. McReynolds was quoted as saying the demolitions were part of the university's "scorched-earth policy,"[9] and the Rev. L. Charles Merrill of the University United Methodist Church, our longtime neighbor on the west side of the campus, wrote to Ed Sharpe that UT was creating "a blight over the landscape." "It is a bit incongruous for a university supposedly dedicated to alleviation of the human predicament to be tearing houses down," he wrote.[10] I was shocked and actually amused that Merrill would write a letter to one of his parishioners when he had virtually no knowledge of the facts in the case.

By December 1988 I had decided to make another fundamental shift of policy that I hoped would resolve the rest of the Blackland controversy. The new policy limited UT's expansion, with one small exception, to the western half of the sixteen-block area, that is, the eight blocks between Comal and Leona streets. I announced this decision to neighborhood and NAACP leaders and also informed them that UT was prepared to sell or trade all the property that it had already acquired in the eastern half of the area (except for a small parcel east of Leona along Manor Road), thus supporting the continued residential character of those blocks. In announcing that UT's long-term plan was now to acquire only eight blocks instead of sixteen, I was agreeing in most respects to a proposal that the neighborhood had made in September.

Five key factors had combined to make it possible for us to adopt this new approach:

- The fortuitous acquisition of the 6.57-acre Villa Capri Motel site in October 1987 had made acquisition of the full sixteen-block area east of I–35 much less important. It had been sold in 1984 for more than $12 million to a company that planned a more intensive development, but those plans fell through, and when the property was offered for sale in late 1987 to avoid foreclosure, UT bought it at a bargain price of $6,027,396. We spent an additional $209,827 in early 1988 to tear down the motel. (No protesters showed up for *that* demolition, although I think Wales Madden might have been tempted to picket the bulldozers, since over the years the Villa Capri had practically been his home away from home.)

- The acquisition in 1987 of the industrial site in Southeast Austin that was to be partially occupied by the Sematech consortium offered UT a new option for eventual development of facilities that did not need to be located on the main campus.

- The development of telecommunications technologies had made remote locations for some UT facilities much more feasible. This had already been demonstrated through microwave links with Balcones Research Center (now the Pickle Research Campus).

- UT had determined that more intensive use of campus land west of I-35 was feasible. We could rely more on parking garages than surface parking, fill in some low-density areas, and construct taller buildings than UT had typically built.

It had become clear that an ongoing dispute with the Blackland Neighborhood would not serve the interests of anyone concerned. The need for additional land was certainly important for UT, but it was not and had never been so important as to disregard the consequences. UT had enough raw power to take as much land as it wanted, but at what price in reputation, good will, and fairness? It was time to end this dispute.

The neighborhood's leaders certainly seemed pleased with our new direction when I explained it to them during a meeting on December 22 with representatives of the neighborhood association, the community development corporation, and the NAACP. I was particularly gratified by the comments of Katherine Poole in the newspaper the next day. "I think it's just wonderful," she said. "I am especially pleased about the divestment of lots that they own on the east side of Leona. That makes me feel that this is for real and that there will be no more lies. It's one of those things where you've worked so long and things have been so unstable, and now I feel like I can go on and live my last few years in peace." And I could not help but be pleased by the way she went on to describe my presentation at the meeting: "He just laid it out on the table, and he was very sincere . . . what he said was clear and honest, and he looked us in the eyes and answered our questions with patience. I think we still have a lot to do to help the neighborhood, but so long as Dr. Cunningham is president, I have an awful lot of faith. I hope he is there forever." University presidents don't hear that kind of compliment very often, so I treasured those comments.[11]

It would be more than two years, however, before a definitive agreement was reached with the city and the neighborhood for the disposition of UT property east of Leona Street. The delay was partly caused by an adverse real estate market, as some of the property was worth less than we had paid for it. By late 1990 I asked James S. Wilson, executive director of endowment real estate at the UT System offices, to see if he could bring his expertise to bear in concluding an agreement that would finally bring the Blackland matter to an end. Wilson wrote on December 11, 1990, to Charles Smith, then president of the Blackland Community Development Corporation, explaining our constraints because of current appraised values, but assuring Smith that we were willing to consider the sale of land east of Leona at a later date if we could "recover a greater portion of the funds expended on the lots." Wilson also stated our willingness to trade parcels east and west of Leona based on current market values, as well as our willingness to lease land east of Leona to the city or the corporation at a nominal cost for up to thirty years.[12]

The idea for a lease of that extended length rather than a sale evolved because of the depressed property values; we thought that might be a reasonable alternative, and the corporation agreed. The final arrangement as negotiated in early 1991 provided for the lease of eleven lots east of Leona (including five lots that were already under lease to the city under previous agreements) for use as low-income housing for thirty years for $1—not $1 per year, but a total of $1 for the entire thirty years—with an option for the corporation to renew the lease for an additional thirty years at an annual rate of 8 percent of the appraised value of the land at that time. The university could only hope that in sixty years the land might be worth enough to be sold.

By June 1991, all the relevant documents were sent to the city, and the City Council approved the agreement without discussion in December. In March 1992, we closed the deal. A day that some people had long ago given up on had finally arrived, and UT was now officially at peace with its neighbors to the east.

CHAPTER 9

The *Hopwood* Case

ll the efforts of the University of Texas to achieve a more diverse campus could have been derailed by the *Hopwood* case, which for almost ten years loomed over UT Austin and all of Texas higher education, and whose indirect effects have persisted into the twenty-first century in the form of the top 10 percent rule, which governs admissions to state-funded universities.[1]

The case arose on September 29, 1992, when Cheryl J. Hopwood, an Anglo applicant who had been denied admission to the UT Law School earlier that year, filed a lawsuit charging that she had been discriminated against. The case was a direct assault on the Supreme Court's landmark ruling in *Bakke v. Regents of University of California*, which held that universities may consider race in admissions in order to maintain diverse enrollment or to remedy past discrimination. That 1978 decision had been the legal basis for affirmative action programs at universities across the country. In addition, Texas universities had agreed since 1983 to comply with a federal desegregation order. Under an agreement between the state and the federal Department of Education's Office of Civil Rights, Texas schools were committed to affirmative action in professional school admissions and to achieving set goals for increasing minority enrollment.[2]

The decision by the U.S. 5th Circuit Court of Appeals in the *Hopwood* case in 1996 cast aside all the precedents and assumptions of the previous eighteen years when it outlawed affirmative action programs based on race and effectively overturned the U.S. Supreme Court ruling in *Bakke*. The ban applied, effectively, only in Texas—leaving the state's universities at a serious nationwide disadvantage in recruiting minority students and faculty.[3] Although the case dealt only with admissions policies of the UT School of Law, Texas Attorney

General Dan Morales interpreted the 5th Circuit's decision as applying to all colleges and universities in Texas.

The impact of the ruling on the law school was immediate and severe. In the first year after the ruling, African American enrollment fell more than 90 percent (from thirty-eight to four), and Mexican American enrollment fell almost 60 percent (from sixty-four to twenty-six). From the early 1980s to 1995, Mexican Americans usually made up more than 10 percent of the law school's students, while African Americans had been between 6 and 8 percent of the total since 1988. In 1997, Mexican American enrollment was 5.6 percent of the total and African American enrollment was 0.9 percent. These percentages improved a little in succeeding years but did not recover to pre-*Hopwood* levels until the mid-2000s, when the *Hopwood* ruling was no longer in effect.

The U.S. Supreme Court twice (in 1996 and 2001) declined to hear the university's appeal, and the ban on affirmative action remained in place until the court, ruling in a Michigan case in 2003, reaffirmed the constitutionality of very carefully drawn affirmative action programs that did not use quotas (which UT Austin had never used).[4] Since then UT Austin has reinstated many of the affirmative action programs that were in place before *Hopwood*.

Thus, the *Hopwood* case stemmed from decisions made while I was president of UT Austin, continued in the courts throughout my tenure as chancellor and beyond, and left the state with the top 10 percent rule, a well-intentioned but ill-advised legislative effort designed to compensate for the loss of affirmative action programs.

Throughout the case, the university and the people of Texas were fortunate to have the legal services of the firm of Vinson and Elkins, which by July 1998 had committed approximately $2 million to the defense of the lawsuit and continued to represent the university on a *pro bono* basis. The firm's senior partner, Harry Reasoner, a Distinguished Alumnus of the university and the law school, led these efforts out of his personal commitment to equal opportunity, as well as because of the Houston-based firm's desire to serve the best interests of the legal profession and of legal education in Texas. Reasoner's dedication made it possible for UT to pursue this long and expensive lawsuit without diverting significant resources from our educational mission.[5] Our legal team also benefited immensely from the contribu-

Charles Alan Wright. *UT Office of Public Affairs Records, e_utopa_00028.*

tions of distinguished members of the faculty at the UT Law School, including professors Charles Alan Wright and Douglas Laycock.

The law school had initiated a two-committee system for admissions after 1971 when a totally color-blind admission system had resulted in no African Americans being admitted. Over the years the law school modified its affirmative action policies in many ways, and in 1992 it again instituted a separate committee to review minority applications. Professor Laycock made the following statement in the preface to his collection of material on the *Hopwood* case: "As it happened, in 1992 the Law School had created a separate committee to review minority applications. This two-committee system became the subject of much criticism later, but neither side thought the dispute was about the administrative details of the program, and neither did the Court of Appeals. The Law School's Admissions Committee in 1992 thought that two committees would lead to a fairer and more accurate process. Consolidating consideration of minority files made it easier to identify the strongest minority applicants, and easier to enforce uniform limits on the magnitude of racial preferences. For their part, the plaintiffs objected to any degree of racial preference, however it might be administered. The Court of Appeals in the first appeal adopted plaintiffs' position. The two-committee system was thus irrelevant to the sweeping decision in the Court of Appeals, and it was irrelevant to plaintiffs' decision to sue. But the two-committee system did have procedural consequences along the way."[6]

When the university was sued, the law school immediately dropped the two-committee system. Professor Laycock is a very bright attorney and, like me, a strong advocate for helping minority students gain access to the university. However, I disagree with his analysis of the impact of the two-committee system. At a minimum, the two-committee approach used by the School of Law helped attract the interest of conservative lawyers who were looking for an opportunity to strike a blow against affirmative action. I believe the two-committee structure clearly went beyond the guidelines in the *Bakke* case. When I was briefed on what the law school had done I was very upset. Clearly, this was a mistake and it certainly should not have happened, and I was embarrassed that it happened when I was president.

The university got off to a good start in this long-running fight in August 1994. After a trial, U.S. District Judge Sam Sparks of Austin ruled that while the law school's two-committee admission system was unconstitutional, it could continue its policy of using one committee that would review all applicants. The committee was free to make its decisions on a variety of criteria, including race. Judge Sparks fined the university $1 and ordered it to re-review the plaintiffs' applications without charging them an application fee. This ruling was consistent with *Bakke* and it was welcomed with great relief by campus and UT System officials. My own comment on the ruling was that it was "most gratifying, particularly when one considers that a decision striking down our ability to pursue a diverse student population would have been a serious blow to the state's continuing efforts to eliminate the vestiges of desegregation and discrimination of the past."[7]

At a press conference at which many UT officials spoke, I was even more positive about the ruling: "The judge ordered a $1 penalty, did not order the students be admitted, found the university was acting in good faith, and affirmed the fact that the system we are using now is constitutional. That is as close to total victory as I think we could have ever hoped to have."[8]

This feeling of elation lasted for about nineteen months. The plaintiffs appealed, of course, and in March 1996 the 5th Circuit reversed Sparks's ruling and declared that any consideration of race, even as one factor among many, was unconstitutional. The 5th Circuit's decision had overruled the Supreme Court.

Throughout the public debate over *Hopwood,* as often happens in any public discussion of affirmative action, many people assumed that the law school's admissions policies had enforced quotas based on race. This was never the case. The UT Law School considered each applicant's undergraduate grade point average and score on the Law School Admission Test, as well as many other factors, such as undergraduate major, letters of recommendation, socio-economic background, indications of hard work and persistence, hardships overcome, and race. After the 1996 decision in *Hopwood v. Texas*, and until the Supreme Court's decisions in two Michigan cases in 2003, an applicant's race was excluded from the list of factors considered at the law school.[9]

The 5th Circuit took the unusual action of not penalizing the university for operating an admissions system that it considered to be unconstitutional. The court stated that:

> . . . the law school had always acted in good faith. This is a difficult area of the law, in which the law school erred with the best of intentions. As a result, the plaintiffs have not met the federal standard for punitive damages as stated in *Smith v. Wade.* Thus, we agree with the district court that punitive damages are not warranted. We note, however, that if the law school continues to operate a disguised or overt racial classification system in the future, its actors could be subject to actual and punitive damages.[10]

While I was very pleased that the court did not penalize the university, the statement that if the university did not follow its instructions in the future with respect to admissions, then "its actors could be subject to actual and punitive damage" did get my attention. I made sure that everyone in the chain of command understood what the court had said. We were determined to obey the law, at the same time that we appealed the court's decision.

Changing views about affirmative action among the members of the UT Board of Regents affected the motives for the board's actions during the years that the *Hopwood* decision applied to Texas, but the members' real personal views and motives were often hard to detect because they were usually quite careful about what they said in public. The board consisted of mature, sophisticated people, and they said no more than absolutely necessary, trying to avoid inflaming the public discussion on either side. I believe this helped keep the issue of affirmative action from becoming as volatile as it had been in California and some other states.

In early 1993, a few months after the *Hopwood* case was filed, Democratic appointees of Governor Ann Richards represented a majority on the board and maintained that position until early 1997, when the second set of appointees of Governor George W. Bush took their seats and the majority returned to the Republicans. Under the leadership of Chairman Bernard Rapoport (1993–1997), the four years of a Democratic majority, the board expressed strong support for affirmative action and pursued all the legal avenues available to it. But even after the Republican appointees regained the majority, the board continued to support appealing the case to the Supreme Court. After 1997, several of the regents (including Tony Sanchez, a Bush appointee) were advocates of affirmative action and wanted to see the *Hopwood* decision overturned, but others may well have supported an appeal to the Supreme Court hoping for a definitive nationwide ban on affirmative action. Still others were motivated mostly by a wish simply to have all higher education institutions in the country covered by the same rules, whatever they might be, so that UT Austin would no longer be at a disadvantage in competing with other states for students.

In May 1998 the board of regents spoke about the case with Morales in an executive session. The attorney general made it very clear that he did not support affirmative action and that he would not use state resources to appeal the 5th Circuit decision. Morales did not stand in the way of our appeal in 1998, but acquiesced only after Judge Sam Sparks rebuked him for "putting his personal agenda ahead of his professional responsibilities" in the *Hopwood* case.[11] We continued to rely on the outstanding pro bono work of Harry Reasoner and Vinson and Elkins.[12]

The pursuit of national uniformity in laws pertaining to admis-

From left, Ronnie Krist, G. P. Hardy, Harry Reasoner, Joe Jamail, and Jim Kronzer standing in front of a painting of themselves that hangs in the law school, November 13, 1992. *UT Office of Public Affairs Records, e_utopa_00027.*

sions rules was the official position of the board when it voted 9–0 in May 1998 to pursue a second appeal of the case, and the consensus language of the board's motion allowed all the regents to sign on regardless of their personal views about affirmative action. The motion sought to bring "uniformity and finality" to the issue of affirmative action and to "permit Texas colleges and universities to compete on a level playing field."[13]

The "level playing field" argument was a strong one. While governed by *Hopwood*, UT Austin's law school and the UT System's medical schools generally experienced drops in minority enrollment, and we were unable to compete consistently for the best minority applicants, as they were lured to other states that could still offer scholarships and other incentives based partly on race. This pattern was very dangerous for Texas. As I said in May 1998, "Texas will soon be a majority-minority state. The long-term social, cultural and economic vitality of Texas is irrevocably linked to its ability to recruit and graduate minority students."[14]

I always considered it to be one of my best political maneuvers that I was able to persuade a board of regents that was made up of liberals and conservatives, Republicans and Democrats, to vote 9–0 to appeal *Hopwood*. While the regents had different views, they all understood it was in UT's best interest to get this issue resolved once and for all. One more time our board rose to the occasion and did the right thing. I felt I had spent some significant political capital to ensure this vote, but I was very happy with the outcome.

The practice followed by me as chancellor and by members of the board of regents was not to fight with Morales in public over his approach to the *Hopwood* case, but many others, of all political persuasions, did not hesitate to take issue with him. John Cornyn, who was running for attorney general in 1998 on the Republican ticket, said the attorney general's decisions should be based on legal principles and not on his personal views. Cornyn said that if he were attorney general he would advise UT officials that he thought affirmative action policies were illegal but that he would abide by their wish to pursue an appeal. Former attorney general Jim Mattox, a Democrat, also said an attorney general ought to defer to the client's desires in a case with unsettled legal issues like *Hopwood*.[15]

After the Supreme Court's rulings in the Michigan case in 2003, Texas was no longer subject to the ban on affirmative action mandated by the *Hopwood* case, but some effects of the ruling persisted. Those effects included the state's "Top 10 Percent Law," Texas House Bill 588, which was passed in 1997 under the leadership of Governor George W. Bush. The law, which was designed to mitigate the impact of the 5th Circuit decision, required that any Texas high school student graduating in the top 10 percent of his or her class would receive automatic admission at any Texas state college or university.

UT Austin officials told me they could live with the legislation because the university was currently admitting well over 95 percent of the students in the top 10 percent of the graduates of the state's high schools. No one had the time to estimate what the long-term impact of the new requirement would be as the state population grew at ever-increasing rates. In practice, the top 10 percent rule presented several serious problems for UT Austin: It restricted the university's ability to make admissions decisions on a range of factors apart from class ranking; it prohibited the university from distinguishing among students from high schools of widely varying academic quality; and it largely eliminated the university's control over the size of each year's freshman class. Ten years after the law was passed, more than 80 percent of each year's freshman class was being admitted automatically under the top 10 percent rule.

The *Hopwood* case presents at least three lessons that future generations should heed. First, the governor and the legislature should avoid trying to micromanage higher education. If we ever needed evidence that details of university administration such as admissions policies are best dealt with at the campus or regents' level, and not in the legislature, the top 10 percent law is a prime example.

Second, we should always beware of the fact that well-intentioned ideas can have unintended consequences. It is interesting to reflect on what ultimately occurred because the law school adopted a strategy to recruit minority students that was clearly unconstitutional. If the law school had utilized the traditional *Bakke* remedy to recruit minority students, Cheryl Hopwood's attorney may well have told her that a lawsuit against UT was inadvisable since the Supreme Court had already dealt with this issue. However, the action the law school took by creating two committees made UT an easy target. Once Judge Sparks had ruled in favor of UT, Hopwood had a clear path to a very conservative 5th Circuit Court of Appeals which, in turn, used the opportunity to challenge the precedent in *Bakke*. Without the ban on affirmative action during the years that the *Hopwood* decision was in force in Texas, it is highly unlikely that the legislature would have ever addressed the details of university admissions policies and would not have come up with the top 10 percent law, which caused many significant problems for UT Austin and created an admissions system that had the effect of discriminating against some of the state's best students.

The third implication may be as simple as persistence is a virtue. UT Austin and the UT System never gave up in the fight to attract qualified minority students to UT Austin. Even after losing the support of the state's attorney general and receiving a poorly reasoned decision by the 5th Circuit, we persisted in our efforts to attract and retain minority students and to obtain a positive decision in the U.S.

Supreme Court. The university's ability to persist in this case owes a great debt of gratitude to Harry Reasoner and his law firm, Vinson and Elkins. We are also very fortunate that Judge Sam Sparks was the trial judge in the case. He applied the law fairly and appropriately and his original decision was vindicated by the U.S. Supreme Court.

CHAPTER 10

Progress in the Natural Sciences

The two most important academic advancements of the university during the years I was in the central administration focused on critically important programs in the College of Natural Sciences. The first was the long-anticipated development of a molecular biology program, and the second was the construction of an innovative, world-class telescope at McDonald Observatory. Both projects had begun before I became president, and both required a significant amount of my time and attention during the years that I was president and chancellor. In hindsight, both were extremely complex, controversial, and expensive, and both consumed a great deal of my political capital. However, both endeavors were vital to the research and graduate education mission of the university, and both were highly successful.

As early as 1980–1981, an internal committee of faculty considered options for developing a molecular biology program. Dean Robert E. Boyer of the College of Natural Sciences recognized when he became dean in 1980 that the university was lagging far behind most other major universities in molecular biology. Whether because of lack of leadership or lack of money, the University of Texas had failed to move aggressively in molecular biology in the late 1970s when research universities throughout the world were forging a revolution in the study of biology at the molecular level. UT's departments of zoology, botany, and microbiology had strong national reputations, but those reputations were built largely on expertise in older areas of biological science such as population biology and field studies in ecology, not the new science of molecular biology. The fact that our more traditional departments were so good may have contributed to the early reluctance to invest in molecular biology.

Seeking guidance in how best to correct our deficiency, Boyer assembled an external review committee composed of molecular biologists from Cal Tech, MIT, and the University of Colorado. They observed that although UT Austin was getting into the field very late, the development of a first-class program in a short time was still possible. They noted that "no major university can afford not to be at the forefront of molecular biology, which will provide striking new opportunities to attack fundamental problems in medicine, agriculture, and resource biology. In addition the expanding industrial exploitation of biotechnology will offer unique opportunities for beneficial collaboration with the private sector in generating academic positions, research resources, and new high-technology industries in surrounding communities." The committee recommended creation of a "center of excellence" in molecular biology with at least one endowed faculty chair, a commitment for at least nine other faculty positions, expansion of research space, and start-up funds of at least $3 million.[1]

Boyer and others went to work, and by June 1985 he was able to present to President Flawn a report that cited major progress toward fulfilling the external committee's recommendations. In the area of faculty endowments, the university had exceeded everything envisioned by that committee, thanks to the Centennial Teachers and Scholars Program. In just three years the university had established four endowed chairs in molecular biology (each endowed with $1 million), another $1 million chair in plant cell biology, two chairs with smaller endowments in microbiology, and five other endowed professorships and lectureships. A big problem was that most of these positions remained unfilled, and that was a result of an even bigger problem—the lack of new or renovated research space in which the prospective faculty members and their graduate students would work. Attempts at recruitment for some of the positions, including the four $1 million chairs, would be futile until UT could provide a modern place to work. Boyer recommended two major steps to solve that problem—renovation of the aging Experimental Science Building and funding for a new 100,000-square-foot lab and classroom building.[2]

The critical need for action on molecular biology did not really resonate with me until the first week of March in 1987. Isabella and I had been invited by Jess Hay, chairman of the board of regents, to spend a long weekend at his house in Acapulco, and the other house guests included Michael Brown and his wife and Joseph Goldstein. Brown and Goldstein were faculty members at the University of Texas Southwestern Medical Center at Dallas and winners of the Nobel Prize in medicine in 1985. They had shared the prize for their discovery of the underlying mechanisms of cholesterol metabolism, a discovery that led to the development of statin drugs. Brown, Goldstein, and I were lounging by Hay's pool one afternoon when I asked them what they thought UT Austin needed to be doing in the sciences. Their immediate answer was molecular biology. They said that in their opinion the university would never be competitive in the life sciences unless it did something about this weakness.

I may have been a little hesitant to admit to them that I didn't fully understand what they were talking about, but at the next meeting of the executive officers in Austin I asked Provost Gerry Fonken to tell me about molecular biology. Fonken has always been one to recognize a "teachable moment" and he has always been able to explain the most complicated material to nonspecialists clearly and succinctly. I listened as he outlined where we were in molecular biology, where we had come from, and where Boyer and others wanted to take us. I was quickly persuaded.

When, several months later, I received the report of a committee that Boyer and Fonken had formed in 1986 to work on the matter, my first impression was that the group had decided this was not the time for modesty. The report recommended an expansion that would take place over a period of seven and a half years and involve spending $65 million for teaching and research facilities in the life sciences, including a $46 million, 200,000-square-foot molecular biology building; a $2.85 million, 20,000-square-foot annex to the Animal Resources Center; and a $16 million renovation of the Experimental Science Building.

I didn't think $65 million was realistic under the prevailing economic and budget conditions. We had been struggling since 1985 to obtain minimal appropriations from the legislature, and that struggle gave every appearance of continuing. At the same time, the Permanent University Fund, which had been the main source of capital funding for UT Austin for decades, was facing increasing demands on its resources, and the regents were moving rapidly toward a policy of requiring significant private-sector donations as part of the funding for most new construction. So I wanted to know, first, if we could do molecular biology for less than $65 million in facilities costs, and, second, if it was worth making any significant investment if we couldn't spend as much as the committee had recommended.

One of the basic problems was that we still had no consensus, either in the administration or among the faculty, about how to organize the molecular biology program, while the severe financial crisis dictated an extraordinary level of justification for any investments in new programs and facilities. I asked Fonken to consult again with Brown and Goldstein to get their advice about the best way to proceed, and Fonken reported to me in January 1988 that they felt we should appoint a new external committee to evaluate our program and use that committee's findings together with the building committee's report as a guide for future action. It had been only six months since our last external review, but I thought, "Why not?" Brown and Goldstein had also offered us the excellent advice that we ought to be careful not to spend all our available money on a building, but to hold back a substantial amount to support research and other programmatic needs once the building opened.[3] That was sound advice at a university that, for much of its history, has been better able to finance the construction of buildings than support the academic programs inside them.

That external committee was formed in May 1988 and included prominent biologists from Princeton, Berkeley, and the Whitehead Institute for Biomedical Research in Massachusetts. In October, the panel presented a seventeen-page report that set out a clear plan for achieving excellence in molecular biology, and most of its recommendations drew wide support from the faculty, although it also sparked some significant objections. The consultants' opinion was that our current plans were an inadequate response to the problem and that we needed to take a series of bold steps rather than make merely incremental changes. They recommended a new department of molecular biology separate from current academic departments, with a world-renowned scientist brought in from outside to lead the effort. They recommended building up the department to twenty to twenty-five faculty members within the next seven years, with perhaps 80 percent of these appointments coming from outside. They also stated that the faculty of the new department be required to teach no more than one lecture course a year. This would be about half the teaching load in the biological sciences, but the consultants emphasized that the molecular biology faculty would be even more heavily involved in research and in teaching graduate students than other faculty. The consultants agreed with our internal assessment that successful faculty recruitment depended on a new facility to house the program.

The committee also made it clear that all life science departments at UT needed upgrading, and that the development of molecular biology should not come at the expense of current units. In this regard, the committee's analysis of our faculty/student ratio in the biological sciences was all too familiar. We just did not have the resources that were available to many of our peer institutions nationwide.[4]

In general, the faculty in existing departments reacted favorably to the report, although those in the Department of Botany were skeptical about how serious the administration really was, since they were still waiting, they said, to see some results from the 1982 external advisory report.[5] From the UT System, there was a concern that we avoid duplicating the work of the system's six health science institutions. In addition, the teaching loads that the consultants recommended were judged by system officials to be simply ridiculous.

In late November 1988, Boyer sent me a revised and expanded plan for molecular biology and the other life sciences that built on the external advisers' report and in some ways went well beyond it. He outlined a ten-year plan that could cost an estimated $88.6 million, including the construction and renovation projects that were under review, expansion of the faculty, some $3 million in equipment purchases, and a new endowment fund of $10 million to $20 million to support research and related activities. My response was that I didn't have $88.6 million, any more than I had the $65 million that had been recommended a year earlier. I wrote back to Boyer that even without new ideas, "The University of Texas is straining its resources to fund molecular biology."[6]

We reached an important milestone in August 1989, when the board of regents approved the appointment of architects for the molecular biology building. The project was authorized at $25 million, with $13 million to come from the PUF, $8 million from institutional funds, and $4 million from private-sector gifts.

Deciding where to locate the building was a major issue. It needed to be near related research and teaching facilities, and that meant in the vicinity of Speedway and 24th Street, an intersection just northeast of the Tower where the Experimental Science Building (ESB) and another biology building, Patterson Laboratories, were located. Two other biology buildings are just up the block on 24th Street, the College of Pharmacy is around the corner, and the Animal Resources Center is a little farther north. Proximity to ESB was considered of great importance because it was planned that faculty there and in the new building would be interacting daily, as well as because key equipment in the new building would also serve people housed in ESB.

Four locations were considered, all in the same block as ESB, and the site we chose in August 1990, and approved by the board of regents in December, was facing Speedway, immediately north of ESB. Part of this site was then a parking lot, but another part was occupied, unfortunately, by the indoor swimming pool that was an important element of Anna Hiss Gymnasium. That produced another sticking point in an initiative that, over the years, had its full share of them.

I took some consolation from the fact that the controversy was not as intense as it might have been, since one of the sites we rejected would have required demolition of the entire gymnasium building. That site was, in fact, the first choice of both the Faculty Building Advisory Committee and an ad hoc faculty committee that worked on this project, but the site I decided on was acceptable to them as an alternative.[7] It had not taken me long to decide against the option of tearing down the entire gym, which had been there since 1931 and was named (in 1974) for Anna Hiss, who directed the university's physical education program for women for thirty-six years. The building housed the only campus pool accessible by the handicapped, and the building was being used in the 1980s for physical education (kinesiology) classes as well as a highly acclaimed dance program.

Advocates of leaving the pool undisturbed mounted an extensive letter-writing campaign to members of the board of regents and the newspapers, as well as to my office. One letter came from Barbara Jordan, a former member of the U.S. Congress, who held the Lyndon B. Johnson Chair in National Policy at the LBJ School of Public Affairs. She had a special interest in the fate of the gym, since her mobility was impaired by illness and she was a frequent user of the Anna Hiss pool. She wrote to the regents in November 1989, almost a year before I made a decision: "I strongly believe that modernity and progress should not be destructive of a past that is worth preserving. . . . I am sympathetic to the need of the university to enlarge facilities of various departments in order to meet the study and research needs of students and faculty. However, it should not be necessary to destroy or alter this extraordinary edifice in order to meet these needs. It would be well worth the effort to explore the various alternatives which have been suggested to save Anna Hiss Gym."[8] Louis Beecherl, who had become chairman in March 1989, wrote to Jordan assuring her that her views would be considered as the decision process continued, and I also talked with her about the issues involved.[9] It was of great importance to me that we find a solution that Jordan would be comfortable with.

The need to locate the molecular biology building adjacent to the Experimental Science Building, together with the desire not to totally destroy Anna Hiss Gym, led to two decisions: first, to choose the site that would require only the demolition of the Anna Hiss pool but leave the rest of the building intact, and second, to renovate Gregory Gym (a few blocks south on Speedway) with a pool that would virtually duplicate the pool at Anna Hiss, including handicap access. A key provision of this plan was that the changes at Gregory would be completed before the pool at Anna Hiss was demolished. This proved to be a compromise that was acceptable to Jordan, and that was a key factor in my being willing to take it to the regents and in their being willing to accept it. This episode provides a good example of Jordan's use of her power and her understanding of the need for compromise.

The financing plan that the regents had approved in 1989 required me to come up with $4 million in private donations to help fund the new building, and at the same time I was in need of $2 million in donations to help pay for the badly needed renovation of the Experimental Science Building. The university had often received private donations to help construct nonacademic buildings, but this would be the first time that we would seek donations for academic facilities on the main campus—a result largely of the growing inability of the Permanent University Fund to meet all the demands that were being placed on it. When the regents placed this new requirement on the university for financing buildings, they also agreed to consider naming a building for a donor who would help pay for it. This would violate their rule that a building could not be named for a person until he or she had been dead for at least five years.

I believe some regents were a little embarrassed by asking me to raise $6 million for these two academic buildings. When this decision was made, I tried to look dejected about this new burden that they had placed on me, but the truth is that I was very pleased they had set the bar as low as they had.

I found one-third of the $6 million fairly quickly from James R. (Jim Bob) Moffett, a friend, business associate, and UT alumnus in New Orleans. In April 1990, UT announced the donation of this $2 million for the support of capital projects in the College of Natural Sciences, but we did not specify at that time which project the money would be spent on. I said I would at some point ask the regents to name "an appropriate facility" for Moffett and his wife, Louise, although at that time we were leaving the details to be decided later.[10] I wanted as much flexibility as possible as I pursued the remaining $4 million that we needed for Natural Sciences, so it was convenient to have all the naming options still on the table. Moffett had no problem with that. In fact, he told me it was entirely up to me what the university did with his $2 million gift. He didn't ask for anything in return or place any restrictions on that gift except that it not be spent on athletics.

Finding the rest of the money for capital projects in Natural Sciences was far more difficult than I had expected. After several other possibilities fell through, Shirley Bird Perry and I, with the assistance of Virgil Waggoner, a friend of UT who was the CEO of Sterling Chemical Inc., identified a good prospect in Albert B. Alkek, a Houston oilman and philanthropist who had been a generous supporter of education, health care, and the arts. In September 1990, Waggoner, Perry, Boyer, and I went to see Alkek in his downtown Houston office. We laid out our plan for the development of molecular biology and asked him for $4 million to support our building program. I told him that I would recommend to the board of regents that we name the new molecular biology building after him. Alkek immediately agreed to it. He said he never signed agreements over matters such as this and didn't think it was appropriate, so all I had was his handshake, and that was good enough for me. He seemed genuinely thrilled about being asked to part with $4 million for this purpose. Waggoner, Perry, Boyer, and I were so excited we almost danced out of the building. Our meeting with Alkek had begun at 10 a.m. and by noon I was on a Southwest Airlines flight back to Austin, counting that $4 million in my head. What a country! Who said this fund-raising business was hard?

Then came the 1992 presidential election, in which Bill Clinton

defeated Alkek's old friend, George H. W. Bush. Alkek promptly
wrote to the university to say he was reneging on our deal. He felt the
economy was going to crash under Clinton's leadership and he was
withdrawing all his philanthropic pledges. Perry called me in London
and gave me the news.[11] Alkek did recover from the shock of the 1992
election (and of course the economy under Clinton didn't crash—
far from it), and by 1993 Alkek was feeling well enough to donate
$30 million for a hospital at M. D. Anderson Cancer Center. Mickey
LeMaistre, president of M. D. Anderson, knew about the problem we
had had with Alkek, but there are only so many $30 million donors. I
told LeMaistre that I would recommend that he be very careful when
dealing with Alkek. Alkek committed $30 million to be paid out over
a five-year period. Unfortunately, he fooled us again. He died soon
after his commitment was finalized (with a handshake only—the
Alkek way), and his will instructed his estate to pay M. D. Anderson
$1 million a year for thirty years. As a result, the present value of his
gift was approximately $17 million, which was far less than his initial
handshake pledge.

There was nothing we could do after Alkek's letter but regroup and
go look for the money elsewhere. I called Waggoner from London to
tell him the news, and he was shocked and every bit as disappointed
as I was. I already had the $2 million pledge from Moffett for an
unspecified project, so I called Beecherl later the same day and asked
him if he was agreeable to applying that money to molecular biology
and naming the building for the Moffetts. Beecherl recognized that
Moffett was a bit controversial and thought there might be a problem
with the naming, but he also recognized that Moffett was a respected
business leader and a generous friend of the university, so he agreed.

A few days later, Moffett and I were walking out of the Asia Society on Park Avenue in New York City, where we had held a Freeport-
McMoRan board meeting, and I told him what I wanted to do with
his money, and that I wanted to name the molecular biology building
for him and Louise. His reaction was simply, "Fine, Bill, whatever
you want to do with the money." I was not surprised, because he had
always said the use of the money was up to me. He said the university
has been great to him and he wanted to try in a small way to repay it.
He restated that the gift was totally unrestricted.

Later I dropped the other shoe and told him that I wanted to ask
Freeport-McMoRan to contribute $1 million to go with his own

personal $2 million gift. Moffett said I would need to talk to the company's contribution committee about that. I was on the board of Freeport and a member of that committee, so I discussed it with the other members at the next Freeport board meeting, and they voted to recommend to the board that the company make the donation in Moffett's name. We were then $1 million short of being able to fulfill our commitment to the UT Board of Regents for the new molecular biology building. Waggoner and his wife, June, once again came through for the university. They announced that they would contribute $1 million to the molecular biology building, and our fund-raising was complete. I will always be grateful for their generosity and their genuine concern for the welfare of the university. Several years later, June and Virgil Waggoner made an additional $5 million donation to the molecular biology program, this time to support research into the underlying biology of drug and alcohol addiction. In December 1994, when I was serving as chancellor, the regents named the molecular biology building for the Moffetts. They also named one wing of the building for June and Virgil Wagonner and the other for Freeport-McMoRan.

While the fund-raising for the building was underway, we proceeded with efforts to get the academic program started through the creation, in 1993, of the Institute for Cellular and Molecular Biology, which was led by Dr. Henry Bose, a distinguished professor of microbiology. The institute provided an administrative mechanism for bringing together faculty from numerous departments in the natural sciences, engineering, and pharmacy for interdisciplinary studies centered on molecular biology. The institute was conceived as a way to support faculty hiring in cell and molecular biology, support the university-wide graduate program in cell and molecular biology, and provide staff for the core facilities and shared equipment that faculty and graduate students would use. The growth and achievements of the institute have been phenomenal from the very beginning. For example, the graduate program had nine students in 1994, a number that is now well over two hundred. Some three hundred undergraduates also conduct research in the institute's labs.

Several milestones were reached in 1997, including the opening of the Moffett Building, full funding for the institute, and the appointment of Alan Lambowitz (recruited from Ohio State) as the institute's first permanent director. A full accounting of the later growth of the molecular biology program is beyond the scope of this book, but suffice it to say that Lambowitz and his team succeeded in recruiting senior faculty of international stature for endowed chairs as well as a greatly expanded number of junior faculty. An additional biology building, housing wet labs, was constructed adjacent to the north end of the Moffett Building, and eventually the Experimental Science Building was replaced with a totally new facility, the Norman Hackerman Building. The administrative structure of the entire biology program was reorganized into a School of Biological Sciences in order to better reflect the way contemporary biologists carry out their studies. All these developments represented the culmination of more than twenty years of work spanning the terms of six university presidents. By the early years of the new millennium, it was clear the university had at last caught up with modern biology. A new focus for the university in the early twenty-first century has been an effort to develop a medical school—a possibility that would be highly remote without the groundwork that has been laid by the success of the university's molecular biology program.

My second endeavor in the scientific community involved the construction of a telescope in collaboration with Penn State University, Stanford University, and two universities in Germany. The Hobby-Eberly Telescope represented an effort to build one of the world's largest telescopes at a fraction of the usual cost. The dedication of the telescope in October 1997 brought some 350 scientists, politicians, and academic leaders to the remote West Texas site that is the home of McDonald Observatory, and many others watched by satellite back in Austin. We heard an eloquent address by Nobel laureate Steven Weinberg; we were regaled by Congressman Jake Pickle; and we heard Frank Bash, the observatory director, state that the telescope had been completed "on time and on budget." I leaned over to Bill Hobby, the former lieutenant governor for whom the telescope was partially named, and said: "Yes, but it was the ninth budget and the eighth timetable."

Soon after I became president in September 1985, Harlan Smith, then the director of the observatory, briefed me on his long-held hopes for a new telescope. Since 1978, he told me, the observatory and the university's Department of Astronomy had been hoping to construct a giant telescope (nicknamed the Eye of Texas) with a mirror in the range of 300 inches (7.6 meters), but the prospects for funding the

$50 million project had been hurt by the state's economic woes. The UT Board of Regents had authorized a fund-raising campaign in 1980, but by October 1985, only a little more than $1.3 million had been assembled.[12] It was clear to everyone that in the current economic environment we weren't going to be able to build a $50 million telescope.

It was troubling to have to reach that conclusion, because the university really did need a new telescope. Smith could explain the reasons for this better than anyone, and he excelled at explaining it to nonastronomers, always infecting them with some of his own enthusiasm. The larger a telescope's mirror, the more light it can collect, thus revealing fainter and more distant objects than a smaller mirror. McDonald had two major telescopes, but they were quickly being dwarfed by newer instruments around the world. Our 82-inch telescope (named for Otto Struve, the observatory's first director) was the second largest in the world when it was completed in 1939, and the 107-inch scope (now most fittingly named for Harlan Smith) was the third largest when it began operation in 1969. By the mid-1980s, these instruments had dropped to thirty-first and sixteenth place, respectively—still respectable but no longer at the cutting edge. Without a new telescope, it was doubtful UT Austin would be able to maintain for long the high quality of its astronomy program.[13]

A solution was found almost immediately after we closed the file on the 300-inch telescope, when Smith forged a partnership with astronomers at Penn State for development of a large telescope of a design that had never been built before, at a fraction of the cost of conventional telescopes. Bash had learned about the Penn State idea at a professional meeting and relayed information to Smith, who seized on it as a way to advance our astronomy program, even without $50 million.[14]

A partnership between Penn State and UT Austin had numerous advantages. Penn State had astronomers who had come up with an innovative and economical design, had experience with the fiber optics and other technologies to be used, and had a unique facility for making and testing telescope mirrors. UT Austin had an astronomy faculty that could help plan and design the telescope, and had an excellent place to put it: McDonald Observatory was renowned for its dark skies far from the "light pollution" of big cities and its large number of nights each year with weather suitable for observing. And even though the cost as advertised in 1985 was a mere $6 million, the idea for the two universities to share that cost had immediate appeal. On the administrative side, UT officials were delighted with the prospect of working again with Bryce Jordan, who served as president of Penn State from 1983 to 1990, after distinguished service as president of UT Dallas, interim president of UT Austin, and executive vice chancellor for academic affairs at the UT System.

The concept for the telescope was devised by Penn State astronomers Daniel W. Weedman and Lawrence W. Ramsey, who borrowed ideas from the design of a radio telescope and applied them to a reflecting telescope with an innovative type of mirror. Their design would be cheaper to build than a conventional telescope because it was dedicated to only one purpose—spectroscopy, or the study of the component wavelengths of light, which was what most telescope time was used for anyway. The design sacrificed greater flexibility for cost savings.

Much of the "astronomical" cost of a conventional large telescope was related either to making it move in complicated ways or to the fabrication of the large mirror. By departing from those design elements, the Penn State design could be built, it was estimated, for perhaps one-tenth or less of the cost of a conventional telescope. The Spectroscopic Survey Telescope (or SST, as it was first called) was to achieve these economies through a series of technical innovations—such as eliminating the single large mirror and replacing it with an array of many smaller, mass-produced mirrors in a honeycomb pattern.

In the spring of 1986, with the design still in the "proof of concept" stage, Jordan and I agreed that UT Austin would join the project and help pay for the planning and design. In December, the board of regents agreed with my request to authorize UT Austin to raise $1.5 million in private gifts (with a deadline of January 1, 1989) and to match that with $1.5 million from our Available University Fund resources to pay for our half of the total cost.

It may not seem now that raising $1.5 million should have presented much of a challenge, but the campaign was slow to make progress. The astronomers may have remained cheerfully optimistic, but the professional fund-raisers at Penn State and UT were struggling to think of likely donors. By early 1989, at least sixteen potential donors rejected our proposals. As a Penn State official wrote, "Frankly, I'm not terribly optimistic about the project. Please don't misunderstand,

Bill Hobby and the Otto Struve 82" Telescope, Fort Davis, c. 1997. *Courtesy of the Hobby family.*

we have not given up, but it certainly looks like slim pickings when you start taking a look at the number of prospects we have left."[15]

The opportunity to have one's name on the telescope was always a selling point. In July, George Christian suggested that we name the telescope after Hobby. Christian did not have to explain his idea twice. It would be an appropriate way to pay tribute to Hobby's many years of support for Texas higher education. In addition, the Hobby Foundation had already committed $100,000 to support the telescope, and we were hopeful that it might contribute additional funds. We also felt that many lobbyists and other friends of Hobby's would be interested in donating to a telescope named in his honor. Christian had been a good friend of Hobby's for many years, and he was also chairman of McDonald Observatory's Board of Visitors. I immediately asked Christian if he would agree to take charge of our fund-raising efforts, and when he said yes my confidence in our ability to deliver the funds went up dramatically.

Christian's assignment was to work with a fund-raising team put together by Hobby to pursue donations to the telescope to honor him on the completion of his career as an elected official. The emphasis was on finding a small number of major donors who would make pledges before Hobby retired from office in January 1991. While Hobby would always command the greatest respect throughout Texas, gifts in his honor would be more likely while he still held the state's most powerful elective office.

Later in 1990, Penn State also made a decision about its share of the name, when Robert E. Eberly, a longtime supporter of that university, agreed to donate almost $2 million to the project, and then we were able to designate the SST as the Hobby-Eberly Telescope.[16] Meanwhile, Smith had announced his decision to retire as observatory director in August 1989. After a long international search, Gerry Fonken recommended that we offer the position to Bash, whose familiarity with the telescope project from its inception was a strong point in his favor. I agreed, and Bash served with distinction through the dedication and opening of the telescope in 1997 and for six years beyond that.

Also in August 1989 we were surprised to learn that Penn State had decided to limit its contribution to no more than $2.25 million. This unsettling news[17] arrived at about the same time that the astronomers were discussing among themselves the likelihood that several "add-ons" would be necessary, increasing the original estimated cost by $2 million or more. There was also a realization within the astronomers' group that the design work had not progressed far enough to yield "really accurate costing." "In fact, it is likely to be about a year before these large uncertainties can be resolved," according to a draft of a letter to the other astronomers from Smith. "There is not the slightest desire on the part of the Texas astronomers to overrun the original estimates, but *it would be folly in the extreme to build a telescope which does not work or which works so poorly as to be an object of ridicule*" (emphasis in original).[18]

I agreed at this point with Fonken's recommendation to hold periodic reviews of the project with the design team in order to determine "with essential certainty that the telescope can be built and what it will actually cost."[19] At the end of the year, Fonken laid out clearly what was at stake. "In my opinion," he wrote to me, "closure of the work seems to have persistently slipped in each of the past several years despite repeated assurances from Harlan Smith that the 'end was in sight.' . . . I believe that we are faced with a dilemma. Expectations that UT and Penn State will in fact construct the SST extend back at least three years and numerous donors, the McDonald Board of Visitors, the general public, and others have continued to adhere to those expectations. Yet, at present, we seem to be still short of a completed design and cost analysis of the project. The very speculative cost estimates appear to be growing well beyond the original $6,000,000 and Penn State appears to have drawn back from the understanding that the project be 50/50 cost shared. I suggest that we convene another review in mid-to-late January. Unless that review provides convincing evidence that the design work can be rather quickly brought to closure and that the project costs can be rigorously contained, I believe we should consider steps to discontinue the project."[20]

We also began to try to identify additional university partners who would be interested in contributing financially in return for use of the telescope.[21] Eventually Bash secured commitments from three new partners—Ludwig Maximilian University in Munich, followed by George August University in Göttingen, and then Stanford. Based on the commitments as of 1992, UT Austin had a 52 percent share, Penn State had 31 percent, Stanford had 7 percent, and each of the German universities had 5 percent.[22]

By mid-February 1990, the new cost estimate from the astronomers' team was a maximum of $8.2 million, but others, including Fonken, thought the cost was likely to rise to as much as $10 million. UT Austin's fund-raising efforts up to that time had yielded $1.04 million, so we were about two-thirds of the way toward qualifying for the $1.5 million in matching money from the regents. The UT money together with the $2.07 million that Penn State had promised brought the amount in hand or pledged to $4.59 million. Christian reported that the new cost estimates had been quite a shock to Hobby's team, but they were still hoping to raise $3.5 million.

The project received a major boost from the Texas Legislature in 1991 with the creation and funding of a Center for Advanced Studies in Astronomy. The center was a source of continuing money, so as well as helping fund the construction, it also provided operating money after construction was completed. This was a new special-item appropriation, and it may very well have saved the project from eventual cancellation. During very difficult economic times, the legislature committed $958,000 for the project for the 1992–1993 biennium—far more than we could have realistically expected when budget deliberations began in early 1991. Senator John Montford, a friend of Hobby's and a strong supporter of higher education and research at the university, agreed to support the new funding. The fact that Montford was also chairman of the Senate Finance Committee increased our odds of success from negligible to virtually certain.

By the fall of 1991, UT Austin had raised a little more than $2.4 million, more than qualifying for the AUF matching money. Together with other funds and the new appropriation, the UT Austin contribution now exceeded $5.6 million.

Unfortunately, costs were continuing to rise even above the $8.2 million "maximum" that Bash and others had forecast in 1990, and even exceeded Fonken's most dire predictions. In the fall of 1991, we were facing a total project cost of about $11.8 million. By early 1992, UT and Penn State stepped back to have another external panel of astronomers review the project. This panel recommended that we hire a full-time project manager and establish an engineering team charged with turning the plan into reality.

The new team included representatives of the astronomy programs, but we also brought in engineers from the aerospace industry and elsewhere. Tom Sebring, an engineer with wide experience in telescope building, was named project manager in 1992, and he saw the telescope through to its dedication in 1997. Sebring brought numerous changes to the project, and most people welcomed his approach. The site for the telescope was moved from Mount Locke (where McDonald's other telescopes are located) to a next-door peak, Mount Fowlkes, and several key details were redesigned while preserving the original concept.[23]

With the new project team and the new design—and a new cost estimate of $13.5 million—the project was finally ready for a groundbreaking ceremony in 1994 and then the three years of construction leading to the dedication in 1997. However, for more than two years after that "on time and on budget" dedication, the telescope underwent detailed "shakedown" and "commissioning" periods, during which engineers and astronomers determined it had serious problems related to its efficiency and the quality of its images. About $2 million was spent during those years to solve a host of problems of the sort that can arise with any sophisticated scientific instrument, as well as problems unique to this one. Another $6 million (as much as the entire project was supposed to cost at first) was spent on new spectrographs and a new system to keep the mirrors aligned. Additional fixes, known collectively as the Hobby-Eberly Telescope Completion Project, cost an additional $2 million. The total cost since the inception had risen to $24 million—four times the original budget.[24] Fonken was kind enough not to tell me "I told you so."

Eventually, the UT fund-raising was brought to completion through the generosity of seven "founding donors"—the Abell-Hanger Foundation, M. D. Anderson Foundation, Brown Foundation, Cullen Foundation, Hobby Foundation, Houston Endowment, and an anonymous donor in Dallas—as well as major gifts from twenty-five other foundations, companies, associations, and individuals, and more than one hundred other smaller benefactors. The university and the faculty members in the Department of Astronomy owe these donors a great debt of gratitude.

All the difficulties associated with the telescope should be kept in perspective. Building large state-of-the-art telescopes is one of the most complicated of all scientific and engineering challenges. Each design is unique, so experience in building previous telescopes is not always of great help. There may have never been one anywhere in the world that was finished "on time and on budget." Because of its radically new design, it is fair to say that the Hobby-Eberly Telescope was not so much designed as constructed by trial and error. Without the optimism and intellectual firepower of Harlan Smith and Frank Bash, and the engineering and construction skills of Tom Sebring, the Hobby-Eberly Telescope would never have been completed. I am confident that few, if any, of the university administrators who helped bring the Hobby-Eberly Telescope into being would be eager to get involved in another telescope project. This is not to say that UT Austin should never build another telescope, but I know a number of people who are thankful they have already had their turn at telescope-building.

CHAPTER 11

Teaching English and Political Correctness

My relationship with the College of Liberal Arts was closely watched throughout my presidency. As I have mentioned in earlier chapters, my background in business led some individuals to doubt that I was sincerely interested in strengthening the College of Liberal Arts. A few months after I became president, as I discussed in Chapter 3, *Texas Monthly* magazine published a long, mean-spirited article about me, the main point of which seemed to be that my background as a marketing professor made me thoroughly unfit to lead a great university. I knew from the beginning that I needed to make a special effort to persuade people that I had a vision for the university that encompassed its entire mission, including its pursuit of excellence in the liberal arts.

The record of my presidency demonstrates that I did, in fact, consider the liberal arts to be of central importance to the life of the university. For example, I strongly supported the effort to bring the renowned Pforzheimer Collection of early printed books to the Harry Ransom Humanities Research Center and focused much energy on raising the money that made that acquisition possible. I was able to help make possible the acquisition of the Natchez Trace Collection of historical documents by the Center for American History. And I made the initial contact and "the ask" for $10 million that Robert and Nancy Dedman of Dallas donated for liberal arts scholarships. I will discuss these and other fund-raising successes in more detail in Chapter 13.

Other developments in liberal arts during my presidency that I am particularly pleased with include the James A. Michener fellowships for writers; scholarships for the Plan II liberal arts honors program; renovated facilities for faculty in economics, French, and Italian as well as a facility for a liberal arts placement center; the development of new academic initiatives such as the Center for Social Philosophy and Policy, the Texas Center for Writers, the Edward Clark Center for Australian Studies, and the Conservation Education Program to help protect and preserve library materials. I am also proud that I was able to place the President's Office at the service of the successful effort to create an endowment for the interdisciplinary seminar in British Studies, and that Isabella and I were able to contribute to this effort personally.

Much of my effort to work with Dean Bob King and his successor, Dean Standish Meacham, to strengthen liberal arts involved crises in the Department of English. While presidents of large universities will often disagree about many things, they almost always agree that faculty members in English can be very difficult to manage. There are at least three reasons for this. First, as Betty Sue Flowers, one of UT Austin's most distinguished faculty members in the Department of English, once told me, faculty members in English are "social critics." They are attracted to the role of literature as providing insights into, and critiques of, society, and in some cases they are carried away by the process of debate and argument so that the process becomes at least as important as the actual outcome. My experience is that many English faculty members would rather fight than win.

Second, English faculty, like some other liberal arts faculty, are consistently upset over their absolute pay as well as how they are paid relative to faculty in the professional schools. Early in my presidency I met with the senior faculty in the English Department for breakfast. One of the first questions was how could I justify paying a twenty-six-year-old assistant professor in the Department of Accounting twice as much as the average full professor in English. I told the group that if the university paid the English faculty the same salaries that it paid the accounting faculty, we would have the highest paid English Department in the nation. In contrast, if we paid the accounting faculty what we paid the English faculty, we would not have an Accounting Department. I explained that this is how the market works, as a university competes for talent not only against other universities but also against the private sector. If there were more of a private market for experts in literature, universities would pay more for English professors. My answer was received with deafening silence.

A third issue that leads to friction with an English Department is the traditional role of teaching writing to students from across the university. This is at best a tough job that requires intensive student-faculty interaction, and it involves instruction to a very high percentage of the university's total undergraduate population. English faculty members in research universities, like UT Austin, have received their doctoral degrees from prestigious schools where they focused on highly advanced and specialized topics in the study of language and literature, and now they are faced with twenty-five freshman business and engineering majors who really do not care about learning how to write a cogent memo. It is not a pretty picture.

The standard solution to this problem is for an English Department to hire a large number of teaching assistants to teach writing so the faculty can remain focused on the specialty of their choice. This solution works reasonably well if the TA's are dedicated to their jobs and are properly supervised. The alternative of taking basic writing courses away from the English Department is almost always resisted by the English faculty because it is a clear statement to the world that the faculty do not care about the teaching of writing and because it represents a significant loss of resources. The TA's who teach the course are always doctoral students in the department. If they are not needed to teach writing, then the size of the department's doctoral program will be reduced.

This issue of teaching writing was combined in the 1980s with a nationwide debate over "multicultural" education in a way that brought the UT Austin Department of English to the verge of self-destruction. A controversy within the department over English 306, the main rhetoric and composition course for freshmen, veered off into a contest over what was widely described as "political correctness" and "multiculturalism," including a proposal to use a highly disputed sociology anthology on racism and sexism as the central text for the course. The textbook was eventually dropped, in favor of a packet of readings to be assembled by faculty, but the controversy continued until the end of my presidency.

The controversy was part of a larger debate at universities across the country over how to guarantee that undergraduates received a broad education that included exposure to cultures other than their own. From this seemingly simple and universally accepted goal, the nationwide "multiculturalism" movement quickly descended into academic warfare over charges of indoctrination and political bias. At UT, the debate was heavily influenced by other factors, including the desire to finally overcome any vestiges of the institution's legacy of racial discrimination, debate over affirmative action programs for recruiting minority students and faculty, long-running internal divisions in the English Department, and the department's budgetary challenge of providing writing instruction to most of the university's growing number of freshmen.[1] These complexities of the debate meant that the dispute was not simply a matter of political liberals versus conservatives, but that oversimplified view often prevailed. I believe the campus and media debate that could be placed under the headings of "political correctness" and "multiculturalism" generated far more heat than light, more confusion than insight, and more sloganeering than clear thinking. There was widespread agreement with the venerable idea that a university education should broaden students' horizons and make them conversant with cultures and ways of life different from their own. Beyond that ideal, it often seemed, there was nothing but disagreement.

Strong personalities among the faculty also shaped the debate. Among the department's most passionate advocates for a new, multicultural approach to teaching writing was Linda Brodkey, at one time the head of the committee charged with drafting a new course syllabus for English 306. On the other side, favoring more traditional approaches to teaching rhetoric and composition, were equally determined faculty members such as Alan Gribben, a distinguished Mark Twain scholar and later the author of a biography of Harry Ransom. Brodkey and Gribben, as well as a number of others who were highly active in the debate over English 306, later left UT for faculty posts at other universities, and it may be that such changes in the personality of the faculty contributed a great deal to the ultimate outcome of the issue at UT.

The matter took numerous twists and turns over the years, most of which I will spare the reader, but it reached a climax during the two years (1989 to 1991) that Standish Meacham was dean of liberal arts. King had served as dean with great distinction (and considerable heroism) since 1979 and richly deserved an opportunity to put aside administrative burdens and return to his teaching and scholarship in the Department of Linguistics. I named Meacham as his successor in June 1989 and he took over in September. Meacham had been on the history faculty since 1967 and had twice served as chairman of that department.

In the late spring of 1990, Dean Herbert Woodson of the College of Engineering announced that if English 306 was going to be turned into a "multi-cultural sociology/anthropology course," his college would ask the central administration to drop English 306 as a required course and would hire its own faculty to teach writing. The deans of the College of Natural Sciences and the College of Business immediately followed Woodson's leadership and stated that they wanted to examine the possibility of creating their own writing courses. I responded that it would be difficult for the central administration to mandate a writing course that a college did not want as part of its curriculum.

By July 1990 it was clear that the plans for overhauling the teaching of English 306 were so divisive across the campus that more time was needed to decide what to do with the course. Meacham postponed any changes for at least a year so the faculty could further refine its plans and hopefully develop a course that would have broader support across the campus. The postponement was widely hailed as a victory by the more conservative factions.[2]

The postponement was followed a few months later by Meacham's decision, which was announced on January 8, 1991, to step down as dean and return to his faculty role in history. He cited "personal reasons" for this decision and dismissed talk that he was being forced out because of his liberal views.[3] While I agreed with Meacham that a change was desirable, I believe he found it more difficult to continue as dean after members of the committee that was charged with redesigning English 306 decided to resign as a group. The committee members' decision predated Meacham's but became public on February 5, 1991, less than a month after Meacham's own announcement.

The committee, led by Brodkey, had had a contentious history, with two members resigning in the spring of 1990 over a dispute with the group's procedures. Some fifty faculty members from various departments signed an advertisement in the *Daily Texan* that spring criticizing the work of the committee.[4]

The resignations of the committee and of Meacham eventually provided an opportunity to take control of this seemingly never-ending issue and cut through the tangle of campus politics that seemed to be preventing a reasonable course of action. The first step I took was to persuade King to return as acting dean effective June 1991 while a search committee sought candidates for a permanent dean. At first,

Dean Robert D. King. UT *Office of Public Affairs Records, e_utopa_00030.*

our hope was to fill the position by the fall of 1992, but after a few months it was clear that more time would be needed, and King agreed to continue as acting dean until the fall of 1993.

In the fall of 1991 a University Council committee proposed a multicultural course requirement that would begin in the fall of 1992 with a three-hour course and would increase in later years to six hours. I always felt this was one last attempt by the same group of people who had been working so hard to modify English 306 to force the university to require a multicultural ethnic studies course on the entire campus. The University Council approved the proposal in October, but there were enough letters of protest from faculty members that the proposal was required to be submitted to a vote of the entire faculty.[5] This resulted in the first called meeting of the faculty that had a quorum in many years, as several hundred faculty gathered in the LBJ Auditorium. Gerry Fonken and I were concerned that a vote only by those who were motivated enough to turn out for the meeting would result in approval of the course requirement. We felt that while the goal of exposing our students to a varied cultural experience

was a noble one, we were also strongly convinced that the proposal
that had passed the University Council was politically motivated and
would not represent a significant academic advancement for our students. In addition, there were many practical logistical questions that
remained unanswered, such as who would teach the courses and how
they would be paid for, that were not even discussed in the University
Council's proposal.

In order to avoid a vote at that meeting, Fonken and I decided that
he would ask Austin Gleason of the Department of Physics to make
a motion at the General Faculty meeting that a ballot be mailed to all
faculty members to deal with the issue. Fonken and I felt confident
that if the faculty as a whole was ever given an opportunity to speak
on this issue, they would vote it down.

The meeting took place on December 6, 1991. There was clearly a
quorum of the faculty in attendance. I opened the meeting and called
for discussion. Gleason immediately raised his hand and made the
motion that a mail ballot be sent to all of the faculty concerning the
University Council's proposed multicultural course. I asked for and
received a second, and while I did ask if there was "any discussion,"
I waited less than five seconds before calling for a vote. I am not sure
that everyone in the auditorium knew exactly what they were voting
on, but as chair I heard the motion pass. I then said that seeing no
other business, the meeting was adjourned. The meeting was concluded in less than seven minutes.

We were correct about the results of the mail ballot. The vote was
759 (64 percent) against to 434 (36 percent) for, with about 900 eligible faculty members not voting. Because of a glitch in the list of
eligible voters, some 430 faculty members did not receive ballots, but
they were invited to vote in person at the office of the University
Council secretary, Paul Kelly. Among those, the vote was 30 in favor
and 33 against. Proponents of the multiculturalism requirement inevitably complained about the voting process.

I felt that we had made a great deal of progress just in avoiding
the implementation of a radical multicultural course either under the
label of English 306 or some other required courses as envisioned by
the University Council. However, the fundamental issue still existed—
how to teach English 306 effectively to a large number of undergraduates. King, Fonken, and I had discussed this issue on numerous occasions during the spring semester in 1992.

King felt that the only way to solve this problem once and for all was to create a separate division for this purpose apart from the English Department and under direct control of the dean's office. The course would be taught by professional full-time teachers, many of whom would have a Ph.D. in English but who would be focusing their attention on teaching writing, not research. King, Fonken, and I met on August 31, 1992, the last day I was president of UT Austin. I wanted this problem solved before I officially left office at midnight that night. King was a little nervous over this issue because he knew that the English Department would go ballistic, but I was ready to approve his proposal. My concern was that if we did not solve it now with King in control, we would never get another chance. After much discussion, I finally said, "The stars are aligned. If we don't do this and do it today, it will not happen. Bob, if you will recommend it to Gerry, and Gerry, if you will recommend it to me, I will approve it." King then made his recommendation, and Fonken made his, and I kept my word and it was done.

The creation of the Division of Rhetoric and Composition was the last official act of my presidency, just before I fed the turtles one last time on the fourth-floor balcony outside my office and turned out the lights. Some people may still debate whether that was the best way to handle a seemingly intractable problem, but some people just like to debate. Everyone can thank me, King, and Fonken for the fact that undergraduate students are receiving excellent instruction in rhetoric and composition from professional instructors who enjoy teaching writing to undergraduates. On a personal note, I was greatly relieved that King was there to oversee the college with a steady and forceful hand during this difficult time of transition, and I will always be grateful for his willingness to sacrifice his own scholarly pursuits for the welfare of the college and the university. When he returned as acting dean, he had already served as a dean for a total of thirteen years, having been dean of the old College of Social and Behavioral Sciences for three years before his first stint as leader of the College of Liberal Arts, and he had taken far more punishment than any one university administrator should be expected to suffer. The fact that he was willing to come back as acting dean for two additional years shows how deeply devoted he was to the university's liberal arts program and the education of all UT students.

CHAPTER 12

Crisis and Progress in the Fine Arts

The university's Performing Arts Center (PAC) opened in 1981 as the fulfillment of a dream by Frank Erwin for the campus to have a world-class performance space that could accommodate any type of theatrical or musical production, including his beloved grand opera. The PAC quickly became known as one of the finest centers of its kind on any university campus, and it allowed Austin to attract the finest touring productions from Broadway and the world of classical music, thus serving as a valuable cultural asset not only for the university but for the entire city and region. The stellar success of the PAC had become tarnished, however, by the mid-1980s because of serious operating deficits of more than $600,000 in 1986 and 1987.

The center, which was managed through the College of Fine Arts, had always been envisioned as a facility that would support its annual operating budget largely through ticket sales. The economic crisis that had developed at the PAC was clearly a problem that demanded my attention as president—for the welfare of the college and the cultural life of the campus, and, indeed, the larger community.

Our first approach to the deficit as it developed during the 1986–1987 performance season was to consider it primarily as a problem that was the responsibility of the College of Fine Arts, so that the college would have to make up the deficit by reconfiguring its overall budget and shifting funds around as necessary. This approach was consistent with the way any college or school at the university would manage its affairs, with the dean making decisions about how to allocate funds to meet competing demands. Under this approach, we developed a plan in 1987 with Dean J. Robert Wills through which the college would pay off the accumulated deficit by 1990, largely by transferring funds from other programs in the college. It was also decided that the PAC would not schedule any new touring events until the deficit was eliminated.

The prospect of several years with no more New York dance companies and world-renowned classical pianists performing for UT and Austin audiences woke up many in the community about the seriousness of the financial problem. In one sense, the solution was simple—the audiences that cared so deeply about such cultural opportunities would have to support them by buying tickets, or the opportunities would go away.

When the depth of the financial problem became public in November 1987, the university received criticism from the arts community and some civic leaders for what was sometimes seen as a cold-hearted approach and for what it meant for the arts in Austin. While concerns about losing the PAC's cultural benefits were certainly understandable, it was clear that most of the criticism was poorly informed. The PAC had never been entirely alone in meeting its financial requirements. Bonds from the Permanent University Fund had been used to build the $41 million facility, so it had no burden of capital costs. Because it was primarily an instructional facility, state appropriations paid for most of the facility's general overhead, including air conditioning and heating, electricity, maintenance, and custodial services. In addition, an allocation from the Available University Fund of more than $1 million a year provided support for the permanent staff of the PAC.

The fact that the PAC was "losing money" despite these substantial subsidies indicates just how poor the programming decisions had been. Managers of such facilities always have to balance their programming decisions, so that ticket sales from some highly popular shows help to subsidize events that draw a more limited audience and will predictably lose money but nevertheless have extremely high cultural value, for at least a limited audience. This is particularly true at an academic performing arts center, which is expected to present events that will be of keen interest to fine arts faculty and students but not necessarily popular in the general community. The university was simply expecting the PAC to do a better job of balancing its programs, while also expecting the PAC and the college to take responsibility for paying off the accumulated deficit.[1]

By December 1987, it was clear to me that that approach was not going to work. The financial demands on the PAC were too great, given the economic realities of a recession and diminished ticket sales, while the importance of the PAC to the university and the community as a cultural asset had never been greater. In addition to all the traditional values of such facilities, the PAC had developed into one of the important selling points for attracting high-tech companies and other corporations to Austin. Weighing more heavily in my mind was the danger that the PAC's problems could harm the academic programs of the College of Fine Arts. If paying off the deficit within the current administrative and budget structure was going to mean disrupting those academic programs and interfering with the education of students and the preeminence of their professors, we really had no choice but to find another direction.

When it became clear at the end of 1987 that a new approach was going to be necessary, Wills and I agreed on December 16 to appoint a special committee to take a fresh look at the PAC and its operations and advise us on our options. I was fortunate to be able to rely on Ed Sharpe as the chairman of this committee—just one more in a long list of examples of my calling on him as a special troubleshooter. Sharpe's diplomatic and organizational skills, as well as his gentle but forceful way of getting people to face reality and reach a consensus, proved very useful once again. Sharpe had a highly dedicated and knowledgeable group of people to work with on this committee: Oscar Brockett, professor of drama; John Murphy, professor of advertising; Randi Shade, president of the Students' Association; Maline McCalla, chair of the Fine Arts Foundation Advisory Council; and Bob Dorsey, a member of the advisory council. We also named two ex officio members: Ronald Pearson, director of the PAC, and Dean Justice, director of the Frank Erwin Special Events Center.

It was essential that the committee work quickly, and they wasted no time, presenting Wills and me with a report by January 8, 1988. This was another benefit of having Sharpe in charge of the committee. We couldn't afford to wait for the usual six months or year that university committees often require to finish their work. Wills and I agreed with the direction that the committee had recommended, and on February 16 I met with the faculty and staff of the college to announce our new plan.[2]

A central part of the plan was our commitment to raise at least $3 million for an endowment to help underwrite the PAC's concert

From left, Jack Blanton, Perry and Nancy Lee Bass, and Van Cliburn at Bass Concert Hall, September 20, 1988. *UT Office of Public Affairs Records, e_utopa_00038.*

series. We began the endowment with $500,000 from university funds that matched a gift of $500,000 to the Department of Drama by Mary Lewis Scott Kleberg of Kingsville. Mrs. Kleberg, who was a strong advocate for education and the arts, graciously agreed to the Drama and PAC endowments as uses for the proceeds from the sale of Sweetbrush, her family's historic home in Austin. In addition to those endowment funds, I decided to seek permission from the UT Board of Regents to set aside an additional $833,000 in university funds to provide matches for contributions to the PAC endowment.

Shirley Bird Perry and I did not know where to turn to raise the remainder of the endowment. While we hoped the Austin community would collectively make a significant gift, we were not confident that this would happen. As a result, we turned once again to Perry and Nancy Lee Bass to bail us out. The Basses were true friends of the fine arts, and they loved the university. They also had shown a willingness to come to the aid of UT when we had had previous problems. They were very receptive to the idea of helping create an endowment in the college, and they very quickly agreed to donate $1 million to the endowment. Based on a one-for-two match and the Basses' very generous gift, we quickly raised $2.5 million of the goal of $3 million.[3]

I also agreed with the committee's recommendation to create a Programming Advisory Board, to be chaired by the PAC director but also to include students, faculty, staff, and community representatives. In broader terms, my announcement on February 16 shifted the focus from the PAC's past deficit and placed emphasis on how to ensure a viable operation for the future. As for the deficit, I simply told the press, "We're not dealing with that for the moment."[4]

A number of other more detailed steps were taken to help put the PAC on a sound financial basis. Following the committee's recommendations, these included reducing the number of events produced annually, broadening the range and appeal of events, attracting more students to events, reinstituting an optional student fee for PAC events, offering season tickets to the public, and sharing the risk of high-investment events. I also decided that because of the university-wide importance of the PAC, the central administration ought to have more oversight and input into its operations. So, while the PAC director would continue to report to the dean, I made it clear that the director would also have regular communications with Sharpe.

The crisis may or may not have been a factor in decisions later in 1988 by Ronald Pearson and Dean Wills to pursue their careers elsewhere. Pearson resigned in July to take a comparable job as director of a new arts center at the University of South Carolina. He told the Austin newspaper that the PAC's problems were "probably all mixed up in it somewhere" as he decided to accept the new job, but the job also had attractions as a chance to begin operating a performing arts facility from the ground up.[5] Gerry Harris, who had been associate director of the PAC, became acting director. By this time, Sharpe was playing a very active role in supervising the operations of the PAC, and Harris was very comfortable with this arrangement. He understood the need to book a series of Broadway plays and musicals that would have a broad appeal to Austin and the Central Texas community. Throughout the next few years, Harris played a critical role in helping resolve the PAC's financial problems.

Pearson's resignation did not surprise me, but Wills's resignation did. Wills and I met in my office in late November 1988. While I was very direct with him, I felt I was making good progress in helping him understand the need to improve the financial controls in the PAC. About one hour after he left my office, I asked Sharpe to step in, and I told him that I felt I had had an excellent meeting with Wills. Sharpe said, "Well, it may not have gone as well as you think. Bob just called and resigned."

Wills announced that he would leave UT to become provost at Pacific Lutheran University, a small private university in Tacoma, Washington, with an emphasis on teaching. The church affiliation, the concentration on teaching, and the chance to have a broad academic position were strong attractions for him, he told the Austin newspaper.[6]

The year 1988 saw another momentous development in the College of Fine Arts, this one thankfully not a crisis but a sign of the college's enduring strength and value. We were able to announce in June 1988 that a donation of $1.65 million would be made to the college by an anonymous donor, a gift that would result in endowments totaling $4.4 million after the addition of the university's matching funds and other money that the college's advisory council had agreed to raise. These funds represented a 42 percent increase in the college's overall endowment, from about $10.6 million to almost $15 million. We used the funds to create four endowed faculty chairs, increase the funding for two existing chairs, and establish an endowment for graduate student fellowships. In keeping with the donor's wish, we never announced the source of the gift, but the local newspaper reported that its "sources" said the donor was the O'Donnell Foundation of Dallas, led by longtime UT Austin supporters Peter and Edith O'Donnell.[7] The gift could not have come at a more fortuitous time, as it gave the College of Fine Arts and all of its friends some much-needed good news after months of controversy over the financial problems of the PAC.

I *did* announce that the donor had told me that before making a decision about the gift, he had commissioned a panel of independent experts to evaluate the college's five-year plan for academic programs, and that their positive report had convinced him that his money would be put to good use. The donor told me that his motive for the gift was "to help the College of Fine Arts become one of the finest in the country and to serve as a model for other public institutions to follow. The quality of the college will be determined largely by the quality of its

Peter O'Donnell Jr. *UT Office of Public Affairs Records, e_utopa_00050.*

faculty and students. Therefore, it is our hope and expectation that these endowments will help the college attract professors and graduate students of the highest ability and reputation."

The gift to the College of Fine Arts was announced at the same time as a $4.5 million gift from the same donor for endowed faculty and students positions in the College of Engineering. The far larger gift to Engineering did not receive as much public attention, probably because it was deemed less "newsworthy" than the gift to the College of Fine Arts, given the definition of "news" as something out of the ordinary. I never considered any multimillion-dollar gift as "ordinary," but there was no doubt that big gifts to the fine arts were quite rare. We were very grateful for both gifts, and I know the College of Fine Arts has made outstanding use of that "seed money" through the years.

The search for a new director of the PAC was delayed, at first because of the financial crisis at the PAC and also because we wanted a new dean of fine arts to be in place to help with the decision on hiring a PAC director. In addition, Sharpe and I both felt Harris was doing an excellent job as acting director, so there was no immediate need to start a search for a permanent director.

We began actively looking for a permanent director in 1990, after Jon Whitmore took office as the new dean. We were fortunate to attract Whitmore from the State University of New York at Buffalo, where he had served as dean of arts and letters, and his five years as dean of fine arts at UT Austin were highly successful. While there were several very impressive finalists for the position of PAC director, Pebbles Wadsworth was the finalist everyone fell in love with. She had experience, pizzazz, style, and the willingness to work with both the President's Office and Dean Whitmore. She had helped build the UCLA facility to a position of national prominence, and she was attracted by the opportunity to have a similar impact at UT, particularly given the unsurpassed physical facilities of the campus. She also brought to the job well-developed ideas about closer ties between the PAC and the university's academic programs in the fine arts as well as reaching out more effectively to the larger Austin community. One goal that she emphasized from the beginning was to use the arts programming of the PAC to help break down barriers between cultural groups, and she proved especially adept at making the PAC an

Pebbles Wadsworth in the Performing Arts Center at the University of Texas, February 1992. *UT Office of Public Affairs Records, e_utopa_00032.*

important venue for the arts from Latin America. Once Wadsworth was on the scene (beginning in January 1992), Sharpe and I both realized that we could move on to other activities. She quickly had the situation well under control and continued to provide dynamic and inspired leadership for the PAC until her retirement in 2008. There were numerous attractions in the UT job for Wadsworth, and she proved every bit as successful as we had hoped she would be.

During the years that I was president, the university witnessed the culmination of efforts to correct a decades-old problem that arose in the College of Fine Arts but involved the entire university and its legacy of racial discrimination. I refer to the decision by the university administration in 1957 to bar Barbara Conrad, a black student, from appearing in a student opera production. The role that she had prepared for, Dido, Queen of Carthage, involved duets with a white student playing the hero Aeneas, and this interracial stagecraft proved more than the segregationist leaders of the state and the university could accept. As shameful as the incident was in the university's history, Conrad refused to let it deter her from her dreams, and she graduated from UT in 1959 with a degree in voice and went on to a highly acclaimed career as an operatic mezzo-soprano with the Metropolitan Opera, the Vienna State Opera, Teatro Nacional in Venezuela, and many other companies around the world. In the 1980s, the university sought to make amends for its past wrongs and reached out to Conrad. She returned to the campus in 1984 for a campus recital, and in the spring of 1985 she was named a Distinguished Alumnus of the university. She was chosen for this honor a few months before I became president, but I was proud that she was one of the honorees at the first Distinguished Alumnus ceremony that I attended as president.

Conrad and the university continued to develop a close relationship in the ensuing years. She returned to the campus numerous times to perform with students, and by the end of the 1980s she was working with the College of Fine Arts in planning special performance projects involving the African American community and others. At the spring commencement ceremony in 1987, Conrad was seated at the front of the Tower with other dignitaries from the Ex-Students' Association. After the official party had marched in and was seated, I decided that it would be a wonderful idea to ask Conrad to lead the graduates and their guests in singing "The Eyes of Texas" at the end of the gradu-

Opera singer and UT Distinguished Alumnus Barbara Conrad singing "The Eyes of Texas" at the 1987 Commencement. *Prints and Photographs Collection, di_08396.*

ation ceremony. After all, this is "The University" and having a star from the Metropolitan Opera sing just made sense to me. I stepped off the stage and walked down and asked Conrad if she would do this for me. She immediately agreed. Then at the end of the ceremony I invited Conrad up to the podium. It took only a few seconds for the huge audience to realize that they had an opportunity to listen to one of America's great mezzo-sopranos. The crowd went silent as Conrad stole the show. It was my most memorable graduation.

I was delighted that UT Austin invited Conrad to perform at the commencement ceremony in May 2000, the last commencement that I attended as chancellor. This time the university was gracious enough not to ask Conrad to sing without any notice. Once again, she was spectacular. Many stories from history lack a happy ending, or they are never resolved to our satisfaction, but everyone associated with the University of Texas can be proud that that painful episode from

1957 had a happy ending at last—thanks in no small measure to the generosity and resilience of Conrad herself.

I am very proud of the progress that was made in the College of Fine Arts during my tenure as president of UT Austin. The central administration took an aggressive role in helping resolve problems that the college could not solve on its own, but we were also quick to withdraw once we had the right people in place to manage the college. This is the proper role of the central administration, and I believe we played it very well.

CHAPTER 13

Fund-Raising at UT Austin

One of my highest priorities as president was increasing the amount
of private-sector funding for the university. There was no doubt
that one of the reasons the board of regents appointed me was the
success I had had with fund-raising in the business school. I was
extremely fortunate as president to have at my side Shirley Bird
Perry, whose knowledge and skills had been so important in the success of the university's centennial fund-raising campaign under President Flawn and who agreed to continue as vice president for development and university relations. We made a good team, and I will
always be grateful for her tireless efforts on behalf of the university.

Many people may not realize how much effort a president of a
public university puts into fund-raising. There is still a fairly common
perception that while private universities must rely on donations,
public institutions are supported by state tax dollars and, therefore,
don't need private support. This perception is even more prevalent for
UT Austin because of the misperception that the Permanent University Fund has made UT Austin a "wealthy" university.

All the leaders of UT Austin in the modern era have worked hard
to combat this myth and to explain to the public why fund-raising is
essential to the continued health of the institution. When I became
president in 1985, appropriations from state taxes accounted for about
43 percent of the university's budget, and they declined to approximately 30 percent by my last year as president (1992), and then to
less than 24 percent by the end of my term as chancellor in 2000. A
second myth about funding is that the Permanent University Fund
is dedicated exclusively to UT Austin. The truth is that Texas A&M
and most of the UT System's component institutions also benefit from
the PUF. While the PUF is a large endowment fund, it has many thousands of students and faculty to support, as well as the administrative

offices at the UT System. As a result of UT Austin's unending drive for excellence, supplementing state appropriations with donations from the private sector has been increasingly important.

The first major strides in coordinated fund-raising at UT Austin were made under President Flawn with the Centennial Teachers and Scholars Program, which raised money for endowed chairs, professorships, and scholarships. The special centennial fund-raising effort produced some spectacular results including a UT record of $89 million in donations in 1984, the year before I became president, but the yearly totals fell off immediately after that campaign. For example, in 1986–1987, UT Austin raised only $32 million in donations and ranked twenty-first among public universities while Texas A&M was in eleventh place with $47 million.[1]

There is a common misperception that major donors are given special privileges on campus. With minor exceptions, this really is not true. I did receive many calls from wealthy donors inquiring about the chances of their son, daughter, or grandchild being admitted to the university. My standard response was to begin by asking them to tell me about the applicant. I found that very few of the calls concerned National Merit Scholarship finalists who were ranked in the top 2 percent of their high school class with scores of 1600 on the SAT. The easiest case for me was when it was clear the prospective student was not qualified, or, at best, had been an underachiever in high school. I made it very clear that my experience indicated that very few people went from being subpar high school students to excellent college students over a summer. In addition, while the young man or woman had done only marginally well competing against high school students from their hometown, if they attended UT Austin, they would be competing against the state's very best students. I concluded by saying that it was important that the young man or woman have a successful academic experience, and that it was in their best interest to attend a smaller, less competitive school, where they would get more personal attention. This approach worked most of the time.

I did try to return calls from major donors very quickly while other people may have had to spend more time in the UT bureaucracy before their problems ever reached my desk. To illustrate, Ross Perot called me in November 1990 and asked if I would help place Bob Peck in our administration as an intern. Peck was considering pursuing a graduate program in either public affairs or law and he wanted to have exposure to higher education administration. Shirley Bird Perry and I agreed that this individual had a very unique background (he is the only person Perot ever asked me to accept as an intern) and he was hired within twenty-four hours.

A second illustration of a call I quickly returned was from my good friend Dee Kelly in June 1990. Kelly had been a longtime supporter of the UT Law School and he was Perry Bass's attorney in Fort Worth. After a few moments of pleasantries, Kelly said that "Perry" (I did not have to ask Perry who) would like UT Austin to take over the management and ownership of the Sam Rayburn Museum in Bonham. I had never been to the museum, but I immediately recognized that it would be of great value to the university and our program of preserving important archives related to Texas and United States history. I told Kelly that I would make arrangements to visit the library as soon as possible. Kelly met me, Shirley Bird Perry, and Don Carleton, director of UT's Center for American History, at the library on July 13, 1990. I asked Carleton to lead a team of UT Austin experts to do a careful, thorough review of the library's assets and report to me as soon as possible on how the library could be integrated into UT Austin. I felt comfortable with Carleton in charge. He was a true academic entrepreneur, and he never saw an important historical collection that he did not want to acquire for UT Austin.

On September 14, 1990, I found myself at a podium in Bonham officially accepting UT Austin's newest asset. I called the museum "the University of Texas at Austin at Bonham." In addition to making a wealth of scholarly resources available for study, the museum has also helped UT Austin continue its service responsibility to the people of Texas by making sure that one of the state's unique historical treasures will always be properly maintained. Bass, Kelly, and their colleagues on the Sam Rayburn Library Board transferred not only the physical assets of the library but also enough permanent endowment resources to ensure that the library never becomes a financial drain on the university.

Perry and I spent most of our fund-raising efforts in trying to help the colleges such as liberal arts and fine arts that did not have a history of operating successful fund-raising programs. Professional schools such as business, engineering, and law raised numerous endowments during the centennial. They also had mature yearly fund-raising programs that appealed to alumni and businesses.

One of the first initiatives I asked Perry to get involved in was helping raise relatively small amounts of money from an annual fund campaign based on letters from the deans and telephone calls from students. We started such an effort when I was dean of the business school, relying mainly on solicitation letters sent to alumni from me, and then following up with calls from student volunteers. Our initial efforts in the college were not very sophisticated, but we did succeed in involving a large number of students in the college fund-raising efforts and we did raise a significant amount of unrestricted donations. I first met Connie Saathoff at one of these business school fundraisers. Saathoff was twenty-two years old and had volunteered as an employee in the Assistant Dean's Office to attend the event. She took charge of the volunteers and of coordinating the effort to send thankyou letters to the people who had agreed to donate to the college. I was impressed with her organizational skills and her willingness to volunteer to help the college, and I hired her a year later to work in the Dean's Office. She stayed with me as my assistant throughout my career at UT Austin and the UT System and beyond that when I returned to full-time faculty duties.

Perry hired Michael Meadows, who was a freshly minted liberal arts graduate of UT Austin, to lead our first university-wide telethon effort. As was my experience in the business school, I found as president that our students and recent graduates made fantastic solicitors. A student understands from his or her own experience many of the financial needs of the university. Students have a personal stake in the success of the fund-raising effort since the money raised will enhance their educational experience, and they typically are very enthusiastic, which makes a good impression on alumni. It is harder for an alumnus to turn down a bright, articulate, highly motivated student than an anonymous older person who has been hired to work a phone bank.

The university's centennial fund-raising campaign had been concluded by the time I became president. That campaign, the Centennial Teachers and Scholars Program, far exceeded its original goals for new endowments to support faculty positions, student scholarships and fellowships, and other activities. After June 1985, the centennial campaign had been replaced with a Regents Endowed Teachers and Scholars Program, which was also marvelously successful. In 1990, I announced a new campaign called An Investment in Students, whose goal was to raise $100 million for student scholarships and fellowships. As usual, the deans played an important role in working their donor lists to generate endowments for this campaign. The university matched one dollar from the AUF for each two dollars that were raised. Once again, it was proved that matching funds always help stimulate donations. Larry Temple chaired the committee, and it was very successful.

Throughout the years I was president, we had successes in securing major gifts that allowed the university to move forward academically in dramatic ways. Perry and I met regularly to discuss potential opportunities where I could be of help in raising money. I will briefly discuss several fund-raising efforts that illustrate the different ways major gifts come about in liberal arts and fine arts, as well as the intriguing motives and generosity of donors.

Two months after I became president, Decherd Turner, director of the Humanities Research Center, breathlessly informed me, Perry, Ed Sharpe, and Bill Livingston that there was a fabulous collection of rare books and manuscripts available—the type of collection that could be obtained "only once in a lifetime." It was late on a Friday afternoon and the setting sun contributed to the mystique of the meeting. Turner told us that the Pforzheimer Library was "truly the finest collection of Elizabethan literature available anywhere in the world," and that the books were so rare and so unusual that he would "crawl to New York City to simply have an opportunity to see them."

The Pforzheimer Collection, as Turner patiently explained to me, was amassed by Carl Pforzheimer Sr. and his son and was owned by the Carl and Lily Pforzheimer Foundation of New York. The collection contained 1,100 volumes printed in Europe between 1475 and 1700. Yes, all this could be ours, Turner announced. And the cost? A mere $15 million. Turner assured me this was a bargain. I asked Livingston to be the point person on doing the "due diligence" to make sure Turner had not gotten ahead of himself. An independent appraisal by an expert at Christie's in New York placed the market value of the collection at $16.4 million.

The university had been interested in acquiring the Pforzheimer Library for many years. UT's Gutenberg Bible had been part of the Pforzheimer Library, and it had been purchased from the Pforzheimer Foundation in 1978. Harry Ransom maintained cordial relations with the Pforzheimer family throughout the years that he was building the rare book collections of the university. After Ransom retired, Chancellor Charles LeMaistre continued the contact with the Pforzheimer family, and in 1974 he and Ransom made a new series of inquiries about the possibility of acquiring the books in the Pforzheimer Library. I became excited about the possibility of completing a transaction that Ransom and LeMaistre had tried to bring to fruition years ago. Still, the question remained: Where was I going to get $15 million?

Turner informed me that he had been talking with Ross Perot about a way the university could acquire the collection. The plan involved a purchase of the collection by Perot, who would agree to house the books at UT Austin, and then the university would have time to raise the money to pay him back. I immediately realized that raising money to pay Perot $15 million for "used books" would be a very difficult assignment. However, it was the kind of project that would receive a lot of attention in the liberal arts, and I was assured by Livingston and Turner that it was worth pursuing. If I could pull off this fund-raising challenge, it would be more than a symbolic statement and would positively impact the life of liberal arts on the campus forever.

After the regents gave the go-ahead to pursue the acquisition, Perry and I asked Hayden Head, the former chairman of the UT Austin Development Board, to become the volunteer leader of our fund-raising campaign. Head was a well-known Corpus Christi attorney, and his experience and contacts throughout Texas made him very well qualified to take on the assignment. To our delight, he agreed to help, and Perry, Head, and I went to visit Perot in Dallas on November 7, 1985.

On January 21, 1986, we announced the agreement with Perot and the plans to reimburse him. Perot attended a press conference in Austin that day to announce the acquisition, and Governor Mark White, House Speaker Gib Lewis, and Lieutenant Governor Bill Hobby as well as other dignitaries also attended, most of them probably drawn more by the desire to interact with Perot as by their love of fifteenth-century books.[2]

Perot talked about how pleased he was to be a conduit to help the books come to the University of Texas. He made it clear that the books were on loan to the university. Nevertheless, many people saw the pictures and read the headlines and thought Perot had given the university the books and that all was hunky dory.

When Head, Perry, and I had initially visited with Perot, he told me he would help us raise the money to pay for the collection. I didn't

Pforzheimer Library press conference, January 21, 1986. From left, just beyond the lectern, Decherd Turner, William H. Cunningham, Jess Hay, H. Ross Perot, Governor Mark White, Lieutenant Governor Bill Hobby, and Speaker Gib Lewis. *UT Office of Public Affairs Records, e_utopa_00034.*

see how this would work. Was Perot, one of the nation's wealthiest individuals, going to ask people to give him money so he could give books to the University of Texas at Austin? I did not think so. Despite my misgivings, we glossed over the issue and moved ahead.

Perry, Head, and I met with Perot a few weeks later in his office. The purpose of the meeting was to begin to discuss strategy as to how we would raise the money to pay for the Pforzheimer Collection—to pay back Perot. The meeting took a very different turn after a few pleasantries when Perot said he could not help us raise the money. This did not surprise me. I could see it coming, and I was very sympathetic with him. I never felt Perot reneged. But he did change his mind, and he was not going to help, so now we were on our own. Perot had been caught up in the enthusiasm of the moment and said he would help us raise the money, but I'm sure he later came to the same conclusion I did and said there was no way he could help us. He would have had a huge conflict of interest calling his friends and asking them to contribute to a fund to pay him back for books that he had helped the university obtain. I said, "Ross, I understand," and I did. I said it was my responsibility to raise the money and that I did appreciate everything he had done for the university. In addition, I had Head and Perry on my team, and I was confident that we could accomplish our objective.

We immediately began a fund-raising effort to focus on individuals who had the capacity and the interest to make major gifts for this purpose. That is a fairly small crowd. My first thought was that the only people I know who had more money than Perot were the Basses. I called Perry Bass and he very generously agreed to arrange a meeting with himself, Nancy Lee, and Val Wilkie from the Sid Richardson Foundation. We made a presentation to them and very shortly thereafter the Basses agreed to donate $5.5 million from the Sid Richardson Foundation to support the purchase of the Pforzheimer Collection. This was one of the numerous times that Perry and Nancy Lee Bass bailed me out when the university faced a major problem.

We also had success with the Amon Carter Foundation of Fort Worth, which contributed $1 million. Turner, Perry, and I took the UT plane to Fort Worth to make a presentation to Bob Crow, executive director of the foundation, on May 27, 1986, and we took along $3 million worth of some of the most interesting books for our "show and tell." The books filled two hard-sided Samsonite suitcases. The weather was stormy, and the flight was very rough. At one point Decherd expressed a fear that if we crashed these rare and priceless books would be lost to civilization. While I tried to show concern for the books, I was much more interested in my own survival.

When we arrived at the airport, we didn't have security, police, or private vehicles. Hayden flew himself to Fort Worth in his private plane. We met him at Meacham Field and had a brief strategy conference, and then we took a taxi. That is the way we did things in those days. We never considered hiring a limousine or asking one of the UT institutions in the Dallas–Fort Worth area to provide transportation around Fort Worth. It was simply not our style. So I put $3 million worth of rare books in the back of a yellow cab and went to the foundation, where we had a very successful meeting. Then, on the way out of Fort Worth, we stopped for lunch at the Cattleman's Restaurant in the old stockyards section of town. I told the taxi to wait for us, but I did take the books inside just in case the taxi drove away. I didn't know how I would explain to the regents that I had lost $3 million worth of rare books in a yellow cab while I was eating brisket and sausage.

After those two major foundation gifts, the funding prospects dropped off considerably, although we eventually approached just about every large foundation in Texas. Margaret McDermott and the McDermott Foundation of Dallas contributed a very generous $500,000, and we received $5,000 from C. W. W. (Tex) Cook of Austin. The prospects for any more major progress were exceedingly slim, and we were still well short of the $15 million goal. Fortunately, the board of regents, under the leadership of Jess Hay, agreed to let me use some of the proceeds from the Available University Fund to pay for the Pforzheimer Collection. With these funds we finally cobbled together the $15 million to reimburse Perot.

I called Perot and told him that we had raised the money. He said we lived up to our end of the bargain. He did not charge any interest and could not have been more of a gentleman. In hindsight, we should have rushed up to Dallas to present him a check as well as a pitch about how he should invest this money at UT Austin for excellence in liberal arts, the HRC, or whatever sector of the university he was interested in. If we had done that, we might have been successful in getting Perot to give us the money back.

However, another group, from the UT Health Science Center at San Antonio and led by Glenn Biggs, visited Perot, and our efforts paid off for them. They met Perot and talked about the importance of the rapidly growing Health Science Center and asked him to make a major contribution to support research in the name of his old friend, Hayden Head. Perot told them he would be pleased to do that because UT Austin had just given him $15 million. In that moment, the money we had raised and the money we had contributed from the Available University Fund came back to the Health Science Center in San Antonio.

Another of our more interesting efforts also involved the College of Liberal Arts and our football program. In my first year as president I learned that the usual procedure for out-of-town football games was for the opposing school's president to invite the president of UT to sit with him at the game. However, when the SMU game came up in the fall of 1985, I was not invited to sit in the SMU president's box. I do not know whether this was an oversight on the part of the SMU President's Office or if it was an intentional snub. It may be that President L. Donald Shields felt his board of trustees would feel it was inappropriate for him to be seen socializing with "the enemy."

A few days before the game I was visiting my personal physician, SMU alum Dr. Kent Beasley, and he asked me about the SMU game. I told him I had not received an invitation to sit with the SMU president. Beasley was furious over the apparent snub, and he called SMU. The next day a call came from the President's Office inviting me to the game. They offered me a box, although it was on the ten-yard line some distance away from the SMU president's box on the fifty-yard line. I called Beasley and invited him and his wife, Mary Adele, to accompany me, Isabella, John, Shirley Bird, and Sam Perry to the game. At halftime, Jere Thompson stopped in and asked me to accompany him to the president's box to meet Bob Dedman and a number of other distinguished people from the Dallas business community. My first conversation with Dedman was delightful and truly enlightening. He told me that he had three degrees from UT Austin—an undergraduate degree in liberal arts, a master's degree, and a law degree—and that he loved UT Austin. He also told me that while he had made a number of high-profile gifts to SMU, he also wanted to make a major gift to UT Austin.

Perry and I began to strategize about a gift from Dedman before we left the game. We understood that Dedman had both the capacity and the interest to make a major gift. We also realized that Dedman would probably want to focus on liberal arts.

Ed Sharpe, Perry, and I met with Dean Bob King, and we designed a proposal to support undergraduate liberal arts majors. We decided to ask Dedman to donate $10 million to create and fund the Dedman Scholars Program. This would be the largest gift ever given to the UT College of Liberal Arts. I called Lowell Lebermann, a longtime supporter of the college, and asked him to go to Dallas with me to help make the pitch to Dedman. Lebermann, Perry, and I met with Dedman in his Dallas office in November 1985 and outlined our request for him to fund the $10 million excellence program. He was very excited about it and agreed to fund it. So, because of Beasley, Thompson, and UT football, the College of Liberal Arts ended up with a new $10 million endowment that has benefitted many students.

Like the relationship with the Pforzheimer family, UT's relationship with James Michener went back to Chancellor Harry Ransom. This

From left, Robert King, Robert and Nancy Dedman, William H. Cunningham, and Jess Hay at the Dedman gift press conference, May 1, 1986. *UT Office of Public Affairs Records, e_utopa_00036.*

story, once again, illustrates that university fund-raisers must focus on long-term relationships. James and Mari Michener were great friends of UT Austin, dating to 1968, and their gift of twentieth-century paintings to the university was a direct result of Michener's fruitful relationship with Ransom. The Micheners' relationship with the university intensified after Bill Clements, who was serving his first term as governor, extended an invitation to Michener in 1982 to come to Austin to write a novel (published in 1985 as *Texas*) commemorating the 150th anniversary of Texas's statehood in 1986.

The university helped introduce Michener to important Texans as he and his team did their research. We also provided him with office space and made him feel very much a part of the university community, designating him as the Jack Taylor Professor Emeritus. He was the only person in the university's history whose first appointment was as professor emeritus.

In February 1986, the Micheners pledged $1 million to UT to help create a graduate program for aspiring writers. We were very excited about the gift, which included $100,000 for the UT Press endowment for fellowships and book publishing in support of a new graduate writing program and $900,000 that was to be used for student fellowships and faculty endowments.

The Micheners came to our house on many occasions when I was president. We would have dinners for regents, donors, and friends of the university. Everyone was thrilled to have an opportunity to have dinner with Jim and Mari Michener, who were both very stimulating conversationalists and great fun to be around.

Livingston and I frequently had lunch with Jim and his assistant, John Kings. This was one of the great pleasures of being president of UT Austin—being able on a regular basis to interact with some of the most interesting people in the world. At lunch at the Tarry House, a private club in West Austin, on March 15, 1991, Michener told us he wanted to make a major contribution to our writing center. He said that if we did nothing else but continue on the path we were on, he would give the university $3 million. If, on the other hand, the university made substantial progress beyond the current trajectory he would donate $5 million, and if the university made really substantial progress he would contribute as much as $10 million in new endowment funds. I told Michener that we would do an excellent job that would merit his commitment of $10 million. He said that was great but that he wanted to wait and see how things progressed before making a final decision. Once again, I asked Livingston to closely monitor the evolution of the writing center. I did not want us to lose sight of this very significant gift.

On Friday, July 17, 1992, Michener called me from his summer home in Brunswick, Maine, and said we had indeed made excellent progress with the writing center and he wanted to give the university $10 million to support the center. He asked me when I could come to Maine and sign the papers. I told him I was confident that I could be in their home before the day was out but if I could come on Sunday, July 19, it would be much easier for me. He said that would be just fine.

Livingston and I flew to Maine on Sunday and we were met at the airport by the Micheners. I could tell at once that something was wrong. Jim Michener's head was down and he was clearly unhappy. When we got to their house he said, "I have bad news. I don't have the $10 million." I told Michener at once not to worry about it, let's just enjoy the day. Then he said, "Bill, I have $10 million in U.S. government bonds, but they don't mature for another thirty days." I said, "Jim, don't worry about it, we are happy to take U.S. govern-

Mari and James Michener with William and Isabella Cunningham, May 19, 1992. *UT Office of Public Affairs Records, e_utopa_00037.*

ment bonds. It is not a problem." I explained that we would hold the bonds until they matured. Michener was greatly relieved. We had a wonderful dinner and a very pleasant evening.

The next day Livingston and I headed back to Texas, and I asked university officials to contact Michener's investment adviser in New York, who had been instructed to give us the bonds. At first the adviser wanted to wait the thirty days and send us the cash, but I wanted to make sure we got control of the bonds as soon as possible, just in case something happened to the Micheners before the time was up, or they changed their mind about the gift. I didn't think either alternative was likely, but you never know. We had to put a lot of pressure on the adviser to get the bonds transferred immediately. He didn't like going through the hassle, but we insisted. The bonds came to the university, and within a month we were able to transfer the money to the endowment benefiting the writing center. In November 1997, a few weeks after Michener died, the regents renamed the center the James A. Michener Center for Writers.

The story of the faithful support from Jim and Mari Michener for the UT Austin art museum also deserves mention. They were among several people who had been urging me for some time to do something about the university's art museum, which occupied cramped and entirely inadequate quarters, split between the Art Building and the Humanities Research Center. A new museum building had been a dream of the university for years, but the long-standing obstacle—money—had not changed. The Micheners felt strongly that we needed a new museum to house the university's art collection, as well as to help attract additional acquisitions.

When Mari died in September 1994, I was among those visiting with Michener in their home after the memorial service, and he asked me to come into the bedroom and speak with him privately. He told me he wanted to give $5 million in Mari's name to support a museum. I told him the university would be very honored to accept the gift and that we would work toward building a museum. I was chancellor at the time, and the details of the gift and of planning a new museum would, of course, have to go through the UT Austin administration, but there was never any doubt that the university was still committed to its long-standing dream. We knew such a project would require much more than $5 million, but Michener's decision to honor Mari with this gift represented the first major step toward realizing this dream. Michener did not ask that the museum be named after Mari, and he certainly did not ask that it be named after him.

I received a call from Laura Lee Blanton in June 1996 telling me that she was very confident that if I would visit with Joe Nelson, president of the Houston Endowment, he would help me draft a proposal to the foundation that would result in a major gift to the university to support the construction of a new art museum. Her husband, Jack Blanton, former chairman of the UT Board of Regents, was chairman of the Houston Endowment at the time. I informed President Robert Berdahl about Laura Lee's suggestion, and we both agreed that because of my personal connection with the Blantons, I should go by myself to make the initial "ask."

I went to Houston on June 19 and again on July 2, 1996, to meet with Nelson and Harold Metts, a director of the Houston Endowment. Jack Blanton was not in attendance. The ask was short, and the response even quicker. They made it clear that the foundation would make a gift of $12 million to the university for the new art museum if it was named after Blanton.

On December 20, 1996, the regents named the museum after Blanton in recognition of his many contributions to UT Austin and the Houston Endowment's contribution of $12 million. The building that houses the exhibition space of the Blanton Museum of Art was appropriately named the Mari and James A. Michener Gallery Building, and the museum's other building, which houses offices, classrooms, a café, and a gift shop, was named for another great friend of mine and a UT benefactor, Edgar A. Smith.

As chancellor I worked with Berdahl and others to raise the additional funds we would need for a first-class museum, and others carried the process forward after I left the Chancellor's Office in 2000. When my dear friend Bernard Rapoport came to me and asked where he should give an additional $5 million that he wanted to donate to the university, I recommended he give it to the museum. The magnificent atrium near the entrance to the Michener Gallery Building was named for Bernard and Audre Rapoport.

The most interesting development trip I ever took involved the Queen Mother and Fleur Cowles, who were two of the most interesting women I ever met, and Tom Staley, who may be the best fundraiser I have ever known. Cowles made her first mark on the publishing world in the late 1940s as associate editor of *Look* magazine. In 1950 she became the first publisher of *Flair* magazine, which rapidly became known as the most innovative and creative magazine of its time. Cowles was also a gifted artist and writer, a pilot, and a close friend of luminaries such as Marilyn Monroe, President Eisenhower, and Queen Elizabeth II. Cowles represented Eisenhower at the coronation of the queen in 1953. When I met Fleur she was married to Tom Montague Meyer, her fourth husband, a highly successful timber executive.

Staley, who had succeeded Decherd Turner as director of the HRC in 1988, knew of Cowles's interest in magazines, books, and literature, and he was able to get her excited about the HRC and his plans for continuing to strengthen its position as one of the great humanities centers in the world. Staley invited Livingston, Sharpe, me, and our wives to attend an HRC Advisory Council meeting in London and to accompany him and his wife, Muffy, to London to call on

Cowles. The visit began with a beautiful lunch at Cowles's home in Albany in London on November 10, 1992. Needless to say, her home was decorated in exquisite taste. Everything was perfect. And on top of everything, Cowles had invited her dear friend, the Queen Mother, to have lunch with us.

Cowles was kind enough to seat me at the head of the table, and the Queen Mother was seated to my immediate right. I felt very important, and I was very honored even to be attending the lunch. After lunch, I had the pleasure of joining the Queen Mother on a settee, and we had a very pleasant chat and a glass of sherry. She wanted to know more about my job. I told her that I spent a lot of my time raising money for the university from individuals and foundations. Her eyes widened in a mischievous way and she said, "Well, you're nothing but a beggar!" "Yes," I told her, thinking of the many beggars I had seen on London street corners, "but I wear nice suits." She chuckled at that, and I felt that I had made yet one more friend for the University of Texas.

The U.S. ambassador, Raymond G. H. Seitz, hosted a reception that evening honoring Cowles and the HRC at the Winfield House in Regents Park. We had a great time. All the members of the HRC Advisory Council recognized what a rare treat it was to go to London with Staley and his great staff. The following evening Isabella and I hosted a reception for Cowles and the advisory council at the Athenaeum Hotel in Piccadilly. Everyone had a marvelous time and our activities in London helped set the stage for several significant gifts from Cowles, as well as from other advisory council members.

Fleur and Tom Meyer entertained us again at their farm in Sussex in May 1996. It was a delightful setting, with beautiful streams, cows grazing in the meadows, and stately old homes scattered through the countryside. Isabella also went to Spain and stayed with Fleur and Tom on several occasions. When Tom and Fleur came to Austin to visit the HRC, they usually stayed with us at Bauer House, the official home of the chancellor of the University of Texas System. We hosted several dinners for Cowles at Bauer House and always included her dear friend, Lady Bird Johnson. It was a treat for Isabella and me just to be in the same room with Mrs. Johnson and Cowles as they told stories about events and people that we had just read about.

I will conclude by briefly mentioning a gift from a longtime faculty member at UT Austin, John McKetta. The university has been blessed

From left, Governor Ann Richards, Isabella Cunningham, Queen Elizabeth II, and Lady Bird Johnson. *Courtesy of William H. Cunningham.*

by the generosity of many of its faculty and staff over the years. However, the gift from McKetta makes it clear one more time that the university is made up of very caring people who think of their roles as not just holding down a job, but far more significantly as being members of an important perpetual community. In addition, the McKetta gift also demonstrates once again that the best thing a chief university fund-raiser can do is get out of the way and let nature take its course.

McKetta retired from the faculty in 1990 after fifty-four years. He had been chairman of the Department of Chemical Engineering, dean of the College of Engineering, and executive vice chancellor of the UT System. McKetta made a very dramatic announcement in 1995 that he wanted to return to UT Austin all the money that he had ever

John J. McKetta. UT *Office of Public Affairs Records, e_utopa_00040.*

been paid as a faculty member, and he challenged his former students to match his donation. The money would be used to create a chair in chemical engineering. After his donation and all of his students' matching gifts, more than $2.2 million was raised for the department. McKetta's unique gift attracted wide attention, and we held a big event at Bauer House on March 2, 1995, to thank him.

I have recounted just a few of the adventures that made raising money for the university so enjoyable for me. Fund-raising was one of the most important aspects of my job, and it was never a burden for me. In fact, I believe one of my greatest natural talents lies in asking people for money—as long as it's for such a worthy cause as the University of Texas. Asking people to join me in our shared quest for excellence came naturally to me.

Throughout my experience in raising money for the university—and in carrying out all the related work that attracts loyal supporters—I was extremely fortunate in having Shirley Bird Perry by my side every step of the way. I cannot adequately express how important she was to me as a trusted adviser, as a source of valuable and practical information, as a dedicated administrator, and simply as a friend. We worked side by side throughout the fifteen years that I served as president and chancellor, and except for those occasional vacations when she accompanied Sam Perry on his fly-fishing trips (she packed plenty of books to occupy her time), we conferred many times every day on ways to provide the essential financial support that would allow the university to maintain and enhance its status as a center for excellence in higher education. Whether as part of a patient and well-planned routine or in response to one of the numerous dramatic crises that landed on our plate, Shirley Bird was always there when I needed her—and that was just about all the time.

CHAPTER 14

Intercollegiate Athletics—Let
The Games Begin

I brought to the presidency of UT Austin a lifelong enthusiasm for sports, including college football. I attended every home football game at Michigan State from 1962 to 1970 and numerous away games, as well as one Rose Bowl game against UCLA in 1965. This enthusiasm served me well throughout my years as a university administrator, providing a basis for numerous relationships with alumni, politicians, and donors, and serving as a focus for the socializing that helped lay a foundation of support for the university. If I had not already been a great fan of UT athletics programs, I would have needed to acquire such an interest. As Peter Flawn advised, "If you don't like football, fake it."

I never had to fake it. Occasionally as president, however, I found myself needing to resist an overemphasis on college athletics displayed by some fans and boosters, including some in high places. As important as football and other sports can be for creating a sense of unity and reinforcing the positive image of a school, one must always guard against the tail wagging the dog. Despite persistent criticism from some quarters, there was never in my mind any question that our most important objective was to provide world-class educational opportunities to a wide variety of students, including student athletes. In addition, the university offers a number of service activities that include entertainment provided by intercollegiate athletics, and there was no question that athletics help the university bond with its internal and external constituents.

UT Austin is different from almost all other universities in that it aspires to play at the highest level in every sport in which it participates. Excellence on the playing fields has been no less important than excellence in the classroom and the laboratory. I know some

William H. Cunningham with Darrell Royal. *Courtesy of William H. Cunningham.*

people have always turned that around and said the university places too much emphasis on athletics, and that it even uses athletics as the standard by which to measure academic achievement. Frank Erwin's famous statement that the football team needs a university it can be proud of is funny, but it is wrong, and I am confident Erwin knew that when he said it. The simple truth is that the university wants to excel at everything it does. This is not a win-at-all-costs mentality; it is an attitude that says we expect to be able to compete fairly with the very best and at the highest level whether in the classroom, in the laboratory, or on the athletic field.

This ambition for excellence is expensive, and that means football revenues have to carry the athletics program. Except for men's basketball and baseball, the sports other than football are true nonrevenue sports, and they depend on football for their livelihood. It is also true, of course, that fielding a team in cross-country or tennis is relatively inexpensive, but even the least expensive sport has its costs. This is not an issue of women vs. men. The men's tennis team does not generate any more money than the women's tennis team.

My first interaction with UT athletics and Darrell Royal came soon after I arrived in Texas. I had great football seats as a graduate student at MSU, but when I received faculty seats for our first season at Texas (in the fall of 1971) I realized we had been demoted to the end zone. The next spring I decided to visit with Royal about this. I made an appointment, and when I arrived in his office he greeted me with a professional but warm "Dr. Cunningham, how can I help you?" I said, "Darrell, do you know where my seats are?" I explained to him that the few faculty who supported him and the football program were all sitting in the end zone. It did not take Royal long to figure out that this was a problem worth solving. The next fall, Royal moved all the faculty to seats between the thirty and fifty yard lines on the east side and moved the visiting team supporters who had been in those seats to the end zone.

At the same meeting, Royal asked me if I would be willing to do a marketing research study for the men's athletics program. I told him I would be pleased to do so, and he said that I would receive a call from Bill Ellington, who was the associate athletics director. Ellington was a true gentleman, and I was honored to work with him on the project. In hindsight, I am very embarrassed about my behavior toward Royal that first day. The whole conversation was backward, but Royal was very polite to me. I should never have been so disrespectful to Royal as to call him Darrell. We later became good friends, and I was finally successful in getting him to call me Bill.

I received a call from Royal soon after I completed my research. He was going to meet with President Rogers in the afternoon, and he was interested to know if I had any data about the fans' preferences for day or night games. Rogers wanted to play all the games during the day, but Royal felt that because of the typically warm weather in September the season should begin with night games and then transition to day games. The data on fans' preferences supported Royal's position, and this was the first time that any of my work made its way to the President's Office. Rogers accepted my research, and we continued to have our early-season games played at night.

I had an occasion to support Royal soon after I was elected to the Faculty Senate in 1973. Barry Switzer, head football coach at the University of Oklahoma, had been accused by a number of people of violating NCAA rules.[1] Royal challenged Switzer to dueling lie-detector tests. Royal said he would go first and Switzer could ask him any questions he wanted to. Switzer demurred. For some reason this dispute was considered worthy of debate in the Faculty Senate, where

I became an instant supporter of Royal. I didn't have much information about the athletics program in those early years, and my decision to side with the legendary Coach Royal was mostly a knee-jerk reaction to support our coach, but my instincts turned out to be correct.

It was at about this time that I met Lan Hewlett, whom Royal had hired as the first academic adviser in college athletics in the country. His job was to monitor the athletes' academic progress, organize and monitor the athletics tutorial program, and work with faculty members to ensure that our student athletes were given a reasonable chance of academic success. Neither Hewlett nor anyone else in the athletics program ever asked me to do anything improper—never asked me to change a grade or give a student any other kind of break—but it was clear that under Royal's leadership the athletics program was serious about students' academic performance, and he wanted them to have as good a chance as possible to succeed in the classroom and to graduate. Royal cared a great deal about his student athletes, and he knew something that they did not: Most of them would not make a living playing professional sports. Royal wanted his students to graduate and become productive members of society. He also understood that if a student flunks out of UT, he will not be available to play football.

When I became president I knew there was a special relationship between the university and Royal, who at that time served as an assistant to the president. In that role, he had been called upon by President Flawn for advice on a variety of athletics matters, and continued to be available to represent the university in many different settings. No one associated with the university has ever been more popular with the public. Whenever I would ask him to speak to a group or participate in a golf tournament or other event on behalf of UT, he always said without hesitation, "You bet, I will go," and he always did a great job for UT.

Although Royal was "only" the football coach and athletics director, a good argument can be made that he had as positive an impact on UT as anyone in its history. At the same time, however, his very success on the football field, as well as the force of his personality and character both on and off the field, left something of a "curse" on the university for many years. Ever since his retirement, he has remained the model by which all UT coaches are measured, and at least until Mack Brown won a national championship in 2005, this comparison was always dramatically in Royal's favor. There is, no doubt, a certain unfairness in this way of evaluating a coach, but it also makes sense to measure one's own performance by the best.

For the president of UT Austin, football is often more important as a social occasion than an athletic contest. I realized this even as associate dean of the business school, when I was occasionally invited to the president's receptions held before every home game—always an important occasion for meeting alumni and others who had an interest in athletics and the university in general. I still remember the first time that Isabella and I were invited by Flawn to attend the presidents' pre-game football party, then held in the old art museum in the Art Building north of the stadium. This was a clear signal in my mind that the Cunninghams had become part of the power structure of UT Austin.

By the 1980s these parties were major social events—fully catered affairs with hundreds of invited guests. Often, the president's conversations at these events and the donations that would follow would have lasting importance for UT, long after that day's football score had been forgotten. There was always a rumor that one reason President Stephen Spurr was fired was that he served hot dogs at the president's pre-game reception. People didn't expect champagne and caviar, but they did want something a little fancier than boiled wieners. I doubt that the hot dogs themselves sealed Spurr's fate, but they might have been a symbol of the relatively low importance he placed on both the reception and the game that followed. A president facing difficulty over more substantive matters needs all the help he can get, and laying out a nice spread for the home folks, and then showing some real interest in the game that follows, can be a valuable investment. Isabella and I both enjoyed the games when I was president, and we both instinctively knew that we should be among the most enthusiastic fans in attendance. In addition, Isabella personally approved each of the catered menus, and the guests were served excellent food and plenty of it. Shirley Bird Perry did not have to explain the wiener story to Isabella and me more than once.

Out-of-town football games were also often important social occasions. The first out-of-town game that I attended as president was against Stanford in late September 1985, and the trip was an eye-opener for me in many ways. Fortunately, Perry took me under her wing and made sure I did not make a complete fool of myself. Her first revelation to me was that I needed to wear a coat and tie, not only to the pre-game receptions and parties, but also to the game itself. I am sure I had never worn a coat and tie to a football game, but before long I didn't feel comfortable in anything else.

That trip to California began in Los Angeles, where three events were scheduled the day before the game, which was to be played in Palo Alto on September 28. I was going to speak at a luncheon held by Mr. and Mrs. Jack Wrather, whose company owned the ocean liner *Queen Mary*, which was docked permanently in Long Beach, and Howard Hughes's airplane the *Spruce Goose*. The Wrathers were good friends of George and Ronya Kozmetsky, and their son, Christopher, attended the UT business school. The luncheon had been arranged while I was still dean. I was also scheduled to attend a Texas Exes reception and a dinner party that Judd Swearingen, an old friend of the university, was holding in Beverly Hills.

Soon after I took office, Joyce Moos received a call from Swearingen, who said he was very pleased that Bill Cunningham, who had been one of his favorite professors in the 1950s, had been made president. He went on to say that he would like to host a party for Bill to introduce him to his friends in Hollywood. It turned out that Swearingen was thinking about the Bill Cunningham who had been a distinguished UT professor of chemical engineering and had recently retired. When Swearingen learned about his mistake he said he would still like to host a party for me, thinking, I suppose, that one Bill Cunningham would be as good as another.

Perry and I almost didn't make the luncheon at the *Queen Mary*, since our commercial flight was delayed at Austin's Mueller Airport. It was then that I made the first use of some of the remarkable perks that the UT Austin president enjoys. My friend John Watson had previously offered me the use of his Lear jet, which he said would be available to me five to six hours a month free of charge. I called Watson from the airport and explained that Perry and I were trying to make a lunch meeting in Los Angeles in a few hours, and he immediately called his pilots and told them to meet us at the private terminal. Within an hour, the plane was fueled and ready to go, and off we went. I remember thinking as we flew to California that we were pretty big dogs.

The lunch was about half over when we arrived at the *Queen Mary*. Bob Witt, acting dean of the business school, was in attendance and had given a talk about the school, and I was asked to make a few comments on the university as a whole. This was my first UT update speech—a talk that I gave more than a thousand times over the next seven years. Afterward we had a private tour of the *Queen Mary* and the *Spruce Goose*, and from there we went to the Texas Exes' reception, which was in a large and very noisy restaurant and bar. This was the second time I gave the UT update speech. The audience was quite receptive and enthusiastic, but it was the opposite extreme from the palatial accommodations of the *Queen Mary*. We then went directly to Judd Swearingen's party, held at the Beverly Hills Country Club in one of the more elegant sections of Beverly Hills. Some of the most famous and powerful people in Los Angeles were in attendance. There was a ten-piece band and a wonderful dinner, and everyone received a silver Bevo as a party favor. After dinner the bandleader gave me the microphone, and I presented my UT update speech for the third time, and the audience, many of whom I am sure didn't have a lot of interest in UT, was very cordial. I am sure that when I spoke at all the events that day I must have seemed very young, inexperienced, and probably not very polished (all true), but people everywhere could not have been nicer.

We stayed at the party until well past 11:00 p.m. and then finally went to check in at our hotel. When we got to the lobby, there was disco music playing in another room, and Perry turned to me and asked if I wanted to go to the disco. I was exhausted, and I said, "You've got to be kidding, I'm going to bed." Several years later, she told me she had been relieved that I turned down a chance to go dancing because she was also very tired, but that was the first time she had ever worked for someone younger than she was, and she was determined to prove she had as much energy as I did.

The annual UT–OU weekend is also surrounded by social events that are mandatory for a UT president and his staff—events that transcend the mere Saturday football game, which was played at the Cotton Bowl during the State Fair of Texas. The events provide an opportunity for the university to bond with alumni and to interact with members of the Texas Legislature. The UT president's group always arrived in Dallas about noon on Friday and stayed at the Adolphus Hotel, a great downtown spot that provided good access to the weekend's events and was a wonderful place for meeting friends of the university. In those days, two of the key events on Friday were a large and lavish party sponsored by the Dallas Chamber of Commerce in honor of the two universities (a party that always attracted a lot of "power" alums from the two schools) and a UT-sponsored reception in honor of the Texas Speaker of the House. The Speaker and many other members of the legislature would attend, along with lots of other politicians, community people, and local civic and social hangers-on. It was always held in one of the downtown hotels and was basically a big, noisy bash complete with lots of smoke and alcohol. I never enjoyed the event, and I always made only a cameo appearance. My usual procedure was to stop by the event and then Isabella and I would go to a dinner with several important Dallas alums and friends such as Jere and Peggy Thompson and John and Barbara Stuart.

I took Sam Barshop to the Speaker's party in 1989 when he was a new member of the UT Board of Regents, and after one minute he asked me who was paying for all this. I looked at him and painfully said, "The UT System is paying for it." I did make it clear that UT Austin was not paying for it. "This is just ridiculous," he said with a grimace, and I had to agree because we were spending thousands of dollars to help liquor up a vast ballroom full of revelers—most of whom we didn't even know. He told me several weeks later that he discussed the matter with the rest of the board and a decision was made that we should stop sponsoring the Speaker's reception. Overall, I was pleased that Barshop had stepped up and killed that event. We were very fortunate that no reporters ever asked us how much money the UT System spent on this affair.

On Saturday mornings just before the UT–OU game we held a reception for members of the Dallas business, cultural, and political power structure—and this was an event that certainly justified the expense. It was sponsored by both UT Austin and the UT System, and the president and chancellor stood side-by-side in the receiving line. When I first became president, this party was held at the Adolphus, but Shirley Bird and Isabella decided that holding it at Fair Park would be a lot more convenient for everyone. This event was a wonderful opportunity for both the president and the chancellor to keep in touch with the people in Dallas who really made a difference in both local and statewide politics. I always found that nothing could take the place of such local relationships—another example of the truth of Tip O'Neill's adage, "All politics is local."

It was customary for the UT president to do a radio interview at halftime of the OU game. In 1986, at my second UT–OU game as president, Perry informed me about two-thirds of the way through the first half that we needed to start making our way up to the press box for a radio interview. That year the interview was conducted by Doug English, a former UT football player who had also had a very successful career in the NFL with the Detroit Lions. We were getting beaten pretty badly at halftime (the final score was 47–12), so I wasn't sure what to say about football. I asked Perry for advice, and she suggested I say, "We remain optimistic." I looked at her and said, "Shirley Bird, are you crazy? They are killing us." I suggested to English that we talk about our National Merit Scholars program. English was happy to do whatever I wanted, so I briefed the radio audience on how successful we had been in recruiting National Merit Scholars and also bragged about minority recruitment and retention and the quality of our faculty. I don't know if the audience was interested, but with English's help we did find something positive to talk about.

As I was leaving the game, Jess Hay motioned for me to come to his seat. Hay was the chairman of the board of regents and I was always happy to visit with him. UT had been involved that year in a major dispute with Governor Mark White, who had cut our budget as an emergency matter to help balance the state's budget. Hay said to me very sternly, "I know why UT lost." I had been receiving a great deal of pressure to fire Coach Fred Akers, and I thought this might be the last straw. I feared that Hay, who always stated that the board should stay out of athletics decisions, was now about to tell me that I should fire the coach. He looked at me in a very serious and deadpan manner and said, "The team lost because it was discouraged over the budget cuts." Hay and I had a great laugh.

From time to time there was pressure to move the game from the Cotton Bowl and play it in Austin and Norman in alternate years. I always resisted this pressure because of the great social and political value of playing the game in Dallas, but the Dallas venue meant little to OU officials at that time, and they were always of the opinion that playing in Norman every other year would be of more benefit to them. For UT, however, the political heat resulting from leaving Dallas would have been staggering. Whenever I was approached about the possibility of moving the game, my standard line was that UT would be going to Dallas, whether or not Oklahoma showed up. If necessary, I said, we would find someone else to play. This was not just a joke. For a while, we actually considered the possibility of lining up another non-conference opponent such as LSU to play in the Cotton Bowl every year if Oklahoma dropped out. This was, of course, when UT and OU were still in different conferences.

As I have indicated, women's athletics made great strides during these years. During my first year as president, the Lady Longhorns basketball team had a spectacular undefeated season—winning the national championship in the playoffs in Lexington, Kentucky. This was, of course, a great thrill for me and for Isabella, who had been chair of the Women's Intercollegiate Athletics Council when I became president. Isabella greatly enjoyed that assignment and had developed a very good relationship with both Donna Lopiano, the women's athletics director, and Jody Conradt, the coach of the basketball team.

When I became president I found myself in the unenviable position of having to fire my wife, since I felt that Isabella could not remain as chair of the women's athletics council while I was president. Isabella was not pleased about my decision, but on my second day in office I sent her a letter informing her that I looked forward to receiving a copy of her letter of resignation. She wrote back that she would resign but not for another ten days because she had a few matters to resolve first, and I decided that would be acceptable. I am not the stupidest man in America.

G. Charles Franklin, vice president for business affairs, explained the UT Austin budget to me in great detail during the days after my appointment as president. One of the issues he raised was how men's and women's intercollegiate athletics were funded. The bottom line was that men's athletics, thanks to football, was very profitable, while the entire women's program lost money, like most of the other men's sports. The two programs were trying to get along, but clearly there was some tension between them, as the men's program was subsidizing the women's program while it was seeking to expand its own program.

We always announced with great fanfare that intercollegiate athletics received no state funds. This was true, but the women's program was subsidized by the President's Office with nonstate unrestricted funds derived from gifts to the university. These funds were available for use in any academic or nonacademic purpose, but a decision was made in President Rogers' administration that if the university was going to be competitive at the highest level in women's sports, both the men's athletics program and the President's Office would have to

John Cunningham in the White House Rose Garden when President Reagan met with the National Champions Lady Longhorn basketball team in spring 1986. *Courtesy of William H. Cunningham.*

subsidize it. While this was never a secret, it was not well understood across the campus.

One of my priorities as president was to force the men's program to pay for all intercollegiate athletics including the women's program, thus freeing up money that the President's Office could use for academic purposes. I knew this would be a tough burden for the men's program, but I was also confident that it was possible under the leadership of Athletics Director DeLoss Dodds. As funding for men's athletics increased, the subsidies from the President's Office declined and were almost eliminated before I resigned as chancellor in 2000.[2] It was easy to support Dodds's various fund-raising initiatives since he was ethical, creative, and successful.

The trip to Kentucky for the national championship series in the spring of 1986 was delightful, mainly because of the outstanding performance of the Lady Longhorns. Isabella and I also had an opportunity to have lunch with Otis Singletary and his wife, Gloria. He had been a UT Austin faculty member and vice chancellor for academic affairs at the UT System before going on to become president of the University of Kentucky. Isabella and I were new at being a presidential couple, while Otis and Gloria were old hands at it. They couldn't have been nicer, and they took us, at my request, to visit the great racehorse Secretariat. The president of UT Austin has a beautiful office, but it did not even begin to compare to Secretariat's suite at Claiborne Farm in Paris, Kentucky.

Later that spring I went with the team when we were invited to meet with President Reagan at the White House. In addition to the traditional Rose Garden ceremony, I was told that the visit would include a brief meeting with Reagan in the Oval Office, and I arranged to take a signed copy of the special edition of James Michener's book, *Texas*, to present to Reagan. These elaborately produced books were selling for $5,000 each, and my office had paid that amount to the UT

William H. Cunningham with President Ronald Reagan and UT women's basketball coach Jody Conradt in spring 1986. *Courtesy of William H. Cunningham.*

Press out of gift funds so we could present the book to Reagan. Then we got word from the White House staff that only the head coaches of the men's and women's national championship teams would be invited to meet the president in the Oval Office. I called Senator Phil Gramm and told him I had planned to present Reagan with a $5,000 book signed by James Michener, but that I would not go to the White House if I was not invited into the Oval Office.

I felt that it sent a horrible signal about the importance of athletics if the coach was invited into the office, but the president of the university was left standing outdoors in the Rose Garden. I told Senator Gramm that the women's team and Coach Conradt would attend, but I would stay in Austin. He explained to someone on the White House staff, and the White House reversed its position. Reagan was as gracious as anyone could be, and he never let on that he had weightier matters to deal with. The meeting came the day after the United States had bombed Libya.[3]

A university athletics program, even one as well run as at the University of Texas, will encounter much more controversial issues than ceremonies in the Oval Office, and it is to some of those matters that I turn in the next chapter.

CHAPTER 15

Intercollegiate Athletics— Playing by the Rules

iring anyone is no fun, and most university presidents would rather not be in the position of having to dismiss someone who holds a very visible position and may have considerable support among the public. Nevertheless, every football, basketball, and baseball coach knows he or she is in the educational and entertainment businesses, and that being fired is one of the built-in risks of the job. I am confident that the dismissal of any UT coach never came as a complete surprise to the person being terminated. If anything, the university has tended to stay with a coach well past the time that the performance of the coach's teams made a dismissal seem likely. In addition, it was always easier to be more patient with the coaches in the less visible sports than with those in football, but the pressure to win is there, nonetheless.

UT Austin and most other major Division I schools talk about the importance of the "off-the-field" performance of their athletes as part of the equation of evaluating a coach. "Off-the-field" usually means graduation rates and grade point averages for the team. It can also include problems with the local police or other disciplinary issues. Compared with men, women are easy to manage. Female athletes are generally not focused on potential careers as professional athletes, and that may help explain why women's teams tend to have higher grade point averages.

I was fortunate never to have to dismiss a head coach because of violations of NCAA rules, and for that I am grateful to the fine men and women who have coached UT Austin's student athletes and to two people who helped set UT's high ethical standards with regard to athletics—Darrell Royal and DeLoss Dodds. Royal helped establish the tradition of honesty and integrity, and Dodds reinforced that tradition and carried it into the contemporary era.

One of the first issues I faced as president in 1985 was the question of whether to keep Fred Akers, Royal's successor as head coach. Akers had been the coach since 1977 and had recorded eight straight winning seasons, eight bowl appearances, and two Southwest Conference championships, but he remained unpopular with many fans. Part of the problem with some fans may have been that Akers came close in 1977 and 1983 to winning a national championship, but each time fell short because of an end-of-season bowl loss. Fielding an excellent team year after year can still be disappointing if the biggest prize of all remains tantalizingly out of reach.

A second part of the problem was that when Royal retired he had recommended that his longtime assistant coach, Mike Campbell, become head coach, but President Rogers selected Akers. This was a public rebuke of Royal since it was widely known that he had recommended Campbell. The result was that football fans were divided into two camps—those who supported Royal and those who supported Akers. Akers did not reach out to Royal. He probably felt that he was not hired by Royal and that his real boss was not the athletics director but the president of the university. Royal and Akers were both true gentlemen, at least with respect to me. Neither ever made derogatory comments about the other to me.

Among those who were most disappointed with Akers was Regent Bill Roden of Midland. Roden had been one of the five regents who supported me for president before the unanimous public vote of the board in August 1985, and he always wanted me to understand that his had been "the deciding vote." I never argued with him about that, although I knew that any of the five could make an equal claim.

Roden made it clear from the first day of my presidency that he thought I should fire Akers. As the 1985 season developed, I began to feel increasing pressure from Roden and a number of other fans to fire Akers, but I couldn't find any justification for changing coaches at that time. Akers was leading the team to its ninth straight winning season, although for the second straight year UT was unranked nationally. The 1985 season ended with a loss to Air Force in the Bluebonnet Bowl for an 8–4 record. It was the fourth straight bowl loss for UT and added fuel to the anti-Akers flames. Dodds and I talked several times that fall about the unhappiness of many UT supporters, but we

Coach David McWilliams with the Longhorn football team on the sideline, September 5, 1987. *UT Texas Student Publications Photograph Collection, e_uttsp_00008.*

still couldn't see firing a coach who had nine straight winning seasons and had won more games than any UT coach except Royal.

The 1986 season was a different story. The team finished 5–6 and missed postseason play for the first time since the mid-1970s. Dodds and I decided it would be in the best interests of the university to hire a new coach. I felt that we would never bring all the fans back together again if Akers remained head coach. The animosity between the Akers and Royal groups was simply too strong. I never saw any effort by either Royal or Akers to stimulate the conflict, but nevertheless it continued in a manner that I felt was not in UT's best interest. Akers ended his UT coaching career with an impressive record of 86–31–2—at that time more wins than any UT coach except Royal.

David McWilliams, who had been an assistant coach under both Royal and Akers and then had moved to Texas Tech as the head coach, was the only person whom Dodds and I seriously considered as Akers's successor. He had been at Texas Tech only one year, but I think it is fair to say that his heart had always remained with UT. He was a player on Royal's 1963 national championship team, and he was an assistant coach on Royal's 1970 national championship team. His return to UT was widely popular in Austin. Royal strongly supported Dodds's recommendation that UT should hire McWilliams. After Dodds talked with McWilliams I called Lauro Cavazos, the president of Texas Tech. He was not very pleased that we had made McWilliams an offer to return to Texas, and he told me so. The conversation ended rather abruptly.

In early 1987 it became apparent that UT Austin was going to be charged by the NCAA with providing football players with extra benefits as defined by NCAA rules, which could be a very serious allegation, along with a number of relatively minor rules violations that occurred from 1980 through 1986. Several newspaper stories from the previous year had alleged violations of the rules, and I began dealing with the issue by consulting with George Christian, a former press secretary to President Lyndon B. Johnson, and with Professor Charles Alan Wright of the law school. Wright was one of the nation's most prominent scholars of constitutional law, and he had been a member of the NCAA Committee on Infractions from 1973 to 1983 and served as its chairman from 1978 to 1983.

Christian and Wright were extraordinarily talented people with a wealth of experience and excellent judgment, and they were very helpful to a relatively young and still inexperienced president. Very quickly we decided to hire Knox Nunnally, an attorney with the firm of Vinson and Elkins and a former Longhorn football player, to conduct a joint investigation with the NCAA. I made it very clear to all UT Austin employees that they were expected to cooperate fully with the investigation. I had watched Watergate unfold, and no one had to explain to me that a cover-up is often worse than the initial crime. When the NCAA presented its formal charges in March 1987, the university had already established a cooperative and even collaborative role with the association. I believe the fact that we were never really in an adversarial role with the NCAA tended to moderate the association's decisions.

Most of the violations concerned loans of small sums of money to athletes ($670 to football players) and other small benefits, such as the loan of a car for brief periods. Other charges involved the improper sale of complimentary tickets, excessive spending on entertainment related to recruiting, and employment of a prospective recruit by a

UT alumnus. All the alleged violations occurred during Fred Akers's term as head football coach, and they involved, among others, McWilliams; Ken Dabbs, an assistant athletics director who had been recruiting coordinator for football; and various others, including ten "boosters," and a former equipment manager. Knox Nunnally did a thorough investigation.[1] He concluded that there was no "proof" that anyone from UT had knowingly violated any significant NCAA rules.

In late March, I discussed the investigation with the University Council and also met with Dodds and his assistant directors, as well as with McWilliams and his assistants. In these meetings, I announced seven steps to help ensure that rules violations would not occur again. The first was that in the future any employee who knowingly violated NCAA rules or was involved in a cover-up of NCAA violations would be terminated.[2]

I also announced these additional steps:

- I would meet annually with all employees (in groups) of the men's and women's programs to make my no-tolerance policy clear. I wanted everyone to understand perfectly how serious we were, so I often said to them, "Look at me when I say this. I am not winking at you. I mean this."
- UT's legal counsel would meet regularly with all coaches to discuss NCAA rules.
- The university would enforce a no-tolerance policy among the athletes, and UT lawyers would meet with each team at least once a year to explain the rules.
- I was supporting legislation introduced by state Senator John Montford to empower universities to sue an individual who knowingly broke an NCAA rule.
- The university would expand its communications with alumni regarding NCAA rules and their appropriate involvement in UT's programs.
- A special faculty committee led by Wright would study the athletics program and give me recommendations for further action.[3]

The university was indeed fortunate to be able to draw on the expertise of Wright during this matter. Early on, Wright sent me a copy of an article he had written on how a university ought to respond to charges of an NCAA violation, based on his experience in hearing more than 100 cases as a member of the Committee on Infractions.

This article was of immense value to me.[4] One of the main reasons the university emerged from the 1987 investigation in such good shape is that we were being advised by one of the nation's greatest experts on such matters.

We had to file an answer to the NCAA by April 13 and then about ten days later, accompanied by Dodds and Ron Brown, vice president for student affairs, I made a presentation to the NCAA. Our position was that we had done an open joint investigation with the NCAA and had found no evidence to support the serious allegations concerning financial incentives for student athletes to attend UT, but that we were guilty with respect to a few of the minor charges. For example, when McWilliams was an assistant coach he loaned his car to a student athlete to drive another injured student to class. McWilliams was completely transparent with both the university and the NCAA concerning the incident. I had no interest in firing our head football coach because he was trying to help a student get to class. I also felt confident that if this was all the NCAA had, then we would be in good shape.

I told the NCAA that it would be naive to think our joint investigation had uncovered every instance of a violation. However, I also stated that we believed steps already taken had corrected the great majority of problem areas. In the end, the Infractions Committee agreed with our position that the violations had been minor.

By hiring Nunnally and instructing all employees to cooperate with him and the NCAA, we were trying to signal to the NCAA that we wanted to know exactly what was going on so we could take swift and appropriate action. Everyone had read about the recent problems with the athletics program at SMU and how the problems were compounded by efforts to cover them up, which led to the "death penalty" for the SMU program. I had wanted to be in a position to tell the NCAA, when its Infractions Committee addressed the allegations, that we had already taken specific corrective measures.

One of the good things that came out of the NCAA investigation is that Dodds and I determined that we needed more bench strength in the compliance area. Dodds hired Butch Worley to lead this effort. Worley had a law degree from Texas Tech and had lettered in football and baseball at Austin College in Sherman. When he joined the UT athletics department in 1987, he had been assistant director for compliance at the NCAA, being the staff person who presented cases to the Committee on Infractions, so it's safe to say he knew as much about compliance with NCAA rules as anyone in the country. It quickly became apparent to all of us that Worley was too talented to remain pigeonholed in one position, and he steadily moved up in the organization and assumed more and more responsibilities. Most recently he has been deputy director of men's athletics.

McWilliams had a winning season and a Bluebonnet Bowl victory his first year, but two losing seasons followed. Things turned around in his fourth season, with a 10–2 record and a No. 10 ranking nationally, but the next year (1991) saw another record below .500. The football team's record under McWilliams stood at 31–26–0 for the five years he had been the head coach. McWilliams decided he wanted to resign as coach but would like to remain with the university, and I was pleased that he stayed because his considerable talents continued to be of great benefit to the athletics program. He became associate athletics director for development and led the "T" Association, an organization of former letter-winners.

We turned next to John Mackovic, who took over the football program as head coach in 1992. Mackovic came from the University of Illinois, where he had been the head coach and athletics director. He was the last head football coach hired during my presidency. During his five years at UT, he compiled a record of 41–28–2 and led UT to three bowl games. In 1997, when I was in the chancellor's office, Acting President Peter Flawn informed me that he and Dodds had decided to change coaches. I was, of course, very interested, but this was their decision, not mine.

The Mack Brown era began in 1998. I am one of many people who would like to be able to take credit for the wisdom of hiring Mack Brown, but the individuals who deserve the real credit are Tom Hicks, Dodds, Flawn, and Royal. Hicks, who was then on the board of regents, understood that it was critical that the university recruit a football coach who could win, but who would also be a fine representative for the university as a whole. As usual, Dodds displayed his mastery of succession management. He quickly identified each of the prospects that should be considered, and he was able to create a back-channel communication system that identified which of those coaches were interested in Texas. Royal and Flawn filled the role of true professionals who were only interested in doing what was best for the university in the long run.

I also wish I could say I had hired Dodds, but the fact is that Flawn did that in 1981. Very few universities have had a men's athletics director for that length of time (some, in fact, seem to go through athletics directors about as fast as football coaches), and the stability and continuity of leadership at UT has been a key element in the success of the entire sports program. Dodds has run a high quality, clean program that has been competitive at the highest level in most sports year in and year out.

As president, one of my responsibilities was to help deflect some of the pressure that members of the public placed on the athletics program. Pressure usually came from poorly informed alumni and boosters, from fans whose only interest is in winning football games. The pressure also came from a small group of Texas fanatics who would have never been satisfied with an athletics director who had not grown up in Texas, punched cows, roughnecked in the oilfields, gone to UT, and played football for Darrell Royal. Dodds came to UT from Kansas, and he was always more comfortable staying behind the scenes and letting his coaches have the spotlight. One result of this was that his key role in leading the whole program was often poorly understood by the public.

Dodds was also very protective of his coaches. As president, I made the final decisions when we changed football or basketball coaches, but I never contradicted Dodds's advice and counsel. When a change was in the offing, Dodds always had a list of five or six prospective coaches in his pocket. With each name, he could give me a concise but thorough analysis of the person's strengths and weaknesses, their recruiting and leadership skills, their assistant coaches, and other details. And he would have a strong opinion about which person on the list ought to be our first choice. He sometimes observed that a common danger in looking for a new coach was to concentrate too much on someone who had undeniable strengths in an area where the old coach had been weak, so he tried to present a very carefully balanced assessment, hoping to recruit a truly multidimensional coach who could do everything.

Dodds had an extraordinary network of contacts through which preliminary discussions could be arranged with a prospective coach, and more often than not the people on his list were interested in talking with him. He always handled these initial discussions on his own,

From left, Jack Taylor, William H. Cunningham, and his father, Earl Cunningham, serving as guest coaches at a Lady Longhorns basketball game, c. 1987. *Courtesy of William H. Cunningham.*

and if there was a second round, I would join in (but only for the football and basketball coaching positions).

Isabella and I had been regularly attending the women's basketball games ever since she was appointed chairman of the Women's Athletics Council in 1978. While I was president and chancellor we sat in the section on the floor next to the coach and the scorers' table, next to other loyal fans such as Governor Ann Richards. We had the best seats in the house, close enough to the action that we could hear what Jody Conradt was saying to the team. The basketball team and the entire women's program were very oriented toward marketing, and regularly invited special guests to dinner before the games and did everything possible to provide a close-up and highly entertaining experience. We also regularly joined other guests during visits to the locker room at halftime. This was a particularly interesting experience because we all got to hear Conradt talk with her players about what they were doing right or wrong. She frequently mentioned they needed to "box out" on defense. I would always nod in an approving manner at Conradt's comments, but it was also clear to me that my high school basketball skills were not sufficient to make me a student of the game.

At the end of Conradt's interaction with the students, she would inevitably ask any of the guests if they had any suggestions for the team. The only time I ever saw anyone respond was when James Michener offered several thoughtful and cogent comments about a specific defense strategy. I later learned that Michener had some special credentials in the field, having written with great insight about women's basketball in his book *Sports in America*.

Donna Lopiano resigned in 1992 after seventeen years as director of women's athletics to become chief executive officer of the national Women's Sports Foundation. I regretted her departure but was delighted that in her new job she would have a national leadership role in promoting sports for women. I talked to her before she left, and she thanked me for the support I had given her and for all the progress we had made in women's athletics over the years. We both agreed that UT Austin had the nation's premier program in women's intercollegiate athletics. Lopiano was always an aggressive and strong leader, and I like those kinds of people, so I always got along well with her. She had received a lot of support from my two immediate predecessors, Lorene Rogers and Peter Flawn, and I like to think that I helped to continue and expand their support for women's athletics.

When Lopiano announced her decision to leave, it was clear that we had only one real option for her successor and that was Conradt, who accepted the job and also continued as head basketball coach. I thought that at some point the university would need to combine the administration of men's and women's intercollegiate athletics and have only one athletics director. We had, however, made much of the fact that UT Austin was one of only three or four major universities that had separate men's and women's programs, and it would have been difficult to back away from that commitment. We did begin to coordinate a lot of the functions, such as ticket services and fund-raising, for the sake of collaboration and efficiency.

In April 1992, Ed Sharpe and I had lunch with Conradt and had a long discussion during which I told her I thought it would be best for the whole women's program if she would step down as athletics director and focus only on basketball. My pitch was that she could do whichever job she wanted, but in my heart, I really felt it would be much better for the university if she relinquished the director's position—because it seemed to me that being the head basketball coach was a more important assignment for her, could make better use of her talents, and could be of more value to the players and to the university.

She out-bluffed me and said she just didn't want to relinquish either job. In the end, and out of respect for her and everything she had accomplished for the university, I said, "Fine, if that's what you really want to do, that is fine with me, and I will support you." I had a lot of confidence in her and stood behind her. Conradt was recognized as one of the nation's premier women's basketball coaches, and she had all the talent necessary to be the director of athletics for both men's and women's sports at any major university. If UT had not had Dodds as men's athletics director, Conradt would have been an excellent candidate for leadership of both the men's and women's programs.

Conradt served as the women's athletics director for about nine years, and I believe the basketball program did suffer somewhat because her attention was divided between her administrative duties and her coaching responsibilities. Royal had found out how hard it is to be the athletics director while also serving as a head coach, and I think Conradt may have learned the same lesson—although she certainly gave both jobs everything she had.

A few months after Lopiano went to work for the Women's Sports Foundation, she joined a lawsuit against UT Austin, charging that in our women's athletics program we had not abided by the requirements of Title IX, the provisions of the federal education act barring discrimination on the basis of sex in education programs. I felt the university had been extremely supportive of both Lopiano and women's athletics, and I had thought she felt the same way. We had held a big party in her honor before she left UT, and she and I had a very emotional meeting in my office when she thanked me and the university for everything we had done for her and women's sports. Then to have her leave and sue the university a few months later surprised and upset me.

I did understand, however, that she was trying to uphold the duties of her new job—which was to represent the interests of women's athletics across the nation. I am not sure what she was thinking, because I have not spoken with her since the lawsuit was filed in 1992, but I have been told that she felt that UT had done more for women's athletics than any other school in the nation. So perhaps the strategy was that if you could take on UT in court and win, then, by definition, you would be defeating everybody. This was the first lawsuit of its kind in seeking an across-the-board expansion of women's athletics at a major university. Lopiano is tough, competitive, and smart, and the lawsuit may have been a good decision on her part in light of her new national position, but to me it was like one family member turning on another. I didn't like it then, and I still don't.

Regent Martha Smiley played an instrumental role in the negotiations that led to a settlement of the lawsuit. She had just recently joined the board of regents, and I didn't know a lot about her. However, it became clear to me that she was a very smart and resourceful lawyer who cared deeply about the university, women's intercollegiate athletics, and higher education, and that she was willing to bring all her substantial skills to bear in order to play a positive role in resolving the dispute over Title IX.

Under the settlement reached in 1993, the university agreed to a major expansion of support for women's athletics in financial support, scholarships, and facilities. A key element of the agreement was a decision by UT to speed up the previously planned start of intercollegiate competition in soccer and softball. Major new commitments were made to increasing the number of women's athletic scholarships. All of these provisions were strongly endorsed by President Robert Berdahl, my successor at UT Austin, as well as by me and the UT Board of Regents.[5]

Concerns over minority student enrollment after the *Hopwood* lawsuit (discussed in Chapter 9) resulted in 1997 in an unusual attempt in the Texas Legislature to micromanage an aspect of the university's athletics programs. The legislature that year passed the top 10 percent law in an effort to help protect and expand educational opportunities for minority students, but some minority legislators felt the university had simply not done enough to support minority students. One of those was state Representative Ron Wilson of Houston, who introduced a bill that year that would have restricted the way universities offered scholarships to athletes. In the end, the law as passed neither harmed the athletics programs at UT Austin or Texas A&M nor served to increase minority enrollment. Despite its ultimate ineffectualness, the proposed legislation deserves to be remembered as an example of legislative action that would do far more harm than good and would try to solve one problem by creating a host of others.

The first version of Wilson's bill called for a ban on state-funded scholarships or other financial assistance to student athletes at all Texas universities. This proposal fell flat with almost everyone else in the legislature, including most of Wilson's colleagues within the Texas Legislative Black Caucus. Wilson quickly amended the bill to say that an entering freshman who was receiving an athletics scholarship had to have a high school grade point average equal to or higher than the average GPA of all entering freshmen from the previous year, and in order to keep the scholarship each year, the student would have to maintain a GPA that was at least as high as the average for all under-graduates at the school. At first, this version was given little chance of passage, but it did begin to gain some traction, and we at the UT System began to watch it with interest.

Wilson used some harsh rhetoric in promoting his bill. "Obviously, *Hopwood* means that a lot of average and above-average minority students won't be admitted through the front door of the University of Texas or Texas A&M," he said. "If they don't want us through the front door, then they shouldn't be allowed to bring us through the back door" to play on the football team and other sports. Wilson went on to decry what he called the "plantation education system" in which minority students could still find opportunities as athletes providing "entertainment value," while schools saw a decline in the number of other minority students.[6]

Wilson's amended bill passed the House at the end of April with little opposition and no debate.[7] This surprised us at the UT System, but we were still keeping a low profile on the bill. I continued to be disappointed by the extreme rhetoric with which Wilson was attacking our athletics program. Wilson caricatured the university's actions in a way that was seriously misleading about the academic success of student athletes. In 1998, the overall six-year graduation rate among student athletes at UT Austin was 57 percent, compared to a campus-wide rate of 65 percent. The university's student athletes were working hard in the classroom. In the spring semester of 1996, 38 percent of them had GPAs of 3.0 or better, and 18 percent had perfect GPAs of 4.0. The cumulative GPA for our student athletes was 2.6, compared to a campus-wide average of 2.83 for undergraduates. The university was also pleased that in the fall of 1996, 140 student athletes made the Big 12 commissioner's honor roll (with GPAs of 3.0 or better), while thirty were named Phillips 66 Classroom Champions and nineteen were nominated for the national All-Academic Team. The university's commitment to the all-around development of student athletes was demonstrated by the fact that each year more than $1 million was budgeted from athletic revenues for an academic-support program that included nine full-time professional counselors and more than a hundred part-time mentors and tutors, as well as for a life-skills program that included career development, résumé writing, and job-search services.[8]

We found it fortunate that the Wilson bill began to meet considerable resistance in the Senate, where it was sponsored by state Senator Royce West of Dallas. Senator Teel Bivens expressed his opposition to the bill and his surprise that the House had voted for it. He vowed to keep the bill from coming to a vote in the Senate Education Committee, which did, however, hold hearings on it. Mike Millsap, vice chancellor for governmental relations, and I decided it was time to be more energetic in communicating with legislators about the bill and explaining how it would affect athletics programs at institutions in the UT System, particularly at UT Austin. When Bivens scheduled his committee hearing, we asked prominent coaches and others associated with athletics at UT Austin to come to present their views about the impact of the bill.

Rarely had we brought such an all-star lineup to a legislative committee hearing: Darrell Royal, DeLoss Dodds, Jody Conradt, Tom Penders, and Curt Fludd, an assistant athletics director in charge of academic-support programs for athletes. I joined these distinguished staff members in testifying "on" the legislation, meaning that as university employees we were there to explain the proposed legislation, not to advocate for or against it.

Penders told the committee the bill "would be a disaster." "You might as well blow up the football field and the basketball courts and make parking lots out of them," he said. Royal predicted that the bill would cause athletes to leave the state, after which the coaches would leave, and "then we're out of the athletic business." Conradt said the bill would make it impossible to compete against other states in recruiting, and Dodds predicted that the bill would result in UT dropping out of the Big 12 Conference and out of Division I athletic competition. He predicted that athletics revenues of the football and basketball programs would fall from the then-current $20 million a year to about $4 million a year.

Also testifying against the bill as a private citizen was Alfred Jackson, a former UT Austin athlete who played eight years in the NFL and went on to a successful career in investment management in Houston. Echoing many of his comments at the hearing, Jackson later wrote a very insightful op-ed article for the *Dallas Morning News* in which he pointed out that Wilson's bill was not a useful way to respond to the justifiable concerns about the *Hopwood* case. "There is absolutely no sense in trying to deal with the ill effects of *Hopwood* by punishing student athletes, who include minority athletes. There is no logical connection between the two," Jackson wrote.[9]

Our position was that Wilson's bill presented us with either the option of using the lowest high school achievements of student athletes as campus-wide admission criteria, an option that might have doubled the size of UT Austin, or the option of abandoning the intercollegiate athletics program at UT Austin and Texas A&M and most, if not all, of the other Division I universities in the state. The bill would have had the unintended effect of requiring student athletes to have higher GPA qualifications than many of their fellow students who were not athletes (since all athletes would have to be at or above the campus-wide average).

After considerable parliamentary maneuvering, Senator Bill Ratliff helped craft a compromise for the bill in a conference committee. Instead of saying universities could award scholarships to student athletes only on the basis of their grade point averages in relation to the GPA of other students, the bill now said that *if* a university used the GPA as an admission requirement, it could award scholarships only on that basis. As we read the final language in Ratliff's compromise we concluded that UT Austin would no longer be affected by the bill because the university did not use the GPA as a factor in admissions. Instead, for years the university had used a combination of factors such as class rank in high school, scores on standardized tests, essays, a record of community service, and other life experiences. Nothing in the bill required a university to start using the GPA, and it was safe to say UT Austin was not going to start now.

Ratliff persuaded his colleagues to accept this new language. At first we were not happy with the deal that Ratliff had worked out because we believed there would be great potential for court battles over the interpretation of the law and the legislature's intent, but Ratliff told me this was the best deal he could strike and advised us to go along. I agreed to accept his compromised language. The Ratliff compromise was accepted by the committee on May 29.

There was considerable discussion on the floor of the Senate on May 31 and in the House on June 1 as legislators on different sides of the bill sought to clarify its legislative intent. In the Senate, Judith Zaffirini and Tom Haywood were among those asking questions to clarify that the bill did not require any university to use the GPA as an admission standard. In the House, Tom Uher, Harold Dutton, and Dan Kubiak engaged in a number of carefully rehearsed exchanges to make that same clarification. Uher and Kubiak at one point pursued a series of clarifications that left no wiggle room for anyone seeking to apply the bill to UT Austin or any other university that did not use the GPA as an admission standard.[10]

Governor George Bush signed the bill on June 20, calling it a symbolic measure. I thought he should not have signed the bill, but it was probably the politically expedient thing to do. Bush must have known that the bill did not make any sense, nor would it have any impact on state public policy. Nothing more was heard about the bill as a relevant part of Texas higher education.

The proper role of athletics on a university campus will be endlessly debated, and as in many debates, some of the loudest and most persistent voices in this one are also some of the least informed. On one side, a university president or chancellor must cope with rabid sports fans who demand a win-at-any-cost approach and even sometimes seem to think that the institution's main purpose is to put a winning football team on the field. On the other side are critics of the entire athletics enterprise who fear that it detracts from the institution's academic mission, draining resources away from academics and corrupting the core values of the university. There is nothing a university leader can do to stop this debate, and there is even very little he can say that will satisfy either side.

I found, as president and chancellor, that the only useful approach was to persevere in the university's commitment to excellence in athletics, defined primarily as being honest and competitive, while keeping athletics in perspective as secondary to the university's educational mission. The rabid fans don't want anything to be secondary to their favorite sport, and many critics on the other side don't want to hear the truth about how intercollegiate athletics at UT is not only self-sustaining financially, but the support of student athletes is also consistent with the mission of excellence for the university as a whole. I strongly believe it remains possible for a university to engage in intercollegiate athletics without losing its bearings, and I believe UT has pursued that course with considerable success.

CHAPTER 16

The Demise of the Southwest Conference and the Birth of the Big 12

Anumber of powerful forces came together to cause the dissolution of the Southwest Conference. When James Pickering, president of the University of Houston, said in February 1994 that he was "shocked" that the University of Houston was not invited to join the new conference, it illustrates how bright people can at times just miss major forces that will inevitably cause changes in the institutions they govern.

The true beginning of the end of the SWC started in the early 1980s when Rice, TCU, and the University of Houston failed to attract large numbers of people to their home football games. Rice often had the lowest average attendance, dipping as low as 15,000 in the mid-1980s. Houston's average was often not much better and even sank as low as 13,436 in 1986, while TCU sometimes averaged around 25,000. At Baylor and SMU, the per-game average was often well above 30,000, while Texas A&M and UT Austin consistently averaged well in excess of 50,000, soaring in some years above 60,000 at A&M and above 70,000 at UT.

The second force that led to the destruction of the SWC was the NCAA's decision in 1987 to give the "death penalty" to SMU after its investigation found that SMU's athletics program was "built on a legacy of wrongdoing, deceit, and rules violations." SMU had demonstrated an ability to be competitive at the highest level in football and attract reasonable-sized home crowds to its games. Without a strong SMU, the three other strongest schools—Arkansas, Texas, and Texas A&M—could not carry the conference.

The third force was the widespread dissatisfaction with the College Football Association's TV contract. In 1990, this led to Notre Dame splitting off from the CFA and Penn State abandoning its independent status to become the eleventh member of the Big Ten. In August of the same year, Arkansas announced it was terminating its relationship with the SWC and joining the Southeastern Conference (SEC). The move to create a super conference was alive and well.

On June 30, 1989, I traveled to Washington to participate in a meeting at the French Embassy with several other university presidents to complete an exchange agreement with a French university. My office received a call from Chuck Knapp, president of the University of Georgia, asking if I could meet with him at the law office of Kilpatrick and Kody before our meeting at the embassy. Knapp and I had been assistant professors together at UT and I told his office that I would be happy to visit with him. When I got there we were taken to a private room and we spent twenty minutes reminiscing about our careers as assistant professors, and then I asked Knapp what this was all about. He said the SEC wanted UT Austin, and he wanted to know if I would be willing to consider it. I told him we were honored to be asked to consider such a move, but that I couldn't say one way or another whether we would be interested. I could only assure him that we would give it serious consideration.

When I got back to Austin I met with Shirley Bird Perry, Ed Sharpe, and DeLoss Dodds. The first decision we made was that any move out of the SWC would need to include Texas A&M. This didn't take long to decide, if for no other reason than that the political realities in Texas would demand that A&M be taken care of and be happy about any change. That day I called A&M President Bill Mobley, a good friend, and brought him up to speed and told him that UT would not make any decision that was not consistent with what A&M wanted to do. I assured him it was important to me that moving out of the SWC be a joint decision between the two schools. Mobley appreciated that. He knew he could trust me, and I knew I could trust him.

Sharpe and Dodds were the point people for me in the summer of 1989 as we began to analyze the advantages and disadvantages of the SEC. We quickly decided that if we were serious about examining a move to the SEC, we needed to examine all the possible options before making a decision. Sharpe and Dodds weighed the possibilities of joining various major conferences. After several meetings, I concluded that the most logical option for UT would be to join either the PAC 10 Conference or the Big 10 Conference.

These conferences were attractive to me because most of their members were institutions very similar to UT Austin—large multi-faceted research universities with high academic standards and with strong intercollegiate athletics programs across a broad spectrum of sports. No one liked to acknowledge it publicly, but it seemed to many people, including me, that one of the reasons UT Austin had been having so much trouble winning in the SWC was that many of the other institutions had much weaker academic standards than we did. Along with their higher academic requirements, the schools in the Big 10 and the PAC 10 played high-quality football, and they had strong programs in a broad range of men's and women's sports programs. While there are many very fine schools in the SEC, they did not quite measure up to the academic standards of the Big 10 or the PAC 10, and these two conferences also played very good football. Very candidly, I thought Texas would have a better chance of competing on a level playing field with Big 10 or PAC 10 opponents and, as a result, I was never very interested in the SEC. Dodds began some preliminary contacts with PAC 10 officials, and before long conference officials, athletics directors, and some university presidents were engaged in rather serious discussions.

I had several conversations with Jim Duderstadt, president of the University of Michigan. He made it very clear that if the Big 10 was ever going to expand toward the west or south, he knew that Texas would be at the top of its list. However, he also said the Big 10 presidents were just beginning to talk about expansion and he felt it would be several years before the conference was ready to seriously consider the possibility of adding schools.

My continuing discussions with Mobley, however, revealed that Texas A&M had no interest in the PAC 10 and would prefer the SEC. I am not sure if the SEC was Mobley's personal preference or the consensus of his regents, but the result was that for a while we agreed to keep two sets of discussions going—UT with the PAC 10 and A&M with the SEC. Dodds and I briefed the UT System regents at a board meeting in August 1990 in Odessa, and they gave me an informal nod to proceed with the PAC 10. At that point the board had not discussed the matter in public or taken any votes, but I felt I had their tacit approval to conclude a deal. Mobley was satisfied with our moving west while A&M went east, and both conferences had accepted an arrangement for UT and A&M to continue playing each other on Thanksgiving Day. It would have been a deal breaker for

Mobley and me if the two conferences had not agreed to both schools playing their traditional Thanksgiving Day football game.

At the last minute, after word had leaked out about the negotiations, we began to get pressure from several elected officials, including House Speaker Gib Lewis. It was clear that their lives would be easier if we stayed in the Southwest Conference. I understood this and I was sympathetic to their problems. However, we knew this issue would develop when we began looking at other conferences, and we were determined to take the political heat and "do the right thing" for UT and Texas A&M.

The PAC 10 required that its members vote unanimously to accept a new member. I had been assured that this was not a problem and that all the presidents were excited about having UT Austin join the conference. However, at the last minute, Donald Kennedy, president of Stanford, decided he did not want UT to join, and as a result the PAC 10 commissioner, Thomas C. Hansen, called Dodds and withdrew the offer. Hansen was embarrassed that Kennedy had pulled the rug out from under him. He had also seen a great opportunity for the PAC 10 to expand and flourish blow up in his face.

I do not know for sure why Kennedy changed his mind about UT. My feeling, which was particularly supported by conversations I had with Dodds and several PAC 10 presidents, was that Stanford was afraid of having to compete against UT Austin. I have said UT was one of only a few universities in the country that had high academic standards and also wanted to play at the highest level in every sport that it competed in, and I believe Kennedy was simply afraid of that kind of competition.

I called each of the regents and explained what had happened. Then I called Mobley, who promptly shut down his discussions with the SEC. Next, I went over and met with Gib Lewis and Mike Millsap (Lewis's chief of staff at the time) and explained to them that we had decided to remain in the SWC and were committed to making it viable. That was certainly accurate, because we had no other conference to move to. Following in the tradition of most successful politicians when they don't get what they want, we declared victory. The next day, August 25, 1990, UT and Texas A&M put out press releases that said we had studied all the options and that staying in the Southwest Conference was the best choice for us. Lewis was very pleased. I don't know if he ever really knew how close we had come to leaving.

Two weeks later, Kennedy called me and said he had made a mistake and he wanted to support UT's entry into the PAC 10. I think he must have gotten a lot of heat from his colleagues, and now he said he wanted to make the motion inviting UT Austin to join the PAC 10 at the next meeting of the PAC 10 presidents. I was stunned. I told him I did not appreciate his timing. He had hung us out to dry two weeks earlier, and we had been forced to make a big public announcement about how we were going to remain committed to the SWC. I was curt and to the point with him. I tried to remain pleasant, but not *too* pleasant because I thought he had been extremely shortsighted. I was not about to go down that road again. That uncomfortable phone call was the final act of our PAC 10 romance, at least for 1990.

The SWC's future was clearly affected by the decision of Arkansas, announced on August 2, 1990, to move to the SEC. While Arkansas was not the key player in the SWC, its loss negatively impacted the conference, particularly in light of SMU's self-destruction.

In the fall of 1990, the president of the SWC asked the consulting firm McKinsey and Co. to do a strategic review of the future of the SWC. Their report, which was very well done, concluded that "the Southwest Conference is extremely vulnerable to dismemberment." I always felt that the SEC really did not want Arkansas. Its real target was Texas, and it hoped that by taking Arkansas it would create an environment that would force UT, and possibly Texas A&M, to move to the SEC.

Mobley and I continued to talk regularly about how our two universities should proceed. UT Austin and Texas A&M were great rivals on the field, but Mobley and I continued to recognize that our institutions were joined at the hip. One issue that bothered us was how the gate receipts were divided in the SWC. The conference divided the home gate income for each game equally between the two schools. For example, if UT played the University of Houston at Houston and the gate income was $100,000, each school received $50,000. The next year when Houston played at Texas, the revenue from ticket sales might be $250,000, and each school would receive $125,000. Mobley and I told the other presidents at a SWC meeting that we wanted to change the system so that each school would structure an arrangement with its SWC opponents to pay the same home-and-home income. Therefore, if we paid Houston $50,000 when they came to Austin, they would in turn pay us $50,000 when we played in

Houston, and then each school would keep the balance of its home-game gate revenue. When Mobley and I introduced our new plan at a meeting of the presidents, Ken Pye, president of SMU, said he supported the proposal. George Rupp, president of Rice, asked Pye how he could support this plan, and Pye said simply, "Because I can count to two." His point was that if Texas and Texas A&M wanted to change the rules, the rest of the conference better go along. The rules were changed, and as a result a great deal more money flowed to A&M and Texas.

After Robert Berdahl became president of UT Austin in 1993, I tried to remain mindful of the fact that it was not my place as chancellor to play a lead role in the decision about UT Austin changing conferences. I also recognized, however, that athletics was very important to the campus and to the people of Texas, and I did not trust Berdahl to make a decision about this on his own. I made it my business to make sure the Chancellor's Office and the board of regents were well briefed on any discussions. I was most concerned that UT Austin might stumble into an agreement that we would later regret and would have to withdraw from. As we began to analyze the possibilities, I think Berdahl and I worked reasonably well together. I focused on political activities associated with where we would go and how it would be done, and Berdahl spent a fair amount of time talking with presidents of other institutions in several conferences.

The PAC 10 question came up again in 1993. I told Berdahl and Washington State University President Samuel H. Smith, who had called me about a possible move, that the political realities in Texas dictated any decision UT made and would also have to be acceptable to both Texas A&M and Texas Tech. Texas Tech now had more leverage in such discussions because it had acquired considerable political muscle. State Representative Rob Junnel, chairman of the House Appropriations Committee, was a very strong Texas Tech alumnus and he never liked UT Austin. In addition, John Montford, who received both his BA and JD degrees from UT, and who had represented Lubbock in the Texas Senate since 1983, was chairman of the Senate Finance Committee. Lieutenant Governor Bob Bullock earned a bachelor's degree at Texas Tech, as well as a law degree at Baylor. A decision about athletics that did not make Texas Tech happy could have caused UT legislative problems that it certainly didn't need.

One option that we carefully considered was for A&M to join the

SEC, while UT and Texas Tech went to the PAC 10. Bob Lawless, president of Texas Tech, expressed a strong interest in doing that, and I told PAC 10 officials that I thought there was a very good chance that UT would come to the PAC 10 if they would also take Texas Tech. We had a lot of discussion back and forth, and I kept Lawless up to date on the talks. The problem was that the PAC 10 was not interested in Texas Tech. The PAC 10 looked at a large amount of academic data about Texas Tech and concluded that it would be one of the weakest schools academically in the conference. So once again the possibility of UT heading west fell through.

The catalyst to UT being forced to take some action with respect to the SWC came when other conferences and individual schools abandoned the CFA. By the mid-1990s it was clear to Dodds that we would be forced to take action if we wanted to generate a reasonable amount of TV revenue.

UT was not interested in the SEC, and the Big 10 or the PAC 10 were not viable alternatives. One possibility was to form a super conference by uniting the Southwest Conference and the Big 8, which was also in need of a stronger negotiating position for TV contracts. Most of the SWC schools would have favored such an arrangement, but the Big 8 wasn't interested, preferring instead a merger with only four other schools to form a twelve-school conference. The Big 8 was attractive to UT for several reasons. Although the schools were not as strong academically as those in the PAC 10, they were very good institutions, and most of them had strong athletic traditions. The geography of the merger also made a lot of sense, since most of the Big 8 schools, like those in the SWC, were in the central time zone. And by this time Texas A&M was also increasingly interested in looking at the Big 8. Mobley told me that most people at A&M had come to the conclusion that they really did not want to make a move that would leave UT out, just as earlier we had not wanted to leave *them* out. Once again, the leaders of UT and A&M found themselves each wanting to do the right thing by the other.

The main question soon became which of the SWC schools might be attractive to the Big 8. UT Austin, Texas A&M, and Texas Tech clearly made the cut. We could have formed an eleven-school conference, but the idea had developed for a conference with two equal-sized divisions, so we needed one more school to make an even dozen. The other members of the SWC were Baylor, Houston, Rice, SMU, and TCU. The two that were given the most serious consideration were TCU and Baylor. Houston would clearly not be up to the academic standards of other schools in the new conference, while Rice, one of the finest schools in the nation academically, did not measure up in athletics competition, and SMU was still suffering the effects of its football "death penalty."

It has often been said that Baylor was ultimately selected because of political pressure from Ann Richards or Bob Bullock, and that other politicians such as Pete Laney and Rob Junell made sure Texas Tech was included.[1] Despite the persistence of these myths, and despite the obvious strengths of Tech and Baylor in the legislature and among the state's political leadership, the truth is that I never received any significant political pressure over whom to take to the new conference. I realize that some people may not believe this, but it is true. It is accurate that Bullock wanted us to take Baylor, but he was not a strong supporter of athletics in general and it didn't really make a lot of difference to him. For all I know, he may have, for his own political purposes, let other people think he had been deeply involved in the makeup of what was to become the Big 12 conference. He was as light-handed with me on this matter as I had ever seen him, and when Bullock really cared about something and wanted something done a certain way, he was not light-handed. David Sibley, who represented Waco in the Texas Senate and who had played basketball at Baylor, talked to me a number of times about why he felt Baylor deserved to be in the new super conference. Senator Montford had made the same appeals to me about Texas Tech. However, both Sibley and Montford are class people and they never threatened UT in any way. They were good lobbyists for their institutions, and both of them had a strong track record of support for UT Austin and higher education as a whole in Texas. As I have already noted, we were certainly mindful of the potential difficulties for UT in the legislature if Texas Tech were harmed, but this political reality was never expressed to me in the crude terms that popular mythology has imagined.

A meeting that I attended in Bullock's office on the Sunday night of February 20, 1994, led to some of the talk about Bullock being the dealmaker on the Big 12. Mobley was also there, along with several of the A&M regents. Billy Clayton, the former House Speaker who had become an A&M regent, seemed to be leading the A&M delegation. Senators Sibley and Montford were also in attendance.

Former Texas Governor Preston Smith, former Speaker of the House Gib Lewis, Speaker Pete Laney, Senator John Montford, former Lieutenant Governor Bill Hobby, and former Governor Dolph Briscoe at Montford's governor for a day celebration, April 24, 1993. *Hobby (William P., Sr.) Papers, Dolph Briscoe Center for American History, the University of Texas at Austin, di_08756.*

At the outset I stated that UT felt the best option was for UT, A&M, Tech, and Baylor to join the Big 8. Bullock, Sibley, and Montford were very pleased about our decision. The A&M delegation met with Bullock, Sibley, and Montford by themselves in another room. I have been told that Bullock was more than direct and referred to the assembled Aggies as "a bunch of . . . tin soldiers." When they came out of the meeting, the A&M officials told me they were ready to go to the Big 8 and they concurred with UT's recommendation.

I believe the real reason Bullock called the meeting on that Sunday night was that he was concerned that the A&M regents still wanted to go to the SEC. Bullock may have been convinced by Sibley and Montford that this would not be in the state's best interest and, as a result, he may have felt a need to put some of his famous pressure on the A&M regents. Fortunately, UT was out of the line of fire.

After the meeting, Bullock was kind enough to let me use his office

Texas Lieutenant Governor Bob Bullock. *UT Office of Public Affairs Records, e_utopa_00048.*

phone to call Baylor President Herb Reynolds to tell him that Baylor had made the cut. Herb's wife, Joy, told me he was at a prayer meeting (it was, after all, a Sunday night) and I told him later that I now had a new confidence in the power of prayer since I assumed he had been praying that Baylor was going to join the new conference. Herb had a great sense of humor and he was an outstanding leader at Baylor.[2]

An objective look at all the data—from measures of academic quality to athletic attendance and performance at that time—had led us to conclude that Baylor was the best choice from among the remaining SWC schools. Our judgment was that the next best was TCU.

The Big 12 conference was a great success, and I think DeLoss Dodds deserves more credit than anyone for its success. He understood from the beginning why the SWC was no longer viable, why we had to move, and what the viable choices were. He was supportive of the different avenues we investigated, and time and again he facilitated the discussions among the various schools. He had the respect of every other athletics director in the country, and I think that however the final decision had come out—PAC 10, Big 12, or some other arrangement—he would have been able to make it work for the benefit of UT and all the other conference members.

It is also important to acknowledge the UT Board of Regents for its support over a fairly significant time frame. The two regents who deserve the most credit are Chairman Bernard Rapoport and Tom

Hicks. Rapoport understood the political realities of the time and he fully supported UT's efforts. Hicks is a master deal-maker whose great interest in sports is well known. Both of these individuals invested a lot of time and energy to make sure UT analyzed all its options and made the best choice.

The University of Houston may have been the school that was most unhappy with the new conference arrangement, and some people at that school continued to be unhappy because UT did not play them in football after the demise of the Southwest Conference. It is to UT's advantage to play football in Houston, where we have many fans and supporters, and UT's games with Rice in Houston have always been popular and well attended. In addition, our football coaches have always used the game to help recruit players. When I was chancellor, James Pickering, president of the University of Houston, tried to exert political pressure to force UT to play them in a "home-and-home" series. He told me that if we didn't agree, he would make sure we paid for it in the legislature. He specifically mentioned that Montford was prepared to penalize UT in the Senate Finance Committee if we did not play a regular home-and-home sequence with UH.

I called Montford, and he assured me he had not spoken with Pickering about this issue and he had no interest in participating in this fight. This did not surprise me, since Montford had always demonstrated that he was a man of great integrity who would not want to be involved in such political melodrama. I finally called Beth Robertson, the chairwoman of the UH Board of Regents, and told her I was unhappy with these attempts at political pressure, however clumsy they were. She was mortified and put an end to it immediately.

CHAPTER 17

Royal-Memorial Stadium

The 1990s renovation and expansion of Memorial Stadium, which was renamed to include Darrell Royal's name, was a source of considerable strain between Robert Berdahl and me. The tension over this project began very early. I visited Tom Hicks in his office in Austin soon after he joined the board of regents in January 1994, and I found DeLoss Dodds there with a set of rough architectural plans for renovation of the stadium. This was the first I had heard about renovation plans, but there was really no reason for me to know about the plans at that stage since it was a UT Austin venture and most campus departments are frequently dreaming of ways to enhance their facilities.

As the project moved forward, Dodds got caught between the actual needs of the athletics program and his loyalty to the UT president. Berdahl was skeptical about the need to expand the stadium. He probably felt the money could be better spent on other things, although, of course, the funds would not have been available for other purposes because financing of the stadium project was coming from private donations and revenues generated from the athletics program. I am confident Berdahl understood those realities of financing the athletics program, but he may have felt, nevertheless, that spending a large amount of money on athletics would not look good to the faculty or other individuals outside the university who cared primarily about the institution's academic mission.

After an extensive period of planning at the campus level, the regents were briefed by campus officials in an executive session, which was closed to the public, on February 8, 1996. Berdahl made it very clear that he was against renovating the stadium at that time. He turned to Dodds and asked a few questions about what he thought needed to happen, and Dodds dutifully supported Berdahl. Dodds understood who he worked for, and he was not interested in playing politics with the board. His stated position was that renovating and expanding the stadium would be wonderful, but that it was not a priority and that the athletics program would not be adversely affected if the stadium were left as it was. I pulled Dodds aside at the back of the room and told him that we were about to witness a train wreck and I did not want him to be the first casualty. I understood Dodds's need to support Berdahl, but I also knew there was no hope of saving Berdahl from being a casualty of his own presentation.

Hicks was very upset, although he controlled his emotions at the meeting and never let his temper show. He was unhappy with Dodds because they had worked together for a long time on developing conceptual plans for the renovated stadium. He knew what needed to be done to bring the stadium into the modern era, and he also knew that Dodds knew what needed to be done. Still, Dodds was not going to contradict Berdahl in front of the board and the UT System administration. I know it was a difficult time for Dodds, but he had the courage and loyalty to stand with Berdahl. Despite the lack of support from Berdahl, the regents were clearly intent on going ahead with the stadium project and making it one of their priorities. No one on the board or in the system administration disagreed with this decision, which was startling in that it directly challenged the stated view of the campus president.

Later, after he had resigned to accept the presidency of the University of California at Berkeley, Berdahl suggested that I had interfered in the operations of UT Austin. In response to a question from the news media about whether his relationship with me had been a reason for taking the Berkeley job, he said, "It's not always been easy for me to have my predecessor be my boss, and it's not always been easy for my predecessor to be my boss. Clearly, we have different styles, and sometimes styles become substance."[1] Later, as part of a broader reflection on his view of university governance issues, he elaborated on what he considered a pattern of interference in campus affairs: "Trustees should not be second-guessing coaches, systems should not be deciding campus priorities or running academic programs."[2]

It was not fair or accurate to say I interfered with the general operations of the university. I had been at UT Austin for my entire professional career, and I knew the university and its needs as well as anyone. However, I was also keenly aware of the natural tension

From left, DeLoss Dodds, Frank Denius, William H. Cunningham, Mack Rankin, and Jody Conradt at the stadium campaign kickoff. *Courtesy of William H. Cunningham.*

that existed between UT Austin and the UT System and between the president of the flagship campus and the chancellor. I had no interest in inflaming this tension by interfering with the day-to-day operations of UT Austin. In addition, I had a full-time job, which would not have given me enough time to play an active role on the main campus.

Berdahl did, however, have a point with respect to my involvement in plans for the stadium. It was clear to me that the project had to proceed if the university was going to be competitive in football, and that the regents wanted the project to move forward in a thoughtful and expeditious manner. My view is that a vacuum was created by Berdahl's actions and inactions, and the vacuum was filled by the UT System and the men's athletics department. I made my mind up at that meeting in February 1996 that I would invest a substantial amount

From left, Mike Myers, Isabella Cunningham, Sammye Myers, and Jess Hay at the Cunninghams' ranch. Myers is holding a picture of William H. Cunningham and Anna Cunningham, his mother. *Courtesy of William H. Cunningham.*

of my time and the UT System's resources to help plan the renovation of the stadium, raise the money to support the project, and pay close attention to all the details associated with the actual construction. I was determined that the project not fail because of any lack of enthusiasm from the President's Office.

The project was planned to take three years, beginning in 1996, and to be completed in a way that would not interfere with athletic events. It included, in various stages, removal of the artificial turf and replacement with a grass playing field, removal of the track oval and lowering of the playing field to accommodate new seating, installation of a Jumbotron video system, an overhaul of the scoreboards, construction of 66 suites on the west and east sides of the stadium, a new concession plaza and visitors' locker room, the addition of a 5,000-seat upper deck on the east side, and construction of a 13,000-square-foot private club room. The project also included construction of a practice field (now the Frank Denius Practice Fields) and a 20,000-seat track and soccer stadium (now the Mike A. Myers Stadium and Soccer Field), east of the football stadium. When all parts of the project were completed in 1999, the football stadium would officially seat 80,082 fans, the university would have spent more than $100 million, and it would have one of the most modern college football and track facilities in the United States.[3]

The renovation and expansion of the stadium faced a second hurdle from a state law that protected views of the state Capitol so that it could be seen from various "view corridors" around the city. The legislature had passed the law in 1983 to ensure that the Capitol could continue to be viewed from thirty designated corridors and would not be obscured by new buildings.[4]

After the regents had approved the plans for the multistage project in February 1996, it was discovered that the planned addition of an upper deck on the east side of the stadium would partially obstruct views of the Capitol from one of the protected corridors specified in the law, while later parts of the project would interfere slightly with another view corridor. The upper deck was scheduled to be completed by the start of the 1998 football season, but we could not proceed with construction before resolving the conflict.

Rather than change the plans for the stadium, we decided first to explore the possibilities for modifying the law to allow for the upper deck on the east side and for the other parts of the project that would conflict with the view corridors. Lady Bird Johnson was a very important part of the equation because one of the protected views that would be partly blocked by our project was from the plaza of the LBJ Presidential Library, on the northeastern corner of the UT Austin campus. I went to visit with Mrs. Johnson in the fall of 1996 and laid out our plans for her, pointing out that while the view of the Capitol from the plaza would be blocked, the view from the library's eighth floor would remain unobscured. I also told Mrs. Johnson that the view from the plaza had long been blocked by the stately live oak trees on the south side of the plaza. The trees, of course, had continued growing without regard for any state laws.

I asked Mrs. Johnson if she would be willing to support our need to change the law. She looked directly at me and said, "Bill, you know I will do whatever you want me to do." Then she followed up with a letter to me that said whatever the university felt it needed to do about the view corridors would be fine with her. As the legislative session progressed, Mrs. Johnson authorized Harry Middleton, director of the LBJ Library, to tell the news media that the stadium project

William H. Cunningham with Lady Bird Johnson, April 6, 1993. *UT Office of Public Affairs Records, e_utopa_00058.*

had her blessing and that she was "pleased to know that the stadium improvements will minimally affect the view of the Capitol from the Lyndon Baines Johnson Library."[5] I am confident that the legislature would not have approved any change in the law if she had objected. No one else in Texas commanded the respect that she did, and her endorsement of our plans certainly served to deflate whatever opposition there had been.

The other Capitol view that would be affected by the stadium expansion was from the intersection of East 38th and Red River streets, about ten blocks north of the stadium. I believe our case was aided by the fact that the Capitol was clearly visible only from the middle of that intersection, so that southbound motorists (or northbound drivers looking in their rearview mirrors) would be the only ones able to see the Capitol from there, and their view would be fleeting.

The City of Austin also had ordinances restricting construction in the view corridors, but such municipal laws did not apply to state projects such as the university's. We did, however, try to be good neighbors with the city and worked closely with city officials to explain our plans and discuss how they would affect the views of the Capitol, and Mayor Bruce Todd said he thought the intrusion into the views would be "minimal." "I think you have to have some flexibility. It's hard to move the stadium," Todd said.[6] Todd was an excellent mayor, and he always tried to cooperate with the university.

Mike Millsap and his staff in the UT System Office of Government Affairs worked on the language of possible legislation and came up with a simple one-page bill that exempted construction and renovation of the stadium from the provisions of the 1983 law. State Senator Ken Armbrister of Victoria agreed to introduce the bill, and state Representative Tom Uher of Bay City sponsored it in the House. Armbrister and Uher were members of the leadership and were both good friends of UT Austin and of higher education, so they were good choices as sponsors of the bill. There was a brief dust-up, however, over Armbrister sponsoring the bill when state Senator Gonzalo Barrientos of Austin learned about it. Barrientos told a newspaper he had no objection to the stadium plans but should have been advised about any legislation affecting his district. Armbrister said his office had talked to Barrientos's staff, and then he met with Barrientos to try to soothe his hurt feelings. The spat, which had no effect on the progress of the bill, was just one more example of the delicate dance that has to be performed in the legislature to keep everyone happy.

We had little chance of keeping another legislator—state Representative Glen Maxey of Austin—happy about the stadium bill. Maxey had never supported any legislation that UT felt was in its best interest. I really do not know why he was so anti-UT. It may have been nothing more than that he resented the "establishment" as represented in his mind by UT. In this case, Maxey focused his public criticism of UT on the idea that we were spending too much attention on football and the stadium view corridor and said UT ought to be focusing on academic issues in the legislature. We responded in the news media that we were, in fact, involved in dozens of other legislative issues related to academic programs, faculty salaries, tuition, admission rules, and other items, and we tried to keep the stadium bill in proper perspective as a small part of our overall efforts to represent the interests of higher education in our conversations with lawmakers. Maxey remained irritated by our bill.

"I think they could figure out a way to do whatever they want to do for the rich and gentried classes to go watch football on Saturday afternoon and make money for the athletic program without screwing up the aesthetics of this city and this Capitol building," Maxey said.[7] That description of UT football fans as "the rich and gentried classes" made it clear to me that Maxey had never seen the mass of our fans up close and that he was not likely to support our bill, no matter how much we explained it to him.

Once again when the heat was on, the university called on Darrell Royal for help. His name was still magic in the Capitol, and Millsap and I were confident he could help us. Royal and I attended a House committee hearing to speak on the bill on March 18, 1997, and answered questions from lawmakers. Speakers in favor of the bill included representatives of the Greater Austin Chamber of Commerce, the Austin Hotel/Motel Association, and the Greater Austin Sports Foundation. No one spoke against the bill. Maxey was nowhere to be seen.

In the end, the Senate approved the bill unanimously in February and the House passed it in March with only two members—Maxey and Debra Danburg of Houston—on record as opposed. Governor Bush promptly signed the bill, and the way was cleared for the stadium project to proceed.

Management of large construction projects at UT System component institutions is usually handled by the UT System's Office of Facilities Planning and Construction, in conjunction with campus architectural and construction offices. Therefore, it was not unusual or untoward that the UT System managed this complicated stadium project. The professional construction and planning officials on the campus understood this. What was unusual was that the campus president was not engaged in this very large project. Intercollegiate Athletics and Dodds, however, participated actively in every stage as the project developed. At this point, Dodds was a full partner in what was happening. The board of regents and its Building and Grounds Committee were briefed many times by the outside architects and by UT System personnel, as was Hicks individually, on the progress of the project. In addition, I reviewed carefully all aspects of the project weekly in my office. I knew that university presidents and chancellors had gotten into trouble over much smaller issues than football stadiums, and I was going to make sure this project turned out to be one of the finest facilities of its type in the country.

One of our first and most important decisions was to hire Heery International from Atlanta to plan the project and eventually design the renovation. While we interviewed several architectural and engineering firms, it was evident to everyone that Heery was the best, and they did a great job for UT.

The financial projections indicated that we needed to raise almost $25 million in donations to make the project viable, and the athletics department eventually launched a $30 million "Longhorn Legacy" campaign to fulfill these needs. The rest of the money would come from bond proceeds that would be paid off by revenue generated from the renovated football stadium. One of the largest drivers in this equation was the addition of football suites. They are incredibly profitable. It is fair to say that about a hundred suite holders are paying for a significant portion of the stadium's debt.

I was nervous about our ability to raise the $30 million. This was more money than the university ever raised in donations to support any construction project. While pondering how to achieve this goal, I came up with the idea of adding Darrell Royal's name to the stadium as a vehicle around which to raise money. I felt that many people would be more likely to contribute if it was in honor of Royal. I ran the idea by Bernard Rapoport, then chairman of the board of regents, and he immediately embraced it. He felt this would be an appropriate way to honor Royal, one of the most successful coaches in college football history, and it would make it much easier for the university to raise the money to renovate the stadium.

Berdahl and I met with Royal at his home at Barton Creek on January 30, 1996. When I arrived, Royal seemed unusually formal. While I had known him for many years, I had never before made an appointment to visit him in his home to discuss university business. After a few minutes, I told him that I wanted his permission to recommend to the board of regents that we rename the football stadium the "Darrell K Royal–Texas Memorial Stadium." I explained that the stadium should be named after him and that this would give us a hook for raising money for the renovation. Royal was stunned. He said all the politically correct things, but it was clear to me that he was very pleased. Later he told me he thought I was coming out to his house to fire him from his job as assistant to the president! This did explain why he was a bit formal when we arrived.

The stadium, which opened in 1924, was originally named in

memory of Texans who had served in World War I, and it had been rededicated in 1948 in honor of those who had died in World War II, and then rededicated again in 1977 in honor of American veterans of all wars. There was some feeling that by altering the name we were somehow detracting from the memory of veterans. We had not anticipated these complaints. Frank Denius, who had assisted the university on many other occasions, once again came to UT's rescue. Denius, a World War II veteran, is one of our nation's most highly decorated soldiers, having been wounded at Omaha Beach and again during the Battle of the Bulge, and then having continued to fight with his unit until the end of the war. Denius's opinion on how best to honor veterans could not be ignored. He understood the need to expand and modernize the athletics facilities, and he had a great deal of respect for Darrell Royal. Therefore, when we explained to him that the stadium would be named the Darrell K Royal–Texas Memorial Stadium, he agreed to be the external point person as we explained to the community why we wanted to add Royal's name to the stadium. Without Denius's help, we would have had a much harder time changing the name. Denius was instrumental in helping the university establish the Royal-Texas Memorial Stadium Veterans Committee, which is composed of alumni who have served in World War II, Korea, Vietnam, or the wars in Iraq and Afghanistan. This committee works to uphold the stadium's role in honoring the memory of UT students and alumni who died in war. The university also designates one home game each year as Veterans Recognition Day.

Including Royal's name in the stadium proved to be a very attractive approach to raising the donations we needed to help make the renovations a success. The board of regents had made it clear they expected a successful fund-raising campaign, and I took an active part in it to help ensure its success. The first person I called was Tex Moncrief. Moncrief had all the qualities to make him a logical donor. He was a longtime friend of Royal's, he loved UT, he had been an active supporter of athletics for many years, and he was very wealthy. Rapoport and I went to see Moncrief in Fort Worth on May 2, 1996, laid out the stadium plans, and asked if he would consider making a $5 million contribution. He said he would like to but that he had made so many commitments that his tax adviser told me him he couldn't make any more until the current ones were paid off. I told Moncrief, "That is not going to be a problem. If you tell me you're going to

Regent W. A. "Tex" Moncrief. *UT Office of Public Affairs Records, e_utopa_00042.*

do it, then that is all I need. You can give it to us in several years or whenever you want to." He said that on that basis he would commit to contributing $5 million.

About two years later, several members of the board of regents were beginning to get nervous about some of the outstanding pledges on the stadium. Pat Oxford, a regent from Houston, came up with the idea that we should discount the value of these pledges. He was able to convince his colleagues on the board to instruct me to call Moncrief and find out his level of commitment regarding his $5 million pledge. I certainly did not want to do that because I felt it was in bad taste and completely unnecessary, and that it might endanger the university's relationship with one of the most important families in Texas. Moncrief was one of the most generous supporters of the university and the son of the legendary Texas oil wildcatter Monty Moncrief, as well as a dear friend and mentor to me and one of my strongest supporters as chancellor. So there could be fewer activities as distasteful to me as asking Moncrief where his check was. However, I did what the regents told me to do, and I called Moncrief and asked him as gently as I could when he expected to complete his pledge. He said to me, "Are you dunning a Moncrief? No one has ever dunned a Moncrief." I replied at once, "I'm not dunning you, Tex." I am confident that he knew this call was not my idea, and he enjoyed teasing me. Within twenty-four hours, the university received most of the pledge, and the rest of it arrived in the next few days.

After Royal's name was added to the stadium, I was delighted that the regents accepted my recommendation in 1997 to rename the renovated athletic center at the south end of the stadium (containing offices, exercise rooms, and other facilities). This center, which had opened in 1986, had been named the Vernon F. "Doc" Neuhaus–Darrell K Royal Athletic Center, but was now renamed the W. A. "Tex" Moncrief, Jr.–V. F. "Doc" Neuhaus Athletic Center. Adding Moncrief's name to the center was a most fitting way of honoring one of the most significant donors to the stadium renovation project.

Joe and Lee Jamail are another example of individuals who were among the university's greatest advocates and financial supporters. They made many important and lasting contributions to UT Austin during the years I was president and chancellor—a record of generosity that has continued unbroken. Jamail had been a successful attorney since he received his law degree from UT Austin in 1953, but he hit an absolute home run in 1985 when he successfully represented Pennzoil in a lawsuit against Texaco. Jamail has made major gifts to the law school, athletics, and many other programs at UT Austin, as well as to many other higher education and cultural institutions. On two occasions I went to Houston for press conferences when Jamail and his wonderful wife, Lee, announced major gifts to a variety of institutions. UT Austin received a significant portion of the funds at these announcements, but the Jamails' donations also demonstrated their broader interests and their loyalty to Houston institutions. One of these was Rice University, where Lee served as a regent. The Jamails never had any strings attached to any of their gifts. They were all given simply from the heart.

I knew that the Jamails were very close to Intercollegiate Athletics and to Edith and Darrell Royal. As a result, they were an immediate target of mine for a major contribution to the renovation of the Royal-Memorial Stadium. On September 4, 1996, the UT plane flew to Waco to pick up Bernard Rapoport, chairman of the board of regents. In addition to Rapoport and me, Dodds, Royal, Jody Conradt, and Mark Yudof were on the plane. As we flew to Houston to attend a press conference that the Jamails had called to announce

Joe and Lee Jamail, April 14, 1992, UT *Office of Public Affairs Records, e_uto-pa_00039.*

$17 million in contributions to higher education, we all strategized about what roles we would play at the event. While I was designated by the Jamails to be master of ceremonies, each individual was given an opportunity to publicly thank the Jamails for their support of UT Austin and higher education. Rapoport stole the show with his enthusiasm and love for Joe and Lee. UT Austin received $5 million for support of athletics, the Plan II program, and the School of Nursing. We were also very pleased to announce that the board of regents was going to name the football field in honor of Joe.

The suites on the east side (the "sun" side of the stadium) did not sell as quickly as had the limited number on the west side. By the beginning of the 1998 season, we still had twenty-one suites that had not been leased, and judging by attendance at early home games that year many of those who had bought suites had not started attending. I remember visiting with Hicks in his west-side suite at the 1998 Rice game (in late September), and we both looked over at all the dark suites on the east side. It was not a pretty picture. Hicks told me to turn on the lights and, if necessary, to pay people to sit in the seats. I called Dodds the next day and asked him to make sure we had people in all the suites for the next game. Dodds understood the logic of the request. When we played Iowa State the next Saturday, the east-side

From left, Darrell Royal, Joe Jamail, and Willie Nelson with a T-shirt that was given to Joe Jamail at the time Joe and Lee Jamail made a major gift to the university in 1992. *UT Office of Public Affairs Records, e_utopa_00043.*

suites looked like they were the hottest place to be in Austin. Most of them were occupied by undergraduates from various student organizations who were invited up to the plush surroundings by Dodds's office, but it was a beautiful sight, nonetheless.

The renovation of the stadium, the renaming, and the fund-raising effort were all unqualified successes, and they combined to give UT Austin a state-of-the-art and nationally competitive facility. The UT Board of Regents, the UT System administration, and the many private donors who contributed to the project deserve credit for their important roles in this success. I believe, however, that the greatest credit goes to Tom Hicks and DeLoss Dodds. Hicks played his role beautifully as the catalytic regent who propelled UT Austin and the UT System to renovate the stadium, but never tried to micromanage the project. Dodds walked a tightrope between the UT Austin administration, UT System officials, and the regents. Only a true professional who was dedicated to excellence and was a gifted "politician" could have made this work. Dodds delivered.

CHAPTER 18

Economic Development and the Recruitment of Sematech

became president of UT Austin at a time when the fundamental relationship between a strong and expanding state economy and a strong state education system, from kindergarten through graduate school, had begun to be widely recognized in Texas. The relationship had certainly been understood for decades by a few, and especially by those familiar with the history of California since World War II. In Texas the idea that our colleges and universities could be powerful "drivers" of economic development did not really catch on until the 1980s.

As long as the Texas economy was booming, few people saw the need to look ahead and plan for the day when a new basis of wealth would be necessary. But by the mid-1980s there had been enough shocks to the petroleum-based economy—with reverberations deep into the state's tax revenues—that more and more people were seeing the need to lay the foundation for a new type of economy that a few visionary leaders, such as George Kozmetsky, had been talking about for years. This would be an economy in which knowledge and creativity, embodied in a highly educated population and advanced university research, would be the premier stimulants of economic growth—an economy based on human capital more than agriculture or minerals. It would also be an economy that embodied Kozmetsky's long-held idea of a close working relationship among business, government, and academia.

One of the university's first major steps to help the state diversify its economy was the successful effort in 1983 to attract to Austin the Microelectronics and Computer Technology Corporation (MCC), an industry-wide initiative in computer software research. President Peter Flawn was the quarterback of this effort. Flawn asked me, as dean of the business school, to help support the university's efforts to recruit MCC. I attended a number of meetings and made it clear that the college would do anything possible to support MCC. My primary job was to be enthusiastic. This was easy for me because I was smart enough to be enthusiastic with respect to all of Flawn's initiatives and because I "got it" quickly that Texas needed to diversify its economy. My enthusiasm translated into offering executive education programs to MCC officials, as well as making slots available to them in our executive MBA Program.

The importance of increasing state support for colleges and universities in order to develop the educated population and the great centers of research necessary for economic development emerged as a key theme of the budget debate in the 1985 legislative session. This theme would continue to play a role in many subsequent legislative sessions and throughout my years as president and chancellor. Almost everyone today accepts the premise that continued economic strength requires strong colleges and universities. Translating that principle into action, however, is another matter, and while much progress has been made, the record remains decidedly uneven.

One of the leading proponents of support for higher education as a basis for economic development was Lieutenant Governor Bill Hobby. In June 1986, with Texas facing the prospect of a special legislative session to deal with one in a long series of budget crises, I participated in a conference of the Texas Science and Technology Council in Dallas at which Hobby delivered a speech that presented a forceful summary of the economic realities facing Texas and the need for increased investment in higher education. The speech, a copy of which I circulated to deans and executive officers at UT Austin, was typical of the clarity with which Hobby understood the issues. He emphasized the importance of advanced university research through which "we will develop the ideas that will permit us to sustain the prosperity we have enjoyed in the past," and he outlined four steps that he saw as essential "to put Texas in the first rank of the states on which the economic future of this country will depend." Those steps were: continuing to recruit first-rate faculty members, developing additional nationally recognized research universities, expanding research into "new" areas such as biotechnology, and attracting a federally supported national laboratory.[1]

The Hobby plan was simple, practical, doable, and visionary. More

William H. Cunningham with Texas Lieutenant Governor Bill Hobby. *Courtesy of William H. Cunningham.*

than a quarter of a century later, Texas has still not achieved all of those goals, although we have certainly come a long way.

My focus on economic development went up dramatically when I received a telephone call from Governor Bill Clements in May 1987. It was easy to be a philosophical supporter of Hobby's plan at 40,000 feet. All I had to do was applaud loudly at the appropriate time and give a few speeches on the interaction between economic development and the funding of great universities. Clements transformed me instantly into a key player and UT point person in the state's effort to recruit Sematech, initially a consortium of fourteen semiconductor makers to promote research into semiconductor design and manufacturing. I knew I was going to be evaluated by the state's political and business leadership not on how I could articulate a philosophy, but on whether I could deliver, or at least help deliver, Sematech to Austin. The university and I were clearly operating on a much bigger stage.

The story of how Sematech came to Texas is instructive for at least three reasons: for the way diverse state interests came together to leverage their power on behalf of a common goal; as an example of the way science, technology, and business are interwoven in the contemporary economy; and as an illustration of how modern research universities are not only educational institutions but also political and economic forces.

Sematech sent letters seeking bids to the governors of all fifty states in May 1987. The state that succeeded in winning Sematech would be helping to secure its role as a major national and international player in the high-technology economy and could be expected to attract many more high-tech industries as a result of Sematech. The consortium was also expected to be a direct boost for the winning state's economy through its initial workforce of eight hundred and a projected budget of $250 million a year, half from its corporate members and half from federal, state, and local government.

Clements called me because he was concerned that Texas make the most competitive bid that it could, including incentives that would stand up against the proposals expected from powerful states such as California, North Carolina, and New York, and he recognized the central role that UT Austin would need to play. It was known that the leaders of Sematech wanted to locate in a university community with strong science and engineering programs, and the interaction that was envisioned between the consortium and university faculty and graduate students promised to be of enormous importance for both sides.

Other criteria set forth by Sematech made a formidable list that would test the resources of any state. These included a suitable existing building in which an appropriate "clean room" could be operational within six months of the bid award; at least thirty-five acres for eventual location of laboratories, manufacturing units with additional clean rooms, and offices; substantial state and local financial incentives; a pool of skilled workers; and a high quality of life in the community.

One of Clements's main concerns when he called me was that the state, being in the midst of what seemed to be perennial budget difficulties, might have trouble putting together a competitive financial package for Sematech. He asked that UT step forward with financing that would be adequate for buying the land that Sematech would need as well as for building or renovating the sophisticated facilities required for the consortium's research. I responded at once that while the university would be pleased to provide short-term financial help,

William H. Cunningham at Jere Thompson's home in Mexico, c. 1987. Once cell phones became available, I was never unavailable. *Courtesy of William H. Cunningham.*

we were not in a position to underwrite the project out of our permanent capital resources—that is, the university could contribute money to get the project started but would need eventually to be reimbursed.

Clements told me he would work with the legislature during the next session (in 1989) to make sure we got our money back. As the project developed, some at UT had doubts about whether we could really put together a competitive bid and raise all the money that would be necessary and then follow through on all the commitments. I remember Vice Provost Steve Monti expressing such doubts, and I told him not to worry about the financial commitment because Texas would never be selected anyway. As it turned out, Monti and I were both wrong. I did not see how, politically, the university could turn down a request from the governor to help the state diversify its economy. Therefore, rather than being seen as reluctant, I decided at once to become one of Sematech's biggest supporters. I have said on many occasions that it is better to drive the train than to be run over by the train.

That call from Clements was the beginning of what proved to be a long and fruitful collaboration between UT, the state and other government entities, and private industries involved in Sematech—a partnership similar to the one that had succeeded in bringing MCC to Austin in 1983. I looked on Sematech not only as a project of enormous educational importance to the university but also as an opportunity to obtain substantial assets for UT (land and a research facility) that would become part of the institution forever. If Sematech, at some point, went out of business or moved, those assets would revert back to UT. Long-term, it was a no-risk deal, although managing the immediate financing and other arrangements required quite a bit of ingenuity—what real estate investors would call "creative financing."

The Sematech bid involved an army of experts, volunteers, and advocates from all backgrounds, with a committee of some six hundred people organized and led by Pike Powers, an Austin lawyer, and Peter Mills, then vice president for economic development at the Austin Chamber of Commerce. The leadership of Powers and Mills was indispensable in making the bid a true community-wide effort, but I believe it is fair to say that UT Austin was the key player in almost every phase of drafting the bid and meeting with Sematech officials. Once again, I relied a great deal on Gerry Fonken and Steve Monti to help coordinate the university's overall efforts. The university also owes a special debt of gratitude to engineering professors Ben Streetman and Al Tasch, who clearly understood why Sematech would be a valuable asset to UT, and who were also widely recognized as experts in the semiconductor industry. With the Provost Office's knowledge of the university and Streetman's and Tasch's knowledge of semiconductors, I felt comfortable that we would put together a very competitive bid.

The university's role was nowhere more evident than in the task of securing a site and a building that would meet Sematech's requirements. There were two site possibilities—either on a vacant portion of the university's Balcones Research Center (since renamed the J. J. Pickle Research Campus) or acquiring a factory site in Southeast

Austin that had been vacated by Data General Corp., a minicomputer manufacturer that had fallen on hard times. The Balcones site would have had the advantage of being next door to MCC, but the Data General site was eventually seen as having just about every other advantage—including the fact that it already had a manufacturing building on the site. In the end, the acquisition of the site and its renovation were possible only because of the resources that UT Austin had access to through the Permanent University Fund, as well as because of the university's high credit rating.

After extensive discussions among the university, state officials, and Sematech officials, the UT Board of Regents approved an allocation of $12.3 million to acquire the Data General site, which would be leased to Sematech at $1 per year for the first ten years. That left the larger question of how to finance the renovations, including the all-important construction of a clean room, at an estimated cost of at least $35 million. A bill that would have allowed the issuance of special state bonds to finance the project failed during a special legislative session in 1987, so the people putting together Austin's bid had to turn elsewhere. Groups in Dallas and El Paso had also been working on bids, but Sematech had asked that Texas focus on the Austin proposal. The university was prepared to help secure this financing, but the other continuing commitments of the Permanent University Fund on behalf of capital projects across the UT System made it essential that expenses incurred in the financing arrangements would be reimbursed, as I had emphasized with Clements from the beginning.

The plan to achieve these objectives was worked out through an agreement between the university and Travis County, which had the authority under state law to create a county Research and Development Authority that could issue bonds. The county Commissioners Court, led by County Judge Bill Aleshire, promptly created the authority, and they named me its chairman, since the only real business before the new entity was to facilitate the financing of the renovations for Sematech. There was really no role for the county except to serve as a legal mechanism for issuing the bonds, if and when Sematech selected Austin as its home.[2]

Bonds issued by the county authority alone would have carried a prohibitively high interest rate because it and the county had no track record of issuing such bonds and no collateral. However, because we had Clements's pledge that the legislature would reimburse the university, UT was able to make the project affordable by using its triple-A credit rating to guarantee the county's bonds. That meant the bonds would be an excellent credit risk, and as a result they were sold with a very low interest rate.

These bonds proved to be of great importance in the overall bid since they represented not some vague promise of support but a definite financing mechanism that would ensure that the Sematech facilities were renovated by the target date. After Austin was selected as the site for the consortium in January 1988, action on the bonds proceeded quickly, and by mid-February the state Bond Review Board had approved the bond issue, which totaled $38 million. The UT System handled all the details for the county and completed the sale of the bonds in May.[3]

Until the announcement by Sematech that Austin had won the competition, the university's decisions to help finance the project were based only on oral promises by Clements that we would eventually be reimbursed for everything but the $12.3 million that had been spent on acquiring the Data General site. That included interest payments on the bonds, which UT agreed to pay out of the Permanent University Fund on an interim basis. The promises were formalized on January 8, 1988, in a letter that Jack Blanton, then chairman of the UT Board of Regents, sent to Clements, Hobby, and House Speaker Gib Lewis. The letter, which each of the state officials signed and returned to Blanton, made it clear that the "interim funds" made available by UT were to be reimbursed through the General Appropriations Act in the next session of the legislature but would not come out of any higher education appropriations and would not be taken into account when determining any of the appropriations for the UT System.[4] Our attorneys inserted all these carefully phrased stipulations based on long experience in dealing with state lawmakers.

When the legislature convened in 1989, we had to deal with getting our money back, but with this letter in hand we felt confident there would be no problems. I had not anticipated, however, that State Representative Rob Junell, a member of the House Appropriations Committee, might try to object to the deal that we had with the governor, the lieutenant governor, and the House Speaker. Junell told me early in the legislative session that if I wanted to be reimbursed for the Sematech expenses I needed to go see Clements, since he was the one who made the guarantee. Junell conveniently forgot that his "boss," Speaker Lewis, had also signed this letter. In the end, Clements, Hobby, and Lewis rolled over Junell and upheld their end of the bargain and made sure our agreement was reflected in the appropriations bill passed that year.

The university contributed to the bid for Sematech in a host of other ways, principally through the research opportunities afforded by the campus's College of Engineering and its research centers and institutes. These included the Microelectronics Research Center, the Materials Science and Engineering Program, and a program in Manufacturing Systems Engineering. The university emphasized to Sematech the numerous opportunities that such academic centers offered for professional interactions with the consortium's employees. Among other tangible benefits associated with UT, the bid included time for Sematech on the university's supercomputer, valued at $1.5 million over four years; use of conference facilities at no cost for four years; and collaborative research projects that could have a value of $5 million based on anticipated funding by the legislature.[5]

In November 1987, Sematech officials named twelve states as finalists for the project and gave them until December to submit additional information. Texas was among the finalists, and that meant the Austin bid. The others were Arizona, California, Colorado, Florida, Massachusetts, Missouri, New Mexico, New York, North Carolina, Oregon, and Wisconsin.[6]

There was intense speculation about the bids of the various finalists, but little reliable information. Austin officials had heard talk that Massachusetts had put together a package of incentives worth $260 million, but without the details it was impossible to evaluate the competition.[7] The Austin incentives had a value estimated by some at $62 million and later placed at $68 million, well below what other states had offered.[8] Of the total, more than $50 million was accounted for by UT's purchase of the site and its arrangements to finance the renovations.

Sematech's final decision was announced January 6, 1988, and the speculation began immediately in other parts of the country about how Austin could have been chosen when its bid did not appear to some people, at least on paper, to be as competitive.[9] One frequent explanation was that strong support for federal appropriations to Sematech by Jim Wright, the Fort Worth congressman who was then Speaker of the U.S. House of Representatives, and by Austin Congressman Jake Pickle had helped sway Sematech officials, since they were relying on continuing federal appropriations in future years. Also, Lloyd Bentsen, chairman of the Senate Finance Committee, was known to be a strong supporter of UT Austin. Others speculated that Austin's location between the two coasts might have been an advantage, on the theory that leaders of semiconductor companies in the Northeast and California would not want the consortium to be located in the other's backyard.[10]

Some of the speculation might have had an element of truth, but in the end I believe there were three deciding factors. First, the Austin incentives were in the form of guaranteed expenditures on behalf of the state, the university, and others, rather than loans, pledges to seek legislative appropriations, or other less-than-certain promises, as was the case with many other bids. Second, the Austin bid was probably one of the most thorough documents of its kind ever put together. Powers, Mills, Tasch, and Streetman had thought of everything and left no detail to chance. And third, I believe the academic and financial contributions of UT Austin and the UT System were simply overwhelmingly impressive to the scientists and engineers of Sematech.

One small example of how the last two factors came together: Officials at the Chamber of Commerce learned that one member of the site selection team was an avid swimmer, enjoying the exercise almost every day, wherever he might be. So the chamber arranged with UT for the Sematech official to swim in the Olympic-size pool at the Texas Swimming Center—and for UT's women's swim coach, Dick Quick, who was also an Olympics coach, to meet with him at poolside.[11] Multiply such attention to detail (both symbolic and substantive) a thousand-fold and consider how the diverse resources of UT Austin were mobilized on behalf of the project, and reasons for the success of the Sematech bid become easier to understand.

Before MCC and Sematech were brought to Austin, it was customary for Texas and many other states to look to California and the role of Stanford University in the development of Silicon Valley as the premier model for how universities can stimulate economic development and diversification. Reporters from Texas made regular treks to Palo Alto to write about how it was done. After the success of Austin in attracting Sematech, which came so closely on the heels of the success with MCC, reporters from other states started coming to Austin to study our new model. Articles from Florida to Missouri and beyond acknowledged the role of UT Austin in the Sematech bid, and officials in other states frequently faulted the relative weakness of their own higher education systems as factors in their losing bids.[12]

Less than a year after Austin was named the winner of the competition for Sematech, the consortium held an opening ceremony attended by more than a thousand officials from the semiconductor industry, the state, the city, and the university.[13] It was a day of celebration all around, and UT officials were among the happiest people in the audience. We had made a major contribution toward winning the project for Texas, we had delivered on everything that had been promised, and the consortium was opening on schedule. Even on such a day—perhaps especially on such a day—the speeches can run a little long, and several of us in attendance may not have looked as delighted as we really were. The work of an alert photographer for *The Daily Texan* caught me yawning during Chairman Jack Blanton's comments. The *Texan*, of course, ran a large copy of the picture on the front page the next day. Blanton called me and said that he had the photograph examined by his dentist and that I needed a little work on a back molar. I thanked him, but quickly added I was shocked and saddened by the paper's misinterpretation of the picture. I told Blanton that, in fact, I was not yawning, but I was doing the "Sematech yell" in support of his speech. Fortunately for me, he had a good laugh.

The success that UT had in helping recruit Sematech served to reinforce my natural inclination to encourage the university to become more actively involved in helping the state diversify its economy. I also recognized that my role as president of UT Austin put me in a unique position to articulate to the elected leadership of the state, as well as to the general citizens, the importance of linking the development of UT Austin with the state drive for economic development.

Throughout the late 1980s and 1990s, I often elaborated on the economic development theme by listing six fundamental ways that higher education institutions, and particularly major research universities like UT Austin, were intimately linked to the state's economic fortunes:

- By producing an educated workforce, allowing all parts of the state's population to contribute to the growth of the economy and the development of society.

Jack Blanton making remarks at the Sematech dedication ceremony. William H. Cunningham is in the background giving the "Sematech yell," November 15, 1988. Daily Texan *photo by Daniel Byram, copy courtesy of William H. Cunningham.*

- By fostering an intellectual and cultural climate that is attractive to industry.
- By attracting external financial resources, including federal research dollars, that generate spending and job creation.
- By conducting research that broadens society's intellectual, scientific, and technological horizons.
- By assisting in the transfer of new technology from the laboratory to the marketplace.
- By providing public service that assists industry with technical problems, provides medical care, helps strengthen the public schools, and benefits society in thousands of other ways.[14]

During the years that I was chancellor, my emphasis on the economic arguments for the support of higher education intensified, largely because of my expanded responsibilities in dealing with the Texas Legislature. It was essential to tell the story in detail as it applied to all the universities and health science centers in the UT System and, indeed, to all higher education institutions across the state. I wanted to make sure we did everything possible to drive home the messages with fully documented data, justifiable claims, and attention to the human impact of our institutions. We needed to communicate not only directly with members of the legislature and the state's political leadership, but also with the folks back home in communities across the state who could then, we hoped, communicate with their representatives in Austin.

To support these efforts I asked our staff at the UT System to work with the system's institutions to produce regular reports on the economic impact of higher education. I believe two of the most comprehensive of these reports, "The Economic Impact of the University of Texas System" (January 1995) and "The University of Texas System: Service to Texas in the New Century" (November 1998), remain as valuable records of how the work of the UT System was an essential foundation for the state's economic vitality and the progress of the state's people.

The 1995 report consisted of twenty pages of statistics and anecdotal information and was designed to communicate the essential findings of a study that I had asked UT Austin's Bureau of Business Research to conduct on the economic impact of the system and its institutions. Among those findings were the following:

- Every dollar spent at a Texas public university generates $2.929 in direct and indirect economic activity.
- Each job within higher education generates a total of 2.813 jobs throughout the Texas economy.
- Every dollar in personal income created by UT System expenditures and related student expenditures generates $2.310 in personal income throughout the state's economy.

The UT System's import of $835 million a year in federal research funds and spending by out-of-state students generated a total of $2.4 billion in business activity in Texas.[15]

Steve McDonald, a distinguished economist and former chairman of the UT Austin Department of Economics, directed the study for me. McDonald was a classic example of a highly respected scholar who was capable of doing excellent practical research that benefited the state. He was also a gentleman who was more than happy to donate his time to help.

There were always some faculty members and others who were troubled by the university's economic development activities and, in particular, its participation in the Sematech bid. They felt that UT was in danger under my leadership of abandoning its traditional roles of providing a broad, general education for undergraduate students and becoming too closely allied with business interests. Many of these same people had opposed UT's association with MCC, and they sometimes doubted that we had gotten our money's worth from these projects.

My response was that economic development fits within our service mission to the people of Texas, and that I felt very comfortable with the university playing this role, particularly in light of the fact that no one else was in a position to help the state in this way. With regard to MCC, it was true that the university ended up paying for about half the cost of the building because some donors who had pledged to support the project were caught in the downturn in real estate values and other economic problems in Texas in the mid- and late-1980s. However, donations still paid for about half the cost of the building (about $25 million overall), and the university still owns the building, which today is worth far more than its initial construction cost. On those grounds alone, MCC was a good deal for the university. With regard to Sematech, we got all our money back from the state and UT owns the Sematech facilities. Of course, neither of these initiatives was primarily a real estate transaction, and students and faculty have continued to reap enormous benefits through research collaborations, employment opportunities, and other interactions.[16]

I do believe that all the work that was done by so many people when I was president of UT Austin and chancellor of the UT System left an indelible mark on the economic development of Texas. Higher education was important not only for the educational opportunities it provided individual Texans, but also as a key driving force in helping the state diversify and expand its economy.

CHAPTER 19

Appointment as Chancellor

n January 1992 Hans Mark announced that he would retire from the chancellorship on September 1 and would serve full time on the engineering faculty at UT Austin. Mark had been chancellor since 1984 and had focused much of his attention on strengthening ties between the UT System and the federal government, increasing the amount of research funding across the system and enlarging the system to include campuses in the Lower Rio Grande Valley. He had very ably fulfilled the expansionist goals of the regents when they recruited him from Washington, where he had served as secretary of the Air Force and assistant administrator of NASA.

In 1992, the state was in the midst of a severe economic downturn that stemmed from a plunge in oil prices, and the most intense focus of the UT System was on preserving and, if possible, increasing, the level of state appropriations. As a result, the regents, in searching for a successor to Mark, placed a high priority on candidates who they thought would be able to work successfully with the legislature and the state's political leadership. Several regents later acknowledged in the news media that this was an important factor that led the board to focus on me as a potential candidate.

Within a week of Mark's announcement I received calls from four regents asking me if I would be willing to accept the position of chancellor if it was offered to me. My response was always the same. It was not meant to be political, evasive, or even modest. I told each caller that I felt I had a great job and that I still had a great deal of work to do. However, if the board wanted me to become chancellor, I would be pleased to do so. I said what I meant and I meant what I said. I talked with Shirley Bird Perry and Isabella. We all agreed the best thing for me and for the UT System was for me to let the process work. That meant making no attempts to generate any political sup-

From left, Isabella Cunningham, William H. Cunningham, G. Charles Franklin, John Howe, and Kern Wildenthal at the announcement of my selection as chancellor of the University of Texas System, April 9, 1992. UT *Texas Student Publications Photograph Collection, e_uttsp_00009.*

port. If the regents wanted me to become chancellor, great, and if not, that was fine too.

The board advertised for the position nationally in the *Chronicle of Higher Education,* and the names of thirty-eight nominees and applicants were received by the deadline of March 16, 1992. The next day, the regents met in executive session. The board made the decision to interview me and then compare my credentials with the résumés of other people that might be potential candidates. This was an unusual search process. It may have been as simple as they wanted the devil they knew rather than the devil they did not know.

I met with the board on March 17 for several hours. Once I left the room the board decided that I would be the lone finalist for the position. Louis Beecherl, chairman of the UT Board of Regents, came out of the closed meeting and told me he did not think I was necessarily the right person for the job. He indicated that he felt I was too willing to "compromise" with all the various UT constituents and that the job required a more decisive person. I said, "Louis, I understand and I love my job at UT Austin." He responded, "Well, that is fine, but the other eight people in the room just voted to make you chancellor. How much do you want to be paid?" I said, "I accept, and why don't you pay me what you were paying Hans?" He instantly agreed. Neither one of us knew at the time what Mark was making. Our "negotiations" had taken less than five minutes. Technically, the board could not "vote" on my appointment in that executive session, but there are ways for the regents to make their views known and still stay within the law without taking a vote. By law, my appointment could not be finalized for twenty-one days.[1]

Although I did not have Beecherl's initial support to be named chancellor at that meeting, I could not have had a better friend or a stronger supporter than he—both before and after I was named

Louis Beecherl, chairman of the Board of Regents. *UT Office of Public Affairs Records, e_utopa_00044.*

chancellor. Once the board's decision was clear, he acted in every way as if I had been his favorite candidate from the beginning, and he did everything possible to help me and UT succeed. He was not only one of the truly great regents I served with, he was an extraordinary chairman as well.

Soon after my conversation with Beecherl, the board came out of executive session and met in public to select me as the sole finalist for the position. The board asked me to meet with a group of faculty, as well as with student leaders from across the campuses. Both meetings went very well. They asked me candid questions, and I answered them directly. Both groups reported back to the regents that I was more than acceptable to them.

Some political "experts" had predicted a "clash" within the board because Governor Ann Richards would want to have a say in the selection, yet appointees of Bill Clements still held a 6–3 majority on the board. *Texas Monthly* reported that although my name had surfaced as a potential chancellor who had experience in working with the legislature, I was "hardly Ann Richards' type." The magazine's Paul Burka wrote: "No doubt the Republican regents would like to name both the next chancellor and the next president (of UT Austin) while they still have the votes. But UT can hardly afford to snub Richards at a time when its hefty budget is under attack in the courts and in the legislature. Like it or not, the regents are going to have to come to some sort of accommodation with the governor."[2] Burka's report exaggerated both Richards's desire to influence the selection of a chancellor and the extent to which the board needed to accommodate Richards, and in particular the extent to which budget decisions in the Texas Legislature are influenced by such board votes. I was grateful that I enjoyed strong support from both Republicans and Democrats on the board.

After I was named the sole finalist, there were generally two reactions among the press and the public. I received many statements of support from my many friends and associates within the university community, political circles, and among Texas business and civic leaders. On the other hand, there was a flurry of news coverage quoting individuals and groups who were critical about my service on corporate boards and particularly my membership on the board of Freeport-McMoRan Inc., a large mining company that was periodically under fire from environmental groups.

One of the most positive reactions came in an editorial in the *Dallas Morning News*, which said I was "the right man for the times." "During the prolonged economic slump that has made higher education budgets a prime target for budget-cutting legislators, Mr. Cunningham has proved one of the most energetic, effective spokesmen for the state's universities and colleges," the editorial said, while also expressing support for the efforts I had been making to encourage minority high school students to pursue a college education.[3]

Another very supportive editorial appeared in the *Houston Post*, which called the UT System one of the largest and most diversified "businesses" in the state. "Who better to run it than an expert on business?" the newspaper said. "That is why the UT regents have shown unusual common sense in picking Dr. William Cunningham to be the next chancellor."[4]

The same qualities that appealed to the editors of the *Houston Post* drew criticism from others. My service on the board of Freeport-McMoRan was criticized by groups such as the Austin-based Save Our Springs Coalition and Texas Clean Water Action, which were quoted in an article in the *Austin American-Statesman* that was reprinted in various forms in newspapers across the state.[5] However, the article also quoted five members of the board of regents who said my board memberships never came up during the selection process. "It wasn't considered to be important," Beecherl said, and this view was echoed by regents Sam Barshop, Mario Ramirez, Tom Loeffler, and Bernard Rapoport.

With the approach of the April 9 board meeting at which the regents would make my appointment official, I tried to anticipate questions that I would receive from the news media. Shirley Bird Perry, Monty Jones, and Joyce Moos prepared a list of some 150 questions, and they helped me practice addressing the issues that they raised. One of the advantages of having Jones on my staff was that he could draw on his journalism experience to anticipate reporters' questions and knew how to phrase questions in the most pointed and challenging way. If anything, I was over-prepared for the day of the regents' meeting, because the press never got to any of the really hard questions that we had prepared for. All the questions that the press asked me seemed easy after my grilling by my own staff.

I issued a formal statement after the regents' vote and outlined the major challenges that the UT System would be facing in the coming years. These were well known to most people, but I restated them that day just for the record. These concerns included:

- Continuing to develop each institution in the UT System in accordance with its distinct mission and the needs of the area served.
- Dealing with very serious budget constraints, while also upholding and enhancing the quality of educational services.
- Expanding educational opportunities for minority students, as well as increasing the number of minority and women faculty and administrators.
- Expanding collaborations among the system's fifteen component institutions.
- Expanding the contributions that the UT System and its institutions make to the state's economic development.
- Communicating with the public regarding the importance of public institutions of higher education.

When I became president of UT Austin I had less than two weeks to prepare for the job. In contrast, my appointment as chancellor on April 9 meant that I had almost five months to get ready for that job. This was a real luxury and gave me an opportunity to prepare for my new assignment in a more careful and organized manner. In hindsight, it is interesting to me that my approach to my newest challenge did not change a great deal, it just took longer.

There was no "first" meeting with Shirley Bird Perry to discuss the move to the system. Once it became apparent to us that I might be drafted to the chancellorship, we discussed the implications for UT Austin and the UT System. I made it very clear to her that if I went, I wanted her to go with me. Perry was very loyal to me, but she was also very loyal to UT Austin. The UT System administration had not always been viewed positively by UT Austin administrators so it was a big step for Perry to join the "evil empire." However, I was confident that Perry would go with me. She had been my closest adviser, and I could not imagine a situation when she was not right by my side.

As soon as I was named the sole finalist, I also asked Connie Saathoff, Joyce Moos, and Mary Kaszynski to go with me to the UT System. I did not know exactly what role each of them would play, but I did remember Darrell Royal's statement, "Dance with those who brung you." Once again, I had complete confidence in these individuals. Saathoff had been with me since the Dean's Office, and Moos and

Kaszynski had proven time and time again that, like Saathoff, they performed admirably in the most difficult and stressful situations. While I tried to be politically correct by giving them "an opportunity" to go with me to the system, my guess is that they felt they better pack their bags because their leader needed them and I did not want to be told anything but "I am ready to go."

The first person I met with after being formally appointed as chancellor was Hans Mark. He had always been very supportive of me, and I wanted to thank him for his help. I also wanted to make it very clear that I understood the UT System had only one chancellor at a time and that I would support any decisions that he made. Mark was more than gracious and indicated that he would "run by me" any major decisions that he would be making that would affect my administration. We had a very thoughtful discussion about Mark's views on the current administrative team at the system and the component institutions, as well as the major issues that he felt I would be facing in the near future.

I met with Charles A. "Mickey" LeMaistre on March 22 at the Tarry House. I had known LeMaistre for many years and I had a great deal of respect for him. He had been a very successful chancellor of the UT System during a difficult period, and he was also widely recognized as doing an excellent job as president of M. D. Anderson. I wanted LeMaistre's advice on how I should deal with the regents (stay close to them) on the major issues that the UT System would be facing in the foreseeable future (state funding and the need to support excellence at Austin and the medical schools). LeMaistre was very generous with his time that Sunday, and I called upon him many more times for informal advice and counsel.

My visits also included meetings with the people at the UT System who would report directly to me, as well as the component presidents. My meeting with Jim Duncan, executive vice chancellor for academic affairs, was a little unusual. As president, I had worked for Duncan for almost seven years. Now the situation was reversed and Duncan would be reporting to me. He did the professional thing and offered to resign. I told him that I had confidence in him and wanted him to continue in his current position. I did tell him that my style would necessitate me at times working directly with the academic presidents. He assured me this would not be a problem.

The transition with the rest of my direct reports was quite easy and uneventful. I met with Mike Millsap, vice chancellor for governmental relations; Ray Farabee, vice chancellor and general counsel; Dan Burck, executive vice chancellor for business affairs; and Charles Mullins, executive vice chancellor for health affairs. I asked each of them to brief me on major issues that they felt the UT System would be facing in the foreseeable future, and I asked each of them to remain in his position.

My meeting with each of the component presidents also went very well. I felt I knew them since we had all attended countless system meetings, as well as meetings of the regents. I believe most, if not all, of them felt comfortable with my selection as representing one of their own who had become chancellor.

I also visited each of the campuses in the months before I took office. I felt this was an important symbolic statement and I always went by myself. This was the same strategy I used when I met initially with the deans when I became president of UT Austin. I wanted the presidents to know that I had confidence in them and that I needed their help in representing them and their institution effectively before the regents, the legislature, and the people of Texas.

Their styles varied but they were all very good communicators. Kern Wildenthal sat patiently with me and gave me a very well organized PowerPoint presentation about why Southwestern Medical Center was already one of the great medical schools in the country and what needed to be done to make it even better. Miguel Nevárez talked with me passionately and effectively about the needs of the people of South Texas and what UT Pan American could do to materially improve their lives. I quietly realized during these meetings that I was indeed fortunate to have an opportunity to serve the people of Texas as chancellor.

While these large themes would occupy the great majority of my time as chancellor, I began preparing for the job in much more minute detail—such as the question of whether the chancellor should continue to occupy Bauer House in West Austin, and if not, whether the UT System should keep the property. I asked Lowell Lebermann to lead a committee to look into those questions. It would have been my strong preference for Isabella, John, and me to remain in our own home rather than move into Bauer House, but the committee studied the matter and recommended that the chancellor continue to occupy the official residence. They concluded that the house was very valu-

William H. Cunningham with Ray Farabee shortly after I was appointed chancellor. *Courtesy of William H. Cunningham.*

able to the UT System as a site for official occasions, special events, receptions, fund-raising, and other functions. After we had lived there a while I had a better appreciation for just how heavily the property is used for those official purposes. My committee gave me a recommendation that I did not want, but it was the correct one. I followed their advice and never looked at the question again.

From March until I took office as chancellor on September 1, I took a number of steps to plan my team, including asking several key aides and advisers at UT Austin to make the move with me to the system offices in downtown Austin. In addition to Saathoff, Moos, and Kaszynski agreeing to take key staff positions within the Chancellor's Office, Perry became vice chancellor of development and external affairs, so she and I continued to operate as a team on countless issues. Jones also joined the system as director of public information. Within a few years, others on whom I had relied at UT Austin also joined the team, including most notably Ed Sharpe and Lewis Wright. All these highly capable individuals made vital contributions to the success of our initiatives. I will always be personally indebted to them.

I was in a much better position to hit the ground running as chancellor than I had been as president. In addition to having the assistance of the people I have named, I was older and I believe wiser, and I had developed considerable knowledge about the system and the board of regents. I already knew most of the key players at the legislature and within other parts of state government, and I had a strong understanding of the major issues facing the state and higher education, as well as a good feel for the political forces through which those issues would play out. I certainly learned a lot in my initial months as chancellor, but the learning curve was not as steep as it had been seven years earlier.

CHAPTER 20

Working with the Board of Regents

Whenever a new group of appointments to the University of Texas Board of Regents was made by a governor, I contacted the appointees immediately after the announcement and offered any assistance that I could provide in helping them prepare for their confirmation hearing before the Senate. It was common for appointees to face at least a few questions about volatile or highly sensitive political issues, and an unprepared nominee could easily get into trouble. I tried to help them anticipate the difficult questions and to be prepared with answers that would avoid political mine-fields while also being responsive enough to satisfy the questioner. I also made it very clear that they would likely receive some hostile questions from legislators who were upset about actions that the UT System or the board of regents had taken. I did not want them to feel they needed to defend earlier decisions or apologize for them. A reasonable response was to listen carefully and explain that they would be sensitive to the senator's concerns once they were confirmed.

When new regents were confirmed we invited them for an all-day orientation session. Sometimes all three new regents attended the orientation together. The Office of the Board of Regents also had a full sequence of orientations, but I felt it was very important for me to interact with them and give them my perspective. I would brief them on the major issues that I felt the UT System would be facing during their terms on the board. These inevitably included major legislative initiatives and political activities because one of the most important things the UT System does is provide political cover and leadership for the campuses. I also briefed the new regents on campus issues and the quality of leadership that I perceived on each campus. We also scheduled meetings between the new regents and all of the vice chancellors so they could broaden their knowledge of the system and build a relationship with my staff. We also encouraged the new regents to visit as many of the campuses as they could as soon as possible.

My pattern of interaction with the board of regents did not change dramatically when I moved from being president to chancellor. I decided after being named president of UT Austin that I would try to visit with each of the nine regents at least once between the regular meetings of the board, either by telephone or in person. I used these meetings to discuss the agenda for the next board meeting, answer questions, and put my spin on the issues. Once I was appointed chancellor I recognized that I needed to try to meet at least once between meetings in person with each regent. I made it a practice to travel to each regent's home or office to review the agenda for the next board meeting. This took a lot of time, but I felt these meetings helped the regents understand the important issues they would be voting on. Since these were one-on-one meetings, the regents could ask very direct and frank questions and, in most cases, clear up any concerns. This was one reason the regents had few questions during board meetings.

My relationship with the chairman was always much more intimate. I would talk with him at least once a week as president and several times a week as chancellor. We usually visited in person when he was in Austin. While I realized I was hired by the full board, I also realized that I reported regularly to the chairman. I also made it a point to stay out of the board's internal politics, leaving that to the chairman.

The political problems I faced with the board were very manageable and not unusual. The basic structure was difficult because the regents hired the presidents, who then reported officially to a vice chancellor, who in turn reported to me. When I was president of UT Austin I reported to the executive vice chancellor for academic affairs, Jim Duncan, and in turn to Hans Mark, the chancellor, and not directly to the board of regents. However, I also recognized that as president of UT Austin, I was in an unusual position. Many of the regents focused most of their attention on UT Austin and many of the legislative issues were directed at the university. As a result, I felt I needed to have direct unfiltered contact with the board, and I made sure this occurred. However, I did my best to meet regularly with my bosses at the system, to keep them fully up to speed on my contacts with the regents, but I also recognized that for my own political sur-

UT System Board of Regents, May 11, 1995. Standing, from left, Zan W. Holmes Jr.,
Linnet F. Deily, Tom Loeffler, Donald L. Evans, Ellen Clarke Temple, and Lowell H.
Lebermann Jr. Seated, from left, Thomas O. Hicks (vice-chairman), Bernard Rapoport
(chairman), and Martha E. Smiley (vice-chairman). *Prints and Photographs Collection,
di_08398.*

New UT
President
Robert
Berdahl with
William H.
Cunningham,
Peg Berdahl,
and Louis
Beecherl
looking on,
November
8, 1992.
*UT Texas
Student
Publications
Photograph
Collection, e_
uttsp_00010.*

vival and for the benefit of UT Austin, I needed to talk directly with the board and its chairman.

I had a difficult relationship with Robert Berdahl, my successor as president of UT Austin. The difficulties began almost from the start of his appointment. While I am confident in hindsight that both of us could have done things differently that would have improved our relationship, the process that was used to hire him and all other presidents increased the probability of problems. I believe that as president I dealt with the UT System administrative structure better than Berdahl, but I also had the advantage of having been at UT Austin throughout my faculty and administrative careers, while Berdahl came to the presidency from the University of Illinois. I had had from the beginning of my presidency a good feeling for how both the informal and the formal structure had to function.

When I became chancellor, the board's regular meetings were held every two months, with the meetings of standing committees usually held just before the full meeting of the board. This made for two days of meetings that were often quite rushed and tiring for everyone, and it often felt like we were spending most of our time just getting ready for regents' meetings. I asked Regent Lowell Lebermann to chair a committee to determine how we could more effectively organize ourselves, and the result was a change to four regular meetings of the full board each year instead of six. Between these meetings, we also scheduled a separate day of committee meetings where much of the regents' real work was conducted. I am not really sure we accomplished our objective, which was partly to avoid devoting so much time and energy to meetings, but the new schedule did give the committees more time to focus on their work.

I always felt it was my responsibility to make sure the regents were well informed about the activities of UT Austin or the UT System, particularly if the news was bad. I always tried to be the first one to give them any bad news. This was before the days when everyone had e-mail, but it was true even then that bad news traveled quickly, while good news seemed to be delivered by camel. I wanted the regents to feel that they could always count on me to tell them what was really happening with the bark off, and not leave them to try to get accurate information from some other source. This also gave me an opportunity to put my spin on the issue.

I have always been a fan of retreats, which provided an opportunity for the board or for administrators who reported to me directly to get away and have some personal time with each other while focusing on issues in a fresh, and hopefully undisturbed, setting. Successful organizations are made up of people who have confidence in each other and trust each other, and a retreat is an excellent opportunity to develop those relationships. I started holding retreats for administrators and senior faculty when I was dean of the business school. We gathered at an off-campus location and would combine a morning of work with an afternoon and evening of recreation and socializing. This gave everybody a chance to discuss issues in an environment in which the telephone wasn't ringing and there was not a crisis every moment—an atmosphere that is much more difficult to accomplish since the advent of cell phones.

As chancellor I used Bauer House as a site for retreats for my executive staff. These meetings were very productive and usually included presentations by each vice chancellor on current situations and plans for the future. This gave everyone an opportunity to take part in the discussions and led to a real sense of camaraderie. This was consistent with the way I ran our weekly executive officers' meetings. We held regular retreats for the board of regents with a similar format. We would put together PowerPoint presentations that might run to 150 pages, we would bring in various experts to offer their views, and often the vice chancellors would make presentations. I believe these retreats were very useful and helped the regents get up to speed on the range of complex issues they had to deal with.

In the fifteen years that I served as president or chancellor, I worked with dozens of regents of all backgrounds, interests, and political persuasions. Their diversity is partly a reflection of the diversity of the governors who appointed them—Bill Clements (1979–1983 and 1987–1991), Mark White (1983–1987), Ann Richards (1991–1995), and George W. Bush (1995–2000). When I became president in 1985, White was governor, but the board still included three regents who had been appointed by Clements in his first term. An unusual feature of my years of service was that Democrats alternated with Republicans in the Governor's Office, so I dealt with majorities controlled by each party.

During this period the only partisan event that consistently occurred was the election by the board of its chairman. While I never witnessed the process from the inside, it was clear to me that the members of the party that controlled six seats selected the chairman, and then the remaining three members would make the selection unanimous. There were subtle differences in emphasis as the majorities changed, but for the most part the board was focused on making UT Austin and the other component institutions world-class institutions of higher education. The board also consistently recognized that each of the academic institutions played unique and important roles and could not be expected to fit into one mold.

I was fortunate to have the opportunity to work with many excellent regents. While they were all different—with different personalities and different areas of special interest—they all shared some common traits. The great regents were largely independent from the governor, from their political party, and from all other outside forces that might have an impact on the University of Texas. This does not imply that they had not made major financial contributions to the governor who had appointed them, did not remain close to the governor, and were not active politically in the governor's party, but they were, despite such relationships, truly independent in their decision-making and how they approached problems. They based their decisions on principle and independent judgment of what was best for the university—not on mere political loyalties.

The finest regents were willing to use their political connections with the governor and other elected officials to help the university. Instead of taking orders from the governor or other elected officials, they sought to exert influence on those officials. These regents understood that part of their proper role was to help deliver and explain messages from the chancellor or the board or even to put political pressure on an elected official to do what was right.

They also understood from the beginning that the UT System was a large, complex organization that had many different forces operating within it and many different constituents. They realized it would take them a substantial amount of time to really learn how the system operated and what was in the best interest of its institutions. Regents with these qualities also invested the time to read briefing books and study the issues. They tried to acquire an in-depth understanding of the problems within the system and each of its institutions. They were willing to travel to the campuses, meet with the presidents, speak with the other executive officers, and learn about what made each campus distinctive. This implied, of course, that they were willing to listen and learn before jumping in and explaining to university officials how they should deal with complex issues. In contrast, the regents who felt they were ready to make important decisions immediately after being sworn in rarely made an important contribution.

There is a tendency for members of boards of public entities to become much more involved in the micromanagement of the institution than do individuals who serve on major for-profit corporate boards. There were regents, I sometimes felt, who, just because they'd received a bachelor's degree twenty-five years earlier from UT Austin, thought they understood how to run the university. It was also interesting to me that this tendency usually did not exist with the medical schools. The best regents were able to rise above micromanagement behavioral patterns and examine important issues facing UT Austin and the UT System from a broad perspective. They avoided getting bogged down in minutiae, analyzed issues in terms of principles and policies, and were mindful of how a decision on one issue could have larger implications. Most importantly, they listened carefully to campus and system officials before they made up their minds.

The regents who understood that they represented all UT institutions and avoided focusing only on their home region were often the best regents. Those who limited themselves to a more narrow focus were usually from outside of one of the state's major metropolitan areas but had a UT institution in their home community. These regents often knew the president of their hometown institution and had been active on local development boards. People in the community expected them to "deliver" for the home institution, which was often perceived by the community leaders as being neglected by the UT System leaders.

The most admirable regents avoided being caught up only in the interests of specific constituencies—students, minority groups, women, business lobbies, etc.—and tried to represent all constituencies that were of central importance to UT System component institutions. It would have been easy for minority regents to have focused solely on Hispanic or African American students. However, the minority regents I served with realized they had a responsibility to make UT Southwestern an even better flagship medical school, just as they had a responsibility to help UT Austin recruit more African American students from Houston.

There were many opportunities for conflicts of interest for regents, ranging from the hiring of architects to the awarding of construction contracts to the admission of children or grandchildren. The best regents never permitted a conflict of interest to develop between them and any segment of the UT System. They were as concerned about the perception of conflict of interest as much as any real conflict. I am fortunate that even with the regents who were not as sensitive to these types of issues as their colleagues, they never asked me to do anything that even approached violating any state or federal laws.

The regents who were willing to ask hard questions—even those that the chancellor or the presidents probably did not want to be asked—were always classified as being among the best regents. If their questions led them to conclude that something unwise was going on, then they would bore in and ask more and more difficult questions. They understood down deep that while university officials were human beings and could easily make mistakes, in reality they were hardworking people who got to the office every morning early and did their best to deal with difficult and complex issues and often went out at night to serve the institution at social events.

In summary, the most important quality for separating the outstanding regents from people who simply served in an acceptable manner was the willingness to put the UT System ahead of everything but their families. It is interesting to me that many of the best regents had experienced success in many other parts of their lives. While serving as a regent was a "big deal," these people were used to "big deals." Such people were not only more sophisticated than regents who had not had an opportunity to be exposed to complex entities, but they were less susceptible to the idea that all of a sudden they had become a big shot by being appointed to the University of Texas Board of Regents.

In focusing on the great regents, I could single out any number to illustrate the qualities of outstanding leadership and selfless service that they brought to the board. I will focus on Bernard Rapoport, who was not only an indisputably outstanding regent but also one who became a very close friend of mine and with whom I developed something of a father-son relationship.

Often I knew the new appointees to the board from their previous involvement with the university, but I did not know Rapoport when he was nominated by Governor Richards to serve on the board in 1991. This was clearly my fault. Rapoport, known to his friends as B., had made several major financial contributions to UT Austin, including providing the funds for an endowed chair in the LBJ School for Ray Marshall when he returned to the university from serving as secretary of labor in the Carter Administration. Rapoport, who lived in Waco, had been very closely aligned with the liberal wing of the national and state Democratic Party and particularly with Senator Ralph Yarborough. He had also been a financial sponsor of the liberal publication the *Texas Observer* for many years. Despite his contributions to the university through the years, he had not been closely involved in the institution in the same way that other prominent conservative Democrats had, particularly people associated with the inner circles of John Connally and Ben Barnes.

Once Rapoport was appointed, I reached out to him and scheduled a briefing for him, as I did with all new regents, and we bonded immediately. It turns out he bonds with everyone immediately. He did not know any of Clements's Republican regents, and I am sure they felt he was some kind of extreme liberal. After all, he had made most of his money selling insurance to labor unions—not the kind of business that interests most Republicans. The interesting thing to me was how easily Rapoport bonded with all of his colleagues on the board. It was quickly apparent to everyone that he was not some dangerous radical. He said to me when we met, "Don't worry about me, Bill, I didn't make all of this money by being some crazy person." Rapoport's moderate, reasoned positions on issues, together with his outgoing personality and his obvious delight in interacting with people, won over all of his doubters.

Rapoport quickly developed a warm relationship with Tex Moncrief. Their friendship was fascinating to watch because many people had perceived Moncrief as a right-wing extremist, which was not true, just as they had perceived Rapoport to be a crazy leftist, which also was not true. The truth of the matter is, Moncrief is one of the most caring and thoughtful individuals I have ever met, and Rapoport was much more moderate than people think. Moncrief and Rapoport sealed their friendship over the decision to eliminate smoking in all buildings on the UT System's campuses. Both came to the realization after hearing a presentation by President Charles LeMaistre of M. D. Anderson that it was in the UT System's best interest, because of health, safety, and insurance issues, to enforce a smoking ban in all buildings—even though the Permanent University Fund might continue to purchase equity in tobacco companies.

One of the first issues on which I worked with Rapoport concerned an inquiry he received from the *Daily Texan* about tuition. The *Texan* called him soon after he joined the board asking what he thought about potential increases in tuition. Rapoport used the opportunity to launch into a tirade about the fact that tuition was too high and that we needed to have lower, if not free, tuition. After he gave the reporter all kinds of juicy and exciting quotes, he called me and said, "Bill, I just talked with the *Daily Texan*, and I just told them about the problems we have with tuition and that we've got to lower it." Then he asked me what I thought. I paused for a moment and thought, here is the test. Do I tell our new regent that he made a horrible mistake and that the policy he has espoused to the student newspaper would not be in the best interest of the university, or do I just keep my mouth shut? I decided that if I was to have a good relationship with Rapoport I would have to tell him the truth. So I said, "Let me explain to you the problems associated with what you're proposing." He listened patiently as I talked about the fact that we provided significant tuition relief to students from lower socioeconomic groups, about all the financial aid and other assistance we provided to minority students, and about our efforts to raise scholarship funds for economically and socially disadvantaged students. I explained that if we did not charge tuition to students, we would not be in a position to offer the educational services that we did on campus. While tuition was not the biggest portion of our funding, it was significant. After I discussed all that, Rapoport told me, "Bill, the next time, before I talk with the press, I will call you." I told him that however he wanted to handle such calls was fine with me, but I never had to explain an issue to him in such circumstances again, because he was a very fast learner and he realized it would be smart to talk with people at the university about issues before going public with his first impressions.

After Rapoport had served on the board for a year and a half, Richards asked me during halftime at a women's basketball game at UT Austin if I thought he would make a good chairman. I told her I thought Rapoport would make an excellent chairman because of his maturity, thoughtfulness, and deep concern for the university. I did not tell Richards that his greatest asset was that he had always put the university ahead of any political considerations. What separated Rapoport from less successful regents was not just the extent of his enthusiasm or his love for the university, but the fact that UT always came first. I did not feel the need to mention that quality to Richards, and if I had it might have hurt his chances of being elected chairman. Richards did indicate to me that she was not sure he should be named chairman when she asked me, "How long does he need to serve?" I told her the usual term was two years, but that the chairman serves at the pleasure of the board. This was not a very politically correct message to the governor, but I was consciously trying to make the point that the board appoints its own chairman, not the governor.

I recognize that Richards was not the first, nor will she be the last, governor to think that he or she should influence, if not decide, who should be chairman. In February 1985, soon after George W. Bush was elected governor, he tried to get Rapoport to resign as chairman, much the same way Bill Clements had tried to remove Jess Hay from the chairmanship in 1987 (see Chapter 23). Even with three new Republican appointees taking their seats on the board in early 1995, the Democrats were going to maintain a 6–3 majority for the next two years, and Rapoport was clearly the consensus choice for chairman among the Democratic majority. While the long-accepted practice was for the party in the majority to select the chairman, it was evident to me that Bush did not understand or care about regental protocol and he did not want to wait until the second two years of his term to have his friend and newly appointed regent Don Evans become chairman.

Bush and Evans met with Rapoport in the Governor's Office. I am sure they felt that Rapoport was such a pleasant person that he would agree to the governor's wishes. Rapoport called me before the meeting and asked my advice. I told him that he had the votes and he would be elected chairman if he did not voluntarily give up the job. I told him just to listen and stay strong and that UT needed him more than ever.

Rapoport did not follow my advice completely. He told me shortly after the meeting that they had a two-hour conversation in which he talked mostly about the role higher education could play in promoting economic development and helping people escape the grip of poverty. While Bush raised the issue of Rapoport stepping aside, it became painfully clear to them that Rapoport was not even willing to discuss that issue. Rapoport was a good politician who knew how to count votes. He won the election to a second term, and Evans did not become chairman until February 1997, by which time Bush's second round of appointments meant the Republicans had gained a majority of seats on the board.

Rapoport was always very supportive of our South Texas/Border Initiative. I believe his interest in the initiative was driven by the fact that he had grown up in San Antonio and had developed a genuine concern for the economically and socially disadvantaged people of South Texas. Rapoport felt we had a rare, if not unique, opportunity for the university to step forward and really change the nature of higher education in South Texas. He also liked being involved in big, important projects that relied on his significant political skills to bring them to fruition.

One of the most fun times I had was going to the legislature with Rapoport. While he had focused his vast political energy largely on national politics, he was still very well known by state politicians. Wherever we went and whatever office we visited, people knew about Rapoport, and that was very useful to us. However, even Rapoport's clout was not always enough to ensure success. I remember one meeting with Rob Junnel, who was chairman of the House Appropriations Committee. Rapoport, Regent Tom Loeffler, Mike Millsap, and I went to visit with Junnel, and at the beginning Junnel made it clear that Millsap, who had worked for House Speaker Gib Lewis and was now our vice chancellor for governmental relations, was not welcome in the meeting. That was very rude, but Millsap withdrew from the room as instructed by Junnel. Despite that awkward start, Rapoport launched into a passionate discussion of education funding and why it was important to do the right thing for the children of Texas. Junnel listened for about two minutes and then interrupted and made it clear that those issues were of no interest to him. He said his job was to balance the budget, and that was what he intended to do. Then he said he certainly appreciated us stopping by. We left disappointed, but I also saw some humor in comparing the lofty and grand vision that Rapoport and Loeffler had for future generations of Texans with Junnel's narrow focus on the state's two-year budget. Beyond the humor, it was in many ways a very stark and chilling comparison.

When he was chairman, Rapoport and I used to talk at least two to three times a day. These conversations often lasted only a few minutes at a time because he typically placed as many as fifty calls a day. So when he called, you knew to get down to business very quickly. He was always questioning but always supportive. There was never a question of how an issue might affect the labor movement or whether an action would be in Richards's best interest, or even a question of what the Governor's Office thought. Rapoport would get calls regularly from state labor leaders hoping to get UT to change its policies with respect to unions, fair wage issues on construction projects, and other issues. After a union leader would hammer on Rapoport, he would call me and say, "Bill, do me a favor and call this guy back and meet with him if you can. After that, I don't want to know about it. It is your decision, do whatever is in the best interest of the university." And he really meant that. At the beginning of Rapoport's chairmanship I received a number of these calls from labor leaders. I am confident they thought the UT System would now roll over to all their demands. However, after a few months when nothing happened out of the ordinary, they gave up.

In the same way, when we had our various fund-raising events, Rapoport wanted to be in touch with both Republicans and Democrats, as long as they supported the university. He was always very supportive of David Sibley, a Republican senator from Waco, and Bill Ratliff, a Republican senator from East Texas. Both were very supportive of UT and higher education in general.

Rapoport fit all the other key criteria that I have cited as making a great regent. He was independent, and he always thought on a grand scale and was excited by far-reaching projects like the South Texas/ Border Initiative. He was not interested in minutiae and avoided micromanagement. He also had a broad interest in and appreciation for the entire UT System. Even though he loved UT Austin, he also embraced the medical schools and all the academic institutions in the system.

The immense usefulness of a wise, resourceful, and well-connected regent such as Rapoport to the UT System cannot be overestimated. That truth was brought home to me in January 1994 when I spent two of the most exciting days of my life in the company of Rapoport during a trip to Washington, D.C. Rapoport had called me on January 19 to tell me that the UT System needed to get behind First Lady Hillary Clinton's proposed health care legislation—one of the central legislative initiatives of the first two years of President Bill Clinton's first term. UT officials had been studying the legislation since it had been announced the previous September, and we had serious concerns about the effect the bill would have on our medical schools and their associated teaching hospitals. This was another test for me. Could I speak "truth to power"? I passed the test. I told Rapoport that Hillary's initiative would not be in the best interest of the UT System's medical schools." Rapoport was a quick study. After I explained the problems, he said, "Bill, we will need to modify the bill so that it helps support the mission of our great medical schools." He went on to say that we should have lunch with Senator Kennedy and meet with Senator Rockefeller.

I was certainly surprised about how quickly Rapoport made things happen. One week later, on Monday, January 25, I joined Rapoport, Charles Mullins (executive vice chancellor for health affairs), and Mike Millsap (vice chancellor for governmental relations) in Washington for an early morning meeting with Dick Knapp, senior vice president for governmental relations for the Association of American Medical Colleges. Then we met individually with three key members of the House of Representatives (Jack Fields, Charlie Stenholm, and John Wiley Bryant) who were dealing with the health care bill. We finished the afternoon with Rapoport, Mullins, and I giving brief testimony on the bill to the House Energy and Commerce Subcommittee on Academic Health Centers.

As we left the Rayburn House Office Building, I was impressed with the full and productive day that Rapoport had arranged with hardly any advance notice—and our day was not over. Rapoport took my elbow and asked me if I had any tickets to President Clinton's State of the Union address, which was scheduled to begin in about three hours. I said, "No, Bernard, I do not." I did not call him Bernard very often. I had learned from Rapoport's wife, Audre, that when she really wanted his attention, she called him Bernard. I said, "I may be able to get us some tickets for a UT baseball game in Austin, but I do not have any tickets for the State of the Union address." Then Rapoport said, "Let's go ask Tom Foley (the Speaker of the House). I bet he can get us tickets."

In a matter of minutes we were marching full speed to the Speaker's Office. Rapoport knew where it was. He had obviously been there before. Upon arrival, Rapoport announced to the receptionist that

From left, Bernard Rapoport, William H. Cunningham, Isabella Cunningham, President Bill Clinton, and Audre Rapoport, c. 1994. *Courtesy of William H. Cunningham.*

she was the most beautiful woman he had ever seen. I am not sure that statement was true, but I knew she was at least in his top seven because I heard him say that six other times during the day.

The wide-eyed receptionist quickly left and came back and said Speaker Foley would like to see us. Clearly a fine example of representative government. The four of us visited with Speaker Foley in his private office for about an hour, ranging far and wide on various political topics but working in some of the UT System's key concerns about the health care bill. Then the day suddenly became even more bizarre, when President Clinton himself popped in to the Speaker's office. The president was following a long tradition of handing the Speaker a formal copy of the speech he was about to deliver to the joint session of Congress. President Clinton was delighted to see Rapoport, and Mullins, Millsap, and I were included in the festivities as if we were all old friends of the president too.

Just before it was time for President Clinton to leave to give his speech, he turned to Rapoport and said he really wanted him to serve as an ambassador. I quickly chimed in that Rapoport had a much more important job already—as chairman of the board of regents. Then as President Clinton was leaving he turned back to us and said, "Why don't you all come over tomorrow and have breakfast at the White House?" All I could say was, "Works for me."

We did get to attend President Clinton's speech because Speaker Foley managed to produce four tickets to the House gallery. We never knew who the Speaker might have displaced to make room for us with just minutes before the speech was to start, but the lesson was clear to me—I wanted to stay by Rapoport's side whenever possible.

On Tuesday, we arrived at the White House at 7:45 a.m., and to my great surprise, they let us in. Mack McClarty, the president's chief of staff, and George Stephanopoulos, a White House aide, welcomed us and took us to the White House mess for breakfast. Before long, the call came that President Clinton would like to see us in the Oval Office before we left, so we trooped up there and visited with him for about thirty minutes, until it was time for him to attend a meeting of his Cabinet. Our astounding morning at the White House then continued as President Clinton walked with us down to the Cabinet Room, where half a dozen members of the Cabinet jumped up as soon as they saw Rapoport and came over to say hello. We were holding up the most powerful man in the world and all of his department heads, but everyone had plenty of time for Rapoport.

Finally, we did withdraw from the room and let the Executive Branch go about its business. The rest of that day was a little anticlimactic as we visited individually with key senators—Jay Rockefeller, Tom Harkin, Don Riegle, Tom Daschle, Paul Simon, and George Mitchell (the Senate majority leader). Then we had lunch with Ted Kennedy in his office, and we concluded the day with our friend, U.S. Representative Jake Pickle, one of the most powerful and best friends the University of Texas ever had.

We left for home the next day, and I am sure that Mullins and Millsap were thinking, as I was, that we were pretty important people. For Rapoport, it was not much more than a routine couple of days in Washington. We had a magnificent time meeting in the most informal way imaginable with some of the most powerful people in the country—in the world—and we did manage to get across our message about the health care bill. But for Rapoport, it all seemed just like a visit with old friends.

Rapoport loved the Clintons, and they loved him. However, it took only a few seconds for him to realize that the system's medical schools had significant problems with the new health care initiative. As a result, he instinctively knew that his only obligation was to do what was in the best interest of the medical schools.

The really great regents look at issues only through one screen. How will the decision impact the university's ability to complete its complex mission of teaching, research, and service. Rapoport understood, maybe better than anyone else I have ever known, that political questions and politicians are interesting, but they are transitory, while the university's mission remains central to the well-being of Texas.

The most important ingredients in making a successful regent are the traits and qualities that appointees bring to the position. However, I always considered it to be part of my job as president and chancellor to help every member of the board become an even better regent. To their credit, most of them welcomed constructive advice about how they could do their jobs better and be in a position to better serve the UT System. We were indeed fortunate that all but a very few regents took this broad and selfless view. While they may have loved the honor of serving on arguably the state's most prestigious appointed board, they genuinely wanted to be good public servants.

CHAPTER 21

Early Interactions in State Politics

I was introduced to politics by two of the grand masters of Texas politics—Frank Erwin and Jess Hay. I was also mentored by Senator Lloyd Bentsen, Congressman J. J. "Jake" Pickle, Bernard Rapoport, and Ben Barnes. While my early mentors were all legends in Texas Democratic politics, I never identified myself as either a Democrat or a Republican, and I have been very close to people from both parties. When Isabella and I arrived in the state in 1971, Texas politics was in transition, but by and large it was a two-party state—conservative Democrats vs. liberal Democrats. I voted in the Democratic primaries in the early years because I wanted my vote to count. In those days, winning the Democratic primary almost always meant a victory in the general election. By the time I became president and chancellor, the state had developed a real two-party system, and I made it a policy to forswear voting in primaries in order to maintain a position of official nonpartisanship.

My first real interaction with elected officials came when UT Austin decided it needed to create a Faculty Club that would serve as a social and professional center. In 1972, I was elected by the General Faculty to the new Faculty Club Board of Directors. The board consisted of well-established, highly respected senior faculty members such as Charles Alan Wright, who was the chairman of the board. In those days I was sometimes mistaken for the Bill Cunningham who was a senior member of the Department of Chemical Engineering, and I think that must have happened in this election. Bill was loved by the entire campus, and I rode his coattails to victory.

Erwin attended most of our early board meetings as we planned the Faculty Club. He wanted the club to serve alcohol. The problem was that Waggoner Carr, the attorney general of Texas, was making great political fodder out of the fact that UT was about to build a "watering hole" for the faculty. The implication was that the male faculty would be boozing it up with young coeds and setting a bad example for the campus community.

Erwin was convinced that the faculty did not care about whether the club served alcohol. He asked me to do a survey of the faculty to determine exactly what they wanted in the proposed club, and he felt he could use the results to prove that serving alcohol would not be a problem. This was easy for me because this is what marketing faculty do—interview people about market choices. Unfortunately, Erwin was wrong. It turned out that the top priority for the faculty was a place to enjoy a drink at the end of the day. Gone was the argument that the faculty did not care about alcohol. Once I showed Erwin the data he asked me if "we needed to keep it." I said, "No, sir." This was my first introduction to academic freedom.

Erwin's Plan B was nothing short of brilliant. He asked me in the spring of 1973 to go with him to the Capitol, where we met with Senator Charles Herring of Austin in his palatial Capitol office. Herring was a great friend of Erwin and a big UT supporter. Erwin's idea was to have the senator introduce a resolution in the Senate to instruct the UT Board of Regents to create a faculty club that served both food and alcohol. Erwin felt it would be difficult for Carr to criticize the university since it would just be following the Senate's instructions. My job was to explain to Herring why the faculty club would help UT serve as a place for legitimate academic debate and discussion. In hindsight, I realized that Erwin had everything arranged before we went to the Capitol, but I played my role, Herring played his role, and the Senate played its role and promptly passed our resolution 31–0. The fact that only one week earlier the Senate had confusedly adopted a prank resolution congratulating Albert DeSalvo, known as the Boston Strangler, for his unusual method of "population control" did not diminish our achievement in gaining unanimous support for our own resolution.

I also got to know Jake Pickle quite well when we first came to Texas. As I wrote in Chapter 1, Pickle played a critical role in helping Isabella stay in the United States as a legal immigrant. Isabella and I hosted a fund-raiser for Pickle in our home in 1975. This was our first foray into political fund-raising. It was not controversial, as Pickle was known and loved by everyone in Austin. Thirty years later, when Pickle was gravely ill, I was extremely honored when he asked me if

I would be one of the three speakers at his funeral. He gave me clear directions about what he wanted me to say, and, as usual, I followed his instructions to the letter.

A continuing crisis in state revenue that began in my last months as dean of the business school meant there was seldom a time during my presidency when we were not in the midst of a legislative session, either a regular or special session, trying to recover from the last one, or preparing for the next one. A combination of low oil prices, an outdated state tax structure and a weak economy were responsible for the crisis. The Texas economy was undergoing a fundamental shift away from oil and gas but had not yet found a firm footing in the high-tech, knowledge-based economy that was emerging worldwide. Oil and gas production had been declining in Texas since 1972, but the Arab oil embargoes of 1973 and 1979 had helped keep prices high, obscuring the long-term decline of the state's oil industry. The fall in oil prices beginning in 1982 and turning into a full-scale collapse in 1985, plus the fact that the state's tax structure was still heavily weighted toward petroleum revenues, led to a continuing inability of the state to raise enough money to provide basic services. The problem was exacerbated by the needs of a growing population, increasing demands from new residents for state services, and court-mandated expenditures for prisons and mental health. It all added up to a severe challenge to the state's long-cherished "no new taxes" approach to government.[1]

The Legislative Budget Board (LBB) in late 1984 produced an initial budget plan that included reductions in the support for institutions of higher education. State and national media reported the cuts as a "recommendation," and as such it created a serious public relations problem for Texas and its universities. The LBB report propelled Jess Hay, then chairman of the UT Board of Regents, and others into action to forge a consensus around the economic necessity of maintaining support for colleges and universities. While Texas colleges and universities had been enjoying a remarkable prosperity for at least a decade, they still had many critical unmet needs, and most people could not remember a time when Texas higher education faced the prospect of serious budget cuts. Times had been so flush that the legislature, which in those days set all university tuition rates, had not found it necessary to increase the rates since 1971.

In March 1985, in the midst of making the case that Texas needed

William H. Cunningham with U.S. House Speaker Tom Foley and Congressman Jake Pickle atop the LBJ Library on the UT campus. *UT Office of Public Affairs Records, e_utopa_00057.*

to increase higher education appropriations, not cut them, UT Austin and other universities faced an onslaught of criticism from a report issued by Comptroller Bob Bullock. Sensational headlines across the state repeated Bullock's charge that higher education was in possession of a "$3 billion bowl of gravy" made up of what were called "local funds"—money held by institutions in local bank accounts rather than in accounts controlled by the State Treasury. If one reads Bullock's statements from that time very carefully, it is clear that he was not saying that colleges and universities were doing anything improper or deceptive with their local funds. Nevertheless, many newspaper reporters and editors, as well as members of the public, were left with just that impression. And it was an impression Bullock seemed all too happy to leave.

The facts in this case were that the local funds were audited regularly by the state and supervised by the legislature, and they earned higher interest than money deposited in the State Treasury. In most cases, this kind of income was used to provide a direct service or to support self-sustaining functions such as campus housing. The local accounts did not contain a hoard of money that could be applied to the state's revenue shortfall. All the evidence was that we were managing this money responsibly and in accordance with the public interest and the explicit will of the Texas Legislature.[2]

Bullock had said that all he wanted to do with his talk of "gravy" was to get the legislature to take local funds into consideration when making decisions about state appropriations. It was certainly true that some members of the legislature did not understand the local funds— just as some members did not understand the entire state budget process. Real experts on the state budget can be hard to find—even in the halls of the Capitol—but the irony was that Bullock himself was one of those true experts, and he knew better than anyone that his talk about "gravy" was off base. UT's position was that the term "local" did not in any sense represent a "secret" stash of money that could help solve the state's budget crisis. All in all, the episode was not Bullock's finest hour. Perry Bass summed up the position of many of UT's friends in a letter he wrote to Bullock that March: "Dear Bob: I am in receipt of the report that you sent me entitled 'The High Finance of Higher Education.' I am amazed at how inaccurate and misleading this whole report is, and disappointed for the first time at the incompetency of your office."[3]

I had a close and productive working relationship with Bullock when he was lieutenant governor and I was chancellor, and I never knew him to revert to the tactics that he used that spring. Bullock is remembered today as a great friend of higher education and one of Texas's finest statesmen, and that well-deserved reputation is a result largely of his later actions as lieutenant governor, not his "gravy" headlines of March 1985. In all the years that Bullock was lieutenant governor—and thus in a position to wield enormous influence over the state budget—I never heard him mention local funds even once.

Hay deserves much of the credit for eventually forging a compromise plan in the spring of 1985 that included a tuition increase as well as slight cuts in general revenue appropriations for most institutions, while giving universities flexibility to allocate their appropriations among the various campus functions, rather than having the legislature determine how all the money was spent. In addition to his on-the-ground activity in Austin and the many visits to community groups and editorial boards, Hay coordinated a statewide campaign to line up alumni and other university friends, encouraging them to talk to their legislators in support of the plan. My role that spring, though I was still only dean of the business school, was to accompany Chancellor Hans Mark when he made a series of trips around the state as part of that campaign. I do not know why I was asked to be the second person on Mark's team. My guess is that Peter Flawn or Shirley Bird Perry told Hay that I had an intuitive feel for politics and that I "knew" the state reasonably well. Mark's job was to explain Hay's plan for funding higher education and to emphasize the role that institutions of higher education could play in diversifying the economy. Mark was always very eloquent and thoughtful. My role was relatively limited. I focused on helping Mark answer questions that dealt with internal UT Austin matters, and I introduced him to community and business leaders when that was appropriate.

Mark and I went mostly to what might be called the "minor league" communities, while Flawn and Hay covered the larger cities. I was not involved in the strategic planning for how to deal with the issues that arose during that legislative session. I was amazed and delighted with the highly sophisticated way in which Hay, along with Flawn, Mark, and Perry, attacked the problem. The campaign was one of the most visible and aggressive efforts ever waged by UT in the legislature, and it was a sign of things to come in future sessions.[4] It also gave me an opportunity to learn from real pros about how the university could use its political muscle to benefit higher education and UT Austin. I loved the game as I saw it played that spring, although I had hardly begun to realize how much of a master Hay was at it. While I had virtually no interaction with individual politicians, I saw the political process unfolding before my eyes. The need to build coalitions and to generate support from powerful friends of the university were lessons that I learned quickly and never forgot during my subsequent years as a UT administrator.

The final outcome of that legislative session was passage of a $37.3 billion state budget for the 1986–1987 biennium in which general revenue appropriations for the state's thirty-five universities were cut 5.2 percent, although overall appropriations for higher education rose slightly because of a new capital improvement fund.[5] UT Austin's appropriations were cut 3 percent—a cut that some skeptics said was palatable only because it seemed so much better than the more severe cuts that had been talked about six months earlier.

An estimated $264 million in new revenue was to be raised for the biennium through the increase in tuition—the first substantial tuition increase in almost thirty years. The rate for resident tuition was tripled from $4 per semester hour to $12 in the fall of 1985 and then to $16 the next year.[6] The same law (HB 1147) provided for additional increases every other year until the rate would reach $24 an hour in the fall of 1995, although the pace of increases would later be stepped up. For out-of-state students, tuition was increased from $40 to $120 per hour in 1985 and 1986, and then, beginning in the fall of 1987, it was to be set at the actual cost of education, as calculated by the Coordinating Board. These tuition increases began a trend that would last more than twenty-five years—gradually shifting more of the cost of operating state universities from general revenue appropriations to student tuition and fees. The increases in the resident rates barely moved Texas out of last place among the states in resident tuition and caused no significant economic hardships for students, judging by the continued enrollment increases across the state.

After I became president of UT Austin in September 1985, I learned only too well that the president spends more time than many people might realize involved in state politics, particularly the activities of the legislature. It may not be an accident of urban planning that the state's pink granite Capitol and the limestone-clad Main Building of UT Austin occupy opposite ends of an axis. It is a little unfortunate, for purposes of symbolism, that the Tower and the Capitol are not exactly aligned within the city's street grid, but the President's Office on the fourth floor of the Main Building offers one of the clearest views of the Capitol dome, and it is possible to leave that office and be standing in the Governor's Office in ten minutes, assuming that someone else is responsible for finding a parking place. This easy proximity offers tremendous advantages to the president of UT Austin—compared to, say, the president of Texas A&M or the University of Houston. It can also have its disadvantages. When a state senator feels the need to complain about a loud party that took place at a fraternity house, the president of UT Austin is often an easy person to beat on.

Because of the sheer size of UT Austin, as well as the diversity and quality of its programs, its vast ranks of alumni all over the state, and its location next door to the Capitol, the president of the university is often called upon to serve as an unofficial spokesperson for Texas higher education, at least with regard to the many issues that cross all campus boundaries. The same factors help account for the reason that the chancellor of the UT System is called upon to perform a similar kind of statewide leadership role. There is, however, another reason that they are relied upon in this way: Other presidents and chancellors, and their boards, often prefer to hang back and let UT take the risks that always accompany leadership. They know that if no one else will speak up, UT will. If no one else will challenge a hastily conceived and badly written bill, UT will do it.

These lessons were abundantly clear during the legislative session of 1985, and I learned them again and again during the next fifteen years, when I had the privilege of taking a more central role on behalf of UT and Texas higher education. There were times when the aggressive style of play favored by Hay and my other early political mentors drew strong criticism from those who were not great friends of the university, but I never doubted that this style was necessary—particularly in an era of continuing fiscal crisis.

CHAPTER 22

The Budget Crisis of 1986

Soon after I was named president of UT Austin I attended a fund-raiser for Governor Mark White, but I did not make a contribution. At the time, the UT Board of Regents had six Democrats and three Republicans. I instinctively knew I should not make a contribution, but I also realized that White was an important statewide elected official and I should attend the event. In a few days I received a call from Larry Temple inviting me to lunch at Tarry House. After a few minutes of pleasantries, it soon became clear that Temple was a man on a mission. He saw me at the White fund-raiser, and he wanted to tell me to stay as far away as possible from partisan politics and politicians. Temple's advice was very good, but also very hard to follow.

I did not feel that I could do my job and give major political figures in the state the "cold shoulder." I felt that I could get more out of the political structure if I had a personal, positive relationship with the state's senior elected officials. I knew Temple was trying to tell me for my own good that I would be better off staying away from the political process. I tried to justify my behavior of interacting with politicians by not making any personal contributions to elected officials. I may have been wrong, but I always felt this gave me some protection from being branded as either a Republican or a Democrat or as being for one politician and against another.

My guess is that neither Temple nor I had any idea in September 1985 about what an extraordinarily difficult period the university and the state were about to embark upon politically. Passing an appropriations bill is always a challenge. During the period I was president of UT Austin (1985–1992) there were three regular sessions of the Texas Legislature—in 1987, 1989, and 1991—as well as no fewer than fourteen special sessions.

From left, William H. Cunningham, Larry Temple, Nick Kralj, and Frank C. Erwin III with a bust of Frank Erwin. Nick Kralj donated the bust and Larry Temple spoke at the ceremony in 1984. *Prints and Photographs Collection, di_08477.*

Comptroller Bob Bullock certified the budget passed in May 1985 as in balance but warned that the volatility of the world oil market could produce dramatic changes in the months ahead. The worst of his fears came true at the end of the year when a sudden increase in oil production by the Saudis flooded the world with oil and resulted in a collapse in prices. Spot prices fell from $32 a barrel in November 1985 to $15 in February 1986, and Texas tax revenues promptly spiraled downward. In February 1986 the Comptroller's Office, in the first of a series of lowered revenue estimates, said Texas was facing a $1.3 billion shortfall in revenues for the rest of the biennium. By August, when the first of two special legislative sessions convened, the estimated deficit had grown to $2.9 billion, as the oil price collapse continued to have secondary effects in sharply lowered sales tax receipts and other revenues.

White's response to the first lowered estimate was to issue an executive order on February 18, 1986, calling for all state agencies and universities to reduce spending by 13 percent for the biennium. Since

almost one-fourth of the biennium was already over, the impact of
these cuts was significantly greater than it would have been if they had
been spread out over the entire two-year budget period. To achieve
the 13 percent reduction, the executive order mandated an immediate
hiring freeze as well as a moratorium on promotions and merit pay
raises and cuts in travel, construction projects, and other purchases.[1]

UT Austin implemented the hiring freeze and other measures that
White had ordered, but there was no way we could afford to cut our
budget by 13 percent and still remain a major research university with
aspirations toward excellence. A cut of that size would have been a
disaster and very likely would have required eliminating major academic programs or other drastic measures such as dropping summer
school. I had not accepted the presidency of UT Austin in order to
preside over its demise, and I did not accept the idea that contrac-
tion and lowered expectations represented an acceptable course into
the future. Fortunately, Jess Hay and other regents saw things the
same way, and the board of regents increased the university's allocations from the Available University Fund to offset the general revenue appropriations that we had to give back to the state. Using AUF
resources in this way could help keep UT Austin on track until such
time as the legislature again recognized its obligations toward higher
education, and it sent a very important signal to all observers—UT
Austin was the flagship institution in the UT System and it would be
supported even to the detriment of other institutions if necessary.

This challenge to our budget pushed me faster and farther into
politics than I had been expecting. I certainly benefited from the leadership and encouragement of Hay, who was never shy about getting
into the political arena to advocate support for higher education. Hay
made it very clear to me, Hans Mark, and the entire UT System Office
of Governmental Affairs that UT and higher education were in for a
protracted fight with the legislature and the governor over how to
fund higher education and what level of funding would be appropriate. Hay knew we had only a few months to convince the public of
why higher education had to be adequately funded before the start of
the 1987 legislative session.

I spent a great deal of time traveling the state during the spring
of 1986 to visit with alumni, business groups, and other forums to
tell the university's story, and the task was made easy by the fact
that the university had a solid message, and it was one in which I

Chairman of the UT Board of Regents Jess Hay presiding at a regents meeting. *UT Office of Public Affairs Records, e_utopa_00049.*

deeply believed. These speaking engagements gave me an opportunity to present UT's case through statistics, and I found that this approach appealed to decision-makers and community opinion leaders.

I have always been comfortable with numbers, and it was easy for me to make presentations that focused on the university's performance in this way. Critics frequently said the university was "wasteful" or "fat," so I found it useful to back up my comments with well-researched numbers that were developed by Marsha Moss, director of the university's Office of Institutional Studies. I liked to focus on administrative costs, because everyone seems to be against spending money on administration. The facts were that Texas universities were spending far less for administration than schools in other large states. We were fourteenth among the fifteen largest states in administrative costs per student. For every key measurement that helped paint a picture of UT Austin—state appropriations, faculty salaries, tuition rates, graduation rates, minority enrollment, and so forth—I sought to place our performance in perspective by showing how we compared to peer institutions across the country. In every case, UT Austin and Texas institutions generally were among the most efficient and most productive universities in the nation—and among those with the least state support. This was a message that people needed to hear—especially when several politicians were calling for deep cuts in our budget.

I told audiences that spring that UT Austin's ability to serve its students and the state was being put in jeopardy by the proposed cuts. In a talk to alumni in San Angelo a week after White's executive order, I said, "We're past the bare bones cuts already. We're out of the fat and into the muscle. At some point, we (in Texas) are going to have to raise taxes or significantly cut services." A key part of my message was that UT Austin played a fundamental role through its education and research programs in helping attract high-technology industry to Texas. Continued strong investment by the state in the university was one of the surest paths toward the economic diversification that represented the only long-term solution to the state's economic difficulties. The future lay in information and innovation, not just in oil and agriculture. The way out of the present crisis lay in increased investment in higher education, not in budget cuts. I was also not afraid to use the "T" word—for taxes.

This economic development message had been effective in the spring of 1985, and it proved persuasive again in 1986. It continued to be one of my major themes throughout the years I was president and chancellor. The message was not always appreciated among the faculty, and I am sure it reinforced the misperception among some faculty that all I cared about was business, engineering, and natural sciences. The lofty arguments in favor of a liberal education are sound and true, but they often sail right over the heads of legislators. I always had better luck talking to legislators about inventions and factories and jobs. It is also a fact that when lawmakers voted to protect the engineering and computer science budgets, they also automatically voted to help the liberal arts—in some cases despite their own preferences. So I had little time for those perennial whiners who thought we emphasized economic development too much, at the expense of a supposedly more elevated vision of what higher education is all about. There were, of course, many experienced faculty members in the liberal arts such as Bob King and Betty Sue Flowers who understood how the "crass" economic argument was ultimately of great benefit to their programs.

White recognized the economic role of higher education in his State of the State speech to the legislature on January 15, 1985, at the beginning of the regular session of the 69th Texas Legislature, when he said that "research is the oil and gas of our future." Lieutenant Governor Bill Hobby also often demonstrated his keen understanding of the way university investment can pay off in economic diversification, as I have discussed in Chapter 18. On June 12, 1986, as everyone was bracing for a special legislative session to deal with the budget problems, Hobby addressed a meeting of the Texas Science and Technology Council in Dallas and made a forceful case for the need for Texas to expand its university research enterprise.

"There is good reason to believe that Texas is on the threshold of a period of development in entirely new directions," Hobby said. "Our great universities—both public and private—will be at the center of these new enterprises. We must make the necessary investments in these institutions so that we can properly manage and control our future. . . . The choice seems clear. Either we have the courage to invest in research and development at this key point in our history, or we abandon the enterprise and watch our state once again become, in the economic sense, a colony of the East and West coast financial and industrial centers."[2]

At that same conference, I had the opportunity to participate in a discussion of ways to improve the quantity and quality of research at Texas universities. One of the ideas that was adopted by the legislature had to do with the accounting for research grants. At that time all of the overhead funds the university received were "deducted" from its appropriations. Overhead was a real dollar cost, and the university needed the money to support the research enterprise. While this was not the sort of issue that was ever likely to capture the public imagination, it was a very important issue for UT Austin.[3]

By June 1986, it was clear that the state would not be able to balance its budget—or even pay its daily bills—without legislative action, and White called the legislature back for a special session, to begin on August 6.[4] I met in early July with the executive officers of UT Austin to discuss our legislative concerns and strategies. The notes that were prepared by a staff member after that meeting are highly revealing of our thinking at the time, and indicate that we focused on the following key issues: (1) University research and economic development, (2) UT Austin's mandate to become a "university of the first class," (3) UT Austin is not "fat," (4) excellence requires an investment, (5) politicians are focused on jobs, taxes, and votes, (6) politicians can be influenced by contributors, (7) UT and A&M "hearts must beat as one," (8) biotech and biomedical are critical to the state, and (9) which legislators attended UT or A&M and how loyal will they be.

On August 5, just two days before the start of the special session, Hay organized a legislative briefing—actually a campaign rally—of some four hundred friends of higher education. Gathered in the auditorium of the LBJ Library, the audience heard an impassioned speech by Hay denouncing the possibility of spending cuts of up to 34 percent at all state agencies and universities. Hay called this "a meat-axe approach" and said "all that we've done to enhance our programs would be negated in a single legislative act." The cuts, he said, would be a sign that Texas was retreating "to the backwaters of also-rans, content to reside there with recollections of a glorious past." Instead, he advocated a package of relatively small cuts in spending, together with a range of tax increases. His plan was basically the same as one advocated by Hobby, who had just been promoting it on a tour of seven Texas cities.

Hay told the audience to make sure they let their legislators know that they would have strong political support after voting for a tax increase. "We'll be there to support them in November when perhaps they may, in fact, be under attack by demagogues who would suggest dishonestly to the people of the state of Texas that there really is any other rational solution to the problem," Hay said.

I laid out for the audience as clearly as I could what drastic budget cuts could mean for UT Austin: a higher student-faculty ratio, fewer student scholarships, shorter library hours, an end to spring and summer admissions, reduction or cancellation of summer school, reductions in programs designed to broaden educational opportunity for the state's minority students, a dramatic slowdown in faculty recruiting, and an almost certain departure of many of the university's leading faculty members. "The heart and soul of the University of Texas at Austin and the University of Texas System are at risk," I told the group.

Other speakers included Peter O'Donnell Jr., a Dallas philanthropist and longtime supporter of higher education, who compared university research programs to a slow-growing but long-lasting tree and said budget cuts on the order of 34 percent would be like a chainsaw that would destroy years of effort in a few minutes. Bob Inman, then chairman of Microelectronics and Computer Technology Corp., told the audience that the development of high-tech industry in Texas depended on sustained support for university research. Reminding the audience that MCC, a national computer software consortium, had selected Austin as its home because of a perceived commitment to excellence in higher education, Inman observed: "Nobody said that commitment depends on oil continuing to sell at $30 a barrel."

Some eyebrows were raised by the fact that the university's leaders were openly advocating a tax increase and were organizing an effort to call and write lawmakers with the message that the budget crisis could not be solved with spending cuts alone. But Hay was confident about the wisdom and necessity of this approach. "Some would think we ought to relax and play dead, but we are looked to by the people of this state to nurture excellence. It really is obvious that there are not sufficient state revenues for that," he said.[5]

On August 6, the day after that meeting, the Ex-Students' Association took a step toward energizing one of UT Austin's greatest assets—its alumni—by sending to association leaders a four-page summary of the meeting and suggestions for how individual members of the association could help. The letter, from Executive Director Roy Vaughan, began with an urgent appeal for help: "The current budget crisis threatens the very existence of UT as a first class institution of higher learning. It is now time for those of us who care about the University to stand and be counted." His letter ended with a call to action, in which leaders of the association were urged to contact their friends in the legislature with a strong message of support for a tax increase as part of the solution to the budget crisis, and support later at the polls for those who voted for such a tax increase.[6]

In conjunction with that mailing, a special letter appealing for support was sent that week to the more than 150,000 UT alumni who lived in the state (35,000 in Travis County alone). The letter—signed by me, Hay, and association President Gordon Appleman—alerted the alumni to the threat to UT appropriations and advised them that we expected to be calling on them during the session for their support. These letters were early steps in organizing the formidable army of our alumni, so that we could put them into action if and when they were needed during the special session. That day came sooner than we expected.

When the special session opened, there were three budget proposals being discussed. The one advocated by Hobby would not have

Ex-Students' Association President Gordon Appleman and William H. Cunningham
with a scholarship recipient, fall 1985. *Courtesy of Gordon Appleman.*

required any cuts in the UT System beyond those planned under
White's executive order of the previous February (about $91 mil-
lion across the system). A plan put forward by the governor would
have required $25 million in additional budget cuts in the UT System,
beyond those mandated by his executive order. And a proposal from
House Speaker Gib Lewis would have resulted in additional cuts of
up to $30 million across the system, as well as the sacrifice of almost
$300 million from the Permanent University Fund. This proposed
"raid" on the PUF would have resulted in lower bond ratings and
a sharp reduction in the amount of money available for new buildings and other capital projects at all system institutions. Hobby's and
White's plans would have required tax increases to go along with
the spending cuts, but Lewis's proposal was aimed at making up the
state's revenue shortfall without any new taxes. Each of the three plans
would cancel a scheduled pay raise for state employees and would roll
back salaries to their level before the previous year's raises.[7] Hobby's
plan was the least damaging option for UT Austin. It would have cut
our general revenue appropriations for fiscal year 1987 by $12 mil-

lion (7.4 percent), which together with the cuts in general revenue that we had made in the second half of FY 1986 would have added up approximately to the 13 percent reductions called for in White's executive order. The most damaging proposal was Lewis's. It would have cut UT Austin's general revenue for 1987 by $55 million (34 percent) as well as seriously hampering our construction and renovation programs. There was no doubt which plan we favored.

During the second week of the special session I published in the *Houston Chronicle* an op-ed article in which I tried to explain what was at stake in the legislative deliberations and how budget cuts for higher education would have far-reaching effects on the economic health of the state.[8] I sought to leave no doubt about the fact that the quality of education provided to students at UT Austin and the ability of the university to help diversify the state's economy and create jobs were in serious jeopardy. And I directly challenged the view that our budget could easily be cut (by eliminating the so-called "fat") without harming the institution. I also reminded readers that we had some measure of success in recent years in recruiting highly talented junior faculty, but with budget cuts we would begin losing many of these people to other institutions, and would not be able to recruit senior faculty to fill endowed chairs and professorships. In addition, the result of failing to remain competitive in faculty salaries would be a decline in research grants and contracts, and students would experience larger classes, fewer scholarships, fewer counselors and other support staff, and shorter library hours.

I had prepared that article and sent it to the newspaper before one of the biggest legislative firestorms in the university's history struck. On August 11, the House Appropriations Committee included in its budget bill a plan that would have taken almost $298 million from the PUF to help close the budget gap for the current biennium. This was equal to all the capital gains of the fund for the previous five years. I don't know how these budget experts arrived at the five-year period, except that that would give them the amount of money they were seeking. The PUF was worth about $2.5 billion at the time, so the raid would have reduced its value by about 12 percent. Lewis was on record as supporting the plan, but fortunately White and Hobby came out against it, as did many other legislative leaders.[9]

I was in Dallas on August 11 in a meeting with Hay and Jere Thompson, the CEO of Southland Corporation and a longtime supporter of UT, when I got a call that the House Appropriations Committee had voted to include the raid in the bill. We had been aware that such plans were being talked about, but I didn't know lawmakers were really going to go forward with the idea until they voted on it. I talked to Hay about it, and we saw no option but to implement the plan that Roy Vaughan, Gordon Appleman, and others at the Ex-Students' Association had devised. This was the era before anyone had e-mail or cell phones, so they made ingenious use of traditional land-line telephones. By placing calls to a limited number of alumni, and having each of those persons call others on a list, and then repeating the process, the Ex-Students' Association quickly got word to thousands of alumni that it was time to call their legislators and demand that the PUF be protected. The one major problem with this technique was that once it was launched it was impossible to stop. Even if we were making progress in our budget negotiations, there was really nothing we could do to call off the operation.

On August 13, two days after the House Appropriations Committee had voted, more than three thousand phone calls and telegrams arrived from alumni and other university supporters to members of the House and Senate, as well as the offices of the Speaker, the lieutenant governor, and the governor. For three days the calls kept coming in, and the lights on Capitol telephones did not stop blinking as we shut down the Capitol telephone system in the process.[10] The alumni association at Texas A&M had also mailed 120,000 letters to former students and had begun a similar telephone campaign to oppose the raid on the PUF.

The urgent and blunt messages from alumni had an impact on the legislature, where many members had never seen that kind of outpouring of public sentiment or the obvious organizational abilities that were implied by all those phone calls. Also highly persuasive were the solid arguments against the raid that Michael Patrick, the UT System's executive vice chancellor for asset management, and Hay delivered at the Capitol. Perhaps the most telling argument was that the raid would violate the Texas Constitution, which specified that PUF expenditures were limited to "interest, dividends, and other income." If that were not enough, other arguments marshaled against the raid were that it would result in reducing the amount of interest earned by PUF investments; would result in lower ratings for construction bonds and thus an increase in the cost of borrowing; would make the sale of new bond issues more difficult because of the loss of the fund's credibility; and could result in lawsuits by bond holders charging breach of contract, since they had bought the bonds with the understanding that all capital gains would be reinvested in the PUF. It would be hard to imagine a less wise public policy proposed by the House Appropriations Committee, or one that was more politically unfeasible.[11]

On August 12, I briefed deans and other faculty and administrators on the state of affairs in the legislature. My message was simple and to the point—the university faced serious threats but there was no reason to panic. I told them that UT Austin had a great deal of support, and the alumni were behind us. I also emphasized that the business community, as well as many of the most powerful people in the state, were on our side. I concluded by saying, "I am confident that everything will work out all right, but it's going to be scary for a while."[12] I felt like a general whose primary responsibility was to try to keep morale up among the troops.

Hay and I were asked to meet with Gib Lewis and Mike Millsap, who was Lewis's chief of staff, on August 15 in Lewis's office. Lewis had come to realize that the political realities were such that it would not be possible to "raid" the PUF, and he had a new plan that would not require a tax increase—for the university to "loan" the state enough money to help solve the budget problem. Hay looked at Lewis in a deadpan manner and said he thought this might be possible but UT would require collateral. Lewis asked what collateral Hay had in mind, and Hay replied, "The State Capitol building." Lewis got the point. The new plan was dead on arrival.

The campaign against the raid on the PUF as well as against deep budget cuts was joined on the same day Hay and I met with Lewis and Millsap by students at UT Austin and several other UT System campuses. Andrew Chin, the president of the student government at UT Austin, and other student body presidents across the state announced their own letter-writing and telephone campaign against the cuts and in support of a tax increase. Later, students staged a march from the West Mall to the Capitol to dramatize their position.

The August special session ended without a final resolution of the budget problems. The two houses of the legislature were more than $300 million apart in their approach to the problem, with the Senate favoring spending cuts of $418 million and the House holding out for

$740 million in cuts. White promptly called another session to begin on September 8. The comptroller issued a new revenue estimate that now placed the shortfall at $2.3 billion for the rest of the biennium.

In the September session, lawmakers took up where they had left off, and most observers simplified the debate as a contest between Lewis, who remained adamant against any tax increases, and Hobby, who favored a combination of tax increases and budget cuts. In his anti-tax position, Lewis was perceived as reflecting the viewpoint of most House members, but it was also widely understood that he could lead those members to vote for a tax bill if he chose to. The gubernatorial and legislative elections were only two months away, and this may well have influenced the stalemate over the budget. Lewis's Fort Worth district had voted for Ronald Reagan in 1984 by 79 percent, and Lewis had a Republican opponent who was actively campaigning, something that was still a novelty in many Texas legislative districts. In the race for governor, Bill Clements was said to be far ahead of White, and people who wanted to characterize the contest in terms of taxes could point to White's support for small tax increases in the first special session and Clements' "no new taxes" slogan.[13]

Lewis and others kept insisting that higher education was "crying wolf" about the damage that would be done by deep cuts, and they frequently argued that reductions could be absorbed in many agencies after a long period of rapid growth in the state budget. They cited, for example, that annual state spending had grown from $6.2 billion in 1976 to $16.3 billion in 1985—a 163 percent increase in a time when the state's population had grown just 28 percent.

Hay picked up the challenge of those numbers and threw them back at the "no new taxes" supporters. He translated the total budget figures into expenditures per capita and adjusted the 1987 figure for inflation and mandatory expenditures since 1976. This resulted in an annual average increase of less than three-eighths of 1 percent since 1976. Hay's calculations clearly showed that state government had not been on a runaway spending spree.[14]

By the third week of September, it had become clear to Lewis and others in the House that a tax increase of some form was going to be necessary in order to at least patch up the state budget well enough to last until after the election and until the legislature came back for its regular session in January.

There were other factors at work. At one point in the special ses-

From left, William and Isabella Cunningham, Jere and Peggy Thompson, and Wales and Abbie Madden at the Thompsons' home in Beaver Creek, Colorado, after the 1986 legislative session. *Courtesy of William H. Cunningham.*

sion, I called Perry Bass to see if he could help us. Bass and I discussed the university's financial predicament on several occasions. He understood the role that higher education and UT Austin needed to play in helping the state diversify its economy. At the time, Bass was on a hunting trip in a remote area of Africa, but he had left word with his Fort Worth office that if I called, his lobbyists were to do anything they could to help support the university. I explained our problem to one of Bass's lobbyists who indicated that he would be pleased to call Lewis to make sure he understood Bass's position with respect to higher education. This was all that I could ask, and it demonstrated one more time how Perry and Nancy Lee Bass loved UT Austin and understood its role in the state.

The September session resulted in a tax bill that raised the basic sales tax rate by 1 and ⅛ percent to a total of 5¼ percent, raised fuel taxes from 10 cents per gallon to 15 cents, and provided for additional local-option sales taxes. The taxes were scheduled to expire on September 1, 1987, so the next session of the legislature would have to revisit the same issues. The special session also incorporated in the state budget the spending cuts that agencies had made under White's executive order and adopted other finance and accounting measures that helped bring the deficit to "a manageable level," as the Legislative Budget Board put it.[15] That meant that a deficit of only about $980 million remained for the rest of the fiscal year, which ran through the next August.

For the UT System the final outcome was a reduction in general revenue appropriations of about 13.2 percent for FY 1987. The total reduction was $107 million for the biennium, about $16 million more than had been cut in response to White's executive order. Hay called these reductions "serious but not devastating." In a press release summarizing the work of the two special sessions of 1986, Hay commented: "To members and observers of the national academic and research community we say that it would be premature and unwise to eliminate Texas from the intense competition for national and international ranking. The current deficit problem has resulted in the perception of a temporary slowing of our quest for excellence, but we fully believe that the leadership of this State has not abandoned it historic commitment to higher education and will, at the earliest opportunity, provide the resources essential to a full scale and unrestrained pursuit of excellence in the delivery of educational, research, and patient care services. All interested observers should know that we remain on course and that we are still fully committed to providing the very best academic environment in the nation."[16]

On November 13, 1986, White rescinded the portions of his executive order having to do with budget cuts and the hiring freeze, but he left in place the provisions relating to efforts to search out cost-savings in utility contracts, purchasing, and other support operations. White declared that the September 1986 special session of the 69th Legislature "successfully completed a series of budget reduction, accounting, and revenue measures which address the immediate budget deficit and cash flow problems of the State of Texas." In about two months, the 70th Legislature and a new governor, Bill Clements, would pick up where the 69th and White had left off.

The real victory of 1986 was not that we had been successful in reducing the budget cuts to a "manageable" level, but that we had fought off a serious attempt by the Texas Legislature to "raid" the Permanent University Fund. Shirley Bird Perry had always told us that once every two or three generations UT would be called upon to do whatever was necessary to protect the PUF. We all knew that without the PUF, UT Austin would lose any hopes it had to become a world-class university and the UT System would lose much of its independence. I was determined not to be the president of UT Austin who lost the PUF. Hay, Mark, Appleman, and all of Hay's colleagues on the board of regents were equally determined not to permit the university to be destroyed under their watch. We knew that we needed not only to defeat the proposed raid, but we had to inflict pain on the politicians who favored the raid so that our victory and their pain would be remembered for many years to come. That sounds arrogant, but that was our strategy, and there has not been another attempt to raid the PUF in the ensuing quarter of a century.

CHAPTER 23

The Budget Crisis Continues

A s a result of the election in November 1986, Bill Clements returned to the Governor's Office in January 1987 after a four-year hiatus. I had met Clements on several occasions during his first term as governor, when I was associate dean of business. He was always brash and to the point, and I found that rather refreshing for a politician.

The governor of Texas nominates the members of the numerous state boards and commissions that are ultimately responsible for the operation of large segments of state government. While some governors have done a better job in selecting members of the Board of Regents of the UT System than others, I am sure they all have taken this responsibility quite seriously. If an individual is a graduate or supporter of UT, the appointment to the board is a distinct honor and a highly sought-after appointment. Governors frequently appoint friends and/or major financial contributors to the board. These people usually are sophisticated individuals who are quick studies, and, with a few exceptions, the ones appointed during my time were a pleasure to work with.

Clements had a reputation during his first term of making excellent appointments, and he continued this during his second term. His first three appointments to the board of regents during his second term (in March 1987) were Sam Barshop, Louis Beecherl, and W. A. "Tex" Moncrief Jr., each of whom served with distinction. His next three appointments (in February 1989) were Robert Cruikshank, Tom Loeffler, and Mario Ramirez. Once again, Clements did all he could do to help UT by appointing thoughtful, sophisticated individuals who cared deeply about higher education. As I will discuss below, Clements may have appointed stronger, more dedicated and more independent-minded individuals than he had expected.

During my presidency, one of Ed Sharpe's many jobs included

functioning as head of government relations for UT Austin. When the 70th Legislature convened in January 1987, Sharpe and I realized it was not enough for me to have a good working relationship with the governor, lieutenant governor, and House Speaker. I also needed to get acquainted with as many members of the Senate and leaders of the House of Representatives as possible. Our theory was that if we took time to meet the members of the legislature in their offices at the beginning of the session we would have a better chance of working with them as the session unfolded.

Sharpe and I were political novices, but our strategy worked out well, with one dramatic exception. One of the most eye-opening and memorable of our get-acquainted visits was with Senator Chris Harris of Arlington. When we walked into his office, Harris immediately began a profanity-laced attack. This is the only time I ever met with an elected official who acted in this manner. It turned out that Harris was known for having a bad temper and being a bully, and he treated many state officials in that manner. Sharpe and I were stunned, and when we left we agreed that we would never go back to see Harris again. As long as I was president or chancellor, I did my best to make sure that no courtesies were extended to Harris. I later surmised that Harris may have had me confused with Wendell Nedderman, who served for many years as president of UT Arlington. Nedderman and Harris had had several run-ins. I am tall and somewhat bald, as is Nedderman, and when I was introduced by a staff member as the president of "UTA," Harris may have thought I was UT Arlington's president. Perhaps he never really took a good look at either one of us. Harris's bizarre behavior did not scare me away from trying to make friends with other members of the legislature or going to the Capitol to ask for support for higher education and UT Austin.

The actions of the September 1986 special session had fixed the problems with the state's tax and cash flow for the time being, but as the Legislative Budget Board stated, "the next Legislature would start work on the 1988–89 budget 'in the hole' and with an impending 1988 cash flow crisis."[1] It was very clear to everyone at UT Austin and the UT System that we would face a new round of challenges when the 70th Legislature convened in January. We expected that the debate would cover much of the same ground, and Bob Bullock's first revenue estimate confirmed these fears and more. The state still needed $1 billion to balance the books in fiscal year 1987 and $5

billion more to continue the current level of state services, meet statu-
tory requirements, and comply with federal mandates for the next
biennium (fiscal years 1988 and 1989). Seven months later, after the
regular session and two special sessions, the legislature would pass,
and Clements would sign, despite his campaign pledge of "no new
taxes," the largest tax increase in Texas history. Getting to that point
was not easy, to say the least.

Jess Hay remained as chairman at the beginning of the 70th legislative session. Nothing had changed from the previous year. Hay
was spending four or five days a week in Austin advocating for UT
Austin, higher education, and tax increases, and I was fully vested
in his program. Hay firmly believed that university research and economic development were inextricably linked. On numerous occasions,
Hay invited members of the legislature to accompany me, Shirley Bird
Perry, and him to attend presentations by Bill Weldon, who was in
charge of the university's homopolar generator and rail-gun research
programs at Balcones Research Center. Weldon would explain how
the homopolar generator could produce more energy in a flash of a
second than Austin used in a month and how the rail gun could launch
a projectile into space. Weldon was working on a new-generation electric tank gun that could destroy its opponent using kinetic energy. He
was always impressive and persuasive in these presentations.

Hay and I would emphasize to lawmakers that the homopolar generator was just one example of what could be accomplished if the university was properly funded. On most nights when the legislature was
in session, Perry and I would accompany Hay to the Headliners Club
for dinner, where he would give a pitch to two or three legislators
about higher education and the need to increase taxes. At some point
Hay would turn to me and ask me to explain the homopolar generator. While I had no idea what a homopolar generator was before I
met Bill Weldon, I had heard enough of Weldon's presentations that I
could talk the talk at 50,000 feet.

Hay understood the need to build strong personal relationships
with as many members of the legislature as possible. He also understood the need to create a broad coalition to support higher education. He met many times with the board chairmen of Texas A&M
and the other universities and junior colleges in Texas. We knew there
would be a very positive impact if all institutions of higher education
would stick together. However, higher education in Texas consists of

a larger number of diverse and independent entities, and all the others happen to be jealous of UT Austin and the UT System to one extent or another. I remember one occasion in February 1987 when Hay called a meeting of higher education officials from across the state. Hay knew exactly what he wanted and what he was going to do, but he played perfectly the role of the host who wanted to understand what his guests wanted in the plan that was to be presented to the legislature. After a little more than an hour of discussion, with all the officials participating vigorously, Hay got up and left the room. I followed him out and he said, "I hate democracy." Hay was used to being in charge, but he was an expert at playing the part of the coalescing agent. Perry and I called his efforts the "Grand Coalition" or the "Hay Ride." Two of Hay's basic concepts—focusing on politicians one at a time and building a coalition of support among competing institutions of higher education—became key principles of mine in every legislative session in which I was involved. I know that UT was accused at times of being arrogant and uncooperative, but I believe we tried very hard to be team players if for no other reason than that we recognized it was clearly in our best interest to do so.

The UT Board of Regents was going through a very dramatic evolution during this time. Clements and Hay were both from Dallas, but they represented different political parties and philosophies, and they did not get along well. Soon after his election, it was clear that Clements would have preferred to have Hay removed from his position as chairman. However, Clements at first accepted the advice of Regent Tom Rhodes, his longtime friend and business associate, to encourage other board members to vote for Hay for another term as chairman.

At the first meeting of the board after newly appointed members have been confirmed by the Senate, the board traditionally elects its chairman, vice chairman, and the chairmen of its standing committees. When there is a mixture of Republicans and Democrats on the board, the regents from the party with the majority of seats selects the officers and everyone goes along and votes for them. It is a very collegial process and takes only a few minutes in closed session for the board to confirm its decision, at which point the board will vote officially in public.

In February 1987, the board was composed of six regents appointed by White and the three who had just been appointed by Clements. By then, Hay had been quoted again in newspaper articles stating his aggressive position regarding the upcoming budget battle and the related need for a tax increase, and Clements informed Hay that he was withdrawing his earlier support for him as chairman and would back, instead, the candidacy of Jack S. Blanton, another Democrat but one whom Clements apparently thought he could work better with.

Clements had met with Blanton, who was on good terms with many Republicans, and told him that the new Republican regents that he had just appointed, plus one other Democratic appointee, would vote for him if he would agree to run against Hay for chairman. This would give Blanton five votes and Hay four, and Blanton agreed to the deal.

The board met on April 9, 1987, at M. D. Anderson Cancer Center's Science Park in Smithville, east of Austin, where it was dedicating a conference center in honor of Jake Pickle. The board met in executive session for over two hours to discuss the election of officers. All of us waiting outside the meeting room knew something had gone wrong with the process because it usually does not take more than a few minutes to count to five. When the board finally reconvened in open session it was clear that the members had not been able to select a chairman. The collegiality of all-for-one and one-for-all was gone.

Hay convened the meeting and asked each of the members how they were going to vote on the chairmanship. When Hay came to Sam Barshop, he "passed." The vote was four to four, and Hay asked Barshop again who he was voting for. Barshop was a lifelong Republican and a strong supporter of Clements. However, he chose to abstain a second time. Hay then ruled that he would remain as chairman until the board selected a new one. When Tex Moncrief stated that the board's rules called for the selection of new officers at the February board meeting, Hay said, "The regents make the rules, the regents change the rules. Next issue."

Barshop knew exactly what he was doing. While he had never met Hay before joining the board, he had a great deal of respect for what Hay had accomplished during the special sessions in 1986. He was convinced that it would be better for UT if Hay remained as the chairman through the 1987 session. That evening, Barshop received a call from George Bayoud, Clements's chief of staff, who was very upset and told Barshop that the governor was furious and wanted to talk with him. But then Bayoud came back to the phone a few moments later and said Clements did not want to talk with him after all.

Sam Barshop, Isabella Cunningham, and Ann Barshop at Bauer House, c. 1994. *Courtesy of William H. Cunningham.*

Barshop taught all of us a lesson that day. He made it clear that UT was more important to him than his relationship with the governor who had just appointed him. Throughout the board's history, the great regents inevitably have to disagree with the governor who appointed them, and Barshop was certainly one of the university's great regents.

The issue of whether Hay or Blanton was going to be elected chairman that February was really of little importance, so long as the board remained united in its dedication to the best interests of the UT System and its institutions. Despite the governor's preference for Blanton, there was never any doubt about that fundamental unity within the board. This unwavering focus on the welfare of the UT System was always the greatest strength of the board of regents, and in this regard Clements's new appointees in 1987—Barshop, Beecherl, and Moncrief—were among the most dedicated regents in the history of the board. The same can be said of his 1989 appointees—Cruikshank, Loeffler, and Ramirez. With that caliber of individual as regents, a governor really cannot "pull the strings" on various decisions that come before the board.

The battle over the chairmanship was ultimately settled two months later. Throughout the legislative session, the board had supported Hay's ultimately successful efforts to increase funding of higher education, and, with the battle won, Hay withdrew his name from consideration at the June meeting and Blanton was elected unanimously as the new chairman.

Unfortunately, the budget battle in the 70th legislative session did not play out as quickly or easily as the fight over the regents' chairmanship. Clements was initially against a tax increase, while Hobby supported one, and Gib Lewis was somewhere in the middle. I attended a number of legislative budget hearings of the Senate Finance and House Appropriations Committees that spring. The routine was always the same. Hay and Chancellor Hans Mark would make presentations about the need to enhance the higher education budget so that the institutions could help diversify the state's economy and improve the quality of life for all Texans. These were always uplifting and eloquent presentations, and they were usually well received. My job, along with the presidents of the other institutions in the UT System, was to answer specific questions from lawmakers. These ranged from why UT Austin did not have more minority students to when were we going to buy a new bus for McDonald Observatory. It always seemed to me that I was asked more than half of all the questions, but rarely was I asked what it would take to build UT into a great research university. UT Austin was clearly the big institution that many legislators either loved or hated.

I had a great deal of confidence in Mark and his governmental relations team at the UT System. However, I knew they had other institutions to worry about, while my sole concern was UT Austin. Unfortunately, it was apparent that the legislature might ultimately refuse to pass a tax increase and fund higher education appropriately. I had always felt that if the state's budget ever got into really serious problems we could raise tuition again, above the schedule of annual increases that had been approved by the legislature in 1985. In 1987, the total UT Austin undergraduate tuition and mandatory fees was $29 per credit hour and it was probably 50 percent less than tuition and fees at comparable institutions.

I asked former UT Austin presidents Pete Flawn and Norm Hackerman to go with me to meet with Hobby on May 14, 1987, to discuss the possibility of giving UT Austin the authority to immediately double its tuition above the current rate—and "keep" the money rather than have it count against the university's state appropriations. Flawn and Hackerman understood my logic and readily agreed to attend the meeting. Hobby asked Senator Carl Parker, chairman of the Education Committee, and Senator Grant Jones, chairman of the Finance Committee, to participate. I made the pitch that tuition was well below competitive institutions in other states and if Texas could not fund higher education adequately we needed to be able to increase tuition and keep the money. I told Hobby and the senators that the UT administration and the board of regents could take the political heat for the legislature because it would only be passing enabling legislation while the actual tuition increase would come from the campus administrators and the regents.

Hobby would hear none of my arguments. He wanted nothing to do with any new flexibility in tuition for undergraduates. He felt the state had an obligation to provide a low-cost undergraduate education to its citizens, and he thought it would be a political disaster to raise tuition beyond the increases that had already been approved. He told me it was politically more difficult to pass a tuition increase than a tax increase, and he was definitely not persuaded by my argument that the administration and the board of regents would take the heat since they were the ones that would actually set tuition under my proposal.

Hobby did not resist when it came to raising tuition for graduate students. He thought that giving the university flexibility with respect to graduate tuition was an idea that deserved serious consideration, and Parker and Jones agreed. Jones agreed a few days later to put language in the committee's appropriations bill that gave universities the flexibility to double graduate tuition and keep the additional revenue. The graduate tuition language in the Senate Finance Committee bill ultimately passed the legislature with little discussion. I did point out that almost half of our graduate students were from outside Texas. The obvious implications were that they could afford to pay a significantly higher rate, that they and their parents had not been paying taxes in Texas, and that most of them did not vote in Texas. There was relatively little political downside to my proposal and a lot of upside financially for the university.

The 1987 regular session ended in deadlock. The legislature was not able to pass a budget without a tax increase, but the governor was not willing to support a tax increase. Clements called the legislature back into special session on June 2.

As president of UT Austin, I was not usually involved in tax bills. I used to say with some pleasure to members of the legislature that it was my job to propose funding, and it was their job to provide the funds. However, in this case, it became clear to me as the legislature entered its second special session in the summer on June 22 that I needed to try to help pass the tax bill. If there was no tax bill, there would be no additional general revenue funds for higher education. I met with Mike Millsap, whose boss, Lewis, had become a convert that spring for tax increases. He knew that the only way to solve the state's fiscal problems was to pass several broad-based taxes. Millsap asked me to contact eight to ten members of the legislature who he thought might respond positively to my encouragement to support the leadership's tax bill. I called each of these members and asked several leaders in their home communities who were true "orange bloods" also to call them. Local power brokers will usually trump university officials in the eyes of politicians.

I have no idea if my efforts helped persuade even one person to vote for the tax bill. However, I was determined to do anything I could to lay out for the politicians the ramifications of *not* passing a tax bill. In one case my efforts backfired. I talked to R. C. Allen of Corpus Christi, a good friend of mine and a great supporter of UT, and told him I was very disappointed with state Representative Todd Hunter's position on the tax bill. R. C. called Hunter and told him that UT was very unhappy with him and that he should vote for the bill. In the end, Hunter did support the bill, but he was very upset with me. The two lessons for me were that even sophisticated friends of UT often need "coaching" before they deliver a message and that pressure from hometown supporters often works.

The appropriations bill for the 1988–1989 biennium that was finally approved that summer raised state spending almost 6 percent, to $39.5 billion. It required $5.7 billion in new tax revenues, an increase in the statewide sales tax to 6 percent, expansion of the sales tax base, and increases in numerous other taxes.[2] As a result, the sales tax for the first time accounted for more than half of all state revenues. Texas colleges and universities received an aggregate increase of 11.8 percent in general revenue appropriations, while the total of all appropriated funds, including tuition revenue, increased by 6.8 percent. At UT Austin, general revenue appropriations grew 12.5 percent.

Clements, to say the least, was never enthusiastic about the tax increases, but he did eventually withdraw an early threat to veto any increases, thereby allowing increased funding for higher education to become law. The legislature probably could not have overridden a veto, so this was a crucial decision by Clements. I believe he was influenced by the compelling arguments made to him by Peter O'Donnell Jr. O'Donnell, a former chairman of the Republican Party of Texas as well as a great visionary leader on the important role of higher education to the social and economic well-being of Texas, deserved credit for presenting cogent arguments to Clements, and Clements deserves credit for listening.

Many others also played key roles in the final approval of the tax bill and the increased appropriations that it made possible. Many of the young, very conservative Republicans in the House vowed to oppose Clements, Lewis, and Hobby to pass the tax bill. Beecherl came to Austin at my request on several occasions to meet with these Republicans to try to persuade them to be flexible and support an increase in the sales tax. He was frustrated in a number of these efforts, but he did all he could do to help the state pass a tax bill.

The legislature also established two peer-reviewed grant programs for science and technology research, with funding of $59.5 million. In the first year of the program, 1987, UT Austin was awarded 29 percent of the total awards and through the years, UT Austin research faculty remained highly competitive for the grants. From 1987 through 2000, UT Austin researchers garnered awards for a total of $101.3 million. This equaled approximately 23 percent of the funds awarded to all eligible Texas institutions of higher education and more than one-half of the grants awarded to all UT component institutions.

The graduate tuition bill largely flew under the radar until the fall of 1987. I told the deans in the summer that if they wanted to give any raises to their faculty effective in fall 1987 they would have to fund them out of increases in their graduate student tuition. Only Dean Robert Witt in the College of Business and Dean Mark Yudof in the School of Law agreed to increase the tuition of their students to support faculty raises in their colleges. The reactions of the two student groups was very interesting. The student government leaders in the Graduate School of Business thanked me and encouraged me to add additional "user fees" so that the college could attract more and better faculty and take other steps to improve the quality of education offered to the students. The law students threatened to sue me.

When I met with the deans a year later in the spring of 1988, I told them that, once again, they would have to fund faculty raises out of increases in graduate tuition. It was clear to me that they had met and, with the exception of Witt and Yudof, they were going to hold the line and not increase tuition. I told them I was "proud of them" and I was also very concerned about putting any additional financial pressure on their graduate students. I concluded the meeting by telling the deans that I would like each of them to explain to their faculty why they had elected not to give them raises. As I adjourned

Mark Yudof, Page Keeton, and William H. Cunningham at Bauer House celebrating Keeton's birthday. *Photo by Cary Hazlegrove, copy courtesy of William H. Cunningham.*

the meeting I told the deans that I would approve significant raises for the faculty in the College of Business and the School of Law. By noon the next day each of the other deans had called me and said they had reconsidered their positions and would be recommending tuition increases for their graduate students, along with pay raises for their faculty. The deans' coalition against tuition increases had collapsed.

The balanced budget produced by the 70th Legislature was to prove to be only a temporary relief. As the Legislative Budget Board put it with masterful understatement: "The tax system that emerged from measures passed by the Seventieth Legislature is not widely viewed as a long-term solution to the state's revenue needs."[3] For the state to provide the current level of services in the next biennium that would begin on September 1, 1989, $1.1 billion more in general revenue would be required than the state was forecast to have on hand. Once again, the chief culprit was low oil prices. Oil was selling for about $12 a barrel in November 1988, and Bullock's revenue forecast was based on the assumption that it would climb to only $17.50 by the end of the next biennium.

The result was that after a great deal of work by the UT System's governmental relations staff, with the support of the board of regents, UT Austin and the rest of Texas higher education had a reasonably successful legislative session in 1989. General revenue appropriations for state universities rose 12.6 percent. At UT Austin, however, general revenue was increased only 7.8 percent.[4] Despite the relatively modest gain in appropriated general revenue, total expenditures for UT Austin ultimately increased by 16 percent for the biennium. Within the appropriations were dollars for staff and faculty pay raises. The money for faculty helped continue the trend of recovering the ground that was lost as a result of budget cuts from 1985 to 1987. In the early 1980s, the state had actually come within reach of the average for faculty salaries in the ten most populous states, and by 1984 Texas was only 3 percent below that average. But the gap grew to 8.3 percent in 1985 and then to 15.7 percent by 1987 before the trend turned around again. It was estimated that the state was 10.8 percent below the average in 1988 and 9.6 percent below in 1989.[5]

Also during this session, the legislature transferred Pan American University in Edinburg and its Brownsville campus to the UT System. This was a great accomplishment for Chancellor Hans Mark and Jim Duncan, the executive vice chancellor for academic affairs. In addition, as chairman of the board of regents, Blanton also invested a great deal of time and energy to make this happen. We were also lucky that Duncan, Mark, and Blanton had three very honorable and reasonable people to deal with—Miguel Nevárez, president of Pan American University, Juliet Garcia, president of Brownsville Junior College, and Mary Rose Cardenas, chair of the board of trustees of Texas Southmost College. Nevárez and Garcia continued as president of, respectively, UT Pan American and UT Brownsville. The stage that was set by these leaders made it possible for the UT System several years later to push the South Texas/Border Initiative through the legislature.

I had a very interesting and productive interaction with Clements in October 1989 when he called and said he wanted to come to my office that afternoon for a meeting. I immediately demurred and said that I would go to his office, but he insisted on coming to the campus. I told Connie Saathoff and Joyce Moos to "clean up the office, the governor is on his way."

Clements brought with him the director of the Normandy Foundation. Clements was very interested in history, and he had become a supporter of efforts to create and support an academic program in Normandy to further the study of the Allied invasion in World War II. I sat there and listened attentively. I was saying to myself, "Where is this going," when Clements said he would like UT Austin to develop a Normandy Scholars Program, through which we could work with the foundation to send students and faculty to Normandy to study the history of World War II.

I told Clements that this sounded like a very exciting program, but we did not have the funds to support it. This had become my standard response to governors—a great idea, but we have no money. This was a bit of an exaggeration, but it normally worked quite well. I am sure we could have found the money somewhere, but our budget was very tight as a result of the ongoing state budget crisis, and the money for this new program would have had to come out of some less glamorous, but probably more worthy, project. Clements said, "Don't worry about the money. I will raise the money, you design the program." I said okay.

I asked Bill Livingston to develop the program. I used Livingston a number of times to head up special projects, and, as usual, he did an excellent job with this one. The program he designed was first class. We had an excellent faculty, and UT paid for the transportation and

William H. Cunningham and Texas Governor Bill Clements at a Normandy Scholars press conference, February 1990. UT *Office of Public Affairs Records, e_uto-pa_00051.*

housing of all the students as well as the salaries and expenses of the faculty.

Clements asked me if I would go to Dallas to meet with him and some potential donors to the program. On January 16, 1990, we met over lunch with Perry Bass, Peter O'Donnell Jr., Louis Beecherl, and Tex Moncrief—any one of whom could have funded the program by himself. Clements introduced the topic, and I made the pitch about what an exciting program we were entering into. I mentioned that all the students would be given a scholarship to pay for their travel and living expenses in France and we would also be sending faculty members from the Department of History, both to supervise the students (I doubt they did much of this) and to give lectures on World War II (I am confident they did this). I explained that the total annual cost of the program would be approximately $350,000.

When I finished my comments I turned it back to Clements for the close—but there was no close. He thanked our guests for coming and we all left. I did not understand what had happened, but I assumed Clements was going to call the lunch participants privately and ask them to contribute. It was not my job to tell Clements how to raise money; I assumed he was very good at raising money. I would have been happy to make these calls myself, but Clements did not ask me to do so.

Several months later the program was coming rapidly to maturity. We had selected the faculty and students and had made most of the logistical arrangements, but we still had no money to pay for transportation, housing, and all the other costs of the program. I finally decided to call Clements and ask him when we could expect to receive the cash, but when I reached his office I discovered he had gone to Africa. I left a message with his chief of staff, Mike Toomey, that I was concerned that we did not have any private money to support the program.

Clements called me a few days later. He said, "Bill, I told you not to worry about the money." I said, "Governor, that is good enough for me." What else could I say? We proceeded with final plans for the program. At this point I felt that UT would have to fund the Normandy Scholars Program out of our own pocket. I was not going to get into an argument with the governor of Texas over $350,000. A few days before the students were to leave I received a hand-delivered personal check for $350,000 from Bill and Rita Clements to fund the entire program. Clements was certainly a man of his word, and I greatly appreciated this generous donation.

When that spring's group of thirty-four students returned from Normandy we had a party at our home on April 25 to thank Governor and Mrs. Clements for their very generous gift. Almost all the students attended the dinner, and we had a great time. The students told stories about the wonderful time they had in Normandy learning about World War II and French culture. They were thrilled to meet the governor and first lady of Texas, and I believe Governor and Mrs. Clements enjoyed hearing all about the great adventure that they had made possible. Unfortunately, student fees now make up a much larger percentage of the funding of the Normandy Scholars Program than they did originally. This seems to be a pattern that began in the budget crisis of the 1980s and has continued to this day throughout the university.

CHAPTER 24

The New Grand Coalition

On my first day as chancellor, Charles Mullins and Dan Burck came rushing into my office. They told me the regents were just about to sell to Jim Duncan the UT-owned home that he had been living in and it was going to appear to be a "sweetheart" deal. The question was—was I willing, on my first day on the job, to tell my former boss, Duncan, and my new bosses on the board of regents that they were about to make a terrible mistake?

It took me only a few seconds to decide I needed to do the right thing. My backbone may have been strengthened by the fact that Mullins and Burck were looking me in the eye to determine if I was going to pass my first test—to see if I was big enough to be the chancellor of the University of Texas System. I went across the street and pulled Louis Beecherl, the chairman of the board of regents, out of a board committee meeting. I told him that without sufficient independent appraisals the sale was not going to look good no matter how meritorious everyone's motives were. It did not take Beecherl more than a nanosecond to understand the issue, and the sale of the house was pulled down from the agenda. The house was eventually sold to someone with no connections to the university.

Once I passed my first test, I spent the next few weeks (with emphasis on "few") enjoying my honeymoon period. Politicians, state officials, and university officials whom I had not met wanted a chance to meet me. I also attended a number of social events at the campuses where I was introduced to community leaders and campus administrators. While I was doing my best to listen to their concerns and understand their priorities, I was also expected to deliver a well considered speech that clarified the UT System's position on a variety of issues while also expressing my total support for the local institutional president and his or her aspirations. For the most part, this was not a burden, but it did take a fair amount of time.

While I was running around the state being UT System Ambassador No. 1, I also recognized that I needed to develop a strategy for dealing with the 1993 legislative session, which was going to convene in a very short five months. Mike Millsap and I had talked extensively and we were determined to follow Jess Hay's precedent of forging a broad coalition that could create the political will in the legislature to address the state's long-term needs in higher education. We also knew that by virtue of its size and political strength, the UT System would have to be the key organizing force behind any such coalition, and that meant persuading the other university systems, community colleges, and private institutions that we could all benefit more by working together than by going our separate ways. It was never easy to get all the UT System schools to work toward the same political agenda, and Millsap and I knew it would be even more difficult to get all the rest of higher education to focus on one strategy. The members of the higher education community can be very jealous of their not-so-friendly in-state competitors—one institution's best interest may not always be another's.

Unfortunately, my best-laid plans to develop a strong higher education coalition in the fall of 1992 were overtaken by events. The event was a meeting in Bullock's office, which I describe in detail in Chapter 26, that propelled me, Millsap, and the entire UT governmental relations team into a frenzy that lasted until June 1993, when Governor Richards signed the bills that funded and approved the South Texas/ Border Initiative. Bullock's focus on South Texas effectively destroyed my goal for the moment of developing a long-term strategic plan that would be embraced by the majority of higher education institutions in Texas. We moved instantly from strategy to tactics. Gone was the big picture, the grand Jess Hay strategic coalition. We were knee-deep in tactical planning regarding how we could find the right mix of senators and representatives to tackle one of the state's most pressing problems—equitable higher education programs for South Texas. A contributing factor to the unusual nature of the 1993 session was that the Senate convened outside the Capitol building for the only time in modern history, while portions of the Capitol were being restored. The Senate met in an office building on 15th Street four blocks from the Capitol, while the House was able to stay in its Capitol chamber,

University Outreach Center in McAllen. William H. Cunningham with President William Mobley of Texas A&M and Regent Mario Yzaguirre, September 28, 1988. *UT Office of Public Affairs Records, e_utopa_00019.*

so that kept everybody a little out of sync and made legislative business that much more difficult to conduct.

I instinctively knew that UT needed to get along with Texas A&M. A&M was a first-rate university and, unlike many UT people, I had never developed an "us versus them" attitude with respect to the Aggies. In addition, A&M President Bill Mobley was a trusted friend. Mobley and I had been contemporaries as members of our respective business school faculties and then as associate deans, deans, and presidents of our institutions. We had worked together at each level in our administrative careers in a positive and constructive manner.

Herb Richardson was the chancellor of the Texas A&M System, and he was an honest and professional academic executive. The Cunningham/Millsap hopes of having a grand coalition were going to have to be satisfied during the January 1993 session just by having UT and A&M work together as closely as possible. This was not as broad a coalition as I wanted, but it was an acceptable compromise, and clearly Texas A&M was always our most important partner in any coalition that we were ever going to be able to build. Richardson and I met regularly during the session, and we did support each other's efforts.

Mobley was appointed chancellor of the A&M System in September 1993. While I knew Mobley would have a lot on his plate, I was confident that once he was finished with his initial rounds of speaking and campus visits, the UT and A&M systems would be able to sit down and develop a thoughtful strategic plan for higher education that would eventually incorporate Texas Tech, the University of Houston, and all the other universities and community colleges in the state. Unfortunately for these plans, the musical chairs continued at A&M. Mobley was out in September 1994 and Barry Thompson was in as the new chancellor. Mobley never had a chance to hit his stride as chancellor, and my hopes for a grand coalition were dead again.

Thompson had been president of West Texas State, later named West Texas A&M. He did not have Mobley's panache. The first time we met for lunch at the Headliners Club, Thompson told me a story about a fistfight he had in the eighth grade. Mobley and I never discussed altercations on the playground. In addition, as a former president of one of the A&M System's smaller schools, Thompson felt that the A&M regents had shown favoritism toward College Station. This was probably accurate, but it was well beyond my scope of interest.

Ray Bowen became president of the College Station campus in June 1994. He was very smooth and sophisticated. Bowen understood the importance of flagship institutions as well as the importance of the UT and A&M systems working together. When I was working with Thompson on legislative issues, I often found myself thinking about how I needed to find a way to help the College Station campus. Many people will not believe this statement, but it is true.

Change was everywhere, and it was dramatic. In addition to new leadership at Texas A&M, Texas elected a new governor, George W. Bush, in November 1994. My first interaction with Bush had been on April 2, 1991. Bush was then the managing general partner of the Texas Rangers, who were playing UT at Disch-Falk Field. The game was billed as "Ryan versus Ryan," since Nolan Ryan was a star pitcher for the Rangers and his son Reid was playing for UT. I invited Richards as well as Bush to be my guests at the game. We had great seats—the same ones that had been used by Frank Erwin. We had a good time, but nothing occurred to suggest that I would be seeing more of Bush.

While I may have met Bush's close friend Don Evans at some UT event before he joined the UT Board of Regents in 1995, I certainly didn't know him. I did know that he was close to Bush and that he would probably play an important role in the university during Bush's administration. I remember meeting Evans at the Four Seasons Hotel in Austin after the 1994 election, and he seemed like a very affable, pleasant, energetic, and warm individual. I was hopeful that we would all get along very well.

Soon after the election, Tom Loeffler, who had been appointed to the board of regents by Bill Clements, advised me to visit with Bush before he took office in January 1995 so that I could try to establish a personal relationship with him. I decided that I needed to prepare a full-blown presentation that would update Bush in detail on the current state of higher education in Texas and provide us with a vehicle for discussing the issues in depth. This proved to be a mistake.

I met with Bush and Loeffler in Bush's office in Dallas on December 16, 1994. I told Bush that I would like to walk him through a presentation to give him an update on the status of Texas higher education and what could be accomplished at the state's colleges and universities. As everyone in Texas knows, the state constitution gives the governor relatively little real power, but a visionary governor can still exercise enormous influence by using the position to advocate bold actions. I was hopeful that Bush would see himself in that mold and might want to make his mark as governor by becoming an advocate for higher education the way John Connally and Dolph Briscoe had been. This was not as foolish a hope as it might seem today. While Connally and Briscoe were fiscal conservatives, they recognized the important role that higher education must play in creating opportunity for all citizens and were determined to leave the state's colleges and universities stronger than they had found them.

As I began to talk through my presentation, Bush's eyes began to wander and I could tell he had little interest in the subject. Instead of giving up and cutting my presentation short, I moved across to his side of the desk so we could look at the pages of my presentation together, and I almost physically forced him go through it one page at a time. This was clearly a mistake. I am sure Bush resented my actions, and this was a case in which my enthusiasm for higher education was counterproductive. I made the mistake of thinking I could make sure he got off to a good start by helping him understand important public policies and issues associated with a fundamental area of state government. He was not even slightly curious about what I felt should be done to improve higher education.

I learned later that Bush was not a policy wonk and that he liked to receive memos and presentations of no more than one or two pages. In hindsight, I should have tried to find out ahead of time more about Bush's preferences and style, and then should have tailored my presentation to his way of working. Unfortunately, higher education in Texas involves rather complex issues, and it is quite difficult to make the case for the kind of changes that needed to be made using only one or two slides.

I also made the mistake in that meeting of calling Bush by his first name. I actually thought about addressing him as "governor-elect," but that seemed very awkward. Loeffler had advised me to call him George. Loeffler is a good friend of mine, and I know that he very much wanted me to get along with Bush. I had a first-name relationship with many Texas politicians, and I had called Bush by his first name when he had been my guest at the Ryan vs. Ryan baseball game in 1991. In February 1995 Joe Allbaugh, Bush's chief of staff, called Millsap to let us know that I was not to address the governor as George. This seemed very petty to me, and it may have been more Allbaugh's preference than Bush's, but if this is what they wanted it was fine with me.

Partly because of that meeting in Dallas, Bush and I did not get off to a good start, and our relationship got worse over time. Bush may have perceived me as a Democrat, and that may have bothered him. I wasn't a Democrat, but neither was I a Republican. It was true that I had worked closely with Democratic politicians—governors, lieutenant governors, and members of the Senate and House—if for no other reason than that there weren't very many Republicans in positions of power in Austin in those days. Under those conditions, you either worked with the Democrats or you didn't work at all. The two clear exceptions were Tom Craddick and Kay Bailey Hutchison. Craddick was first elected to the House in 1968, and he was a powerful, effective friend of higher education. Craddick's door was always open to me and to UT. Hutchison was elected state treasurer in 1990 and U.S. senator in 1993. She loved UT and was always willing and eager to help the university.

Bush may also have perceived me to be a Democrat because I

William H. Cunningham with Jim Bob Moffett and former Texas lieutenant governor Ben Barnes. *Courtesy of William H. Cunningham.*

had excellent relationships with Bernard Rapoport and Ben Barnes. Rapoport had been a very strong regent and was very supportive of what I was trying to accomplish as chancellor, as well as being a close friend. He was also a strong supporter of our South Texas/Border Initiative, which had begun during Richards's administration. Barnes, a former lieutenant governor, was a high-profile Democratic lobbyist and power broker as well as a strong UT supporter and a good friend of mine.

My next formal meeting with Bush was on March 15, 1995. I asked his chief of staff to arrange a meeting with Rapoport and Lowell Lebermann and me to discuss UT System priorities and budget needs. In hindsight, I should have asked one of Bush's new appointees to the board to go with us. However, Rapoport was the chairman of the board and Lebermann was vice chairman. Both had sponsored a fund-raiser for Bush only a few months earlier and both were highly respected Texans who had a good relationships with both Democrats and Republicans.

We were ushered into Bush's office, and he asked us to sit in front of his desk. He unwrapped a cigar and began to chew it, and then he put his boots on his desk in front of us. Rapoport never lost his cool. He continued to push for more money to support the UT System and its students and faculty. Lebermann, who was blind, missed some of the show, but he joined in with a discussion of how Governor Connally's legacy as a great governor was built on his support for higher education, and how Governor Bush could follow the same pattern. I tried not to look offended, but it was clear to me that Bush wanted to send a message.

We faced one more very difficult and unpleasant political problem during the initial segment of the 1995 legislative session. This problem kept Barry Thompson from talking to me for two months and might have made the chairman of the A&M Board of Regents, Mary Nan West, want to shoot me. It all started when I received a call from Bullock in February. Bullock told me that Senator Judith Zaffirini would be introducing a bill the next day that would transfer Texas A&M International University at Laredo to the UT System. Bullock told me he was going to support the bill and it would pass the Senate. He also told me to stay away from the issue and let the politicians deal with it.

I knew this was going to present a huge problem for A&M and probably for my relations with the Aggies. I did not follow Bullock's advice. I called Thompson as soon as I hung up from talking to Bullock. I told him what Bullock had said, and I told him there still might be time to pacify Zaffirini and stop the potential train wreck. Thompson thanked me for the information, but in hindsight it is clear he never trusted me again. As Shirley Bird used to say, "no good deed goes unpunished." He felt UT was behind a power play to gain control of the Laredo campus. We had nothing to do with Zaffirini's bill or her efforts to transfer Laredo to UT. It would have been a big problem for the UT System to absorb the fledgling Laredo campus, and ultimately we might have felt pressure to allow Laredo access to the Permanent University Fund, placing even more strain on an already overburdened endowment fund.

The Laredo bill did pass the Senate as Bullock had promised, but it lingered in the House the entire session as a result of opposition from Irma Rangel of Corpus Christi, chair of the House Higher Education Committee. Representative Henry Cuellar, who was a good friend of UT as well as a longtime rival of Zaffirini in Laredo and Webb County, was also opposed to the bill. His relationship with Zaffirini became even more stressed during this session. After my unproductive call to Thompson, I followed Bullock's advice and stayed out of the matter, and the most the UT System did was "stay close to the bill," as they say. The staffs of the two university systems continued to work together on other issues, and the bitterness over the Laredo bill was, for the most part, forgotten once the session ended.

When former lieutenant governor Bill Hobby became chancellor of the University of Houston System in September 1995 and former state senator John Montford became chancellor of Texas Tech in August 1996, the "Hay ride" was once again under way. It was very easy to have constructive meetings with Hobby and Montford. They were political pros who understood the need for all of higher education to get along and present a united front to the Texas Legislature.

Tom Scott, associate vice chancellor for governmental relations, and I began meeting with these and other higher education leaders in September 1996 to lay the groundwork for the coalition in anticipation of the difficult legislative session that would begin in January 1997, and we soon put together working groups that included representatives from UT, Texas A&M, the University of Houston, and Texas Tech. Periodically we would try to involve governmental relations staff from the Texas State University System, North Texas State, and community colleges. While it always sounded good to invite those institutions, they did not have as much in common with the UT System, A&M, Houston, or Texas Tech, and they tended to be very suspicious of our "elitist" motives. Usually it was just easier to tell them what was happening rather than try to make a serious effort to involve them in the decision-making.

Hay's grand coalition just naturally came back together. Hobby and Montford wanted to work with UT. They respected UT and its statewide influence, but they also expected to have a seat at the table for their institutions. Thompson cooperated although he was suspicious of UT's motives. Despite problems, we worked together to develop a plan for the January 1997 session.

Scott, at the time an assistant vice chancellor for governmental relations at the UT System, coordinated the work of several task forces that involved administrators from all members of the coalition in formulating statewide goals for higher education, and these task force reports became the basis for the legislative agenda that we developed later in the fall of 1996. Scott did most of the work. He had the intellectual capacity and the political skills that were required to work effectively with the staff members from the other institutions, and he had the expertise to develop the plan. Scott had worked for Hobby for ten years, and before that he had worked in the Governor's Budget Office in the administrations of Preston Smith and Dolph Briscoe, so he was intimately familiar with the state budget process and the legislative arena. Hobby and Montford trusted Scott completely. They knew that while he worked for the UT System he was genuinely focused on doing what was right for the state and that he would never spin the numbers in a dishonest manner. Without Scott's skills in policy analysis and political strategy, the coalition could never have been a success.

The coalition's program was named "Back to Basics." It was focused on meeting the educational needs of the state's population, and it was largely a response to the disturbing implications of the demographic studies conducted by Steve Murdock, the state demographer and director of the Texas State Data Center (then at Texas A&M and later at the University of Texas at San Antonio). Murdock's latest and most comprehensive study, "Texas Challenged," was published in the summer of 1996 and was widely influential in focusing the public, the media, and policy leaders on the need to dramatically enhance educational opportunities at all levels for the state's ethnic minority populations. These groups were, and remain, the fastest growing segments of the Texas population, yet they were historically the most poorly educated and thus the most poorly prepared to help Texas develop a new economy based on the high-technology, information-age trends of the twenty-first century. Murdock's study foresaw a bleak economic and social future for Texas in the first third of the new century unless the state took bold steps to improve the levels of educational attainment of its minority population.[1]

The coalition's report estimated that Texas would need to increase the number of students earning bachelor's degrees by 23 percent to remain competitive economically with other states and in the global economy. Reaching that goal would require more money for scholarships, increased remedial education and retention programs, and new programs to facilitate students' progress from public school to community colleges and universities. That would mean more money for full-time faculty, particularly for freshman and sophomore classes.

The Back to Basics plan also called for new programs for intervention with freshmen who were at risk of dropping out; increased funding for reading programs in elementary school to better prepare the next generation of college students; new workforce development programs and support for research related to economically critical industries; and better funding for the state's health science institutions. These and other elements of the plan were directly tied to efforts to address the needs identified in Murdock's study. The coalition went to the legislature with a request for $926 million in new appropriations to fund the initiative.[2] Neither the Legislative Budget Board nor Bush recommended any additional funding for higher education.

Many lawmakers welcomed the approach of the coalition. State Senator Teel Bivins, R-Amarillo, chairman of the Senate Higher Education Committee, said the coalition's united plan represented a "refreshing change." He went on to say, "Sometimes they work against each other. When you have all of higher education working together it makes it easier for legislators, so you don't have to choose. Here you have everybody speaking with one voice, which is going to give them visibility and credibility."[3] The plan also drew strong support from newspaper editorial boards.

The coalition held together remarkably well throughout the session, and while the legislature was able to fund only about two-thirds ($593 million) of the increased appropriations that the coalition had sought, that was still a significant increase for higher education and more than had seemed realistically possible before the session began. Total general revenue appropriations for higher education were increased by 9 percent (more than the overall growth in state spending of 7.6 percent) in 1997, and the appropriations ended a decade-long erosion of general revenue support for the state's colleges and universities. The legislature also approved a new series of revenue bonds totaling $638.5 million for higher education construction projects, authorization for a regional academic health center in the Lower Rio Grande Valley (see Chapter 28), expansion of academic programs at UT Tyler and UT Brownsville, and new funds for residency programs and other graduate medical education expenses.

Perhaps as important for the long term, the session demonstrated that a coalition involving all the state's higher education institutions was indeed possible, and that a united approach based on sound research and well-argued, statewide policy goals could serve the best interests of all the institutions. Having Hobby and Montford on the team was critically important to our success. They not only knew how Texas politics functioned; only a few short months earlier they had both been key members of the Texas Senate power structure. They were still referred to as Governor Hobby and Senator Montford by many of their close friends in the Senate, such as Teel Bivens, chairman of the Senate Education Committee, and Bill Ratliff, chairman of the Senate Finance Committee. The Hay ride was alive and well.

The UT System and its coalition partners began to work in earnest for the 1999 legislative session in the spring of 1998. Earlier in the fall of 1997, I received a call from Junell and Ratliff indicating that they wanted to explore alternatives for creating additional comprehensive research universities and also address disparities in funding for capital improvements. My assumption was that Ratliff was interested in stimulating the development of additional comprehensive research universities, while Junell was focused on providing additional capital funds for Texas Tech. Scott was once again in charge of putting our coalition's plan together. My top priorities consisted of increasing the funding for higher education and to begin to allocate funds for creating real excellence at institutions other than Texas A&M and UT Austin. Everyone seemed to agree with my idea that Texas needed additional comprehensive research universities that would be in the same league with UT Austin and Texas A&M, but there was no agreement about how to allocate available state money to allow other institutions to reach that level. The top contenders for such status were often listed as Texas Tech and the University of Houston, but many others envisioned themselves as worthy of such enhancement. These included several institutions in the UT System including UT Dallas, UT Arlington, UT San Antonio, and UT El Paso. My position was that Texas needed to provide funding to develop at least two more flagships, but that it was important to fund these institutions without taking resources away from UT Austin and Texas A&M.

Scott developed three plans, which we called Red, White, and Blue. They called for additional excellence in capital funding ranging from $127 million (Red) to almost $400 million (Blue). The total increase in funding for the most ambitious plan for all senior and health-related institutions would require an additional $1 billion in funding for higher education. We took the UT plans to a summit meeting at John Montford's house on Lake Bridgeport on August 7, 1998. Scott,

Millsap, Randy Wallace, and I represented UT. Chancellor Lamar Urbanovsky and Vice Chancellor Jack Morton from the Texas State University System flew up to the meeting on the UT plane. I wanted to go to Montford's home to show respect for him and Texas Tech. By the meeting's end, the chancellors from UT, A&M, Texas Tech, and Texas State had agreed on a plan that would increase the excellence funding for the state universities and begin the process of possibly building additional elite universities. The University of Houston was not represented at the meeting. Houston had a great deal of turnover in the president's and chancellor's positions. Once Hobby left the position of chancellor in 1997, Houston brought very little to the table politically, and it was just easier to meet without them.

The UT System Board of Regents, including Don Evans, whose two terms as chairman included both the 1997 and 1999 legislative sessions, had been supportive of the higher education coalition's initiative in 1997. I outlined the coalition plan for the 1999 session to Evans in Los Angeles on September 12, 1998, at the Beverly Wilshire Hotel at a breakfast before a football game between UT and UCLA. Evans bought into the plan that day, even though I made it very clear that Bush might find it at odds with his legislative agenda. UT lost to sixth-ranked UCLA 49–31, but I did not take that as an omen for the upcoming legislative session.

Evans and I agreed that our legislative effort could benefit from a greater concentration on selling our plan directly to the public. To coordinate a public communications campaign on behalf of Texas higher education, Evans approved the hiring of Jack Martin and his firm Public Strategies Inc., and we were able to use gift funds from the UT Foundation to pay for this project. Martin, a former assistant to U.S. Senator Lloyd Bentsen, is one of the most skilled and politically savvy managers of public relations campaigns in the nation, and his firm helped pioneer many trends in modern public relations. Our efforts included a series of public service announcements and coordinated visits to newspaper editorial boards, and these activities were valuable in expanding the base of support for higher education.

The coalition was very disappointed but not surprised when Bush outlined his budget proposal for the session that would begin in January 1999. Once again, Bush's budget proposal included no increases in funding for higher education. The coalition responded with a proposal for an increase of $1.2 billion for public senior universities and health-related institutions and for public school partnerships, and a total of $1.4 billion for all of higher education, including community and technical colleges. The coalition called for $150 million in new "excellence funding" for universities, with the exception of UT Austin and Texas A&M. As consolation for being left out of this pot, the two existing public flagship universities won support from the rest of the coalition for a constitutional amendment that would lift certain restrictions on the way proceeds from the Permanent University Fund could be spent. This is discussed in detail in Chapter 27.

Scott and his colleagues provided a detailed plan for how the new excellence funds would be used across institutions, the level of excellence that we could attain, and the number of new students we could support. We believed we had produced a very thoughtful document that would be useful to the decision makers in the legislature.

The coalition renewed our arguments that had been so successful in 1997—that new funding was needed to meet the economic and social challenges raised in the report "Texas Challenged"—and we again placed emphasis on basic initiatives such as minority student recruitment and retention programs, faculty salaries, and research. Some people considered our plan for $1.2 billion in new spending to be too ambitious, but the institutions in the coalition knew that meeting the rapidly growing needs of Texas for an enhanced system of higher education was going to require investments on that scale.[4]

Bush was getting ready to run for president of the United States in 2000, and his primary proposals for the legislature in 1999 involved tax relief. He had engineered a package of tax reduction programs in the early part of the 1999 session that were going to generate more than $1 billion in tax relief. The problem was that he was not satisfied with this—he wanted an additional billion. This was approximately the same amount that the higher education coalition was seeking in increased funding. As chancellor of the UT System, I shouldered most of the burden for speaking out for higher education's plan—and thus opposing Bush's plan. In late April, the chancellors attended a meeting called by Bush in his office to discuss the funding of higher education. Montford, Hobby, Urbanovsky, and Thompson attended. We were all gathered around Bush's big coffee table, and I began to lay out the program that the chancellors had agreed on, including the $1.2 billion funding increase. We knew we were there just for the formality of giving Bush a briefing because in reality he had never

William H. Cunningham with Texas Speaker of the House Pete Laney, world champion heavyweight boxer George Foreman, and Texas Governor George W. Bush, inscribed by Bush: "To Bill, an educational heavyweight." *Courtesy of William H. Cunningham.*

expressed any real interest in higher education—an attitude that was reinforced at this meeting. As I was outlining our budget proposal, Bush, with his boots up on a credenza, rolled his eyes at Millsap in a clear signal of his boredom.

After I had explained our $1.2 billion plan, Bush asked me, "How much money would you take? Would you take $500 million?" I said, "Governor, we will take whatever funds you give us, and we will spend them as effectively as we can." Soon after we left his office, Bush told numerous people that he obviously put too much money on the table, because Cunningham sold out so quickly. The truth is that I had not sold out. I had merely been respectful. I had no interest in negotiating with Bush, since it was not certain that he would even have a seat at the table when the actual budget decisions were made. When I heard Bush's comments, I called in Millsap and said, "Tee it up, I want $1 billion." We went back to work and never met again with Bush.

When all was said and done, the public senior colleges and health-related institutions received $843 million in new money for higher education, two-thirds of the amount of new money requested, and a record amount of new state aid for colleges and universities.[5] The "excellence funds" were not enough to make major strides forward at the various institutions hoping for flagship status, but the appropriations were a start. Texas Tech, for example, had sought $20 million to further its aspirations as a flagship institution, but received $4.4 million in "excellence funds."

The grand coalition had once again proved to be the best way to present the Texas Legislature with proposals for support of higher education. I believe our experience during the 1997 and 1999 sessions remains a valuable guide for higher education on how to develop a comprehensive legislative program that incorporates a statewide vision and gives lawmakers a practical and sensible way of sorting through competing priorities. Our experience is also evidence that the UT System can and must be an effective statewide leader in forging such coalitions, moving toward overcoming decades of harmful competition and rivalry among the state's higher education institutions.

It is worth noting that Bush, as well as other governors under whom I served, had very little to do with the budgetary process. This may reflect the fact that higher education simply was not a priority for these governors or that the legislative process simply does not give the governor much of a role to play. The chairs of the Senate Finance and House Appropriations committees were important, as was the lieutenant governor and the Speaker of the House. Unless a governor decides to use the office's bully pulpit to influence the public debate over higher education, he or she will not be a very important player.

During the entire period that Bush was governor he did not propose any additional funding for higher education, and the simple truth is that he was not a player in setting the priorities and direction of higher education. We had very few dealings with the Governor's Office during legislative debates over higher education appropriations because the office was not interested or supportive. On the other hand, we were confident that Bush would never veto a higher educa-tion bill. This would have been a political disaster for him and, as a result, we really had very little concern about any negative impact from actions he might take.

In many ways my entire relationship with Bush can be summed up in a meeting that Larry Faulkner and I had with him, soon after Faulkner became president of UT Austin in April 1998. I wanted to introduce Faulkner to Bush, who graciously welcomed Larry back to Texas (he had served at the University of Illinois for twenty-five years) and then told us (and this is very close to an exact quote), "I don't really care very much about higher education. My priority is on public education—on reading." Then Bush glanced at me and said something close to, "Chancellor Cunningham gets more money out of the legislature for higher education than it probably needs, so it is not a concern for me, and I wish you well in your presidency."

I would be the first person to say that every elected official cannot and probably should not make higher education his or her number-one issue, so I do not fault Bush for having his own list of priori-ties. However, higher education is an important part of the state and many people believe it has the unique power to change the lives of thousands of people each year. If this is true, and I believe it is, Texas would be better off if every governor understands what higher edu-cation is all about and how colleges and universities can shape the future of the state.

CHAPTER 25

Politics: The Great American Game

I became chancellor in September 1992. By the early part of that year, Mike Millsap and I had begun to strategize about what we could do during my time of leadership to make the UT System more powerful and more politically successful. We were not afraid of politicians or the political process and, in fact, we embraced the process. We recognized that UT's success in the Texas Legislature in both the Frank Erwin and Jess Hay eras involved participating in the political process, and we were ready and willing.

We concluded that we needed to have some "skin in the game." If the UT System was to become a serious political force we needed to have a vehicle for supporting our friends and, perhaps, "punishing" our enemies. As state employees, we could not use state time or university resources to create a political action committee, so I encouraged several longtime supporters of UT, headed by John Fainter, to establish a PAC that would be empowered to raise money for the political campaigns of Texas politicians who were working to help further the mission of the UT System and its institutions. The result of that initiative was the Friends of the University Political Action Committee, established in June 1992. We now had a formal and legal way of expressing our appreciation to the politicians who supported our initiatives.

Political action committees were not new to the UT System or its component institutions. During his tenure as chairman of the board of regents, Jess Hay had established the Higher Education Legislative PAC to support UT, and several groups of friends of the UT System's medical schools had created PACs that focused on their issues. Millsap, Shirley Bird Perry, and I visited with Hay at the Petroleum Club in Dallas on January 4, 1993, to get his views on how we could best use the new PAC during the upcoming legislative session. He was

William H. Cunningham with Wales Madden. *Courtesy of William H. Cunningham.*

very helpful and encouraged us to develop the PAC for the maximum advantage.

Fainter became the initial treasurer and president of the UT PAC in June 1992. He did an excellent job of getting the PAC organized, and he made sure we did not violate any laws or regulations. The first board members were Fainter, Larry Temple, John Chase, Hal Hillman, Beryl Milburn, Wales Madden, John Harbin, Michael Cook, and Bob Inman. The individuals that we asked to serve on the board, technically called decision makers, were well-respected longtime supporters of UT, as well as being good friends of mine. When Fainter became chief of staff for Governor Ann Richards in 1993, he resigned as an officer of the PAC, and his former law partner, Roger Moore, took over and served as treasurer from 1993 to 1995. Fainter and Moore alternated as treasurer during the rest of the decade. We were very fortunate to have their judgment and expertise.

One of the first decisions related to the PAC was that it would contribute only to members of the Texas Legislature. This meant we did not contribute to federal or statewide elected officials, with the exception of the lieutenant governor, who presides over the Texas Senate. We stayed away from gubernatorial races because we felt we would have too much to lose. We were confident that the university would have "friends" running in the primaries of both parties and in the general election, and we did not want to make some of our friends unhappy, or even worse, create an enemy. The PAC, by law, was not allowed to contribute to campaigns for federal offices, and we decided not to try to organize a separate PAC for that arena—partly because we did not have the financial resources to be a significant player at that level, but mainly because our primary focus was the Texas Legislature.

A fundamental priority for Millsap and me was to keep our work on behalf of the PAC strictly separate from our work for UT. This meant doing work related to the PAC outside the office and after 5:00 p.m. or on vacation time. We never used any state resources to support the PAC. The laws related to political activities by state employees are very clear, and we were careful to follow both the letter and the spirit of the law.

Initially we raised most of the money for the PAC primarily from friends and supporters of UT Austin. We were never very successful in tapping into alumni of the medical schools or the other academic institutions. I felt it was important to position the PAC as a "system" entity but, in reality, it was supported almost exclusively by friends of UT Austin. I made fund-raising calls using my personal long-distance credit card from home. I asked people such as Jim Bob Moffett, Joe Jamail, and Harry Reasoner if they would be willing to raise or give $10,000.

The UT PAC always had strong financial support from members of the board of regents. Louis Beecherl, Tex Moncrief, Bernard Rapoport, Tom Hicks, Sam Barshop, Tom Loeffler, Martha Smiley, Don Evans, Robert Cruikshank, and Lowell Lebermann gave consistently and generously to the PAC. As the PAC developed, additional people from around Texas were invited to serve on its board. These people understood that by accepting this position they would be expected to raise or contribute money to the PAC.

The PAC was always strictly nonpartisan. Its only objective was to support politicians who supported the UT System. Millsap and I would meet at the Headliners Club when it came time to distribute money, and he would have a complete analysis that included which politicians had been supportive of the UT System and how the proposed contributions broke down by political party. We would then call a meeting of the PAC board and make our recommendations for how the money would be allocated. Out-of-town PAC board members would often participate by teleconference. Once again, all of Millsap's and my efforts to support the PAC were done on our own time, off state property, and with no state resources. As university officials, we had not given up our right to participate in the political process, we just had to do it away from UT.

Our PAC board discussions on how to distribute the money frequently focused on the issue of whether to "punish" the people who failed to support higher education. Millsap always argued that the PAC's goal was to make friends, not to create enemies. He also felt that, while a member of the legislature did not support our position on a specific issue, he or she might become one of our best friends in the future. A second issue frequently discussed at PAC board meetings was whether we should concentrate our money on a relatively small number of our very best friends in the legislature or spread the wealth among a larger number of legislators. Millsap's strategy was to make as many friends as possible even if some of the contributions were relatively small. When we were done with the debate we never tried to "punish" or beat any elected officials. Although we made larger contributions to key committee chairs and the lieutenant governor and Speaker, we also spread the money among a large number of politicians.

Millsap and I always tried to deliver the checks personally. We wanted a little face time with the politician, and we wanted to talk about issues that the UT System expected in the next legislative session. We always gave the check at the beginning of our conversation because we did not want any feeling of quid pro quo. The politician received his or her check regardless of what their position might be on the issues that we would raise.

Once Bernard Rapoport became chairman of the board of regents in March 1993, we became more politically active. Rapoport liked most politicians, and he loved the political process. In addition, he recognized that we needed to be supportive of politicians who supported the UT System's political initiatives. Rapoport began hosting a series of events at his home in Waco to help raise money for elected officials who were strong supporters of UT and higher education in general. He would always ask my advice about whom to honor at these events, and he scheduled them at a time that I could attend. Rapoport did most of the work, calling his friends and assembling at his home a group of thirty to forty people who were likely donors. After a short period of socializing, Rapoport would introduce me. He always began by saying that I was the greatest chancellor in the history of the university. I am not sure he believed that, but I never got tired of hearing it. I would make some laudatory comments about the politician being honored, and then that person would make a few remarks. By this point we would have counted the checks, and Rapoport would always make up the difference between what we had hoped to raise and the actual amount of contributions. We had more than ten events in Rapoport's home while he was chairman. Rapoport was a well-known liberal Democrat, but he would host an event for anyone we felt was on the UT team. Many conservative Democrats, such as John Montford, made the trip to Rapoport's home, as well as Republicans, including senators Bill Ratliff and David Sibley.

After the 1993 legislative session, Millsap received a call from Susan Longley, who was Bullock's political fund-raiser. She asked Millsap if UT was planning on making a contribution to Bullock's campaign fund. I am sure she felt we would want to either use PAC resources or "bundle" some checks together for him. Longley suggested that Bullock hoped UT could raise $20,000. Bullock never once called me or Millsap about this, nor was there ever any type of quid pro quo. Still, we knew we had our marching orders, and we were determined to succeed.

I called Rapoport and he instantly agreed to host a reception for Bullock at his home. Since Longley had suggested the figure of $20,000, Millsap and I wanted to overachieve, and we raised and gave to Bullock more than $35,000. Almost all of the checks were "bundled." I would call friends of UT and ask them if they would please send me a check made out to Bullock's campaign. Rapoport did the same thing with his Waco friends and, as a result, both the donors and the UT PAC got credit. It was all a game, but at least we were players and we understood the rules.

At the end of the cocktail hour and Rapoport's and my brief comments, I invited Bullock to come to Rapoport's study. All the UT officials who were in attendance were lined up and I made a few additional comments about how grateful UT was for Bullock's support of higher education and the UT System institutions. The vice chancellors and campus presidents in attendance were nodding on cue, at which point I announced that we had raised a total of $35,000. Bullock was very grateful and told the assembled group that he would continue to do all he could to support the UT System and its institutions.

There was one unintended consequence of our trip. When Longley called the next year, she upped the ante significantly—and our response was totally predictable. We again raised more money than had been suggested. This inflationary spiral continued every year Bullock was lieutenant governor. The last fund-raiser we had for Bullock in Rapoport's home was in 1997, when we gave him more than $150,000 in bundled checks.

Almost five years after its creation, the PAC came under intense scrutiny and considerable public criticism, largely as a result of articles published in the *San Antonio Express-News*. These articles questioned the propriety of the PAC and its activities. The stories began in February 1997 when the newspaper reported that a lawsuit had been filed by an unhappy employee of UT San Antonio. The employee, Jude Valdez, said in his lawsuit against UTSA President Sam Kirkpatrick that he was pressured in 1992 and 1993 into donating $100 to the PAC (donations said to have been given to Bullock's campaign), and that he was "demoted" after his contribution was late. Kirkpatrick refuted the idea that he had put pressure on anyone for political contributions, and he indicated that changes in Valdez's job duties were related to management issues. I investigated the incident. It was true that in 1994 Kirkpatrick had changed the areas for which Valdez was responsible. However, Valdez, a vice president, had in fact not been demoted. He had kept his title and pay level. Despite the allegations of pressure to donate as part of the PAC's efforts to support Bullock, the newspaper did make it clear, three paragraphs from the end of a seventy-two-paragraph story, that other UTSA vice presidents had not made any contributions at the time that Valdez alleged his contribution was due.[1] I found no evidence that supported Valdez's claim that Kirkpatrick had put pressure on Valdez or anyone else to make a contribution.

By the time the story ran, the PAC had been operating for almost five years. All of the required reports had been filed with the Texas Ethics Commission in a timely manner. Its existence and activities may have come like a "revelation" to some, but the public record had been there since 1992.

The *Express-News* focused a lot of attention on the fact that donations by the PAC, its directors, and various UT employees were often transmitted to Bullock's campaign at roughly the same time or even on the same days. This was the result of the PAC's effort to solicit and coordinate such donations, and it implied nothing about use of state time or resources in political activities. While donations from the PAC to Bullock were the focus of most of the news coverage, the PAC had made contributions to more than a hundred other politicians of both parties.

A fund-raising event in 1994 became the focus of a follow-up story in the San Antonio newspaper's 1997 series of articles about the PAC. A van rented by the UT Foundation, a not-for-profit independent foundation that supports the UT System, was used to drive seven presidents of UT institutions from a system retreat in Austin to Rapoport's home to attend a fund-raiser for Bullock on August 12, 1994. Several system and campus officials made modest contributions to Bullock's campaign at that event. The article seemed to imply that there was something improper about the transportation arrangements, but, as the newspaper acknowledged, the cost of the van was paid for with gift money from the UT Foundation, and no state funds were involved. The article also made it clear that some UT officials who attended the event did not make contributions to Bullock.[2] Three days later, the newspaper found a tax law expert who offered the opinion that the foundation's expenditure was inappropriate, but several other experts interpreted the expense as permissible.[3]

After several articles had run on the front page of the *Express-News* criticizing UT and the UT PAC, I came to the conclusion that I needed to do something to try to stop the barrage of bad publicity. I decided to visit the editor and publisher of the paper. A reporter named Russell Gold had written most of the articles, and I had talked to him on several occasions. I had been open and transparent with him, but I had come to the conclusion that he was clearly biased and UT had no chance of having a balanced story if he was the only point of contact with the paper. In my opinion, Gold thought he had uncovered a major story that would bring down me or other officials, perhaps even giving him a shot at a Pulitzer Prize or some other recognition for investigative reporting. The only problem for Gold was that we had not violated the law, and we had not made any mistakes.

I called San Antonio businessman Red McCombs and told him I wanted to meet with the newspaper's senior staff. He felt this was a good idea, but he made it clear it was a strategy that had some significant risks and all he could do was help set up the meeting. I drove to San Antonio on April 10, 1997, with Shirley Bird Perry, Monty Jones, and Teresa Burroff, who was an associate vice chancellor for business affairs. I told the publisher, Larry Walker, in advance that I felt the university would not get a fair hearing if Gold continued to be the primary author of the articles. We agreed that all my responses to the paper's questions would be on the record, and I stated that I would do my best to answer any and all questions.

I had met with the newspaper's editorial staff and the publisher on many previous occasions, and I felt I had a good relationship with them. There were approximately twelve people from the paper in the room, including Walker, Editor Robert Rivard, and various members of the staffs of the editorial page and the newsroom, including Gold. The meeting lasted more than an hour and a half, and I answered all their questions. I made the case that UT had not violated any laws and that members of the UT administration had not given up their rights to participate in the political process just because they worked for a state agency. When the meeting was over we shook hands and left. The paper did not run any more major articles on this subject.

The *Austin American-Statesman* could not resist an opportunity to bash me and the university. It weighed in on the PAC debate with some belligerent and poorly informed comments. Richard Oppel Sr., the editor, editorialized on March 3, 1997, that "The PAC is a disaster, an outrage, an offense to higher education, and it should be dropped now." He went on to say, "The University of Texas System is trapped in old values, the values of good ol' boys who ruled from frontier days and knew only politics, micromanagement and control." Oppel said in a later editorial, "The sight of UT officials muscling their way through the Capitol halls in pursuit of a bigger stadium and better athletes, more money and more power, is troubling. University of Texas leaders should be pursuing loftier aspirations."[4]

The editorials failed to understand that, at least in Texas, money and power are at the heart of attaining those "loftier aspirations." Oppel was already upset with me over the naming of UT Austin's new molecular biology building after Jim Bob Moffett and because President Bob Berdahl had left for the University of California at Berkeley. Oppel never asked me one question about the PAC or why Berdahl left, and I never saw him at the Capitol.

Despite the fact that all the activities of the PAC had been proper, the newspaper stories and editorials were having the effect of casting doubt on the propriety of the PAC, and the articles quoted various public "watchdog" groups such as Public Citizen and Common Cause, whose officials knew nothing about the PAC, except what they had read in the newspapers, but always assumed the worst. Although I was confident that nothing improper had occurred, I issued a reminder to all UT System and campus employees that any political fund-raising while on the job is forbidden by state law and UT System policy.

In April 1997, Pat Oxford, a newly appointed Republican member of the UT Board of Regents, expressed a desire to make doubly sure about the propriety of all actions of university officials related to the PAC or other political fund-raising, and I agreed that we ought to review the entire issue to ensure that no employees were ever being pressured to make donations, and that the laws and policies against political activity on state time were being strictly followed. I stated at the time that, "It is very important that no university official apply any pressure on employees to participate in any political activity. I remain confident that no such pressure has been exerted. Nevertheless, we are reviewing all our procedures to make sure that everything we do is appropriate and proper."[5] I was reluctant to do one more review only because I knew what the facts were and this was just a waste of valuable time and energy. However, I had no choice but to respond to Oxford's request.

Our review found no indication of pressure being applied for donations, but as the weeks passed it became clear to me that such an air of suspicion had come to surround the relationship between university employees and the PAC that I decided to stop making donations to the PAC and recommended that other university leaders do the same. This decision, which I announced in July, pleased several members of

William H. Cunningham with Texas Governor Ann Richards at UT Commencement, August 27, 1992. *UT Texas Student Publications Photograph Collection, e_utt-sp_00011.*

the board of regents. Oxford had been doing his own "investigation" of the activities of the PAC. I was always suspicious of his motives, but the good news is that he found no irregularities.

When I announced that I would stop making political donations through the PAC, I also sought to clarify the activities of the PAC and its relationship to university employees since its beginning. From the news coverage, one might have assumed that the PAC was heavily financed by university employees. In fact, less than 8 percent of the PAC's contributions since its inception had been from UT employees, and no UT employees had worked on PAC business on state time. In addition, the volunteer board of the PAC was composed of UT alumni but no UT employees. Millsap and I did consult with the PAC board when it determined how to allocate contributions, but we did this on our own time and the final decisions were made by the board.[6]

I felt sure that the PAC could continue to serve its purposes without donations from me or other university leaders. The day after my announcement the Associated Press asked Bullock for his reaction, and he made some very kind comments about me. "He works not just for the University of Texas but for overall improvement in higher education for our state, and I think he is one of the best if not the best chancellor that I have ever seen . . . in this state." Bullock said. He also defended the existence of political action committees and the work of the Friends of the University PAC in seeking to support higher education. "If you're appointed on [a] board of regents today, then you ought to spend a lot of time fund-raising and giving to political candidates. As long as the legislature is as stingy as they are with higher education and with education in general, then by golly they ought to do it."[7]

All of us at the UT System knew that our work with the PAC had been legal and appropriate, and we were in effect vindicated when, despite several months of inflammatory headlines, none of the entities responsible for enforcing the laws and regulations related to ethics and official conduct saw any problem with the PAC. A lot of newspaper ink was used up, but the Texas Ethics Commission, the Texas Attorney General's Office, and the Public Integrity Unit of the Travis County District Attorney's Office, which is charged with pursuing cases of official misconduct by state officials, evidently knew the difference between "a good story" and the truth. We never received an inquiry from any of these entities related to the PAC.

While some people feel that the PAC invested most of its efforts to support Bullock, and there is no question that Bullock was very important to UT, we also worked hard to "bundle" money for a number of politicians other than Bullock. For example, after George Bush was elected governor, we realized that we needed to make some effort to raise money to support him. We had stayed out of the election campaign between Richards and Bush, but now it was politically important to try to help Bush. Working with Don Evans, we put together a fund-raiser at Lowell Lebermann's house in Austin on October 7, 1996.

We had a very successful event for Bush, raising almost $200,000 in bundled checks. Bush spoke at the event, but he was a bit uncomfortable and off his stride, probably because most of those in the audience were UT supporters with whom he never had much connection. In addition, most of the people were probably Democrats from the

Regents Bernard Rapoport and Lowell Lebermann, *UT Office of Public Affairs Records, e_utopa_00047.*

moderate to conservative side of the party, with a few actual liberals mixed in, and they really were not part of the governor's political base. Rapoport made a speech in which he said Bush was going to be a great governor and we all needed to support him and get behind him. Rapoport also said that Bush was a real "liberal" when it comes to trying to help people. This was B.'s gracious and good-natured way of reaching out to Bush and trying to make a positive connection between Bush and the audience, but Bush didn't get it, or he got it and didn't like it. The word "liberal" seemed to burn under his skin. He jumped up as quickly as he could and announced, "B. doesn't speak for me. I am not a liberal." I think he was scared that someone outside the event might hear that he had been called a liberal, regardless of the context. He grabbed the bundled checks and almost ran out of Lebermann's home. I felt that, for the first time since I had been at UT, we did not have a governor who fundamentally supported higher education.

The PAC was quite successful in raising and contributing money to politicians and making friends for the UT System. The PAC made political contributions of more than $698,000 between 1992 and 2000. In addition, we "bundled" more than half a million dollars for Bush, Bullock, and other politicians. The money was never given to punish people, and I do believe that it helped make some friends for UT. Finally we were careful to make sure that our resources went to both Republicans and Democrats. The only real criterion for receiving a donation from the PAC was that the politician had an interest in supporting the UT System. I have never felt that PAC contributions "bought" the university anything. I do feel that our contributions may have opened some doors for UT and, as a result, we got a chance to make our pitch. In reality, the impact may have been nothing more than that we were able to thank the legislators who had supported UT System institutions.

I do believe that Millsap and I set the UT System on a course to become much more politically active than it had been since the Jess Hay era. Some newspapers, primarily the *Austin American-Statesman*, and its editor, Rich Oppel, felt this was inappropriate. I believe that the attitude that UT should be above it all—that UT should not be an important player at the legislature—is very naïve. Left to its own devices, the legislature might very well not do the right thing. First, many of UT's natural friends in the legislature will not know the first thing about the UT System's needs and aspirations unless someone educates them. And second, the budget realities of the state dictate that there will always be competing needs for scarce state resources. The only real questions are which agency is going to receive the money that is available or how large the tax reduction will be if the state is generating a surplus.

It is also important to understand that most governors do not like powerful state agencies advocating their own position on statewide issues. Governors want to tell state officials and boards about how their agencies should operate. However, with respect to higher education, the governor's power is primarily persuasive rather than dictatorial. Bush never once recommended spending increases for any UT System institution. However, during his time as governor (fiscal years 1996–2000), the UT System and its institutions' budgets from state appropriated tax dollars increased by more than 16 percent over FY 1995 levels, and the total budget increased from all sources by 38 percent. During the same period, the cost of living increased by 12.6 percent. The easy thing for the UT chancellor to do would be to thank

From left, Chairman of the Board of Regents Don Evans, President of M. D. Anderson John Mendelsohn, and William H. Cunningham at the Alkek Hospital dedication in 1998. *Photo by Pete Baatz, copy courtesy of William H. Cunningham.*

the governor, accept his or her budget recommendation, and return to the office. However, I believe the more responsible action is to say respectfully, but firmly, "Let the games begin." If UT is going to meet its enormous obligations to the state it needs to be proactive in obtaining support from the legislature.

I did always feel an obligation to tell the chairman of the board of regents everything about what the UT System was trying to do politically. I felt it was unfair and inappropriate to let the chairman be blindsided even if I felt he might ultimately decide to tell us to back off and let the governor's position prevail. This is why, for example, I briefed Evans in detail in September 1998 about our plan to bring all of the institutions of higher education together to put pressure on the Texas Legislature to fund higher education properly. I recognized that Bush probably would not have wanted us to proceed in this manner. However, I wanted to make sure that Evans, and through him the UT Board of Regents, was fully briefed on our plans to try to build a coalition that would strengthen higher education's ability to obtain more resources from the legislature and ultimately begin the creation of at least one new flagship university. I fully understood that it was my obligation to propose a plan and eventually execute the plan, but only it if was approved by the board of regents. Evans never asked me to back off my efforts to raise additional money from the legislature. My guess is that he may have had some pressure from Joe Allbaugh, Bush's chief of staff, and possibly from Bush himself, to make UT soften its efforts to get additional state funding. But if that was the case, Evans never passed the pressure on to me.

CHAPTER 26

The South Texas/Border Initiative

I had always been interested in South Texas. As I discussed in Chapter 7, I made many trips as president of UT Austin to the Lower Rio Grande Valley to meet with high school counselors and students to encourage them to continue their education at UT Austin. On March 11, 1992, I took most of the UT Austin deans with me to Edinburg to meet their counterparts at UT Pan American. Our mission was very simple: to determine what UT Austin could do to help UT Pan American improve its academic programs. I met with UT Pan American President Miguel Nevárez in his office for almost three hours while the deans met with their counterparts. The meetings led to long-term collaborative programs between the institutions. It was also a clear statement by UT Austin that it recognized it had a responsibility to assist other institutions in the UT System.

I met again with Nevárez in his office on June 22 after I had been named chancellor. Nevárez spoke with great passion about the need to develop excellent academic programs at South Texas/Border institutions. He emphasized that UT Austin could never be large enough to provide educational opportunities for all of the very best students in the state. He also made the strong point that while the area from San Antonio to the Mexican border and from Brownsville to El Paso was among the fastest growing parts of the state, the region had a severe shortage of undergraduate and graduate programs that could meet the needs of the students who did not want or could not afford to attend UT Austin. I came away with the realization that dramatic steps were necessary to deal with these fundamental needs. I was even more confident in Nevárez's leadership skills and his understanding of what needed to be accomplished.

In 1987, the League of United Latin American Citizens filed a class-action lawsuit (known as *LULAC et al. v. Richards et al.*) charg-

William H. Cunningham with Texas A&M President William Mobley, Monica Gonzalez (director of the University Outreach Center in McAllen), and UT Pan American President Miguel Nevárez. *UT Office of Public Affairs Records, e_utopa_00052.*

ing that the State of Texas had deprived Mexican Americans of their rights by inadequately funding higher education institutions in South Texas.[1] Many high-powered people testified against the state, including Henry Cisneros, who was a member of the Board of Regents of the Texas A&M University System. The state expected to lose the case since the trial was being held in a Brownsville court and LULAC was represented by very aggressive and effective counsel. The Brownsville jury found in 1991 that there had been no discrimination because there was no constitutional requirement for regional distribution of state funds for higher education, but the jury did conclude that the state had failed to establish "universities of the first class" beyond UT Austin and Texas A&M. The state had won, and justice had prevailed. However, the trial judge, Ben Euresti Jr., threw out the jury verdict and held for the plaintiffs on all aspects of the case. The defendants viewed this as merely a political decision by an elected state district judge with one eye, if not both eyes, on the next election in his hometown. The state appealed Euresti's ruling to the Texas Supreme Court.

The immediate impetus for me for the expansion of higher education initiatives in the 1993 legislative session (my first as chancellor) was a meeting I had with Bob Bullock in September 1992. After serving for sixteen years as the state comptroller, Bullock had been elected lieutenant governor in 1990, and at the time of our meeting he was busy preparing for his second legislative session in that position. He asked me and Herbert H. Richardson, the new Texas A&M chancellor, to meet with him in his office. I had met Bullock a number of times, but I did not know him well, and it appeared to me that this was Richardson's first meeting with him.

I had anticipated that the meeting would run no longer than an hour. Bullock, however, was very interested in public policy. He wanted as much information as we could provide on the status of our universities and what it was going to take to improve higher education across the state. After a wide-ranging discussion of these topics, he asked if we would like to stay for lunch, and although I am sure Richardson and I had other plans, we both readily agreed to stay.

After lunch, which consisted of fried and refried food, Bullock lit into Richardson over the fact that the Texas A&M System reserved the A&M name for its two original institutions, the flagship university in College Station and Prairie View A&M University, as well as the recently renamed West Texas A&M University in Canyon, while leaving the system's three South Texas institutions with the names they had before they joined—Laredo State University, Corpus Christi State University, and Texas A&I University. I remember very distinctly Bullock's exact words: "At least the UT System has the decency to call all its institutions by the UT name." I felt extremely uncomfortable. Richardson was new at his job, and Bullock's outburst seemed to come out of nowhere. And the more he talked, the more of a tirade it became. "You are the chancellor, aren't you?" Bullock demanded. Richardson, quite properly, said he would take up the matter with the Texas A&M regents, but Bullock was clearly not satisfied with that response. I kept quiet, wondering what Bullock might have in store for me when it was my turn.[2]

After Bullock had worked over Richardson, he turned to me, and without any preamble said, "Do you have a plan for South Texas?" I responded immediately "Governor, we have a detailed plan." Bullock

said, "Great. I want to see both of your plans in the morning," and
I automatically said, "Fine," and Richardson agreed to return in the
morning as well.

The only problem was that there was no plan, and I mean there
was "no plan." I was extremely lucky that Bullock didn't ask me to
have a copy of the plan brought to him that afternoon. We did have
a sketchy, incomplete discussion document which dealt with new academic programs at universities in the South Texas/Border region that
the UT and A&M systems had worked on with Attorney General Dan
Morales. Bullock wanted more than an incomplete wish list of programs that had been discussed with his political adversary, Morales.
He wanted a realistic, detailed plan that would be introduced in four
months in the 73rd legislative session.

I had about eighteen hours to come up with a legislative proposal,
so I rushed back to the office and talked to James Duncan, executive
vice chancellor for academic affairs. Unfortunately, it became clear
that the UT System had not yet focused any serious attention on the
development of an initiative for South Texas.

I called the presidents of the five UT System institutions in the
South Texas/Border region—Diana Natalicio at UT El Paso, Miguel
Nevárez at UT Pan American, Juliet Garcia at UT Brownsville, Sam
Kirkpatrick at UT San Antonio, and John Howe at the UT Health
Science Center at San Antonio—and explained the situation to them.
I said this was an opportunity for them to be expansive, and that I
wanted to know what it was going to take to dramatically improve
their institutions, and I had to know now.

Several of the presidents had been complaining for years about
how slowly the UT System and state government bureaucracies
worked. Now I was telling the presidents they had only a few hours
to start faxing their campus priorities to Austin so we could create a
plan that I could present to Bullock the next morning. The presidents
recognized that this was a unique opportunity to move their institutions forward, and before dark we started receiving their ideas for
how the state needed to strengthen their educational programs and
facilities. The phone calls and faxes in both directions continued far
into the night.

Most of the work in Austin that night was done by Associate Vice
Chancellor Joe Stafford; Monty Jones, who worked in our public
affairs office; and Mary Kaszynski, an administrative assistant in my

office. Stafford organized the substance of the plans sent in by the presidents and kept an eye on how the Coordinating Board would react to our proposal. Jones did most of the writing—translating outlines, lists, and other raw material into a readable and persuasive document suitable for giving to the lieutenant governor. Kaszynski kept track of the phone calls and faxes, did typing and organizing, and applied her expert proofreading skills as we went through multiple drafts.

My role was to keep the communications flowing with the presidents. I spent most of the evening on the phone with them, as well as reading and editing the drafts that the team in Austin was producing. I left the office just after 2:00 a.m., but Stafford, Kaszynski, and Jones stayed the rest of the night. When I returned a little before 6:00 a.m. they had a complete and polished document ready for me to read. I made two or three changes, and the proposed South Texas/Border Initiative was completed. The staff did a remarkable job, working at a feverish pace to produce one of the most important and far-reaching documents ever to emerge from the UT System.

The campus presidents had not been timid. The proposal called for $212 million in capital and operating expenditures over a ten-year period. These expenditures would lead to a vast array of new facilities, colleges, and undergraduate and graduate programs across the South Texas/Border region at UT System component institutions.

At 8:00 a.m., Herb Richardson and I met again with Bullock in his office. I presented him with our plan, and he was very pleased. I do not think he heard my sigh of relief when he pronounced that UT had produced an "expansive and detailed plan." A&M's plan was not as well developed as ours, but Bullock seemed to have gotten the anger from the previous afternoon out of his system, and he didn't give Richardson any more grief.

Our proposal did not make suggestions about how the legislature would fund the initiative. At the end of our meeting Bullock turned to me and asked, "How are we going to pay for this?" I gave him an answer that I came to rely on often during legislative sessions—that I was on the spending side of the equation, not the funding side. Bullock did not seem to particularly enjoy my sense of humor.

Funding the South Texas/Border Initiative would have been a challenge in any legislative session, and the conditions that the legislature would face in January 1993 were formidable. Governor Ann Richards and other political leaders wanted to avoid raising taxes, and there were many pressing needs besides higher education in South Texas, including prison construction, public school finance, and children's immunizations.

I received a call from the commissioner of the Texas Higher Education Coordinating Board, Ken Ashworth, in October 1992. Ashworth said that he and several of the new members of the Coordinating Board would like to visit with me. I was to learn and relearn many times that very few people just wanted to "visit" me; most of my visitors wanted something from me.

A few days later, I met with Ashworth and three board members. All they wanted to talk about was tuition revenue bonds. Ashworth explained that the legislature had authorized the issuance of tuition revenue bonds to finance construction projects at several universities through the years, mostly for new institutions or campuses that did not have access to the Permanent University Fund. The bonds were guaranteed by future tuition from all of a system's campuses to back the bonds issued by any one institution. In addition, the legislature had a long-standing informal agreement to reimburse institutions yearly for any tuition revenue that was expended on paying debt service on the bonds.

The message from the Coordinating Board delegation was that tuition revenue bonds were bad for the state and that higher education's leaders should unite against the use of them by the legislature. They were concerned that the legislature had relied too heavily on these bonds to pay for capital payments in recent years and that the commitment of the legislature to pay the debt service on the bonds from general revenue was an unsustainable expense. In addition, they felt the state should not be issuing debt of any kind to support capital projects.

As soon as Ashworth and the board members left, I called Mike Millsap, vice chancellor for governmental relations, and Dan Burck, executive vice chancellor for business affairs, and asked them to come to my office. I told them I had just found the answer to the funding problem for our South Texas initiative—tuition revenue bonds. They were the perfect funding vehicle. Tuition revenue bonds would permit members of the legislature to vote for a high-dollar program without having to pay for it up front. In addition, the legislature had never reneged on its promise to reimburse universities for the bond payments. It was a win-win deal. We could issue the bonds using our credit, and the state would reimburse us. I could never again say the Coordinating Board had never been helpful. I would not have learned about how to fund a major portion of the South Texas/Border Initiative if Ashworth and his colleagues had not come to "visit" with me.

I went to see Bullock soon after my meeting with Ashworth and his colleagues. He liked the plan to use tuition revenue bonds to help fund the initiative, and he said he was confident he could get the Senate to vote for them, but he was concerned about the House. Bullock felt we were going to face serious opposition to the funding plan if not also to the academic goals of the initiative. I asked Millsap to develop a legislative strategy to pass the plan to be funded by tuition revenue bonds. Millsap and Armando Diaz, assistant vice chancellor for governmental relations, began by touching base with the legislative leadership from the South Texas/Border region. We benefited from a small group of very dedicated legislators from South Texas who worked together to unite the region behind the main elements of our plan. These included, among others, Senators Carlos Truan, Judith Zaffirini, Frank Madla, Greg Luna, and Eddie Lucio and, in the House, Irma Rangel, Henry Cuellar, Eddie Cavazos, and Hugo Berlanga. Many lawmakers from outside South Texas, such as Senator Bill Ratliff, were also strong advocates for the needs of the region.

Unfortunately, Bullock was right about the problems in the House. When Millsap and I visited with Rob Junell, chairman of the House Appropriations Committee, he immediately declared there was no way the proposal would pass the House in the form we had devised. He said he supported efforts to enhance the institutions in the South Texas/Border region, but he told us the House would not fund any tuition revenue bond program to "bail out" the UT System. As he saw it, the UT System simply had a "distribution problem," and the solution was simple: Take money away from UT Austin's "excellence funds" to pay for the capital needs of the South Texas/Border region.

Junell was, of course, correct that we could free up resources derived from the Permanent University Fund by cutting the amount of money UT Austin received each year to underwrite academic excellence, but that would mean striking a blow at the state's premier university in order to promote others. This was an absolute nonstarter for me. It was not going to happen. It would not have been acceptable to the board of regents and all Texans who understood the fundamental role that UT Austin played in the economic, scientific, and cultural life of the state. Even without Junell's idea of diverting money for the South Texas/Border region, UT Austin was facing intense budget pressure in those years, as a decline in interest rates and increasing demands on the PUF had already resulted in some reductions in the Austin campus's annual excellence money.[3] Junnel's plan was dead on arrival. I often felt Junell was opposed to UT almost as a matter of principle. It may be that he felt that schools such as Texas Tech were "good enough" and that it was not a wise investment for the state to fund major graduate research institutions such as UT Austin and Texas A&M.

The biggest public run-in between Junell and me was a short impromptu meeting in the first-floor hallway in the Capitol when Junell stated he intended to place a rider on the appropriations bill that would require the board of regents to divert money from the Available University Fund at UT Austin to the support of capital programs at schools in the South Texas/Border region. He then said "What do you think of that?" I said, "Rob, we will obey the rider if the regents want to, but it is clearly unconstitutional." Junell went ballistic. He yelled at me and said he would "force UT to obey." I had called his bluff in public and, like many bullies, he did not like it.

After Junell's tirade, I called Morris Atlas of McAllen, a great friend of the university and one of the most highly respected attorneys in the state. Atlas concluded that I had been correct and that the rider would not be enforceable. I asked Atlas to come to Austin and explain his view of the proposed rider at a meeting that we planned to hold at the Ex-Students' Association. We invited all members of the House Appropriations Committee, and about one-third of them showed up—but Junell did not attend. This was an unprecedented event. Atlas made a detailed and thoughtful presentation that left no one in doubt about the constitutional status of the rider.

Millsap also obtained a letter from Steve Collins, who was chief legislative counsel and executive director of the Texas Legislative Council, an agency that provides nonpartisan legal and research services for the legislature. Collins's letter also advised us that the proposed rider was inconsistent with the state constitution. We did not want to use this letter because we were afraid of the ramifications for Collins if he was put in the position of publicly opposing the chairman of the House Appropriations Committee and possibly the Speaker of the

House. Fortunately, Atlas's presentation was a great success and we never heard any more about Junell's rider.

Millsap, Diaz, and Tom Scott, associate vice chancellor for governmental relations, and I began early in the session to hold a series of meetings with legislators to explain the purposes of the initiative. Every night Millsap and I took at least one or two members of the House or Senate to dinner, and as the session developed we were frequently at dinner with various members from Sunday through Thursday nights. We were following Jess Hay's plan of spending informal time with legislators to sell our plan. They always seemed to care about higher education, even if they thought it was going to be difficult to afford what we wanted to do. We had a tremendous amount of data to share with the members—including detailed information about how the UT System and other institutions of higher education in Texas were funded compared to other states. We had a good story to tell, and we enjoyed telling it.

We sought support for the South Texas/Border Initiative the way professional politicians would run a political campaign. Shirley Bird Perry and Diaz organized a series of meetings that brought community leaders from South Texas to Austin to visit with their legislative delegation. We usually held these meetings over dinner with members of a local delegation, and I would speak about the initiative generally and the presidents of our campuses would explain what the initiative would do for their institutions. Then the community leaders—mayors, county commissioners, business and professional power brokers—would make it clear to their assembled state representatives and senators how much they wanted their delegation to support the plan.

Most of these meetings were a great success. Joe Krier, who was then the CEO of the Greater San Antonio Chamber of Commerce, was the best. He rallied his community leaders on multiple occasions to come to Austin and tell the San Antonio delegation how important our initiative was to UT San Antonio and the San Antonio Health Science Center. The only community meeting that I recall not going well was one we held with El Paso leaders and legislators. Former El Paso mayor Jonathan Rogers stood up at that meeting and attacked me and the entire UT System for what he said was a failure to support adequate funding for UT El Paso through the years. This was definitely not part of the script, and it threw the meeting off stride. Either Rogers did not understand the goals of the South Texas/Border Initiative and how it would strengthen UTEP, or he was just angry about the past and saw this as an opportunity to make a public statement about it.

In an effort to build support for the initiative, Perry, Diaz, and I also traveled during the session to all the South Texas/Border communities where we had institutions. We talked with groups of community leaders, elected officials, and newspaper editorial boards in an effort to overcome some initial suspicion and misunderstanding. Some believed the UT System must have an ulterior motive and the initiative couldn't be as good as it sounded. We always included the presidents of the local UT institutions. We were fortunate to have excellent presidents who had good relationships with most members of their local delegation and the local media. We were smart enough at the UT System to realize that while legislators might be interested in hearing what the chancellor had to say, they were keenly interested in the views on an issue held by the president of the local UT institution and local power brokers who often had a first loyalty to the local institution. Therefore, we worked hard to make sure that presidents were on board with our message and plan, and we relied on them to help generate local support.

The central legislative issue for the Coordinating Board was the way the South Texas/Border Initiative, by providing for academic program development and new buildings through special-item appropriations, bypassed the usual formula system for allocating appropriations to colleges and universities. The formulas took into account various factors, such as the number of students enrolled and the number of semester credit hours taught, in calculating how to divide available money among the institutions. In addition to aiming at a rational and largely nonpolitical method of allocation, the formula system fostered incremental development at the institutions and was a response to naturally evolving conditions at the schools rather than a way of forcefully changing those conditions. As a result, schools with growing enrollment were always penalized with the formula system since it paid only for existing enrollments as determined when the legislature was in session, not enrollment growth after the legislature concluded its business. For many purposes, the formula system works well, but those of us at the UT System felt that incremental change was not acceptable in our South Texas/Border institutions and believed that the formula system was inadequate as a way to foster rapid transformation of the universities.

On May 10, 1993, the House approved bills that contained all the provisions of the initiative. Ten days later, the *Houston Chronicle* published an editorial criticizing the House's action as an infringement on the authority of the Coordinating Board. The editorial argued that decisions about new degree programs and facilities should be "based solely on merit and need, rather than politics." The newspaper asserted that the Coordinating Board would make objective decisions about how to spend scarce state resources, while the legislature's decisions would inevitably be tainted by politics. The editorial urged the Senate to reject the legislation "and let this House meddling die."[4] Fortunately the Senate did not take the newspaper's advice. While there had always been some tension between the Coordinating Board and the various universities, no one whom I knew, except perhaps the editorial writer at the *Houston Chronicle*, would have claimed the Coordinating Board had done its work free from politics.

Junell abandoned his opposition to tuition revenue bonds in late May and even supported a solution to the problem of funding capital projects in the South Texas/Border region that also offered inducements to lawmakers from outside the region. The bill containing the bonds for our initiative (HB 2058, sponsored by Junell and senators Carlos Truan and John Montford) emerged from two and a half months of legislative deliberations containing authorization for a total of $352.4 million in bonds and extended well beyond the South Texas/Border schools. The total, as passed by the House on May 24 and the Senate on May 25, included $239 million for South Texas/Border institutions. There was $161 million for capital projects for the UT System's five schools in the region and $75 million for capital projects for the three Texas A&M University System schools in the region. The cost to obtain Junell's support was to broaden our bill into a statewide initiative that would help schools in all regions meet their needs for new and renovated facilities. The legislature added an additional $113.4 million for nine institutions, of which the Texas Tech Health Science Center received $25 million. While this was fine with me, it was a classic example of legislative log rolling and pork barrel spending.

Apart from the bill containing the tuition revenue bonds for capital projects, the other major spending provisions of the initiative were contained in the appropriations bill. This included $82.9 million for the 1993–1995 biennium to develop new academic programs. We

projected that over the next ten years the money for academic program development would result in expenditures of over $400 mil-
lion and would generate 163 new degree programs at the UT System
institutions, including 59 bachelor's, 65 master's, and 39 doctoral
programs. Richards signed the bill with great fanfare on June 18. We
were very pleased that she wanted to join in celebrating the passage
of the initiative.

I published op-ed articles in the *Dallas Morning News*, the *Houston Chronicle*, the *San Antonio Express-News* and other newspapers
throughout the state explaining the importance of the initiative and
thanking as many elected officials by name as possible. Their support
meant we were stunningly successful in 1993 in securing major long-
term funding for the schools.

Millsap, Perry, and Diaz organized a set of community celebrations
that gave us a chance to publicly express our gratitude to community
leaders and legislators. Bullock attended most of these events, and
we always made sure to acknowledge his central role in the success
of the initiative. It was our practice to praise all public officials for
their contributions, no matter how insignificant, and we even made a
point of thanking Junell for his role in the final success of the initiative, although his most important contribution at the end was finally
just to get out of the way. Expressing our gratitude to Junell was
an acknowledgment of the fact that we were going to have to deal
with him in the future. Our policy was never to publicly embarrass
or criticize a member of the legislature, particularly the chairman of
House Appropriations. We even organized an event in San Angelo on
November 15 to thank Junell for his help. The event went well, and
powerful Austin figures and UT friends including George Christian
and Larry Temple attended.

The tuition revenue bonds were issued later by the board of regents
to fund a science and engineering technology building at UT Brownsville; a new classroom building and renovations to existing facilities
at UTEP; an engineering building and a thermal energy plant at UT
Pan American; a new academic building and expansion of an engineering and biotechnology building at UT San Antonio, as well as a
building at UTSA's downtown campus; and a classroom and research
building and renovations to the nursing building at the UT Health
Science Center at San Antonio.

The initiative approved in 1993 was the turning point in obtaining

From left, William H. Cunningham, former Texas Governor Dolph Briscoe, former Regent Janey Briscoe, UT San Antonio President Sam Kirkpatrick, and Senator Jeff Wentworth at a building groundbreaking at UT San Antonio from funds from the South Texas/Border Initiative, c. 1998. *Courtesy of William H. Cunningham.*

major funding to strengthen the institutions of the region, and the legislature continued to provide significant additional funds for the institutions for the rest of the decade. This continued strong support largely reflected the confidence that lawmakers had in the way the institutions had spent the first funds from the initiative.

This extraordinary infusion of new funding represented an enhancement of educational opportunities through new and upgraded academic programs, new classroom and research facilities, and a range of new research centers, economic development centers, health care programs and other activities. Altogether, the South Texas/Border Initiative resulted in the approval of 197 new undergraduate, master's, and doctoral degree programs from 1990 to 2001. In the ten years from 1992 to 2002, almost 2.5 million square feet of buildings had been added or were being planned as a result of the initiative. The initiative had an immediate effect in increasing the share of state spending going to the region, which had lagged behind the rest of the state throughout its history. From 1990 to 2000, state funding at South Texas/Border schools grew by 108 percent. The schools started the decade of the 1990s with 11 percent of the state's total general revenue spending, and by 1996 that share had grown to 15.2 percent.[5] By the turn of the century, the initiative had fundamentally transformed the institutions in the region, and they had all become significantly stronger institutions that were better able to serve their students and communities, and the entire state, with high-quality and diverse educational programs.

The initiative that we presented to lawmakers in 1993 came while the state's appeal of the LULAC lawsuit was still pending before the state Supreme Court. The appeal was heard on October 13, 1992, but it was not until a year later, on October 6, 1993, that the court issued its ruling, in a twenty-four-page opinion by Chief Justice Tom Phillips. The court unanimously overturned Euresti's ruling and found no evidence of intent to discriminate against Mexican Americans. The court also found that the state's system of higher education was not unconstitutional. By the time the Supreme Court ruled, the UT System was busy implementing the historic initiative that we had persuaded the legislature to pass the previous spring, and while the ruling represented a vindication of the state's higher education system, it had no effect on our continuing commitment to strengthen the colleges and universities in the South Texas/Border region. In fact, on the day the court issued its ruling, I was attending a lunch in San Antonio with campus and community leaders, Regent Tom Loeffler, and members of the Bexar County legislative delegation to celebrate passage of the initiative.[6]

The plaintiffs in the lawsuit and South Texas politicians have always assumed that the South Texas/Border Initiative was a direct response to the LULAC lawsuit and the political activities of certain wealthy, politically sophisticated South Texas individuals such as Tony Sanchez from Laredo. From my perspective, the lawsuit had no bearing on UT's commitment to strengthen institutions in the region. While Bullock's request for a plan for South Texas in September 1992 focused my thinking, the UT System's actions with regard to the region, under both Hans Mark's administration and my own, were undertaken out of a clear and strong conviction that the best interests of the state would be served by expanding educational opportunity in the region, not because a lawsuit had accused the State of Texas of discrimination.

It is impossible for me to know what role Sanchez and other prominent South Texas residents played behind the scenes when the legislature was considering our proposals for the region. Sanchez and I had not met prior to his appointment to the UT Board of Regents by Governor George W. Bush in 1993, but he and I became good friends and shared a mutual dream for the continued growth and prosperity of South Texas. We both have always felt that universities provide the best opportunity for individuals and geographic regions to break out of the bonds of poverty. While Sanchez and I did not work together on the 1993 initiative, I recognize that he and his South Texas colleagues spent a great deal of political capital on our initiative before I became chancellor, and I believe it is accurate to assume they worked feverously behind the scenes to pressure the legislature to pass the initiative. I am confident that their investments in helping communicate the educational needs of the region made my assignment much easier. It is also more than likely that they had a direct impact on Bullock's intent to solve the region's education needs. Loeffler told me in 1992 that if my hopes for our South Texas/Border Initiative were realized, the program would be the most important legacy of my years as chancellor. I believe Loeffler was right.

CHAPTER 27

Asset Management

Major changes in the way the UT System manages its investment assets were adopted while I was chancellor. The stage for the changes was set a year before I became chancellor, when, in 1991, Michael E. Patrick, who had served with distinction for seven years as executive vice chancellor for asset management, decided to leave that position for opportunities in the private sector. Hans Mark named Thomas G. Ricks, who had been responsible for the UT System's alternative investments, to serve as acting vice chancellor. After undertaking a national search, Mark decided that Ricks was the best choice for the appointment to the permanent position, but before asking the regents to finalize that decision he was kind enough to ask me to interview Ricks to make sure I was comfortable with his recommendation. I knew that Ricks had an excellent reputation, and after we met I was very confident that we would be able to work together when I became chancellor in September.

During the transition period, Ricks told me that if the UT System was to be successful in investing its assets it needed to overcome two structural problems. The first dealt with the fundamental organization and governance of his office, and the second was a constitutional prohibition against operating the Permanent University Fund as a total return fund. I understood that these were important and serious issues that I needed to deal with.

Before the creation of the University of Texas Investment Management Company, the vice chancellor for asset management reported to the chancellor. The regents' Committee on Asset Management met periodically to set policies and exercised oversight over the UT investment staff. While the regents were usually sophisticated oilmen, lawyers, bankers, physicians, or other business professionals, they were not experienced in large-scale institutional money management, so their ability to provide guidance to the investment staff was rather limited. This became more and more obvious as investment techniques grew more sophisticated and as the importance of increasing the earnings of the PUF became more critical to the institutions in the UT and A&M systems.

Governor Richards recognized that the system needed at least one regent who was an investment expert, and she appointed Peter Coneway, a former partner with Goldman Sachs in Houston, to the board in March 1993. Coneway stepped down from the board after only a few months because of a technical conflict of interest that existed because of his continuing relationship with Goldman Sachs. Richards then appointed Tom Hicks in January 1994. Hicks was a highly regarded investment professional from Dallas. He was a founding partner of Hicks, Muse, Tate and Furst, a very successful private equity firm. His colleagues on the board immediately elected him chairman of the Asset Management Committee.

Ricks wanted to create an organization to manage the UT System's endowments that would be owned by the board of regents but would have its own board of directors that would be dominated by investment professionals who understood complex investment models and strategies. Ricks argued that he needed to be able to interact with a sophisticated investment board and that this would ultimately lead to improved governance and investment return for the PUF. Ricks also argued that underperformance in the PUF's annual investment return of only 2.5 percent translated into an opportunity cost in the tens of millions of dollars each year and compelled the UT System to adopt the most competitive investment organization structure. He also believed we would be more successful in recruiting investment managers if the system was not constrained by many of the state's rules and regulations. I was in fundamental agreement with Ricks, and he began talking about these ideas with Hicks soon after Hicks joined the board.

Hicks, Ricks, and I visited Duke University's private investment company, DUMAC, to learn how it operated. Hicks picked us up in his private plane on November 18, 1994, and we went to North Carolina in style. We met with Eugene McDonald, president of DUMAC and Benjamin Holloway, chairman of the board of DUMAC. They walked us through how the company was structured and the relationship it had with Duke's board of trustees. At the end of the meet-

Tom Hicks. *Courtesy of Tom Hicks.*   Tom Ricks. *Courtesy of the UT System.*

ing, Hicks and I concluded that Ricks was correct—we needed a new investment structure modeled after private investment companies. Bernard Rapoport, then chairman of the UT Board of Regents, also was an early and enthusiastic supporter of the reorganization plan.

The enabling legislation that we developed to create the new investment entity was introduced in the 74th Legislature in 1995 by state Representative Mark Stiles, chairman of the House Calendars Committee, and Senator John Montford, chairman of the Senate Finance Committee. This was typical of how Mike Millsap liked to pass bills, with the most influential members in the legislature carrying our legislation.

The bill faced four major challenges. Senator Steve Ogden from College Station did not like the bill. I never really understood why, but he felt UT was up to something that ultimately would not be good for the state. I tried to explain to Ogden that with a board made up largely of independent investment professionals there would actually be more oversight of the university's investment practices than there had been in the past. Ogden was not convinced. He agreed to withdraw his opposition only when we amended the proposed legislation to say that at least one member of the board of the University of Texas Investment Management Company would be selected by the Texas

A&M Board of Regents. While Ogden did not trust the A&M regents any more than he trusted the UT board, he did not want to fight with his hometown university, which had now become an active supporter of the UTIMCO legislation.

Two of the remaining three issues dealt with potential conflicts of interest. Lieutenant Governor Bob Bullock never trusted Hicks. He worried that Hicks would be in a position to profit from the new structure. The bill included a section designed to prevent conflicts of interest, prohibiting the new entity from investing in an enterprise in which any of its directors, officers, or employees had a business interest. Despite this language, Bullock was never comfortable with the legislation. The good news was that Bullock both liked and trusted me, and he did not exercise his power to block the bill.

After we had satisfied Bullock, Millsap received a call from Alberto Gonzalez, general counsel to Govenor Bush. Gonzalez also felt there was potential for conflicts of interest in the legislation. He made several suggestions to change the language to strengthen prohibitions against conflicts of interest. Gonzalez made a clear threat that if we did not accept his language Bush might veto the bill. I felt this was a bluff, but we also recognized his suggestions were harmless, so we quickly agreed to them.

The final problem we faced was an altercation between Joe Allbaugh, the governor's chief of staff, and Mark Stiles. Allbaugh let it be known that Bush might veto the legislation, which by then had passed the House and Senate. Allbaugh never told us why Bush had a problem with the bill. It may well have been nothing more than a staff member trying to act like the governor was a player in the process when, in reality, Bush did not care about the UTIMCO bill. When Stiles heard about Allbaugh's comments, he went ballistic and threatened to scuttle a number of the governor's initiatives that were still pending in the House. Allbaugh came over to the House Chamber and Stiles refused to meet with him. At that point, Allbaugh called Millsap and me in for a discussion. He was very upset. We told him that we had not created the problem with Stiles and that he would need to fix it. I had no interest in trying to clean up after Allbaugh. At this point, Allbaugh folded, and the bill was signed.

The legislation drew little, if any, notice from the news media during the session. Instead of focusing on a one-and-a-half page bill that must have seemed like an arcane piece of legislation, most of the media attention during the 74th session was on the way Bush, Bullock, and House Speaker Pete Laney worked together on much more colorful legislative issues such as tort reform, property rights, electricity deregulation, and telecommunication policy.[1]

In May 1996 the board of regents used the authority created by the legislation and established the University of Texas Investment Management Company, a separate entity set up to invest the assets of the PUF and other endowments and funds over which the regents have fiduciary control (then valued at a total of $9 billion). While UTIMCO was modeled after investment companies created by Duke, Harvard, Princeton, and Stanford, it was the first such entity at a public university. The makeup of the board of directors was specified in the legislation: It would consist of three members of the UT System Board of Regents, the chancellor of the UT System, and five outside investment professionals, one of whom was to be selected by the Texas A&M Board of Regents.

UTIMCO's outside directors, while being subject to the ultimate control of the board of regents, enhanced the UT System's ability to participate in an environment of integrated world financial markets, alternative investments, hedge funds, and rapid technological innovation. Hicks said: "As a private sector corporation, UTIMCO is better able to analyze and respond quickly to market information and thereby control fund risk and return profiles."[2] Hicks became the first chairman of the UTIMCO board, and Ricks became its first CEO and president. As chancellor of the UT System, I was the first director of UTIMCO. I had made sure that the enabling legislation stated that the chancellor of the UT System would automatically be a member of the board. Hicks recruited outstanding independent members of the board. They included Richard Fisher and Susan M. Byrne of Dallas, Luther King from Fort Worth, and Homer Luther of Houston. Texas A&M's first appointment was Robert Allen from Houston, who was a member of the Texas A&M System Board of Regents. Ricks's work in planning UTIMCO and steering it through its first five years was a major reason for its success.

In March 1999, R. G. Ratcliffe, a reporter at the *Houston Chronicle*, began to focus on UTIMCO's meeting policies that restricted the media from attending board meetings and its policy of not providing details concerning privately placed investments.[3] UTIMCO's original policies with respect to open meetings and open records was a result of concerns that disclosure of the information would have harmed the performance of our investments by making sensitive information available to competitors. Because of these concerns, the private investment contracts typically included nondisclosure agreements. Two Texas attorneys general—Dan Morales and John Cornyn—had ruled that this information did not have to be made public because of the state open records act's competitive marketplace exemption.

A week after one of the *Chronicle*'s articles, the UTIMCO board announced that it would change its policy on public disclosure of the private investments, so that the names of principals in future investments and the annual rate of return on each investment would be made public. We did reserve the right not to disclose various other details, such as business plans, investment strategies, and projected rates of return over time. In addition to changing the disclosure policy on future investments, all of our current investment partners agreed to release UTIMCO from confidentiality agreements, so information about those investments could also be made public without fear of legal action. In discussing this change, I observed that, "UTIMCO and the UT System are committed to the highest standards of public accountability, as well as to the imperative that we achieve a high rate of return on the funds that we invest on behalf of the public."[4]

The new disclosure policy supplemented other detailed items of information that were already publicly available regarding UTIMCO's private investments. UTIMCO's audited annual reports were available on the company's website, and they contained data on the performance of the private investment portfolio as a whole. UTIMCO also provided an annual report of detailed schedules of investment securities, including the year-end book value and market value of every investment, including every private investment. All this information had been made public for years before any criticism of UTIMCO by the press, and all the reports had always been audited annually by an outside accounting firm and were sent to the board of regents, the governor, the state comptroller, the state auditor, and the Legislative Budget Board.

Ratcliffe continued to write a series of articles that all but accused Hicks and Bush of a conflict of interest involving the allocations of UTIMCO funds to various external investment advisers. I supervised an investigation of each of Ratcliffe's charges, and the findings were published on UTIMCO's website. If Bush was applying pressure for

UTIMCO to invest with certain investment advisers, he never asked me for help and certainly did not call any of the UTIMCO staff members. In addition, every private equity investment decision was originated in a bottom-up process and was thoroughly vetted by the UTIMCO staff. Only investment decisions that were approved by the staff were forwarded for review and possible approval by the board. If the staff felt that an adviser should not be hired for any reason, he or she never met with the board. Finally, detailed reports on investments were public, and all UTIMCO activities were subject to state audits. My investigation concluded that there was no conflict of interest between Hicks and UTIMCO.

In an effort to clear the air and stop Ratcliffe from continuing to write his poorly researched articles and try to answer any questions the paper had, I called Richard Johnson, publisher of the *Chronicle,* and he agreed to set up a meeting. Johnson was a distinguished alumnus of UT Austin. While he was always fair when it came to articles focusing on UT Austin, I knew that Johnson loved UT and he would not approve of any biased activities. On April 7, 1999, Hicks, Ricks, and I met with Ratcliffe, Johnson, Editor Jack Loftis, and David Langworthy, a member of the editorial board, for almost two hours of an on-the-record question-and-answer session. Pat Oxford and Charles Miller, members of the board of regents from Houston, also attended. We answered every question on the record.

On September 3, 1999, the board of regents approved my recommendation that meetings of the UTIMCO board would be open to the public, consistent with the state open meetings law. This meant we could still hold closed briefing sessions on lawsuits, real estate transactions, prospective investments, and other matters specified in the law, but any decisions by the board of UTIMCO would have to be made in public. Ricks and I concluded that we could protect the discussion of prospective investment strategies and, therefore, I felt comfortable with the recommendation. I also realized that we would have a perpetual fight with the *Houston Chronicle* and the *Austin American-Statesman* on this issue, and it was not worth the negative, distorted press that we were receiving or that we would inevitably receive in the future.[5] It seemed to us that the press had adopted an absolutist position that was unwilling to recognize any of the exceptions written into the Texas open meetings act by the legislature.

When Hicks left the board of regents in February 1999, the UTIMCO board elected Robert H. Allen to succeed him as its chairman. Allen, a member of the Texas A&M Board of Regents, was a private investor in Houston with an outstanding record in business and public service. He was the logical choice to be chairman, and everyone felt very comfortable with his leadership. The selection of an A&M regent as the second chairman of UTIMCO clearly implied that the board of UTIMCO and the UT System Board of Regents had a great deal of confidence in Allen and that UT and A&M were working together.

The constitutional prohibition against operating the PUF as a total return fund was the second major issue affecting the UT System's investment assets while I was chancellor. During the period I was president of UT Austin, and for most of my term as chancellor, the constitution of Texas required that all dividends, interest, and other income from the PUF had to be distributed. At the same time, the constitution prohibited the UT System from spending any of the realized capital gains. That meant all capital gains, such as profits on the sale of stock, had to be invested as part of the "corpus" of the fund.

These restrictions caused several major problems. In years when interest rates were unusually high, the board of regents was required to pay out a higher distribution from the PUF than could be sustained over the long term. This was not appropriate because an important priority for the board of regents is to maintain the purchasing power of the fund, and that could not be achieved if the payout rate was too high. For example, in 1981 the PUF paid out 10 percent of the total value of the fund. Although the faculty and students who benefitted from this unreasonably high payout rate enjoyed the largess of the fund, the future recipients of university endowments would be penalized for this carefree spending pattern.

The opposite problem occurred when interest rates were relatively low and the payout rate to the university endowment had to be reduced. In some years, the board of regents found itself paying out less than 3 percent. This presented the beneficiaries of the endowments with the need to cut budgets that had been set according to the higher payouts of previous years, although there was money available from capital gains that could have been used to support the university's academic programs. This boom-and-bust budget pattern was one of the main consequences of not having access to a portion of the capital gains, which could have been used to help even out the annual allocations to the institutions benefiting from the PUF.

The final problem was that the UT System was deterred from investing in growth companies because they traditionally paid very little in dividends. While those stocks often had attractive capital gains, the university could not distribute the capital gains. The only alternative the constitution permitted was the more narrow strategy of harvesting capital gains and reinvesting them in another asset that paid dividends or interest.

Ricks was a persistent advocate for a total return investment policy, which would permit a stable distribution of money to the beneficiaries from one year to the next and at the same time help maintain the purchasing power of the fund over the long term. In hindsight, I should have addressed the total return question immediately upon becoming chancellor. My excuse for not doing so lies in the fact that I was brand-new to the job and had lots of more immediate problems to deal with, such as the South Texas/Border Initiative and the creation of UTIMCO, and I was not confident we could pass a constitutional amendment. However, Ricks was persistent, and his arguments were bolstered by a report from the State Auditor's Office in 1996, which focused on the advantages of a total return fund. The report concluded that, "A constitutional amendment eliminating those restrictions would provide more flexibility in attempting to maximize long-term growth in both the corpus and the distributions" from the PUF.[6] In addition, one of the university's investment advisers, Cambridge Associates, reported that more than 94 percent of higher education institutions used a total return strategy for investment of their endowments.

Hicks, Ricks, and I brought the issue of a total return fund to the regents in executive session in 1998. The board was an easy sell since Hicks supported the constitutional amendment and the benefit to UT and A&M of operating the PUF as a total return fund was so clear. I made amending the constitution a top priority for the 1999 legislative session.

Laying the proper groundwork for legislative consideration of the amendment took months of planning and discussion between UT officials and our counterparts in the Texas A&M System and among the state's political leaders. Texas A&M officials were not initially in support of the amendment. They understood why it was a good idea economically, but they were genuinely concerned that if the PUF ever became "in play" at the legislature, a variety of bad things could happen. A&M President Ray Bowen and I met several times on the issue, and eventually A&M agreed to support the amendment.

We gained support from all the other university systems, even though they had no direct stake in the PUF, because UT and A&M agreed to support legislative appropriations for special "excellence" funding for the non-PUF institutions. This deal, made possible by our statewide coalition of all higher education institutions, eliminated the possibility that other schools would try to shape our amendment to meet their own interests or work to defeat it.

Millsap and Tom Scott felt we should ask Senator Bill Ratliff to carry the amendment in the Senate. Ratliff's only concern was that UT would go on a spending spree and allocate too much of the capital gains from the PUF. To address this we agreed to three provisions that would restrict decisions of the board of regents in determining the annual payout. First, the amount distributed annually must be consistent with the constitutional goal of preserving over time the purchasing power of PUF investments and of distributions to the AUF. If the purchasing power of PUF investments was not maintained, the distributions to the AUF could not be increased. Second, the distributions to the AUF must always be sufficient to pay the principal and interest owed on bonds and notes backed by the PUF. The third restriction was that the annual distribution to the AUF could not exceed 7 percent of the value of the PUF. I did not like this limit because in periods of sustained high inflation we might find it desirable and feasible to spend more than 7 percent. However, Millsap and Scott advised me that we should not fight Ratliff over this provision since he was one of the primary sponsors for the amendment. Once again, politics involves the science of compromise.

In discussing the proposed amendment with lawmakers, we pointed out that the typical payout for a large university endowment was approximately 4.5 percent, while the payout rate of the PUF in 1999 had been set by the board of regents at 3.9 percent. We also said that under normal economic conditions we would expect the board to pay out between 4.25 percent and 4.75 percent with a total return policy.

Creating a more sensible investment strategy that would permit us to even out over time the expenditures derived from the PUF was one of the major selling points for the amendment. We also told legislators that the UT System would be able to increase the number of construction projects across the system that were funded with PUF bonds because we would be able to increase the projected expenditure supporting such bonds, and that the amendment would enable us to increase the amount of money from the AUF that went to UT Austin each year in excellence funds. These allocations had been reduced dramatically during the 1990s, so the amendment was an opportunity to reverse that pattern.

State Representative Rob Junell, chairman of the House Appropriations Committee, agreed to sponsor the bill in the House along with state Representative Henry Cuellar. Cuellar was a great friend of UT and the rest of higher education, and he was a reliable voice in the House for sound public policy. He served on both the House Appropriations Committee and the House Higher Education Committee in 1999. We had concerns, however, about Junell, who had a long history of being a very strong supporter of Texas Tech. Nevertheless, when Junell offered to sponsor the amendment we felt we had no choice but to accept his offer. We had some concern that he might try to use the amendment to change the language of the PUF to include Texas Tech. Through the years, Junell had threatened a number of changes to the PUF that would have seriously harmed the ability of the fund to benefit UT Austin, and we thought there might be a possibility we would have to defeat our own amendment before the debate was over. Fortunately, these fears turned out to be unfounded. In any case, the amendment would need approval in the Senate regardless of the form it took in the House, and we knew Ratliff would do the right thing.

Thanks to the careful preparation of our governmental relations staff at the UT System and Texas A&M, as well as to the leadership of Ratliff, Junell, and Cuellar, the resolution to put the amendment before the voters won unanimous support in both the House Appropriations Committee and the Senate Finance Committee. The full House approved the amendment unanimously on May 3, and the Senate added its unanimous endorsement on May 13.[7]

With those votes, we began considering how to prepare for the November 2, 1999, general election, when our amendment would be listed as the last of seventeen proposed constitutional amendments. Millsap and I talked a lot about what, if anything, we should do to ensure that the proposition would win voter approval. We understood that most proposed amendments win approval and we might be better off not to bring any attention to our amendment. However, we were also concerned that if some group decided to oppose the proposition and we had not done anything to help it win, then we would deeply regret our inaction.

Jack Martin from Public Strategies advised Millsap and me as we developed our campaign strategy. The campaign included direct mail to targeted likely voters, a limited number of radio advertisements, and an effort to communicate with editorial boards and civic groups. These activities were undertaken with an awareness of the fact that in a constitutional amendment election it is not necessary to mount a comprehensive statewide campaign that saturates the airwaves and the print media, the way one would conduct a campaign for statewide political office. Proposed constitutional amendments usually draw a very small percentage of the eligible voters, so a fairly small group of well-informed and committed supporters can carry an election, provided they have no well-organized and well-funded opposition.

To pay for the outside campaign, our plan was to ask A&M supporters to raise $100,000 and to ask UT supporters to contribute $200,000. The difference was consistent with the way the PUF benefits the two systems, with one-third of the fund's bond proceeds reserved for the A&M System and two-thirds for the UT System. Millsap and I met several times off-campus to discuss these goals, and then we met with Howard Graves, chancellor of the Texas A&M System, beginning in the summer of 1999. Graves, a native Texan and a retired U.S. Army general, was a former superintendent of the U.S. Military Academy at West Point, and he had been a faculty member at the LBJ School of Public Affairs at UT Austin. He understood very well the importance of Proposition 17 for both university systems, and he agreed to work with A&M donors to raise his $100,000 share of the budget for the campaign.

I asked a few friends of UT to help us and we raised our $200,000 share in a few days, but A&M struggled to reach their goal. Graves was new to his job, and he may have been given advice by his legal counsel to stay away from politics and let UT handle the problem. Graves and I met weekly on the phone with Millsap and our media consultant to discuss campaign strategy. At the end of each call the media consultant would ask Graves when he could expect to receive

A&M's money. The direct mail and radio companies insist on being paid up front before they run advertisements. Graves was clearly getting tired of the questions, but there was still no cash. Finally, in an act of frustration I told Graves that I would personally donate the money for A&M's share, so long as it was publicly acknowledged that the UT System chancellor had given the money on A&M's behalf. With that, our friends in College Station began to move very quickly and finished raising their $100,000. As often happens with campaigns of this kind, we eventually realized we would need more money, so we raised our budget goal to $430,000, with friends of UT providing $300,000 and friends of A&M contributing $130,000.

Beginning in September, Graves and I went to major newspapers across the state to explain Proposition 17 to editorial boards and ask them to consider publishing an op-ed article in its support. We visited the *Austin American-Statesman*, the *Corpus Christi Caller-Times*, the *Dallas Morning News*, the *El Paso Times*, the *Fort Worth Star-Telegram*, the *Houston Chronicle*, and the *San Antonio Express-News*. I am pleased that we had consistently positive receptions from the newspapers. We also asked the presidents and several of our institutions in both systems to make similar visits to smaller newspapers around the state. Overall, the UT and A&M teams visited with twenty-three newspaper editorial boards in all major geographic regions and population centers. We emphasized to all university employees participating in these visits that our purpose was to provide information so that the voters of Texas could make an informed decision. In addition, the chairmen of the boards of regents of the UT System and the Texas A&M System, Don Evans and Don Powell, wrote an excellent op-ed article titled "Proposition 17, a modern approach to the permanent University Fund" that was published by newspapers across the state.

Proposition 17 drew very little opposition. State Representative Talmadge Heflin of Houston, who had voted in the House to place the amendment on the ballot, came out against it in the fall, as did a conservative, "pro-family" organization called Texas Eagle Forum. The most noticeable opposition came from a UT Austin law student named Marc Levin, an activist on campus issues for several years, who organized two groups called Students for Affordable Education and Texans Against Proposition 17. Levin published an op-ed article in the *Amarillo Daily News* and the *Houston Chronicle,* and he issued a press release on October 11 criticizing Proposition 17 and was quoted in a news article about the amendment in the *Odessa American*.[8] In addition to opposing Proposition 17 itself, Levin charged that university officials had broken state law by campaigning for passage of the amendment—a charge that was not true. We understood the law very well, and all our actions were within the law.

I never knew if Levin was seriously concerned about the passage of Proposition 17 or if he just enjoyed the publicity of opposing the UT System and the Texas Legislature. However, we took his criticisms of Proposition 17 seriously because they distorted the purpose and importance of the amendment and could seriously mislead any potential voter. We rebutted his statements point by point and again sent out accurate information to the news media. His main arguments were that Proposition 17 would promote "speculation" in the stock market and would be inconsistent with the "prudent investor" objective of generating a steady flow of income. He also asserted that the PUF had been mismanaged. We explained in our communications with the news media that Proposition 17 was designed to do exactly what Levin said he wanted—to provide a stable and predictable stream of annual distributions and to maintain over time the purchasing power of the fund's investments. We also easily defended our management of the PUF by pointing out that we regularly met the tests of the state auditor and outside auditors as well as oversight committees of the legislature. In fact, the legislature had so much confidence in the board of regents' good management of the PUF that it asked UTIMCO to manage, on behalf of other state agencies and universities, almost $900 million of the newly created endowments funded by the state's tobacco lawsuit settlement. These rebuttals evidently satisfied most members of the news media. Newspapers across the state endorsed Proposition 17 and encouraged their readers to vote for it.[9]

The results of the election were gratifying to everyone who had worked so hard over several years to modernize the investment and payout strategy of the PUF. The amendment was approved by 61.2 percent of the voters, and it passed in 161 of the state's 254 counties. Most of the counties where the amendment lost were in rural areas with relatively low population, but in many of these counties the margin was extremely narrow. The statewide turnout was very low, with only about 8 percent of registered voters (about 900,000 out of 11.4 million) voting on Proposition 17. The main support came from those urban counties where UT System institutions had a strong presence. The margin of approval was 73.8 percent in Bexar County, 76.2 percent in El Paso County, 66.6 percent in Tarrant County, 64.4 percent in Travis County, 62.9 percent in Dallas County, and 59.9 percent in Harris County. The favorable votes in those six counties alone would have been enough to gain statewide approval.[10] I do believe that our visits to the editorial boards of the state's major newspapers helped convince them of the merits of passing Proposition 17 and they, in turn, were very supportive of the proposition.

Together with the creation of UTIMCO, Proposition 17 allowed us to bring the management of the PUF fully into the modern era, consistent with the best practices at major university endowment funds across the country. The ultimate test of the success of UTIMCO and Proposition 17 will be how UTIMCO's investment decisions compare over time with the performance of the market and other endowment investment funds. While only the future will tell for sure, I am confident that the decisions to create UTIMCO and to make the PUF a total return fund were two of the most important decisions ever made by the UT Board of Regents and the Texas Legislature. My only concern is that a misdirected board of regents in the future will decide that UTIMCO has too much independence and will withdraw its authority to independently manage the investments. From my perspective, this would be a major mistake.

CHAPTER 28

Regional Academic Health Center

n November 1998 the board of regents approved a plan to establish a Regional Academic Health Center (RAHC) in the Lower Rio Grande Valley, with facilities and programs split among four cities—Harlingen, Edinburg, Brownsville, and McAllen. The decision culminated almost eighteen months of planning that began when the 75th Legislature in 1997 approved, and Governor George W. Bush signed into law, a bill providing partial funding for such a center and delegating the details, including the choice of a site, to the UT System. This far-sighted legislation—authored by state Senator Eddie Lucio of Brownsville and sponsored in the House by state Representative Juan "Chuy" Hinojosa of Edinburg—has been justly hailed as a historic victory for the Lower Rio Grande Valley, a region of high poverty, major health problems, a scarcity of physicians and other health professionals, and a history of feeling like a "neglected stepchild" when it came to state appropriations for education, health, and other basic needs.

The first person I ever visited with about enhancing medical education in the valley was Dr. Mario Ramirez. Ramirez was both a political and a medical force in the valley. He had been active in UT Austin affairs for many years, and when he became a regent in 1989, he used that position to gently, thoughtfully, and persistently advocate for a wide variety of improvements in medical services and medical education in South Texas.

Tony Sanchez, a Laredo businessman, picked up the baton from Ramirez in 1997 when he joined the board of regents. Sanchez, like Ramirez, clearly recognized the need to improve medical services to South Texas. Sanchez was intimately involved in all the major decisions that related to medical education and the delivery of medical services in South Texas during his tenure on the board. His keen sense of the political realities in South Texas played a critical role in our success in developing the RAHC. He also made some very valuable practical contributions to the UT System's eventual efforts to explain the benefits of a RAHC to various valley communities and build region-wide support for it.

Valley leaders had been advocating for years that the state build a medical school in the region, but the huge funding requirements had continued to be a fatal obstacle in the state legislature. The UT Health Science Center at San Antonio was envisioned at its inception in 1959 as an institution that would serve all of South Texas, but by the 1980s the Lower Rio Grande Valley had gained a regional identity apart from the rest of South Texas. Its citizens were advocating for a greater share of state resources of all kinds, and health education (whether a medical school, a pharmacy program, public health programs, or other entities) was always high on their list of priorities. By 1997, years of discussion had begun to focus on the idea of building a RAHC in the valley, and this idea had gained traction among lawmakers.

A RAHC falls considerably short of a full-fledged medical school and even more short of an academic health center, which offers degrees across a wide range of medical and health care specialties, often including dentistry, pharmacy, nursing, allied health, public health, and biomedical research. Instead of such a comprehensive institution, a RAHC provides education to third- and fourth-year medical students and medical residents who have completed medical school and are specializing in one or occasionally more areas of medicine. Both the students and the residents provide a significant amount of medical care to the community under the supervision of medical school faculty.

Lucio approached Armando Diaz, assistant vice chancellor for governmental relations, in the fall of 1996 about getting support from the UT System for expanding health education in the valley. Diaz agreed to arrange for Lucio and his chief of staff, Paul Cowen, to meet with Charles Mullins, executive vice chancellor for health affairs; James Guckian, vice chancellor for health affairs, and Mike Millsap, vice chancellor for governmental relations. Lucio said at the early morning meeting that he was flying to Harlingen at 2:00 p.m. and he didn't want to leave until he had a draft of a bill that he could file for the upcoming legislative session.

From left, William H. Cunningham, Senator Eddie Lucio, Coach Darrell Royal, Paul Cowen (Lucio's chief of staff), and Mike Millsap. *Courtesy of Senator Eddie Lucio.*

The UT System was in an excellent position to discuss the options with Lucio because, thanks to Guckian's work, we had on hand a spreadsheet that provided realistic estimates of the start-up costs for various types of heath education facilities—ranging from a RAHC to a medical school associated with a teaching hospital to the most expensive option, a full-scale academic health center. The costs ranged from about $30 million or $40 million for a RAHC to as much as $300 million for an academic health center. The figures were for initial construction costs, other start-up costs, and operations for the first two years. Guckian had had the foresight to be analyzing the options and their relative costs for several months because of the increasing talk in the valley and at the legislature about new health education initiatives. Dozens of people were engaging in such talk, but it is safe to say that only the UT System had any realistic concept of what it would cost to put the talk into action. With these informed estimates already in our back pocket, the conversation with Lucio quickly focused on establishing a RAHC—the option that the legislature would be most likely to find enough money to support.

I joined the meeting with Lucio, and I quickly became convinced that our best chance for getting the legislature to approve expanded health education in the valley was to get behind an incremental approach, and a RAHC serving the region seemed to answer that need. We also emphasized, and Lucio was quick to agree, that for the RAHC to win legislative approval it would need the unified support of legislators from throughout the valley, and that meant the initiative would need to have a regional focus from the very beginning, rather than being seen as benefiting only one city or county. I asked Ray Farabee, the system's vice chancellor and general counsel, and Mel Hazlewood, of our governmental relations staff, to begin drafting the required legislation. Hazlewood was an extremely talented practitioner of the art of drafting legislation, and his work on the RAHC proposal is a model of legislative efficiency and ingenuity. We didn't have a bill for Lucio to take with him on his trip to the valley that afternoon, but it was finished when he got back. Diaz was named the point person to work with Lucio's staff as we crafted the bill and prepared it to be introduced.

Lucio filed his bill to create a RAHC (SB 606) on February 14, 1997. Despite the UT System's participation in drafting the bill, we were not overly enthusiastic about the prospects of a new state-funded medical entity. Our enthusiasm grew over time, but at first we were concerned about whether the state would adequately fund a new entity. Our priority for medical education in South Texas continued to be the strengthening of the UT Health Science Center at San Antonio, and we were wary of any proposal that might detract from that effort. The political forces in support of a RAHC were gaining strength, and it had important support from the legislative leadership. In addition, the valley delegation was demonstrating an unusual level of unity on this issue, as more and more valley leaders came to realize that they needed to unite in order for the region to compete more successfully against other sections of the state.

Lucio's strategy of getting first in line with his bill proved successful, and the Senate held hearings on his bill in early March and passed it on April 15. Meanwhile, Hinojosa had filed his own bill, which was still in committee in the House. Lucio was able to persuade him to become a sponsor of SB 606 and unite behind the bill that was moving the fastest. Other valley legislators who provided critical support for the RAHC legislation during the 1997 session included Renato Cuellar, a state representative from Weslaco, and Roberto Gutierrez, a state representative from McAllen.

We helped Lucio and others from the valley explain to other legislators the significant advantages of building a RAHC in the valley. Our story was that an institution concentrating on students and medical residencies would be considerably cheaper to build and maintain than a full-scale medical school. The RAHC would draw medical residents to the Lower Rio Grande Valley, and it would serve to increase the number of practicing physicians in the region just as much as a medical school. As a smaller and more focused institution, it could concentrate on serving the public health needs of the regional population, and it would represent a major infusion of state resources into the region. In addition, we were confident that the RAHC would be an investment that was certain to be good for the region's economy (creating hundreds of jobs and generating $100 million or more in economic impact); and, in the minds of many valley residents, it would be a significant first step along the way to eventually establishing a full medical school.

With their united front, the House passed the bill on May 7, and by May 27 both houses had approved conference committee reports and had sent the bill to the governor. Bush signed the bill on June 16, to become effective September 1. Lucio's bill gave the UT Board of Regents complete discretion over selecting a site. While the valley was united on the idea of a RAHC, it is certain that any legislation that specified a particular city for its location would have never become law. While the various competing communities could not agree on any one site, they all seemed willing to let the board of regents make a decision. In part they trusted the regents to make an impartial choice based on an objective judgment of what was in the best interests of the valley as a whole. But they really had no other option—if they wanted to see a RAHC built anywhere. It was clear that, left to their own devices, they would never have been able to decide where to locate the RAHC.

Given all the clear advantages of a RAHC in the valley, it might be surprising that the project was controversial at almost every step in its planning and establishment. All the regional unity that helped secure the support of the legislature seemed to dissolve in the next stage—the matter of selecting a location for the center. Because of the political stakes and the absolute necessity that the legislature be satisfied with our decision, we proceeded in as nonpolitical a manner as possible. It was very apparent that we would have to set clear and justifiable criteria for bids and that the entire process would have to be conducted transparently, without any taint of political dealing.

The UT System's Office of Health Affairs was the logical coordinator of the process, and most of the work was handled by Mullins and Guckian. Once the site selection and other start-up work was complete, operation of most of the RAHC programs was to be under the direction of the UT Health Science Center at San Antonio.

Within a matter of months after the legislative session, we had developed the basic criteria for a site—such as that the community would need to provide adequate land and other resources, and the location would need to be near a hospital—and in December 1997 the regents selected the Kaludis Consulting Group of Washington, D.C., to help evaluate site proposals from interested communities. There is absolutely no question that Mullins and his staff were perfectly capable of selecting a location for the RAHC. However, I knew from the beginning that there were going to be winners and losers in the ultimate decision of which site to select. An expert is frequently defined as someone from out of town. I did not want to have my experts—Mullins and his staff—get into trouble over the selection of the winning city. The goal at that time was to make a decision on a site by the following spring, but a decision was postponed until August and then again until the fall of 1998.

Many people in the valley and in the legislature, as well as many at the UT System, thought at the beginning of the process that the RAHC would be located in McAllen. It was the largest city in the region and had a well-established medical and hospital community. In many respects, the RAHC was McAllen's to lose, and that is exactly what happened.

McAllen's initial proposal was less than overpowering, and there was talk that the city had been complacent and had not paid as much attention to the bid as it should have. From the perspective of the UT System, there were two main reasons that the city failed to develop a truly competitive proposal.

First, many doctors in McAllen were vocal in their opposition to bringing the facility to their city. Some were concerned that the RAHC would never succeed because it was likely to be perpetually underfunded and would therefore be a bad deal for the community, while many others were opposed because they feared it would be *too* successful, attracting more physicians to the city to compete for patients.[1] And second, the city lacked the political leadership willing or able to stand up to the doctors and their politically powerful Hidalgo-Starr Counties Medical Society. The opposition of the doctors was expressed in a letter in February 1998 to area legislators from Dr. Alexander Feigl, then the president of the medical society, and nine of his predecessors. "We are sorry that you have wandered into a face-off between subsidized and private medicine which has been brewing for some time," Feigl wrote. "Unfortunately, you have sided with the system that is a predator of private practices. We feel that if your advisors had consisted of practicing physicians, some of the issues that doom the program to failure could have been foreseen." The "predation" that the medical society feared included the possibility that medical care associated with the RAHC might siphon off some of the $334 million that the federal Medicare program was spending annually on health care provided by physicians within the four counties of the valley. Many doctors throughout the valley have a decidedly entrepreneurial approach to the practice of medicine, owning and operating their own clinics and competing aggressively for patients.

The society's letter went on to predict that the RAHC would eventually require a local tax for its support, that the burden for financing indigent care would fall on the local community, and that there weren't enough patients in the Lower Rio Grande Valley to justify the center. The lawmakers who received the letter—Lucio, Hinojosa, and Gutierrez—vigorously disputed the doctors' claims. The letter was written just as the UT System was preparing to receive the first proposals from cities, and it is perhaps instructive that local politicians in McAllen were keeping a very low profile as the medical society fought with the lawmakers in the news media.[2]

Other communities—particularly Harlingen, historically McAllen's bitter rival in almost everything—did a much better job of lining up their local physicians in favor of the RAHC. The different outcome in Harlingen may have been largely because of Bill Card Jr., who served four terms as mayor through May 1998 and proved to be an effective leader on this issue. It was probably a fact of political life that "lining up support" was partly a task of "keeping the doctors in line," something at which Harlingen succeeded while McAllen failed. Another Harlingen leader who had a major impact on keeping Harlingen and valley communities as a whole united behind the RAHC was former Harlingen mayor Randy Whittington, who led a non-profit foundation that worked for establishment of the center. Whittington worked tirelessly in support of Harlingen and the RAHC. He seemed to spend more time in Austin than I did "working the legislature" and then "working the UT System" to try to ensure that Harlingen would always have a seat at the table when the RAHC was discussed. Harlingen also benefitted greatly from a decision to hire J. M. Watt Consulting, a prominent health care management consulting firm with headquarters in California, to advise the city on its RAHC proposal and related issues. Political leaders in Brownsville, led by Mayor Henry Gonzalez, were also strongly in support of the RAHC, and 134 doctors in that city signed a petition in favor of it.

When the initial proposals arrived in the spring of 1998, it was clear that all the cities in the valley were offering less local support for the RAHC than UT System officials and the board of regents had been expecting. By August, our outside consultants, Kaludis, were clearly leaning toward the bid by Harlingen, but Mullins, Guckian, Sanchez, and I remained dissatisfied with all the proposals. Our thinking was that all the communities could do a better job of demonstrating their desire to win and support the RAHC. We decided to give everyone another chance, so they could revise their bids and try again to win the center.

McAllen responded very affirmatively to this second chance and made major enhancements to the amount of land and money that the city would contribute to the project. In the end, however, the continued undercutting of the city's efforts by local physicians made it very difficult to accept the proposal as it was offered. Sanchez summarized the system's perspective when he said, "It's very difficult to go to someone's home if you're not wanted."[3]

Once it was clear that the McAllen proposal was going to continue to lack support from the majority of the city's doctors, it was widely assumed that Harlingen, home of Valley Baptist Hospital, would have the best shot at winning the RAHC. The other possibilities, Edinburg and Brownsville, were generally seen as having hospitals that were too small to fully support the work of the RAHC in training residents. It was at this time that Sanchez, Mullins, Guckian, Diaz, and I began to develop the idea of sharing the RAHC among all four cities that were in contention. I don't know who thought of it first, but it proved to be an inspired idea. One of the dangers in breaking the RAHC into pieces was that the available resources might be spread too thinly, so a key element of this new multisite plan was for the regents to commit $20 million from the Permanent University Fund to supplement the $30 million in revenue bond funding that the legislature had appropriated. We would also go back to the legislature for additional start-up funding ($5 million that lawmakers eventually authorized from the state's share of a massive tobacco lawsuit settlement), but the importance of the regents' farsighted decision in August 1998 to make a $20 million commitment from the PUF to ensure the success of the RAHC was not lost on anyone, either in the valley or at the Capitol.

If the question of adequate funding could be answered satisfactorily, the idea of splitting the RAHC among four locations had the advantage of diffusing the rivalries among the various valley communities—rivalries that could potentially jeopardize continued state support if only one city won the prize. There were certainly good arguments for concentrating all the resources in one location, and that was the first choice of the health professionals and other administrators within the UT System, but given the complex realities of valley politics the four-site plan had a lot going for it. After some discussion, the board of regents was persuaded that this would be the best choice, and the new plan was approved at the board's meeting on November 11, 1998.[4]

The final arrangement placed the primary component of the RAHC (a $25 million investment) in Harlingen on land donated by the city, with training for third- and fourth-year medical students and new residency programs to be operated in conjunction with Valley Baptist Hospital. Brownsville was awarded a $10 million RAHC division dedicated to public health research and treatment, including development of a School of Public Health to be operated in conjunction with the UT Health Science Center at Houston. In Edinburg, $15 million was committed to a medical research division of the RAHC, to be operated in conjunction with UT Pan American. And in McAllen, $5 million was committed to a new building and new residency programs, contingent on the city's approval of $5 million in matching funds. The total investment of state and UT System funds was $55 million, apart from land and funding provided by the communities. In addition, we supported in the 1999 legislative session Senator Judith

Zaffarini's successful efforts to establish a Laredo Campus Extension of the UT Health Science Center at San Antonio. The eventual goal of Zaffirini's efforts was to provide medical residencies, health-related degree programs, research, and other health education services for Laredo and the surrounding area. This new program was initially funded by using $5 million from the state's share of the settlement from tobacco litigation.

While Harlingen was clearly the biggest winner, McAllen was widely perceived as the biggest loser in the final plan, and officials of that city continued to be displeased that their proposal had not been chosen. I believe the city could have won the lion's share of the RAHC if it had been united in its efforts. Arrangements for donations of land and cash contributions were completed with Brownsville, Edinburg, and Harlingen in early 1999, but a year after the regents' November 1998 decision, with plans well under way for the new facilities in the other three cities, McAllen officials were still negotiating over how they could meet their $5 million obligation.[5] Eventually we came to an arrangement that included a donation of land as well as contributions of money toward the construction costs. The local medical society was still fighting against McAllen's participation as late as April 2000.[6]

The first building on the RAHC campus in Harlingen was constructed using $25 million worth of the tuition revenue bonds that had been appropriated by the legislature. The site was an eighteen-acre tract donated to the UT System by Valley Baptist Medical Center, which also donated additional land for the RAHC's future needs. Land for the RAHC's facilities in Brownsville was donated by the Southmost Union Junior College District.[7] Classes began at the Brownsville public health school in the fall of 2001, with the facility on the campus of UT Brownsville. In Edinburg, a basic research building was constructed on the campus of UT Pan American, and an outgrowth of the RAHC activities was a collaboration with UT Austin that resulted in establishment of a pharmacy school at the Edinburg campus. The first programs related to the RAHC in Harlingen and Edinburg became operational in 2002.

Twenty-four third-year medical students from the Health Science Center in San Antonio began their formal studies in Harlingen in the fall of 2002. They were followed by twenty-three additional students in the fall of 2003. The initial residency programs were in family

The Regional Academic Health Center in Harlingen. *Courtesy of the UT System.*

medicine, which had been a part of Valley Baptist Medical Center in Harlingen and the Family Medicine Residency Program in McAllen.

The dreams of advanced programs in the Lower Rio Grande Valley for medical education had at last become a reality. The legislature continued to provide biennial funding for the RAHC, and within a few years of the beginning of operations it was estimated that more than twelve physicians who had studied at the RAHC, in addition to many other health professionals, were practicing in the valley. I felt from the beginning that the RAHC would improve the quality of medical care in the valley, increase the number of physicians practicing there, serve as a strong engine for economic development, and eventually serve as a basis for the development of a full-scale medical school. Together with our partners in the valley, and with the political leadership of many in the region, the UT System succeeded in bringing historic change to one of the state's neediest areas and fulfilled most of my dream. I am confident that one day the RAHC will become one of the state's fine medical schools. I am very pleased that my colleagues and I at the UT System had an opportunity to help transform medical education and the delivery of medical services in South Texas. This is one of the most important accomplishments that occurred during the period I was chancellor.

CHAPTER 29

UT System Academic and Health Issues

B eing chancellor of a complex university system means dealing mostly with political and legislative issues that involve external entities—the governor, the Texas House and Senate, the federal government, regional political and economic interests, and various other interest groups that reach across the political and social spectrum. There are, however, important occasions when the chancellor is called upon to take an active role in what are thought of as internal institutional issues. Campus administrators—and, to a much greater extent, the faculty—dread those occasions because they often feel that nothing good can come of a system-wide official meddling in their affairs.

There were three occasions when as chancellor I became intimately involved in academic issues. One was the most sensitive issue ever discussed by faculty members—tenure. Another was the creation of a "virtual" university that would be a vehicle for delivering university educational services across Texas. A third issue that I will deal with in this chapter concerns legislation that reformed the way M. D. Anderson Cancer Center is administered—legislation that I believe helped ensure that this world-renowned cancer center would remain within the UT System.

Tenure has always been a hot political issue. Tenure's most extreme critics see a few examples of incompetent faculty and conclude that the entire system of tenure for university professors needs to be scrapped. The traditional reaction by colleges and universities is to circle the wagons and declare that any change in tenure rules would constitute an assault on academic freedom, and this scares most people away from considering any reforms.

In 1996 we were faced with clear statements from two respected lawmakers that some change in the tenure process was becoming a political necessity. Senator Bill Ratliff, who had been named chairman of the Senate Finance Committee, and Senator Teel Bivens, who was designated to succeed Ratliff as chair of the Education Committee in 1997, both decided that action had to be taken that would require universities to have a post-tenure review process—either a process of the institutions' own devising or one imposed on them by state law.

Bivens and Ratliff were highly regarded Republican moderates with long records of enlightened service in the Texas Legislature. I determined quickly that we would have to respond positively to their call for action, and if we did not we faced the real likelihood that the Senate Education Committee would follow through on its statement in May 1996 that it would consider a bill to create a formal statewide mandatory post-tenure review process. The committee had begun discussing various proposals, one of which provided that a tenured professor could be fired for two consecutive years of "below standard" evaluations.

Ratliff's message to me could not have been more direct: "I do plan to go forward with legislation. All I want to try to do is to communicate standards and allow for flexibility for each institution to determine how to meet those standards." At this point, the Texas A&M University System quickly adopted a post-tenure review policy that left the details to each of its institutions.

The choices facing me were fairly simple: The UT System could develop a tenure review policy on its own, or the legislature would impose one on us. I had no trouble choosing between those options. Some faculty continued to push for a third option—to leave things the way they were—but that option simply didn't exist in the real world of Texas politics in 1996. As soon as it became clear that I was going to pursue a system-wide post-tenure review policy, the issue was seized by a few faculty members who were consistent critics of university administrators, among them, at UT Austin, computer science professors Alan Cline and Robert S. Boyer. The issue provided such critics with an opportunity to bash the campus administration, the system offices, and the board of regents. They accused us of everything from not understanding tenure and its importance in protecting academic freedom, to failing to use our political muscle to do battle with the legislature, to being part of a grand conspiracy to get rid of them and other faculty members who were persistent opponents of administrators. There was absolutely no basis for the fear that our interest in post-tenure review might be a calculated effort to crack down on dissenting faculty members, but the critics were correct in their statement that we had been reluctant to fight with the chairmen of the finance and education committees in the Senate. These chairmen were very reasonable people, both of whom had a long history of being supportive of higher education and the UT System, and they chaired two of the most important Senate committees.

It is also important to understand that the Senate had always been more positively predisposed to higher education than the House. If the Senate passed a post-tenure review proposal we would have had virtually no opportunity to kill it in the House. Unfortunately, our naïve faculty critics had no idea about how the House and Senate really worked.

In my experience, it has always been easier to work *with* the legislature and try to exert an influence over legislative deliberations, than to declare war. It is fundamentally bad policy for a state agency to launch a frontal attack against the people who control its funding. There are ways for a university to achieve its goals in the legislature, and making fiery and insulting speeches at Faculty Senate meetings is not one of them. Unfortunately, Boyer and Cline either did not understand these simple principles of governmental relations, or, worse yet, they just wanted to use the tenure issue to wage war on the administration.

I decided early on that developing a post-tenure review policy and gaining faculty support for it would require a thoroughly transparent process that would involve numerous key faculty leaders all along the way. Without such a process, we could have faced not merely the opposition of a few people who can be counted on to be critical, but a large-scale faculty revolt, despite the political realities at the legislature.

While planning how to deal with the faculty, I also took pains to assure Ratliff and Bivens that the UT System would create a meaningful post-tenure review process that would alleviate any need for the legislature to act when it convened in January 1997. Bivens indicated that he felt that "less than 2 percent" of professors in Texas were a problem. He went on to say, however, that even if the percentage of incompetent or "problem" faculty members was that low, it would still mean that perhaps twenty-seven faculty members at UT Austin were in that bottom category. But, he went on to argue, since the university had dismissed only two tenured faculty for unsatisfactory performance in the past twenty-five years, we were obviously not doing our job.

I don't know whether Bivens and Ratliff promoted post-tenure review because they honestly felt such a system would materially improve higher education across the state, or whether they just decided it was a great political issue, or if they were motivated by some combination of these factors. There is no question it was a good political issue. The population at large has never understood tenure for professors and would probably not approve of it if given a chance to vote on it in a referendum, so coming out in favor of periodic review of tenured faculty members carried little risks. Those of us at the UT System sensed that we were dealing as much with a political issue as with a substantive one, so we tried to approach it from both perspectives.

It was helpful throughout the debate to note that Texas was not the first state to be adjusting the rules to allow for periodic review of a faculty member after receiving tenure. By the time the UT System Board of Regents would act on this issue in the fall of 1996, the system's academic affairs office had compiled a list of other prominent universities around the nation that had adopted some type of tenure review policy.[1] For example, the University of California System conducted an annual review of all faculty with a "more substantive" review at least every five years; the college of engineering at Carnegie Mellon University evaluated all faculty every seven years; and the law school at the University of Minnesota held annual evaluations with a special peer review after a finding of below-expected performance and a lack of improvement over the course of a year. Some policies spelled out conditions under which termination might be considered, while others emphasized a program for improvement for a professor who was performing poorly.

I appointed a committee of faculty and administrators (the Committee on Periodic Evaluation of Tenured Faculty) to advise me on the recommendation I would make to the regents. Among those from UT Austin on the committee were Paul Woodruff, a philosophy professor who was head of the Plan II honors program; Frank Bean, a sociologist who was director of the UT Population Research Center; and Mark Yudof, who was the provost. As the process developed, we made sure that the policy we would take to the regents had been reviewed by committees of administrators, faculty, and students at every campus across the system that would be covered by the policy. M. D. Anderson Cancer Center already had a policy of "term tenure"—under which tenure is granted only for a certain time and the faculty member must apply for a new contract—and the UT Health Center at Tyler did not have faculty appointed under either a tenure or term tenure system.

I decided that we should start from the assumption that our approach to tenure was fundamentally flawed because it did not allow for a periodic assessment of a scholar's goals and productivity. We had a system of yearly reviews that were conducted as part of the process of deciding about raises and promotions, and I think that in most departments these reviews were usually well done and provided useful information about short-term goals. However, it seemed equally clear that except when a faculty member was up for promotion to associate or full professor or was being considered for an endowed position, there was not a thoughtful review of long-term issues such as how the person's research career was progressing, how they were developing as a teacher, and whether they demonstrated an ongoing commitment to service responsibilities. Our aim was to correct that deficiency, establishing a review process that would provide long-term evaluations, include procedures for helping a faculty member make improvements, and, ultimately, make faculty members, academic departments, and the university itself more accountable for upholding high standards of academic quality. Another concern with the system then in place was that the annual reviews had become routine in some departments and they were taken less seriously in years when prospects for significant raises were dim.

By early fall of 1996, we were well along the way toward developing a policy that I thought could gain the support of most faculty members and administrators and the regents, and that would satisfy the concerns of Ratliff, Bivens, and other legislators. As part of the effort to explain what we were trying to accomplish and to be transparent with the faculty and the public, I wrote an op-ed article that was published in major newspapers including the *Austin American-Statesman,* the *Dallas Morning News*, and the *Houston Chronicle*, as well as student newspapers like the *Daily Texan*.[2] I tried to make the points that a properly designed system of post-tenure review would not be a threat to the practice of tenure but would be the best way of protecting it, and that I was confident that the vast majority of our faculty were doing an outstanding job and would have no trouble passing the most stringent review of their performance.

Another effort to keep the discussion of the proposed policy out in the open was an appearance that Frank Bean and I made on cable TV in Austin in early October. The show was called "Texas Politics" and was hosted by Marc Levin, then a Plan II junior in economics, and our appearance was billed as a "debate," but as it turned out Bean and I did not disagree much. I did make the point that efforts by some faculty members to postpone consideration of a post-tenure review proposal was a mistake and that we needed to get the issue behind us before the legislature convened in January. Levin offered the opinion that, "Most faculty are glad that Cunningham is doing the review, rather than the legislature doing it for them. It's the lesser of the two evils."[3] This was at best faint praise.

There was a significant difference between the policy that we developed and the initial proposal that had come from the Senate Education Committee and Ratliff in May 1996. The Senate committee's idea had been that a tenured professor could be fired after two consecutive years of below-standard evaluations. The proposal developed by the UT System and approved by the regents in November 1996 called for faculty members to be reviewed every five years and did not focus on someone being fired, emphasizing instead the importance of using the reviews as a basis for making improvements. If a faculty member did not get a positive review at the department level, we proposed a process of further reviews and the eventual possibility of initiating a termination under the system's already well-established procedures.

When the regents met on November 14 to consider the proposal, Dr. William Neaves, dean of the UT Southwestern Medical Center at Dallas and a member of the tenure review committee, was the first speaker. He said that the proposed policy before the board accommodated a number of the concerns expressed by the faculty senates and faculty councils in the UT System institutions and that he personally believed the policy to be workable. Among those speaking against the policy was Alan Cline, leader of the UT System's Faculty Advisory Council, who urged a delay on the grounds that the proposal needed more review and in its current form was an attack on tenure and would harm the university. The specter of "caving in to political pressure" was raised—a warning that is often a sure sign that the speaker fails to understand political realities or was not in a position to make a cogent argument in the matter.

I made no formal comments at the meeting. I had already presented and discussed the proposed policy in numerous forums, and I had talked individually with each member of the board of regents before the meeting about what the policy was designed to do, how it would protect the system of tenure and uphold faculty rights, and why we needed to act on it without delay. Faculty members who wished to speak on the issue were given time to present as much information as they wished and to make their speeches, but in the end the board voted 9–0 in favor of my recommendation.[4]

The new policy instructed the thirteen UT campuses that had traditional tenure systems to develop procedures by September 1997 for a comprehensive evaluation of the performance of tenured faculty members every five years. However, the reviews were designed to do more than merely identify those few faculty members whose performance was unsatisfactory. The plan was that the reviews would provide valuable feedback to a faculty member concerning his or her performance, help determine salary levels and awards, help guide a faculty member in pursuing appropriate professional development activities, and help academic departments re-focus the use of their resources. It was left up to each institution to determine various details.

Concerns among a few faculty that the policy could threaten academic freedom seemed particularly ironic in light of the fact that the board of regents was then chaired by Bernard Rapoport, a staunch defender of faculty rights and a vocal opponent of political interference in academic matters since the turbulent days of the Homer Rainey affair in the 1940s.[5] Rapoport would never have endorsed a policy that jeopardized academic freedom. As he commented after the board's action on November 14: "These guidelines have been crafted so that they support, enhance, and strengthen the tenure system. Tenure is fundamental to the protection of free inquiry, open intellectual and scientific debate, and unfettered criticism of the accepted body of knowledge. As the preamble to the guidelines states, 'Without freedom to question, there can be no freedom to learn.' The new policy will also better enable our universities to satisfy a growing public demand that high academic quality is being maintained, that students' educational needs are being served, and that faculty performance meets expected standards."

In the days after the meeting, Rapoport and I sent an open letter to faculty throughout the UT System to explain the new policy and reiterate that we envisioned it as a way to strengthen the tenure system and enhance the quality of faculty performance. We also emphasized that the policy allows for varying conditions among the campuses, so that they can tailor the system-wide guidelines to fit their needs. This letter was part of a continuing effort to communicate with the university community and the public as fully as possible, and I think we achieved a high level of success in getting the message out about what the policy did and did not do, as well as in addressing the concerns and criticisms that are inevitable with an issue such as tenure.[6]

The whole process of adopting and implementing the post-tenure review policy can also be seen as a textbook example of how a public university can manage a political challenge and head off a political crisis. In the end, the politicians were able to tell their constituents they had helped achieve a meaningful reform of the practice of tenure, and they were right. At the same time, the UT System took action that, apart from the political concerns, was the right thing to do because it has provided constructive counsel to faculty members about their long-term goals and accomplishments—and that will benefit students and enhance the quality of the entire institution.

This issue proved to be a very serious test of my leadership. I was clearly advocating a position that most of the faculty did not like. However, I did feel that I had thought the issue through very carefully and understood the political realities. In addition, I "worked" the regents on this issue very carefully and thoroughly. I would never have permitted this issue to come before the regents if I did not feel I had their overwhelming, if not unanimous, support. The new policy did not create an overly bureaucratic process, and I do not think it has been a burden on the campuses. From all reports, the post-tenure reviews have served their intended purposes, while resulting in none of the abuses that faculty critics had feared.

The dramatic expansion of distance education was not as controversial as post-tenure review, but it had the possibility of dramatically shifting the academic resources of the component institutions and as such needed to be carefully examined. If our faculty critics had ever understood the potential implications of an expanded distance education program, I am confident that they would have been very concerned about our true intentions.

In the late 1990s, the UT System coordinated a rapid expansion of distance education through the use of the Internet and the World Wide Web as a vehicle for delivering instruction, carrying on classroom discussions, conducting conferences between faculty members and students, and providing related educational services. In doing this, we were taking part in a worldwide trend toward online instruction. Internet technologies allowed distance education to come into its own in a way that earlier educators could not have envisioned, and I was easily persuaded that this was an area in which the system administration should take the lead as the coordinator for all the campuses. We often talked about this initiative as the creation of a "virtual university" with an online campus, instead of buildings made of bricks and mortar. Some of this was figurative language and some of it was fact. While the online instruction made use of new technologies, the courses and degree programs continued to be closely tied to campuses and to the academic expertise and teaching skills of faculty members.

While the Internet introduced a new phase of distance learning, the field had been in existence for many years. Beginning in the 1970s, the UT Austin College of Pharmacy, under the very able leadership of Dean James Doluisio, and the UT Health Science Center at San Antonio had been operating a joint program of pharmacy instruction through interactive television using microwave transmission facilities. This program was highly successful educationally and was highly cost-efficient. Twenty years after the start of that program, it was clear that new technologies were going to allow us to leap far beyond that kind of traditional distance education. Many people within the UT System were enthusiastic about these new possibilities, but one of the strongest advocates of a major system-wide initiative was Tony Sanchez, a businessman from Laredo who had been appointed to the UT Board of Regents by Governor Bush.

Part of Sanchez's interest in this issue was his realization that the new technology would give the UT System an opportunity to reach students who would not otherwise have access to advanced educational resources. These could include single working parents, people with disabilities that made travel difficult or impossible, and people from remote areas that simply didn't have access to library resources and faculty members such as those within the UT System. From my conversations with Sanchez, I think he envisioned that the new technology could make it possible for some of the Nobel Prize winners and other internationally renowned faculty members in the UT System to lecture and hold seminars online at all system campuses. In reality, online instruction has been less a vehicle for sharing some of the "celebrity" faculty with other campuses than it has been devoted to more basic types of instruction. Nevertheless, Sanchez's vision and his insistence that the system keep moving on distance education were important factors in the early development of what came to be called the UT TeleCampus.

In 1996 we commissioned Andersen Consulting to study the feasibility of a system-wide online education program and to suggest appropriate pilot projects, and after the success of our early programs we returned to that firm in 1999 for an additional study that helped set the pattern for further growth.[7] As we began to move forward with planning for the TeleCampus in 1997, I asked Mario Gonzalez to be in charge of it. Gonzalez was a professor of electrical engineering at UT Austin and had headed the UT System's efforts to insure that funds from the South Texas/Border Initiative were being properly spent. I knew he was committed to the concept of broadening educational opportunities through new technologies, and, just as important, was thoroughly familiar with what such innovations as the Internet could accomplish. He did a wonderful job of organizing our "virtual university" in its early stages and deserves a lot of credit for its initial success. As part of a broader information technology initiative across the system, Gonzalez began the TeleCampus with $300,000 that we allocated from system funds. One of the best decisions he made was to hire Darcy Hardy to work with him. She had been involved in distance education at UT Austin and took over the TeleCampus after Gonzalez went back to teaching, and she continued to demonstrate why she is considered one of the nation's leaders and innovators in the field.

As the UT System began to establish a full-fledged, centrally managed distance education program, we had to deal with numerous complex issues that had not been concerns when distance education mainly meant televising existing classes and adding interactive voice communications. These included who would teach the courses, how they would be paid, what infrastructure would the UT System provide, how would students register across multiple institutions, who would admit students to various universities, how would the system and the campuses divide the responsibilities (and the financial costs), what computer platforms would be used to provide services, and how the World Wide Web would be used. None of these questions had easy answers.

By the spring of 1998, when the UT TeleCampus was formally inaugurated, there were already more than 200 distance education courses being offered by system institutions, primarily through interactive videoconferencing. About 1,500 students were enrolled, most of them students already enrolled in one of the system's fifteen traditional campuses. They were finding the distance education courses a useful supplement to their regular classes.[8]

The TeleCampus went well beyond simply listing the offering of a variety of courses. When it opened officially in May 1998, it included seven virtual "buildings" that provided distance-learning course schedules, admission and registration information, library facilities, financial aid information, bookstores, a commons area, and other services. The TeleCampus would also serve the public as an electronic gateway to UT System institutions. Through a contract with a private vendor, the system began providing courseware design tools that would allow faculty and staff to develop and produce online their interactive academic courses. Many universities around the world had started distance education programs of one type or another, but we were definitely in the lead in designing a program that went beyond a collection of online courses and included the full range of online services to help ensure the academic success of the distance learner.[9]

Within a year, we were offering two online graduate programs—an MBA in general management and a master's of education in educational technology—as well as five freshman courses in what we then called our "First Year Online" program. By the fall of 2000, we had expanded the course offerings to almost completely fulfill the core requirements for a bachelor's degree, and we had five more master's degree programs—in kinesiology, electrical engineering, computer science, computer science and engineering, and reading. The TeleCampus was also offering a full English-as-a-second-language endorsement program for teachers. The master's degree programs were collaborative degree plans to which several system campuses contributed instructors. In these collaborative programs, students applied to the campus from which they would ultimately receive their degrees. Over the course of their study, they could take courses from all universities that were partners in their degree program, giving online students access to a large faculty base and a large pool of other resources.[10]

I was most actively involved with the online MBA program. I

felt that an MBA program would be an excellent choice for online instruction. Traditional MBA programs have only a few electives in their second year, but executive MBA programs and night MBA programs often have no electives at all. That meant an online MBA program could be relatively easy to plan, compared with a broader-based master's program or a complete undergraduate program. The Tele-Campus offered one of the first online MBA programs in the country.

I met with all the deans of the business schools within the UT System and explained that I needed their help in planning an online MBA program, and I assured them that the system would help provide the funding, through, among other things, grants to pay faculty members' salaries in the summer so that they could work on building the courses for the program. All the business schools except UT Austin agreed to participate. Austin's decision to opt out was made by Dean Bob May, a good friend of mine. He felt that participating in the online program would not be a good use of the business school's brand name and its stature as part of a flagship university, and he was probably correct. The decision not to participate was couched in terms of the school's commitment to other programs, such as its executive MBA program, but I think the bottom line was that UT Austin thought it should not participate in a program that would be dominated by institutions of less stature. The other business schools may have benefited from the fact that UT Austin did not participate, since their involvement in an online program gave them a distinctive selling point for their institutions, and they were not overshadowed in this endeavor by the Austin campus. Even without UT Austin it became an award-winning program.

UT Arlington was a leader of the band in the TeleCampus, particularly in the freshman-level course offerings. UTA faculty members were very proactive in distance education and they were doing excellent work in this area. President Bob Witt also recognized the importance of the virtual university for his campus and the system, and he strongly supported it.[11]

The TeleCampus continued to grow in popularity and to expand its course offerings and services to students, traditional and nontraditional. Among the most popular programs were specialized certification programs for teachers. The list of undergraduate as well as professional courses offered online expanded greatly. The TeleCampus represented one of the few strictly academic initiatives undertaken by the UT System during my tenure, and it proved to be highly successful as an example of how centralized system-wide services, in collaboration with the educational expertise at the campuses, can benefit the people of Texas.

One reason the TeleCampus got off the ground so successfully is the advanced initiative at the UT System and UT Austin to expand digital library services. This initiative was developed in parallel with the TeleCampus. A key feature of the initiative was the creation of a Knowledge Management Center at UT Austin in September 1997, based on recommendations of a system-wide Library Affairs Committee. While continuing to maintain traditional library collections and services, the center was part of an effort to extend the knowledge management function to include digital publishing, publishing on demand, and a host of virtual library services.[12] Harold Billings, director of the UT Austin libraries, was not only a visionary librarian, he also knew how to work the political structure on campus and at the UT System. Today, it is hard to remember what the world was like before the rapid expansion of digital information and communication technologies. The UT TeleCampus was a key player in this revolutionary era.

The effort to reshape the state laws under which M. D. Anderson is administered began in the fall of 1995 when I received a call from Dr. Charles A. "Mickey" LeMaistre, president of the cancer center and one of my predecessors as chancellor of the UT System. LeMaistre said the "bureaucracy" of state regulations and restrictions was killing M. D. Anderson and that a plan had been put together by the cancer center's Board of Visitors (a committee of prominent community, business, and professional leaders who advise the center) to ask the state to separate M. D. Anderson from the UT System. The plan included creation of a new private foundation that would govern M. D. Anderson—freeing the institution from state and UT System regulations. LeMaistre told me this effort was being led by former president George H. W. Bush and San Antonio businessman Red McCombs, both members of the Board of Visitors. McCombs, whose extraordinary philanthropic endeavors are reflected in the naming of the business school at UT Austin in his honor, was the chair of the Board of Visitors' committee on institutional initiatives, and Bush also served on that committee. The committee had helped M. D. Anderson make its business systems more efficient and improve its cash flow, and now the idea was that separation from the state would help continue that work.

I was shocked that LeMaistre would even think of the idea of leaving the UT System and separating from state government. The proposal would have been the largest giveaway of state assets in the history of Texas, and possibly the United. States.

Less than a minute into the conversation, I told LeMaistre flatly that this was "not going to happen." I said I would not recommend it, the UT Board of Regents would not approve it, the Texas Legislature would not pass the required enabling legislation, and I was confident that it would violate the state constitution. I do not know to this day who came up with the idea, but I am confident that it was not Bush or McCombs.

Former UT System Chancellor Charles A. "Mickey" LeMaistre, president of M. D. Anderson Cancer Center. *Photo by Frank Armstrong, Prints and Photographs Collection, di_06980.*

While they may well have thought at some point that it was a good idea, my guess is that the seed of the proposal was planted by someone on LeMaistre's senior staff.

LeMaistre told me that I would soon be receiving a call from McCombs and possibly from Bush to discuss the idea. McCombs did call me. I knew McCombs very well and had a great deal of respect for him. He had a long track record of being one of higher education's biggest supporters, and he was a close friend of mine. However, after listening politely as he discussed the proposal, I reiterated my statement, "This is not going to happen." I then explained the political realities that the legislature would never vote to turn over billions of dollars in assets irrevocably to a private foundation no matter how highly respected its board might be or how worthy was the objective. It just was not in the realm of possibility.

However, I did tell LeMaistre and McCombs that we needed to examine carefully the "bureaucratic problems" that were causing so much trouble for M. D. Anderson. My assumption was that some of them were generated by M. D. Anderson's own policies and procedures while others came from the UT System or were a result of state law. I told LeMaistre that if we could not fix the problems associated with M. D. Anderson and the UT System bureaucracy, we (LeMaistre and I) should be replaced since we were apparently the problem. In addition, I felt that if we went to Lieutenant Governor Bob Bullock and explained that M. D. Anderson needed some help from the state in freeing it from unnecessary bureaucratic controls, Bullock would be more than supportive of our efforts.

I was correct about Bullock. LeMaistre and I met with him in January 1995, just as the 74th session of the legislature was getting under way. He understood the problems, and he liked the solutions that we had developed for freeing M. D. Anderson from some state regulations. Charlie Evans, a highly respected lobbyist, was hired by a private group of Texans to assist the UT System's efforts to pass the proposed legislation. Charles Miller from Houston was kind enough to solicit and handle the money. I made the first $1,000 contribution to the special fund to illustrate publicly that I wanted to resolve M. D. Anderson's problems as soon as possible. The legislation that passed during that session was known as Senate Bill 192, sponsored by Senators Don Henderson of Houston and Carlos Truan of Corpus Christi. In the House the sponsors included Tom Uher of Bay City, Hugo Berlanga of Corpus Christi, Garnet Coleman of Houston, and Tom Craddick of Midland—clear evidence of M. D. Anderson's strong statewide constituency.

When Bullock expedited the Senate's consideration of the bill, I felt quite confident that we were well on our way to solving the state's portion of M. D. Anderson's bureaucratic entanglement. When Bullock was behind you, things tended to happen fast. Henderson filed the bill in the Senate on January 11, and it was passed thirteen days later, on the 24th. The House took a little longer, not passing its version of the bill until March 2.

In addition to the legislation, LeMaistre and I put together two teams of people to identify and resolve any internal bureaucratic problems that might be interfering with M. D. Anderson's efficient operation, apart from the changes we were advocating in state law. Executive Vice Chancellor for Heath Affairs Charles Mullins assigned James Guckian to head the UT System team of bureaucratic crime fighters. The teams functioned efficiently and resolved most of M. D. Anderson's internal bureaucratic problems by the time the legislature

From left, Stella Mullins, Shirley Bird Perry, and Charles Mullins at the Alkek Hospital dedication, 1998. *Photo by Pete Baatz, copy courtesy of William H. Cunningham.*

had adjourned in 1995. Governor George W. Bush signed Senate Bill 192 on March 20. The new law went into effect that day, so M. D. Anderson was immediately free to function in a manner that permitted it to focus its marvelous resources on curing cancer rather than being tied up in bureaucratic red tape.

The legislation made changes in regulations related to the treatment of indigent patients, the cancer center's institutional funds, and hospital fees; provided for an incentive retirement plan; and instituted a "best value" purchasing system instead of relying only on the low bid. Four years later, in the 76th legislative session, we continued this pattern of helping M. D. Anderson when bills were passed to give the cancer center the authority to grant degrees in allied health fields and to acquire land in Houston for expansion of clinical and research facilities.

The 1995 legislation and other steps taken internally helped place M. D. Anderson on a firmer foundation that allowed it to make its administration more efficient. This helped protect the state's massive investment while also freeing the institution from onerous regulations that failed to recognize the unique role that M. D. Anderson plays for the state, the nation, and the world. I am very proud of what we accomplished. This was an excellent example of how private citizens (Bush and McCombs) can effectively put pressure on the UT System and the legislature to resolve major institutional issues that help make the UT System a much more effective vehicle for delivering services to the people of Texas.

CHAPTER 30

The Freeport-McMoRan Controversy

y service on the board of directors of Freeport-McMoRan Inc. became a highly controversial matter for the university in 1994 and 1995, when well-organized opposition to the company's mining operations in Indonesia and its development interests near Austin were reflected in local political issues on and off the UT Austin campus. As I discussed in detail in Chapter 10, the board of regents approved my recommendation in 1994 to name the new molecular biology building at UT Austin for Freeport-McMoRan's CEO, James R. Moffett, and his wife, Louise, in recognition of the $2 million that they had personally contributed toward the construction costs, as well as the $1 million contributed by Freeport-McMoRan. Jim Bob and Louise, who were good friends of mine, had been extremely generous to UT Austin on many occasions through the years, and the regents agreed with me that it was appropriate to honor them in this way.

The campus opposition to Freeport-McMoRan and the naming of the building for the Moffetts arose from at least five factors:

- Environmental and human rights organizations believed the company's gold and copper mine in Indonesia was polluting forests and rivers and that the firm was collaborating with the government of Indonesia in mistreating the indigenous population.
- Environmental groups and some members of the Austin City Council opposed the company's subsidiary, FM Properties, and its Barton Creek development near Austin.
- Environmental groups attacked Freeport-McMoRan, noting that the Environmental Protection Agency had listed the company in 1990 as the largest polluter in the United States in connection with the dumping of waste material in the Mississippi River.

- Freeport-McMoRan had made generous donations to the geology program at UT Austin (Moffett was a graduate of the program), and part of the company's relationship with the program included opportunities for faculty members and graduate students to do research at the company's properties in Indonesia.
- Freeport-McMoRan's critics felt that my membership on the company's board while serving as president and chancellor created a conflict of interest that could only be resolved by me resigning from either the university or the board.

The extent of the campus opposition to the naming of the molecular biology building and to my board membership was difficult to gauge. Certainly some faculty and students cared passionately about the issues, and the editorial pages of the *Daily Texan* and the *Austin American-Statesman* sided with them consistently, as did the *Austin Chronicle*, an alternative weekly paper. While a few very vocal faculty members in the Faculty Council helped organize opposition in 1995 and 1996 to the naming of the building, most faculty and students went about their business without taking a public stand on this issue. The controversy drew only a few large student rallies, although the intensity and energy of the activists at times made up for the lack of a sustained mass movement. At one point, student organizations claimed to have three thousand signatures on a petition to the regents to take the Moffetts' name off the building. Opinion among external constituencies of the university—alumni, donors, and state elected officials—was muted throughout the controversy. I received strong support from the board of regents on all the issues until December 1995, when developments led at least one regent to change her mind.

I do believe that the opposition never rose to the level of a widespread campus movement, never caused even a ripple in the operation of the university, and left the vast majority of faculty and students indifferent.

I joined the Freeport board in 1987, when I was serving as president of UT Austin, at the invitation of Moffett, whom I had met at my first meeting of the UT Development Board. Moffett was a new member, and I was a new president. Moffett was a 1961 graduate of the university with a degree in geological sciences, had played football for Darrell Royal, and had maintained a close relationship with UT Austin through the years as a donor to an array of academic and

From left, Mack Rankin, Jim Bob Moffett, Willie Nelson, and William H. Cunningham at a golf outing at Barton Creek Country Club, April 21, 1995. *Courtesy of William H. Cunningham.*

athletics programs. The company was based in New Orleans and had operations in Louisiana, but its largest activity in the late 1980s was the development of the Grasberg Mine in the Indonesian province of Irian Jaya (since renamed Papua Province), which occupies the western part of the island of New Guinea.

I found service on the company's board to be intellectually exciting and personally stimulating. Freeport was a large multinational corporation with a larger-than-life CEO. The company owned one of the largest copper mines in the world and, as a by-product of copper production, it operated the world's largest gold mine.

At the time I joined the board, I did not even think to inform or ask permission from Executive Vice Chancellor James Duncan or Chancellor Hans Mark, my direct supervisors. The regents had no rules associated with outside employment for component presidents. I always complied with the state laws on ethics, use of state property, and related matters, and I always took vacation time when I attended company board meetings. No one asked me to do this, but I knew instinctively it was the right thing to do. Service on the Freeport board was beneficial to my role as president of UT Austin in several ways, including the opportunity to introduce the university to important figures in national and international affairs. Other board members included Benno C. Schmidt Sr., president of J. H. Whitney & Co.; Henry Kissinger, the former secretary of state; George Putnam, chairman of Putnam Investments; and Mack Rankin, cofounder of Freeport-McMoRan. Membership on the board also gave me an excellent opportunity to learn about how large, sophisticated multinational corporations operated and to expand my personal contacts that would prove useful to the university in my capacity as UT Austin's chief fund-raiser.

When opposition to Freeport heated up in Austin in 1994, my membership on the board became a popular topic for left-leaning activists and the local print media. The charge was frequently made that I somehow had a conflict of interest because I served both as chancellor and as a member of the company's board, and because I had asked Moffett and Freeport for donations for the university and/or I had recommended that the regents name the molecular biology building for the Moffetts. The research arrangement between Freeport and the UT Austin Department of Geological Sciences was also cited as a conflict of interest for the university. The allegation that I was involved in a conflict of interest was discussed in the media a great deal in 1994 and 1995, but the charge always remained vaguely defined and no one could give a satisfactory explanation of exactly how a conflict might have existed. None of the state authorities whose job was to enforce laws and regulations against conflicts of interest ever expressed any interest in the matter.

Bernard Rapoport, chairman of the board of regents during the height of the controversy, was particularly helpful in defending me against claims of conflict of interest. In an op-ed article published in the *Daily Texan*,[1] he made seven key points about these claims:

- All my private business relationships had been publicly disclosed in annual statements filed with the Texas Ethics Commission.
- I had never had a financial interest in any of Freeport's relationships with the university, and my ability to carry out my responsibilities as president and chancellor had not been impaired by any of my business relationships.
- The research that Freeport sponsored in the Department of Geological Sciences was, in itself, unlikely to represent a financial

William H. Cunningham and Henry Kissinger visiting Freeport-McMoRan operations in Spain, October 1993. *Courtesy of William H. Cunningham.*

gain for the company because the research was basic geological research, with the results available to everyone through publication in scientific journals. The company employed its own staff scientists to do applied research such as prospecting for minerals.

- The research contract with Freeport was of immense benefit to faculty and students because it provided an opportunity to study a remote region whose geological features had never before been studied in detail.
- There could not be even a perception that I had a conflict of interest regarding this research because I had played no role in initiating or negotiating the contract, which was approved through the regular channels of the Department of Geological Sciences, the College of Natural Sciences and the Office of the Executive Vice President and Provost.
- With regard to the donations from the Moffetts for molecular biology, I had served the university by helping the Moffetts understand

the institution's critical financial needs, and in doing so I had continued to fulfill one of the main responsibilities of any president or chancellor—to secure private-sector support for academic programs and facilities.

- My recommendation to the board of regents that the molecular biology building be named for the Moffetts created no conflict of interest, and the naming, which the regents approved unanimously, was appropriate in light of the Moffetts' donations. There was no reason to assume the Moffetts would benefit financially from having their names on the building.

Rapoport concluded the article by saying: "I have dealt on an almost daily basis with Chancellor Cunningham for some five years. The totality of his commitment to the UT System is evidenced in every word and action he has ever had with me. On a personal basis, I regret that so much time had to be given to this so-called problem. Based on my first-hand knowledge, there is no problem. The time could have been better spent dealing with substantive issues."

Rapoport's support in this way was of great importance to me. As a major financial backer of liberal causes in Texas and across the country and a person whose progressive credentials were impeccable, Rapoport's op-ed article probably led a number of people to think twice before accepting the criticism of me. It also made it clear that the board of regents was supporting my position. The op-ed article was published just a few weeks after the *Texas Observer,* a liberal magazine that had been kept alive for years by Rapoport's generous checks, devoted two pages to the resignation letter of one of my strongest critics, Professor Steven Feld. The magazine introduced the letter by saying that "two threads of state and corporate tyranny" had come together in the university's ties to Freeport.[2]

Die-hard opponents of Freeport and its relationship with the university were not deterred by Rapoport's op-ed article. Many of them were against large multinational corporations in general, and they were opposed to mining companies as a matter of principle. Many of them were also very young and were at the stage of life where they opposed anyone who was a member of the establishment, was twenty years older than they were, and drove a Buick. I believe a number of people simply didn't like Freeport and its activities as a mining and development company, and they didn't like the fact that UT had several relationships with the company and its CEO, so saying that I had a conflict of interest was a convenient way of trying to promote their views on other issues. Of course, it was easier for some faculty to make this charge because, protected by the principle of academic freedom, they could say just about anything they wanted to. And as a "public figure," I was without much recourse against being libeled.

I was paid for my service on the Freeport board in cash and stock options. A stock option gives a person the right to buy a specific number of shares in a company at a certain time in the future, but at the price of the stock on the day the options were issued. This meant, of course, that if the stock price had risen by the time I exercised the stock option, I could make a profit by buying the stock. Like many companies, Freeport paid its directors in stock options as a way of aligning their personal financial interest with the long-term interests of the shareholders.

No one at the *Austin American-Statesman* seemed to understand anything about stock options and, as a result, the paper pounced on any information about my compensation as if they had discovered some important evidence of wrongdoing. Thus in 1996, after I had left the Freeport board and exercised my options, the newspaper claimed I had earned $650,000 "in one day" by transactions that included selling Freeport stock. The transaction that the *American-Statesman* was interested in occurred on January 26, 1996, and was duly reported in detail to the SEC. The newspaper ran an editorial that called my earnings "unseemly." The fact that my stock transactions had occurred on one day seemed to fascinate reporters and editors even though the money had been earned through my service on the Freeport board over eight years.[3]

Earning that much money seemed especially offensive to some opponents of Freeport, who often used old-fashioned Marxist rhetoric. One unofficial student group (known as the Howlers) that agitated against Freeport and the university based its position on its "Manifesto for a Liberated Education," whose slogans included "Students Before Profits" and "Students in World Solidarity Unite!"[4] The mainstream media didn't use that kind of rhetoric, but their understanding of business and corporate governance often seemed almost as simplistic.

The controversy over the Barton Creek development contributed to negative views of Freeport on the campus, although it was not a direct part of the company's relationship with the university. The development began in 1974 as a project promoted by Ben Barnes and John Connally, and initially involved a country club, golf course, and conference center. Freeport bought the property in 1988 and soon proposed a major expansion that would include houses, condominiums, new golf courses, retail developments, and other amenities. This proposed 4,000-acre Barton Creek Planned Unit Development was opposed by many environmental groups and city officials because of concern about habitat for the golden-cheeked warbler (an endangered species that breeds in Central Texas) and pollution of the Barton Creek watershed.

The Austin City Council passed ordinances to regulate development in the Barton Creek watershed four times between 1980 and 1992. The last of those efforts, known as the Save Our Springs ordinance, was approved in 1992 by voters in a referendum and was a subject of litigation in state courts for the next six years because of its restrictions on development. This litigation, and proposals in the Texas Legislature related to the development project, overlapped with the period in which the public controversy over the university's relationships with Freeport reached a climax.

Protest group against Barton Creek development (Save Our Springs). *UT Texas Student Publications Photograph Collection, e_uttsp_00012.*

Moffett took a very high-profile stance in his fight with the city over the Barton Creek development. In June 1990 he participated in a legendary all-night public hearing that the City Council held on the development plans (before voting against those plans in the early morning hours), and throughout the 1990s he was often the spokesperson for the company in sparring with the City Council and local environmental groups. My own role as a director was less public, in keeping with the usual practice of members of corporate boards when the CEO is the spokesman for the company.

The company stirred strong feelings among many environmentalists in Austin when it helped lead the support for legislation in 1993 that would have exempted Barton Creek and another Austin-area development from the Save Our Springs ordinance. The legislation provided that cities and counties could not impose new regulations on a development after a permit had been filed in accordance with regulations in force at the time of filing. The bill was a direct challenge to Austin's authority to regulate development, and it was seen as one more example of "Austin-bashing" by a legislature that was much more conservative than the city. Developers, such as Freeport, argued that it was clearly unfair for a city to keep changing its regulations in the middle of a project. The legislature passed the bill, but Governor Richards vetoed it, which led to negotiations and legal challenges that kept Freeport and the city engaged for years. In the 1995 legislative session, Freeport and others again backed a bill to win exemption from the Save Our Springs ordinance, and this time the bill was signed into law by the new governor, George W. Bush. Nevertheless, a lawsuit over the ordinance continued, going to trial in Austin in 1995 and eventually being decided by a federal appeals court in 1996 in favor of the city.

This rather complicated background is important because Freeport's involvement in Barton Creek gave opponents of the company's operations in Indonesia a local issue that helped them organize and attract allies. Barton Creek was naturally a lot more important to most Austinites than the rainforests of New Guinea, so it is likely that the Barton Creek issue resulted in more people becoming aware of and criticizing the ties between Freeport and the university. One of these was City Council member Brigid Shea, who knew nothing about the university's molecular biology building or the relationship between UT Austin, Freeport, and Mr. and Mrs. Moffett, but moved

easily from her longtime advocacy against the Barton Creek development to opposing the naming of the molecular biology building for
the Moffetts.[5]

Another Barton Creek critic who effortlessly made the transition
to being a critic of Freeport's activities in Indonesia and of the naming
of the UT building for the Moffetts was Daryl Slusher, who wrote on
these issues extensively for the *Austin Chronicle* before his election to
the City Council as a "green" candidate in 1996. Slusher later drew
criticism from some of his old allies in the environmental movement
because he became more moderate as an office-holder, when he had
to make practical decisions that affected the community rather than
merely offer the public his opinions.

Opponents of Freeport's foreign and Austin-area activities often
cited an announcement in 1990 by the federal Environmental Protection Agency that the company was responsible for more tons of toxic
chemicals released into the environment than any other corporation
in the United States. This label of "No. 1 corporate polluter" showed
up in story after story about the company for years afterward and
was used by environmental groups and other activists as ammunition
against any of the company's activities, without regard for the details
behind the EPA report.

The EPA's "ranking" of corporations was part of its first annual
report under the Toxic Release Inventory (TRI) program and covered toxic releases for 1988. The release of chemicals by Freeport
was related to two of the company's facilities in Louisiana along the
Mississippi River, where gypsum left over from manufacturing fertilizer was being stored. In 1988, the same year covered in the EPA's
1990 report, Freeport had reached an agreement with the EPA and
the Louisiana Department of Environmental Quality to limit releases
into the river to rainwater running off the piles of waste material. By
1994, the sites (then operated by a partnership between Freeport and
IMC Fertilizer Corp.) had been transformed, with the piles of gypsum
waste being covered in clay and grass caps and an internal water-col-
lection system installed. These efforts cost the companies $27 million
through 1993, and there was a ten-year plan to spend an additional
$33 million to continue transforming waste from the fertilizer opera-
tion into more grass-covered hills. In addition, Freeport was under-
writing research at Louisiana State University to try to find uses for
the gypsum rather than merely piling it up and landscaping it.[6]

Environmental groups and the news media rarely reported that the gypsum stacks were operated under sanctions and permits from the EPA and state officials, and that the company had been taking substantial steps to reduce the release of chemicals into the river. In addition, the original "No. 1" ranking was a result of the EPA's decision to include the runoff of weakly diluted phosphoric acid from the gypsum stacks as part of the TRI data, although the phosphoric acid was not itself toxic. Citing scientific studies to that effect, the EPA later decided to remove the runoff of phosphoric acid from its TRI report for the site, and as a result Freeport dropped significantly in the agency's ranking of polluters.

Such details, as well as Freeport's extensive runoff-control program, received relatively little attention in the media. To me, Freeport's actions were evidence that the company was serious about meeting its obligations to reduce pollution and protect the environment, but once the label of "No. 1 polluter" was applied, it was hard to shake. Although as a Freeport director I usually did not comment publicly on company business (leaving that role to the CEO and other official spokespersons), I did comment on the EPA's 1990 report and related environmental issues on at least two occasions. During a student forum on the UT Austin campus, I responded to a question from a student by saying I had never been involved in a project that, in my opinion, would endanger the environment. The next year, I responded to questions from the *Austin American-Statesman* by saying that before becoming a director of Freeport I had "satisfied myself that the company conducted its affairs all over the world in a highly responsible manner." I also said I was confident Freeport "will continue to minimize environmental impacts" in Louisiana and elsewhere.[7]

Criticism of Freeport's mine in Indonesia had surfaced throughout the controversy over Barton Creek. For many years the criticism in Austin over Indonesia had been fairly low-key, being led mainly by Steven Feld, a professor of anthropology and music who directed UT Austin's Center for Intercultural Studies in Folklore and Ethnomusicology. A noted ethnomusicologist, Feld had conducted considerable research over the past twenty years into the music and other cultural life of the indigenous populations of New Guinea, and he was convinced that Freeport's mine in the province of Irian Jaya was a threat to the environment and the human population of the area.[8] He also sided with the indigenous groups in a long-running conflict with the government of Indonesia, and he helped promote the idea in Austin that Freeport and the government of Indonesia's President Suharto were conspiring to destroy the indigenous people of Irian Jaya.

In addition to Feld's criticisms, the early attention to the Freeport issues included a decision in 1991 by the *Austin American-Statesman* to send a reporter, Bill Collier, to Indonesia to investigate the charges of environmental damage and human rights abuses.[9] This project was a significant commitment for a local newspaper such as the *American-Statesman*, and it resulted in a three-day series of long articles at the beginning of September 1991. I thought Collier's reporting was balanced and objective, presenting all sides of the various issues in a straightforward way and avoiding the inflamed rhetoric of other media accounts. His work was very thorough, including interviews with a large number of company managers, workers, community leaders, government officials, and others.[10] Collier's coverage was often criticized by Freeport's opponents. I am sure many of them preferred the coverage in the *Austin Chronicle*, which favored highly charged language, personal attacks, little attention to the facts, and stories that in general were written from an anti-Freeport (and anti-Cunningham) point of view.

In September 1995, after he had secured a new faculty position at the University of California at Santa Cruz, Feld wrote to me resigning his UT faculty position. Feld said he no longer found UT Austin "a morally acceptable place of employment." He said this was because he had dedicated his career "to the causes of ecological and cultural integrity" on the island of New Guinea, while I "had steered the university toward collaboration in environmental destruction and criminal abuses of human rights."

Feld then summarized his opposition to the research contract that Freeport had with the Department of Geological Sciences and the decision by the regents to accept my recommendation to name the molecular biology building for Mr. and Mrs. Moffett. "The building in question," Feld wrote, "is a molecular biology facility. Yet the man for whom it will be named is a molecular biology criminal." After this latest example of calling Jim Bob and me criminals, Feld then expressed his disappointment over the fact that I had never accepted his invitations to meet with him to discuss the company's operations. It is true that I had never responded to these invitations, not being disposed to meet with people who go around calling me a criminal.

I did write back to Feld on this occasion, expressing the hope that he would visit the Freeport mine site and the surrounding area to see for himself what was going on, and I offered to do what I could to facilitate such a trip. I also briefly gave him examples of other views of Freeport's environmental and human rights record that differed sharply from his own. Both letters were supplied to the *Texas Observer* (by Feld, I assume), which printed them on September 29.[11]

It was always hard for me to understand how any reasonable person could take Feld seriously as an authority on Freeport's operations. As an ethnomusicologist, he had no expertise or training in engineering, mining, or the environment. In addition, he had never visited the mine site. How could any serious scholar take such strident positions on a contemporary issue with absolutely no firsthand knowledge or expertise? The only reasonable explanation to me was that he had a political agenda. He did not want this portion of Indonesia to be developed, and he was prepared to do anything or say anything to try to curb development in Indonesia.

There was no doubt that the Indonesian government and army had a troubled record on human rights, but Freeport never participated in any abuses, and had in fact consistently acted through the years to greatly improve the quality of life of the people living in the vicinity of the mining operations—through the establishment of schools, clinics, and other community programs, as well as, of course, by providing jobs and by becoming Indonesia's largest taxpayer. The mining did bring major changes to the way of life of many people in the region, and anyone who wanted the indigenous people to remain completely unchanged by twentieth-century technology, medicine, and economics would be displeased with the presence of the mine. The life expectancy of the people in the region doubled almost at once after Freeport brought in physicians and others with medical training, and there were many other well-documented changes for the better because of the presence of the mine.

As the fall semester of 1995 progressed, several student organizations stepped up protests against Freeport, my board membership, and the naming of the molecular biology building. These organizations—Earth First!, Students for Earth Awareness, the Student Environmental Action Coalition, the Rainforest Action Network, and others—concentrated mostly on holding public forums, distributing misinformation, and sponsoring campus rallies, but some of them

From left, Mack Rankin, William H. Cunningham, and George Putnam at the Free-port-McMoRan Indonesian mine site, c. 1987. *Courtesy of William H. Cunningham.*

occasionally also engaged in more theatrical activities. One evening in October while Isabella and I were holding a reception for Bob Witt, whom I had selected to become acting president of UT Arlington, a group of about fifteen students and others from some of the environmental groups stood outside the gate of Bauer House and shouted slogans as guests arrived. One person held a sign that said, "Earth-raping corporate scum, we know who you are, where you live, and what you do. Watch Out!"[12] On another occasion, a group sponsored a parody of "The Wizard of Oz" on the West Mall, with actors portraying me as "a scarecrow without a brain" and Moffett as "a tin man without enough money to finish polluting the world."[13]

At the end of October 1995, the Overseas Private Investment Corp. (OPIC), a federal agency that helps U.S. businesses invest in developing countries, announced that it was canceling the political risk insurance that it had provided for Freeport's mine in Indonesia because it was concerned about increased production at the mine and the disposal of waste material. Freeport believed the cancellation was tied to U.S. politics, but it did provide more fuel for critics of Free-port and the university. In the spring of 1996, however, Freeport and

OPIC announced an agreement to reinstate the insurance for the rest of the year, along with new investments by Freeport in environmental remediation. The company set up a $100 million trust fund to pay for remediation through the end of the mine's life, estimated at another forty years. This was in addition to remediation efforts the company was already engaged in.[14]

Before this matter was resolved, several of the faculty critics cited the cancellation of the insurance as further evidence that the board of regents should change its 1994 decision to name the molecular biology building for the Moffetts, and that I should resign from the Freeport board. In response, several regents made strong public statements of support for me. Rapoport reiterated his view that the name should not be changed, and Tom Loeffler said he had no concerns about my relationship with Freeport. Martha Smiley said the naming of the building was simply recognition of the Moffetts' longtime commitment to the university. "I realize that the man's company is controversial in Austin . . . but I don't think our job as the Board of Regents is to conduct independent investigations. It just does not seem appropriate," she told the *Austin-American Statesman*.[15] Lowell Lebermann also expressed strong support for me. The regents were receiving an increasing amount of mail during this period demanding that they change the name of the building and force me to step down as a Freeport director, and I was grateful for their steadfastness.

The public debate took a new turn in November 1995 when a Catholic bishop in Indonesia, Hermann Munninghoff, issued a report that appeared to confirm reports that government troops in Indonesia had killed civilians and committed other human rights violations as part of efforts to provide security for the Freeport mine. Munninghoff told the *Austin American-Statesman* that no Freeport employees had participated in the violence but was quoted as saying he thought the company had been involved in rights abuses "only indirectly." He also confirmed that the Catholic Diocese of Austin had written to him seeking verification that he had written a report in August about the violence, but his statements to the newspaper suggested that the English-language version of the report might contain material that he had not written. This was obviously a confused situation, but it provided additional ammunition for those who wanted to believe the worst about Freeport.[16]

Bishop John McCarthy of Austin had contacted me earlier to ask for information about what was going on in Indonesia. McCarthy was a dear friend of mine, but he made it clear that it was necessary for him to make some inquiries about reports from Irian Jaya. I suggested that he contact Munninghoff directly and he did so, but by mid-November he had not heard back. On November 22, Munninghoff made a public statement that his report had been misinterpreted by the media and that he had never made any allegations against Freeport. It was now clear to McCarthy and most other objective analysts that the report that was circulating on the Internet in English under Munninghoff's name had been doctored before it was posted on the Internet and it did not reflect Munninghoff's own work or views.

President Bob Berdahl had stayed out of the Freeport issues as much as he could, but on November 16 he presented an open letter to the campus community, which was printed as a full-page ad in the *Daily Texan* the next day. He declined as a matter of principle to take sides on the debate over Freeport's activities in Indonesia and elsewhere. "The principle vital to the life and future of any university . . . to be protected at all costs, is the principle of institutional neutrality in any debate over what constitutes truth," he wrote. "It is this principle that establishes the moral framework and intellectual environment of The University. It means that The University as an institution does not seek to define truth, *ex cathedra*, but to provide a free and ordered space for individuals to seek and advocate truth as they see it, based upon rational argument."

Berdahl went on to defend the principle of due process as essential to UT's "climate of freedom." "If The University seeks to judge and censor any members of its community, including financial contributors, for their beliefs, or for what is perceived by some to be a lack of social conscience or environmental sensitivity, or for what some consider immoral or illegal actions, we will have sacrificed our commitment to objectivity, rational discourse and due process of law."

Regarding the building name, Berdahl stated that the gift from the Moffetts had been solicited and given in good faith and that the regents had named the building for the Moffetts in accordance with past practice and the regents' rules. He said that to return the gift or rescind the naming decision "as a consequence of public criticism or allegations that have not been proven in any legal tribunal" would compromise UT's neutrality and "would signal all contributors that The University cannot be relied upon to keep its word."[17]

Berdahl had not consulted with me about his open letter. Perhaps predictably, the letter seemed to have little effect on the most severe critics of Freeport and of my relationship with the company. Professor Robert S. Boyer's response was to say that I, rather than Berdahl, ought to be addressing these issues.[18]

Throughout this period in 1995, the editorial page of the *Austin American-Statesman,* under the direction of the newspaper's recently appointed editor, Richard A. Oppel Sr., was one of my strongest critics. I had had good relations with Oppel's immediate predecessors, and I felt they understood the mission of the university and were supportive of it. Oppel's style was much more aggressive, and almost as soon as he arrived there were evident changes in the way reporters did their work and the way the editorial page often sided with critics of the university and found fault with my performance as chancellor.

Oppel had been editor of the *Charlotte Observer* in Charlotte, N.C., and under his direction the newspaper had won three Pulitzer Prizes, including two for reporting that exposed the prevalence of brown lung disease among textile workers and helped to gather the evidence that sent TV evangelist Jim Bakker to jail for fraud. Within a few months of Oppel's arrival in Austin in May 1995, I became convinced that I was the new target of his investigative zeal. It is my opinion that he believed I was engaged in unethical practices and even potentially in criminal acts, and that he wanted to make sure his reporters did everything possible to nail me. I am sure he and his reporters would say they were only seeking the truth, but I am convinced they were seeking my resignation from UT or even my indictment. In the end, they didn't get either a resignation or an indictment, and along the way they probably got a lot less of the truth than they could have if they had not been so obsessed with skewed versions of events.

Oppel came to my office on November 23, 1995, before the UT/Baylor football game, and during our conversation he asked me to come down to his office at the newspaper and debate a group of my critics on the faculty. It was apparent that Oppel wanted to be the reporter, analyst, editorial writer, jury, and judge. Even though Oppel did not recognize this apparent conflict of interest on his part, I did, and I declined his offer. My meeting failed to enlighten him, and the newspaper's off-base editorials on Freeport continued.

On December 13, 1995, it became known publicly that Freeport had sent letters to seven of its critics, including three UT Austin professors, stating that the company might take legal action unless they stopped making "false and damaging" accusations that it had been involved in human rights violations in Indonesia.[19] The letters, from Freeport's senior vice president, Thomas J. Egan, did not cite specific statements by the seven recipients, but Moffett said later: "We've let it go on and on. But there's one place I draw the line. I'm not going to let people accuse me of being a murderer."[20] Freeport also sent the individuals a large packet of information that contradicted statements they had been making.

The threat by Freeport to bring a lawsuit against professors Feld, Alan Cline, and Robert S. Boyer cast the entire controversy in a new light. My first public response, on December 14, was to state that I would not participate in any university or company matters regarding such legal action. This was my immediate response, but I had almost continuous discussions about the matter with regents, Moffett, and others the rest of the day, and events moved very quickly.

Soon after the newspaper story about the lawsuit threat appeared on the morning of December 14, Ellen Temple called Rapoport and told him that because of the lawsuit threat she would resign from the board of regents if I did not resign from the Freeport board. When Rapoport called to tell me about his conversation with Temple, my first thought was that I should resign as chancellor. I told Rapoport that I felt I should do this not because I had done anything wrong, but because public perceptions seemed to have made my position untenable. I felt that Moffett and everyone associated with Freeport were being maligned, and I did not want to run from my friends, Moffett in particular. Rapoport counseled me at once not to think any more about resigning as chancellor. He just dismissed that possibility out of hand. He never instructed me to resign from the Freeport board, but we did have a long conversation about everything that was happening, and it was an immense comfort to me to have someone with whom I could talk through everything without his trying to force his opinion on me.

I called Shirley Bird Perry and asked her to come to my office. I am sure she could sense by the tone of my voice that I needed her help immediately. I never made any decisions that involved the public face of the university without first talking with Perry. She stayed with me the rest of the day.

I next talked with Moffett. I told him I was considering resigning as chancellor. Moffett was even more direct than Rapoport. He told me that this would be a major mistake for me personally and that it would hurt the university. He urged me not to resign from my position as chancellor or from the university. Given all the spectacular and unfounded charges of a conflict of interest that had surrounded my relationship with Freeport through the years, I was always struck by how selflessly Moffett cared about the interests of the university. I next called George Christian, my longtime friend and adviser and someone who had been dealing with crises in government and public affairs for decades. Christian was kind enough to come to my office, and Perry and Rapoport and I talked on the phone several times.

Eventually Moffett, Christian, Rapoport, Perry, and I reached a consensus that in the interests of the university I ought to resign from the Freeport board. I agreed that this had become necessary, since I could not be perceived to be on both sides of a possible legal action involving faculty members. Christian helped me, Monty Jones, and Shirley Bird draft a statement about my resignation from the board, and we issued it that evening (December 14, 1995). In it, I said:

"My professional priority as chancellor has always been to strengthen The University of Texas System and its component institutions. One of my guiding principles has been that nothing I do should interfere with my ability to represent the UT System and to help attract to it the public and private support that is essential for maintaining and enhancing the University's stature as one of the world's great centers of learning.

"In recent months, my membership on the board of directors of Freeport-McMoRan Inc. has been used as an issue against the University. After much reflection, it has become clear that the interests of UT Austin and the rest of the UT System would be best served by my resignation from the Freeport board.

"A few highly vocal opponents of Freeport have distorted the facts and used personal attacks in a continuing campaign to discredit the company. I am convinced that the charges of human rights and environmental abuses leveled against Freeport are totally unfounded.

"I have always maintained that no conflict of interest arose because of my membership on the Freeport board while also serving as Chancellor. I have never been more confident of that fact.

"I have, of course, discussed my decision to resign from the Freeport board with Jim Bob Moffett, the company's chairman and CEO. He agrees that my decision is in the best interest of the University. That attitude exemplifies the high standards and the commitment to the University of Texas that I have always found in Mr. Moffett through the many years that I have been privileged to know him.

"The loyal support of Mr. and Mrs. Moffett for UT Austin has included an extraordinary record of generosity. Their donations have helped meet the critical needs of many of the University's academic programs, and the entire University community should remain grateful to them for the example they have set."[21]

The *Daily Texan*, which was not publishing because final exams for the fall semester were in progress, responded to my announcement by issuing a two-page "extra" edition on Friday, December 15. The edition was produced by the editor, Robert Rogers, and a staff of seven, and was printed through a hastily arranged deal with a newspaper in New Braunfels, since the press operators at the *Texan* were not available. The issue contained two objective news stories about the resignation, an editorial saying I had done the right thing, a column by the editor attacking Freeport on free-speech issues, a timeline of the Freeport issues since 1987, and the complete statement that I had issued the night before.

Reaction to my announcement included some very kind comments by Rapoport—"I think it just affirms what I have said the entire time, that this chancellor is one of the truly great chancellors in the history of the university. His commitment is first and foremost to the university system." Kenneth Ashworth, commissioner of the Texas Higher Education Coordinating Board, issued a very kind and thoughtful comment about me and my dedication to higher education in Texas. Others used the occasion to take a few more swings at me. Bill Bunch, of the Save Our Springs Legal Defense Fund, said my resignation was "a step in the right direction" but that an "investigation" was needed about my role in the naming of the building.[22]

There were two interesting belated reactions to my resignation. In a syndicated column in April 1996, Molly Ivins remarked, with her customary leftist wit, that "Cunningham resigned from the wrong institution," and she questioned whether any university needed a leader with such strong ties to the business community as I had. Two days later, her home newspaper, the *Fort Worth Star-Telegram*, published an editorial stating its opinion that I was "doing a sound and

EXTRA

THE DAILY TEXAN

Vol. 95 Extra   1 Section   The student newspaper of The University of Texas at Austin   Friday, December 15, 1995   25¢

Cunningham resigns from Freeport board

Decision comes after company's threat to sue 3 UT faculty members

KEVIN FITCHARD
AND TOM VAUGHN
Daily Texan Staff

UT System Chancellor William Cunningham resigned from Freeport-McMoRan's board of directors Thursday, one day after Freeport threatened to sue three UT professors who have spoken out against the mining and development company over the last several weeks.

Cunningham could not be reached for comment Thursday, but he issued a statement Thursday night saying that the controversy surrounding his position on Freeport's board has interfered with his ability to represent the University and the UT system.

"In recent months, my membership on the board of directors of Freeport-McMoRan Inc. has been used as an issue against the University," Cunningham said in the statement. "After much reflection, it has become clear that the interests of UT Austin and the rest of the UT System would be best served by my resignation from the Freeport board."

But two of the UT professors threatened by Freeport, Alan Cline and Bob Boyer, said Cunningham's resignation was a direct result of the threats to sue them.

"I believe his service as a director of the Freeport corporation made his role as chancellor of the UT system intolerable after Freeport threatened three of his professors with lawsuits," said Cline, a computer science professor. "How could he maintain both positions? As an officer of the corporation he would have to support any suit against any UT professors."

Wednesday Freeport sent letters to Cline and Boyer, as well as five other activists, accusing them of "malevolent distortions of the truth" about Freeport-McMoRan's mining operations in Indonesia.

Freeport has recently been the subject of numerous allegations of environmental and human rights abuses at its mining operations in Indonesia.

The controversy over Freeport spread to the UT campus when the UT system board of regents decided to name the new molecular biology after the New Orleans based company's CEO, Jim Bob Moffett, after Moffett and Freeport together donated $3 million toward the cost of the building.

"Cunningham can no longer be accused of an apparent conflict of interest if he is no longer on the

> " I have always maintained that no conflict of interest arose because of my membership on the Freeport board while also serving as chancellor. I have never been more confident of that fact..."
> — UT System Chancellor William Cunningham

board," said Boyer. But he added "I'll be happy when the Moffett building is renamed."

Among the others named in the letter are Steven Feld, a former anthropology professor who first launched criticism against Freeport on the UT campus and several, Daryl Slusher and Robert Bryce of The Austin Chronicle; Bill Bunch of the Save Our Springs Legal Defense Fund; and Lori Udall, Washington director of the International Rivers network.

Cunningham, who has been a member of Freeport's board of directors since 1987, owns about 47,000 stock options in the company.

Several UT professors and students claimed that Cunningham's membership on Freeport's board of directors constituted a "clear conflict of interest."

But Cunningham said his resignation was not an implication that such a conflict existed.

"I have always maintained that no conflict of interest arose because of my membership on the Freeport board while also serving as chancellor. I have never been more confident of that fact," Cunningham said in the statement.

The UT System Board of Regents approved the naming of the UT molecular biology building last December after Freeport CEO Jim Bob Moffett and his wife, Louise Moffett donated $2 million to the building's $24 million construction cost.

Cunningham also has repeatedly said the controversy and debate over Freeport is not harmful to the image of the University or that of the UT System.

"Obviously, there is a portion of the community that feels that I should not serve on the Freeport board. There is also a large segment in both the University and the broader communities who believe strongly that it is appropriate for me to serve on the Freeport board," Cunningham said in a prepared statement last month.

Bill Collier, spokesman for Freeport, declined to expand on Cunningham's resignation from the board.

"Certainly we regret not having him on our board," Collier said. But he refused to comment any further saying, "Freeport has not issued a statement on [Cunningham's] resig-

nation."

Collier also said Cunningham's announcement did not damage Freeport's image in any way.

"I don't see how anyone can draw a conclusion that this tarnishes our image," Collier said.

The controversy surrounding Freeport began after local protesters began accusing Freeport of environmental and human rights violations in Irian Jaya, where the mines are located. Freeport has repeatedly denied the allegations. But last month the debate spread to Washington after the Overseas Private Investment Corp. revoked a $1 million political risk insurance policy because of alleged environmental violations.

TSP File Photo

Chancellor William Cunningham resigned from the Freeport McMoRan board of directors Thursday.

Professors hail recent decision

TOM VAUGHN and KEVIN FICHARD
Daily Texan Staff

After months of student protests and faculty debate on the University's association with Freeport-McMoRan Inc., the UT community applauded System Chancellor William Cunningham's resignation from the company's board of directors.

"It removes an apparent conflict of interest," said Bob Boyer, professor of philosophy and computer science. "He is no longer on the board."

"In light of the controversy, I think it's good that he resigned from their board," said Student Government President Sherry Boyles. "I think it doesn't reflect well on the University when he's chancellor and sits on their board of directors."

Ed Sharpe, special consultant to the chancellor, would not comment on Cunningham's resignation, saying only "I respect his decision."

Boyles also said the University's association with Freeport reflects poorly on the University of Texas.

"If the allegations of human rights and environmental abuses ... against Freeport-McMoRan are true, it has the potential of really reflecting poorly on the University of Texas," Boyles said.

"I don't think anybody is going to be quiet about this now," said Alan Cline, professor of computer science.

"[UT President Robert] Berdahl said debate should begin. He invited debate on this campus. Bob Boyer went to the Faculty Council meeting on Monday and presented some of the materials."

Two days later, he and Daryl Slusher [UT professor of anthropology] received threats.

Bill Bunch, attorney for the Save Our Springs Legal Defense Fund, said of Cunningham's resignation "It's a step in the right direction," but it is not an occasion to celebrate.

"Moffett's name is still going on the building."

Of the lawsuits, Austin Chronicle columnist Robert Bryce said, "They're a blatant attempt at intimidation," adding the letters did not offer any specific evidences of misused language.

"I am disappointed that it's come to this," Berdahl told the Associated Press Thursday night.

"I certainly hope that this resignation from the board puts an end to the controversy that has been associated with Cunningham's affiliation with the board," he said.

"It is an unusual circumstance when one of the major supporters and contributors of the university on one side is threatening faculty of the university on the other," Berdahl said. "I obviously puts those of us who care about free debate on the faculty in the cross fire."

Berdahl said he is considering asking a committee of faculty members to look into how other universities decide on building names, including how contributions play into such decisions.

Christina McCatt, vice president for Students for Earth Awareness, said the announcement came as surprise.

"I'm surprised, given the chancellor's lack of response so far to questions about his position on the Freeport board," McCatt said. "I'm glad ... We don't have to worry about the conflict of interest problem any more."

"I'm glad to see [Cunningham] is loyal to UT and its faculty," Boyles said. "There are a lot of people who don't want Freeport McMoRan associated with our University."

With Associated Press reports.

ON THE OTHER SIDE OF THE TEXAN TODAY

Thought We Were Gone, Didn't You? Weather: The Daily Texan will hit the stands today like a cold front.

Hey, there was only a 20 percent chance we were going to pass our finals anyway. I hope I can pull some grades in the 70s.

Index:
Editorials..................................2

A LOOK BACK AT THE FREEPORT DEBATE

■ 1987: Cunningham, then UT president, becomes a member of Freeport-McMoRan's board of directors.
■ 1988: The Environmental Protection Agency names Freeport the top corporate polluter in the U.S., citing its hazardous waste dumping into the Mississippi River.
■ April 11, 1990: The University announces that Jim Bob Moffett, Freeport CEO, and his wife have donated $3 million to the University, $2 million for "a capital project in the College of Natural Sciences."
■ Nov. 25, 1990: Cunningham participates in a student forum concerning his role on Freeport's board of directors and the University's ties with the company. Cunningham said, "I have never been involved with any project, in my opinion, which would endanger or damage the environment."
■ Dec. 1, 1994: UT System Board of Regents approves the naming of the new molecular biology building in honor of Moffett.
■ April 1995: The Australian Council for Overseas Aid cites numerous human rights abuses, including tortures and killings at Freeport's Indonesian mine. The report named the Indonesian military and Freeport security as perpetrators of the crimes.
■ August 1995: Report by the Catholic Church of

Jayapura also cites several human rights abuses at the mine site and confirms many of ACFOA's accusations.
■ Sep. 11, 1995: Steven Feld, UT professor of anthropology, announces his resignation from the University in a letter to Cunningham.
■ Sep. 22, 1995: The National Human Rights Commission of Indonesia releases a report saying "clear and identifiable human rights violations have occurred," on and near the Freeport mine. The commission attributed all abuses to the Indonesian military, saying they were in the process of "safeguarding [Freeport's] mining operations."
■ Oct. 31, 1995: The Overseas Private Investment Corporation, a federal agency which provides insurance for American companies operating overseas, cancels a $100 million political risk insurance policy, alleging numerous environmental abuses at Freeport's mine in Indonesia.
■ Nov. 14, 1995: Freeport officials hold a press conference in Austin denying any involvement by Freeport employees in any human rights abuses.
■ Nov. 16, 1995: A UT student group announces that 3,190 students and faculty members have signed a petition demanding that the regents change the name

of the molecular biology building.
■ Nov. 17, 1995: Berdahl places a full page ad in the Texan saying he "cannot support any effort to reverse commitments already made by the University and Board of Regents with regard to the naming of the molecular biology building."
■ Nov. 22, 1995: Hermann Munninghoff, the bishop of Jayapura, denies in a letter that he made allegations against Freeport. The letter said the bishop had found human rights violations had occurred, but media organizations, and not the bishop himself, have drawn connections between the murders and the company.
■ Dec. 1, 1995: UT System Faculty Advisory Council approves a resolution to "encourage" the Board of Regents to solicit faculty input before naming any building on UT System campuses.
■ Dec. 11, 1995: Berdahl considers a task force to allow faculty members to be involved in naming future buildings.
■ Dec. 14, 1995: Freeport sends letters to seven individuals, including three UT professors, threatening to take legal action against their "false and damaging" accusations of human rights abuses in Indonesia.
■ Dec. 14, 1995: Cunningham resigns from Freeport's board of directors.

Daily Texas extra edition, December 15, 1995, with headline "Cunningham resigns from Freeport board." *UT Office of Public Affairs Records, e_utopa_00060.*

prudent job as chancellor" and that it made sense for a chancellor to have "business connections" and "business sense." "More clearly put," the newspaper said, "a professor may occupy an ivory tower; a chancellor must build it."[23]

The name of the molecular biology building remained a matter of debate at UT Austin in early 1996, even though members of the board of regents had stated repeatedly that they saw no reason to revisit the issue. In January, Berdahl urged the faculty to let the matter drop, but some professors weren't ready to give up. "Some people could read that statement as Freeport has won," said Cline.[24]

A few weeks later the Faculty Council voted 28 to 15 to ask me and the regents to discuss with the Moffetts "the possibility of their voluntarily assenting to a change." There was no interest among the regents in pursuing this. I stated that I was "very disappointed" in the Faculty Council's action, and Rapoport and Smiley were quoted as saying they didn't think a reconsideration of the name was appropriate. The *Austin American-Statesman* ran a headline to a story on February 20, 1996, that said "Faculty opposes" the building's name, but of course there was no way of knowing whether that was true. What was known was that twenty-eight politically active faculty members out of the university's approximately 2,100 faculty members had voted for changing the name.[25]

A week later, it was the turn of the Dean's Council to weigh in on the building naming. The council, composed of deans and senior administrators, voted for a resolution that said it believes "it is vital for the university to honor its commitments to donors and to keep its word when recognizing them for gifts."[26]

Michael Sharlot, dean of the UT School of Law, took issue with the Faculty Council's action in an op-ed article in the *Daily Texan*. He said the council had acted like "a kangaroo court" and had disgraced itself, the faculty in general, and the university. Sharlot did not comment on the substance of any of the issues involving Freeport and UT, but focused exclusively on the manner in which the Faculty Council had acted. He wrote that the allegations of misbehavior by Freeport were based on second- and third-hand reports from groups whose motives were unknown to most of the council members.

"Whatever the actual facts regarding [the Grasberg mine]," he wrote, "the issue for me is whether those who condemn the Moffetts can produce any credible evidence that Freeport, as a corporate body

. . . has participated intentionally in the human rights abuses attributed to the Indonesian military. I have seen and heard none." Sharlot also said "extremely vague charges" had been made with regard to the environmental issues.

"The reason I charge the council with behaving as a kangaroo court is that, having decided to consider resolutions to condemn the Moffetts as unfit to be honored . . . there was no effort to insist on persuasive evidence from those making the charges or to seek contrary views. . . . It is shocking that the council has never, to my knowledge, requested that the faculty with personal knowledge of the area and some relevant academic expertise address the council so as to help inform the decisions and judgments. . . .

"In short, we have witnessed a monstrous public condemnation of two individuals and a company on the basis of a totally one-sided and inadequate investigation."[27]

The end of the controversy came with a whimper. I resigned from the board, and faculty critics realized that if they continued to libel Moffett or Freeport, they could end up in court. This threat did silence the critics whose spouses were intent on their family interest in keeping their assets.[28] Freeport continued with its mining operations and today is recognized as one of the world's leading mining companies, with the world's largest reserves of copper and gold. The people of Indonesia seem to enjoy the prosperity that Freeport has brought to the country as one of its largest taxpayers and most concerned corporate citizens. Most of the students who had been active in the anti-Freeport campaign eventually graduated or moved on to other endeavors, and soon there was little remaining notice on the campus of the issues that had so exercised a few members of the university community for so long. The Moffets' name remained on the molecular biology building, which has become the hub of a magnificent academic program that is providing world-class educational opportunities for thousands of students and is contributing toward expanding the frontiers of the biological sciences. It is safe to say that thousands of people walk past the building every day as a matter of routine and have little if any memory of the great controversy that once swirled around the facility and its illustrious name.

CHAPTER 31

The Numbers Tell the Story

I am fond of saying "the numbers tell the story." The numbers are important because they often give an unbiased appraisal of what has occurred. This is particularly true with respect to financial data. I am very pleased that during my tenure in administration the numbers indicate that both UT Austin and the UT System prospered economically. While I recognize that financial prosperity is not the only way an administrator or an administration should be judged, it is hard for the faculty and staff to provide improved classroom experiences for our students, pursue new research initiatives, and expand on their service responsibilities to the people of Texas if the financial resources are not sufficient.

I will describe below what occurred in total expenditures, state tax dollars, tuition and fees, and research during my tenure as president of UT Austin (FY 1986–1992) and chancellor of the UT System (FY 1993–2000).[1] It will quickly become apparent that not only did our total expenditures go up dramatically, but also the sources of revenue changed even more significantly. I will also discuss the changes that took place in health care funding during my tenure as chancellor.

Total expenditures at UT Austin grew during my presidency from $530.9 million in FY 1986 to $725.6 million in FY 1992 (see Table 1). This represents a 37.7 percent increase in expenditures and a 9.7 percent increase in inflation-adjusted expenditures. During the period I was chancellor, UT Austin's total expenditures increased to $1,071.6 million, an increase of 34.5 percent. This was more than a 15 percent increase in real dollars from 1993 to 2000. While the macro numbers represent significant real growth in expenditures, state-appropriated funds did fluctuate dramatically during my presidency. For example, in 1986 the state appropriated $212.6 million to UT Austin. This declined to $166.3 million in 1987 but rose to $247.3 million in 1992.

In the 1985–1986 fiscal year, the state's tax dollars appropriated to UT Austin represented 40 percent of UT Austin's expenditures, and by FY 1992 these dollars had dropped to 34.1 percent of the university's expenditures. This was largely a function of growth in revenue sources other than state appropriations. To illustrate, while state appropriations increased 16.3 percent from 1986 to 1992, all other sources of funds to finance the budget increased by 50.3 percent. This pattern continued while I was chancellor. State appropriated tax dollars increased 14.3 percent while all other fund sources used to finance the budget increased 43.3 percent. As a percentage of the budget, state appropriations for UT Austin fell from 34.1 percent in 1992 to 25.8 percent in 2000.

The pattern has become clear to everyone by now. The joke I used to tell when I was speaking to UT Austin alumni was that during

TABLE 1
UT AUSTIN—KEY FINANCIAL CHARACTERISTICS, 1986–2000
(millions of dollars)

Year	Total Expenditures	State Appropriated Dollars	Tuition and Fees	Research Expenditures	Capital Expenditures
1986	$ 530.9	$ 212.6	$ 57.6	$ 119.6	$ 103.7
1987	536.2	166.3	60.7	138.5	63.5
1988	566.1	212.8	62.8	133.9	61.1
1989	609.9	210.8	68.2	146.3	49.2
1990	657.6	242.6	72.5	168.1	55.4
1991	708.1	235.4	80.1	184.1	59.3
1992	725.6	247.3	90.4	183.3	63.6
1993	796.6	241.9	110.2	202.3	45.6
1994	813.0	253.6	124.8	203.8	16.5
1995	827.4	247.8	132.3	198.2	80.6
1996	876.6	235.8	165.5	210.7	100.4
1997	918.0	235.5	189.3	225.7	111.7
1998	942.2	255.2	214.9	214.7	152.4
1999	995.1	255.4	220.8	221.1	121.2
2000	1,071.6	276.5	231.7	241.1	206.3

my tenure in administration, UT Austin had moved from being a state university to a state-assisted university to a university that was located in the state. This pattern has only gotten worse in the twenty-first century.

The reduction in the use of tax dollars to support higher education was only one part of the funding story. The Texas Legislature made sweeping changes (HB 1147) in the state's higher education tuition policy that took effect in FY 1986. The bill raised tuition rates for Texas residents from their historic base rate of $4 per semester credit hour to $12 per SCH for FY 1986 and to $16 per SCH for FY 1987. In addition, the minimum tuition for a semester was doubled from $50 to $100. The bill also called for continued graduated increases in tuition through the next decade.

In 1987, the legislature passed a bill (HB 2181) that permitted institutions of higher education to double graduate tuition and "retain" the money instead of having it count against state appropriations. Furthermore, the legislature granted universities the authority to impose different rates among various graduate programs. Such additional flexibility permitted UT Austin to impose different tuition rates as a function of market conditions. Not surprisingly, the first two programs to increase tuition were the Graduate School of Business and the School of Law.

As a result of HB 1147 and HB 2181 and the willingness of the board of regents to increase graduate tuition, income from tuition and fees for UT Austin grew from $57.6 million in FY 1986 to $90.4 million in FY 1992 and then to $231.7 million in FY 2000. In FY 1986, tuition and fee revenue represented 10.8 percent of UT Austin's total expenditures; by FY 1992, this percentage had grown to 12.5 percent, and by 2000 it was 21.6 percent. Tuition clearly became an important element in funding UT Austin during my tenure in administration. Apart from selected graduate programs, many UT Austin students and their families resented the tuition increases that were imposed on them. I was criticized as "Dollar Bill" by the *Daily Texan* once the paper figured out the role that I had played in increasing graduate tuition. The *Texan* even published enlarged images of dollar bills with my face on them.

I had always felt that tuition was unrealistically low and that if the state ever experienced significant financial difficulties, UT Austin would be able to increase tuition to help offset reductions in state

William H. Cunningham addresses graduate students who are protesting reductions in benefits for teaching assistants, April 27, 1988. *UT Texas Student Publications Photograph Collection, e_uttsp_00013.*

spending. I did not want to play the tuition card unless we had to because I was always afraid that the state's political leaders would be pleased to offload the state's responsibilities to our students. Early on in my presidency, however, I concluded that the state would not provide the university with the funds it needed and, as a result, I was a strong advocate for tuition and fee increases and the concept of flexible tuition.

A major change in public policy had taken place during the 1985 and 1987 legislative sessions, as lawmakers adopted on two occasions legislation that put higher education on a clear path to utilize user fees (tuition) to support its operations rather than tax dollars. Without the increases in tuition, UT Austin would have had to dramatically reduce services provided its students. When I became president of UT Austin, its tuition was among the lowest of any major university in the country. When I resigned as chancellor in 2000, tuition at UT Austin was within 5 percent of the average tuition for major public research universities.

The university had a wide variety of grants, scholarships, teaching and research assistant positions, and work-study programs designed to help offset the impact of tuition and fees that were paid by our students. Many of these programs had a financial need component. As a result, we were able to help a significant portion of the relatively low-income students deal with the increases in tuition.

Externally funded research at UT Austin had been an important priority for the institution for many years before I became president. As Table 1 indicates, the university's research continued to increase substantially during my tenure. To illustrate, university research expenditures grew from $119.6 million in FY 1986 to $183.3 million in FY 1992 and to $241.1 million in 2000. This represented a 53.3 percent increase in research during my presidency and another 19.2 percent increase while I was chancellor. In FY 1992, research activity at UT Austin accounted for more than one-third of all research activity in the UT System and 83 percent of the research at all the UT general academic institutions. Research expenditures at UT Austin more than doubled from 1986 to 2000, while the consumer price index increased only 57.2 percent.

I am very proud of Provost Gerry Fonken's efforts to build the research infrastructure all across the campus that permitted the deans and departmental chairmen to attract faculty members who consistently won competitive government and private research grants. I recognize that much of the research infrastructure was built and many of the faculty members who were so successful during my tenure in administration in securing external research funds were hired during the administrations of President Peter Flawn and President Lorene Rogers. Clearly, creating an atmosphere that encourages research is a long-term project. I do feel we did everything that we could to continue to build the culture and the infrastructure that would encourage research and help the state diversify its economy. UT Austin was a major research university when I became president, and it was an even stronger research university at the end of my term as chancellor.

UT Austin always seems to have a large capital expenditure program. It is a large organization and I did inherit a significant amount of deferred maintenance on the campus. In addition, the university is very ambitious, and its deans and faculty are constantly pushing hard to improve the physical facilities so that the institution can increase its research activities as well as improve its students' academic experience. During the period I was president and chancellor, the institution spent almost $1.3 billion on capital projects. Historically, virtually all of the nonathletic buildings on campus had been financed by Permanent University Fund bonds or specific targeted student fees associated with student housing, intramural athletic facilities, the student union, or other student services. During my presidency, the university began its first efforts to raise a portion of the cost of building new facilities from the private sector. Once again, the university began to migrate to the private school model by first asking students to pay the cost of a significant portion of their education and second, requesting donors to pay for a portion of new construction projects.

The university had a rule when I became president that a person had to be deceased for at least five years before a building could be named for him or her. I made it clear to the board of regents that while we had many very loyal alumni, none of them seemed to be interested in following the regents' rules so that they could be recognized with a name on a building they had paid for. The board understood this, and once it became clear that we would need to rely on outside capital for construction it became much easier for the board to waive its naming rules. The molecular biology building, which was named for Louise and Jim Bob Moffett, was the first building named in honor of a donor during my presidency.

While the UT System prospered economically during my years as chancellor, the pattern of funding once again changed dramatically. (See Table 2.) Total expenditures for the UT System during my last year as chancellor exceeded $5.6 billion, which amounted to a 54.6 percent increase in spending while I was chancellor. The academic institutions' expenditures increased 44.4 percent, while the health institutions' expenditures increased 59 percent. These represented an increase in real dollars of 35.4 percent for the UT System—25.2 percent for the academic institutions and almost 40 percent for the health institutions.

In FY 1993, the state's tax dollars appropriated to the UT System amounted to $1.19 billion. (See Table 3.) The total appropriated tax dollars for the UT System grew by $314.4 million during my tenure as chancellor and amounted to a total of $1.5 billion by FY 2000. This represented a 26.4 percent increase in state-appropriated tax dollars.

The funding pattern for the UT System that existed while I was chancellor was similar to what UT Austin experienced during my

TABLE 2
UT SYSTEM
TOTAL EXPENDITURES, 1993–2000
(millions of dollars)

Year	Total, UT System	General Academic Institutions	Health Institutions
1993	3,644.0	1,346.0	2,302.8
1994	3,835.1	1,415.2	2,419.2
1995	4,093.7	1,453.9	2,626.6
1996	4,297.2	1,539.5	2,751.3
1997	4,565.2	1,624.8	2,905.9
1998	4,834.4	1,702.3	3,120.1
1999	5,157.5	1,779.4	3,361.2
2000	5,634.8	1,943.3	3,660.8

presidency. As a result of greater growth from other revenue sources, state tax dollars dropped to 26.7 percent of total expenditures in 2000, from 32.6 percent in 1993. However, even with the decline in state appropriations as a percentage of the system budget, during the eight years I was chancellor (FY 1993–2000), state-appropriated tax dollars to the UT System totaled $10.7 billion, an amount almost one-third greater than for the preceding eight-year period. In addition, state-appropriated tax dollars experienced a real increase of 4.3 percent from 1993 to 2000.

During my tenure as chancellor, the academic institutions received somewhat more favorable treatment from the state in terms of state appropriations than did the health institutions. I am not quite sure why this happened. It may be nothing more than an accident of history or a result of the South Texas/Border Initiative (see Chapter 26) having a greater impact on the academic institutions than on the health institutions. The academic institutions in the South Texas/Border Initiative saw their expenditures increase by 69 percent, compared with only a 37 percent increase for academic institutions not included in the initiative. The South Texas/Border Initiative contributed to a 49.8 percent increase in real expenditures for the four UT System general academic institutions that were part of the initiative.

TABLE 3
UT SYSTEM—STATE APPROPRIATED TAX DOLLARS, 1993–2000
(millions of dollars)

Year	Total, UT System	General Academic Institutions	Health Institutions
1993	1,189.2	502.9	685.2
1994	1,310.5	546.2	763.2
1995	1,293.3	536.2	756.1
1996	1,319.1	545.4	728.1
1997	1,297.5	539.1	712.8
1998	1,369.3	587.5	781.7
1999	1,385.5	596.2	786.9
2000	1,503.6	677.8	821.6

Tax funds made available to all UT general academic institutions grew by 34.8 percent during my tenure as chancellor, and by 19.9 percent to the health institutions. (See Table 3.) In 1993 the state contributed 37.4 percent of the system's academic institutions' budgets. This percentage declined to 34.9 percent of the budget in 2000. The reduction in state support was more dramatic for the health institutions. In 1993 the state funded 29.8 percent of the health institutions' budgets, and this declined to 22.4 percent in 2000. While total tax funding increased for the health institutions by $136.4 million while I was chancellor, this represented less than a 1 percent increase in real dollar support from the state for the health institutions.

Tuition and fee income became a much more significant portion of the budget during the 1993–2000 period. This was a further reflection of the fact that the state leadership was unwilling to invest more appropriated dollars from taxes in higher education, but they were willing to permit the universities to charge their students more tuition and fees. Revenue from tuition and fees in FY 2000 for the UT System totaled $525.3 million and amounted to more than twice the amount collected in FY 1993, when I became chancellor. (See Table 4.)

Tuition revenue to UT Austin rose 302 percent from 1986 to 2000, while the consumer price index increased only 57.2 percent. Once again, the same pattern held for the general academic institutions

TABLE 4
UT SYSTEM—TUITION AND FEE REVENUE, 1993–2000
(millions of dollars)

Year	Total, UT System	General Academic Institutions	Health Institutions
1993	256.5	224.6	31.9
1994	288.7	255.2	33.5
1995	307.9	273.7	34.2
1996	364.3	328.0	36.2
1997	419.7	381.4	38.2
1998	460.9	423.2	37.7
1999	491.5	452.4	39.0
2000	525.3	485.7	39.6

during the period I was chancellor. Tuition increased 162.5 percent while the CPI increased a modest 19.2 percent. My attitude toward tuition as chancellor did not change from when I was president of UT Austin. I felt that if the UT System was going to provide a first-class education for a large number of students, we had no choice but to strongly advocate tuition increases that would ultimately raise our rates to levels that would be more competitive with the other major universities in the country. It was not what I would have preferred to do, but it was the only option available to us to continue to provide outstanding service to the state's ever-growing student population.

Tuition and fees increased in dollar value and in overall financial importance much more dramatically for the academic institutions than for the health institutions. The enrollment at the general academic institutions is much greater and instruction constitutes a greater budgetary activity of these organizations. Tuition and fees amounted to 25 percent of the general academic institutions' total expenditures in FY 2000, a significant change from FY 1993 when they constituted 16.7 percent of total expenditures. In contrast, tuition and fee revenue for the health institutions, while greater per student in absolute terms, did not increase at near the rate of that for students at general academic institutions. Tuition and fee revenue grew by only 24.1 percent in the FY 1993 through FY 2000 period and amounted to a

TABLE 5
UT SYSTEM—RESEARCH EXPENDITURES, 1993–2000
(millions of dollars)

Year	Total, UT System	General Academic Institutions	Health Institutions
1993	602.0	240.9	361.1
1994	615.5	244.5	370.9
1995	628.6	242.7	385.9
1996	656.6	263.3	393.2
1997	704.0	283.6	420.4
1998	708.1	265.1	443.0
1999	744.3	266.6	477.8
2000	849.8	304.1	545.7

Source of financial data in Tables 1–5: The University of Texas System, Office of the Controller. Totals for the UT System in Tables 2 and 3 include amounts for the UT System administration, which are not separately identified in these tables.

little more than 1 percent of the health institutions' budgets in 2000. This is explained in large part by the fact that there are significant noninstructional budget elements within the health institutions. One large example is the M. D. Anderson Cancer Center with a $1 billion budget in 2000 but only $60,000 in tuition revenue.

UT System institutions continued their drive to become even more powerful research organizations during my administration as chancellor. Research expenditures across the UT System went from $602 million in FY 1993 to $849.8 million in FY 2000. (See Table 5.) These expenditures not only contribute to supporting the education of graduate students as they work with faculty members, but also underwrite research that has helped the state diversify its economy. In FY 1993, UT Austin was the unchallenged leader in research, accounting for one-third of all UT System research expenditures; $202.3 million of a system total of $602 million. M. D. Anderson and UT Southwestern Medical Center accounted for $113.6 million and $93.2 million, respectively, in 1993, which in total represented 57.3 percent of all UT health-related components' research activity in 1993.

When I resigned as chancellor, UT Austin was still the clear leader in research among all of the component institutions. However, the other UT general academic institutions and the health institutions had recorded significant increases in research. The research expenditures at all of the academic institutions other than UT Austin grew by 63.2 percent from 1993 to 2000, while UT Austin research expenditures expanded during this period by only 19.2 percent. However, in 2000, UT Austin still spent almost four times as much on research than all the rest of the UT System academic institutions combined.

Research spending also grew rapidly at the health institutions while I was chancellor. It increased from $361 million in FY 1993 to not quite $546 million in FY 2000—an increase of more than 51 percent, while the CPI increased by only 19.2 percent. Research spending by the health institutions amounted to 14.9 percent of their total spending for FY 2000. The clear leaders in research among the health institutions continued to be UT Southwestern and UT M. D. Anderson Cancer Center, where research expenditures increased by 62 percent and 33 percent, respectively. The UT Health Science Center at Houston made the greatest gains in research activity of all the health institutions, growing its research enterprise by 103 percent between 1993 and 2000.

As part of its mission to train health professionals, the UT System operates hospitals and clinics that it owns as well as those it staffs through arrangements with county hospital districts. In 1993, hospital and clinic operations constituted 35 percent of total expenditures at the health institutions, and by FY 2000 hospital and clinic operations had grown to represent 45 percent of total expenditures. Through the hospitals and clinics, the UT System's health institutions spent more than $1.64 billion on health care in 2000. This amounted to an increase of more than 130 percent over expenditures in FY 1993 and became the single largest expense category for these institutions. These expenses during this period were 140 percent greater than in the previous eight-year period and represented an 120 percent increase over inflation.

The UT health institutions also provide a significant amount of indigent care through the hospitals and clinics. Such care was valued at more than $228 million in FY 2000. In addition to the value of the hospital and clinic charges for indigent care, the UT health professionals maintain accounts of charity care charged to the Medical

Services, Research, and Development Programs/Physician Referral Service (MSRDP).[2] Such charges for charity care amounted to $363 million in FY 2000 and averaged approximately $350 million a year during most of the time I was chancellor. In 2000, such charity care was the equivalent of 4 percent of the total of the professional fee charges for health care. It is clear that the UT System's health institutions accounted for a significant portion of the charitable contribution to the health and welfare of Texas's indigent population. Individuals who are seriously ill but lack insurance can often be treated most effectively at university research-based hospitals. We are fortunate to have the facilities in Texas that can deliver this type of help.

Three significant changes occurred in the financing of capital needs during my tenure as chancellor. The first was that, beginning in 1993, the legislature again authorized the use of tuition revenue bonds to finance capital improvements at selected colleges and universities. (See Chapter 26.) The bonds issued for UT System capital improvement projects during this period (all of which were in 1993–2000) amounted to almost $373 million. While the UT System's tuition revenue bonds are guaranteed by the UT System, they are paid for each biennium through a special line-item appropriation. The legislature recognized that it has an obligation to pay the bonds, and it has never reneged on that commitment.

The second change in our capital financing program was the constitutional amendment that passed in 1999, which gave the UT Board of Regents the ability to operate the Permanent University Fund as a total return fund. (See Chapter 27.) As a result, the board could harvest some of the PUF's capital gains, which permitted the system to issue additional bonds to support capital projects.

The third change was that the board of regents was routinely waiving the rules concerning the naming of buildings. Southwestern Medical Center, under Kern Wildenthal's leadership, named twenty-nine buildings, rooms, or centers for donors who contributed significant amounts of money to support these projects. M. D. Anderson was also very successful. Mickey LeMaistre named nine such projects. While the board of regents continued to waive its policy against naming buildings for living persons, it also increased the percentage of a project's cost that donors were required to pay to have their names on buildings. When the molecular biology building at UT Austin was named for the Moffetts, they contributed approximately 10 percent of the total cost of the building. While there was no specific requirement, the cost of naming rose to between 33 percent and 50 percent during the years that I was chancellor.

For the first seven years that I was chancellor, the annual average amount of PUF bond allocations to the institutional building programs was $32 million. With the passage in 1999 of the constitutional amendment regarding management of the PUF, we were able, in FY 2000, to allocate to the building program over $171 million in PUF bond proceeds. With the additional tuition revenue bonds and the added flexibility in the management of the PUF, along with other institutional resources and contributions of donors, the UT System was able to respond to repair, rehabilitation, and growth needs by significantly increasing capital spending.

Overall, capital spending increased by more than 50 percent from 1993 to 2000, compared to the previous eight years, and capital spending was positioned to increase even more during the next decade.

I was quite cognizant of both faculty and staff salaries during my years in administration. I did all that I could to see that compensation was competitive. While I also recognize that the faculty gets most of the press and national attention, I was very aware that the staff is critical to the success of the university. Many of our students interact with staff members as much as or more than they do with faculty. While the staff rarely gets the credit that they deserve, the university needs to be very careful not to play faculty off against staff. Faculty salaries at UT Austin increased by 80 percent between 1986 and 2000, compared to a 57 percent increase in the cost of living; staff salaries increased by 133 percent during this same period.

I am disappointed in two ratios that are associated with students. First, the student/faculty ratio at UT Austin and the other academic institutions was too high. This led to larger and fewer classes. The student/faculty ratio at UT Austin was almost twice that of many of our key competitors such as the University of California at Berkeley or the University of Michigan. We often made the trade-off between faculty salaries and new positions in favor of salary increases. Unfortunately, the same student/faculty ratio problems existed at all the academic institutions while I was chancellor. The argument was that if we were not competitive with faculty salaries we would not be able to retain the best and brightest of our faculty. This was true, but there was a cost associated with this decision.

The second ratio represents the percentage of minority students at UT Austin. During the period I was president, black students on campus increased from 3.4 percent to 3.7 percent of the total student population. The university made more progress with Hispanic and Asian American students. Hispanic students grew from 8.9 percent to 11.7 percent, while Asian American students grew from 3.5 percent to 7.4 percent while I was president. When I resigned as chancellor, in 2000, 3.2 percent of UT Austin's students were black, 11.8 percent Hispanic, and 12.5 percent Asian American.

UT Austin made many attempts and spent a great deal of money during the period I was in administration to recruit African American and Hispanic students. These efforts are described in some detail in Chapter 7. UT Austin had more African American and Hispanic students on its campus than any other flagship nonminority school in the country. This still did not mask the fact that we had a very small percentage of African American students, and we did not make as much progress with Hispanic students as we wanted to.

It is difficult to find any one number or ratio that tells the real story of what happened during the period that I was president and chancellor. With that caveat in mind, I am very pleased that expenditures in real dollars increased 9.7 percent at UT Austin during the seven years I was president and 35.4 percent for all of the UT System's institutions during the eight years I was chancellor. Real dollar expenditures are important because they represent additional services that the UT System was able to provide the people of Texas.

Several major forces helped account for this rather unprecedented period of financial growth for the university. First, Texas had conservative legislators who were not willing to provide tax dollars to the university, but they were nevertheless strong supporters of the university and higher education. This led to their willingness to permit the academic and health institutions to increase tuition and fees. These were considered to be "user fees," which were consistent with the legislature's idea of how state agencies should be funded.

Second, the UT System had a strong board of regents that shared the administration's ambition for what higher education could do to support the state's emerging population, as well as help strengthen and diversify its economy. Most of the board members and each of the chairmen I worked with understood the importance of generating money in the form of tax dollars and tuition and fees. We were also blessed with having regents, and particularly chairmen, who were willing to invest their own time, energy, and political muscle to help the UT System and its component institutions extract more tax dollars from the legislature to support our vital mission.

The third force was that Texans had for many years elected strong and visionary people to serve as lieutenant governor—an office that is recognized as in many ways more powerful in legislative deliberations that that of governor. For whatever reason, the state had a long history of having a lieutenant governor who actively supported higher education in general and UT Austin and the UT System in particular. Lieutenant Governor Ben Barnes was a true partner with Governor John Connally in supporting excellence in higher education. Bill Hobby and Bob Bullock, who served in this important position during the period I was in administration, could not have been more supportive of higher education. Their leadership was often the defining force that permitted higher education to prosper.

During my tenure as president or chancellor, Texas never had a governor who placed higher education as his or her top priority. Connally and Dolph Briscoe had realized when they served as governor that higher education was the key to the future of Texas. In contrast, the governors who held office during my tenure may have been positively predisposed to higher education in general, but it was never their top priority. While I understand this, the simple bottom line was that I am a single-issue evaluator of governors. My focus is not on roads, public safety, tort reform, tax reduction, or helping officials move up to higher office. I have been exclusively driven during my tenure as a university administrator to improving the availability and quality of higher education in Texas and, specifically, at UT Austin and all the institutions in the UT System. I do not apologize for my myopic behavior. I recognize that being a single-issue advocate is not appropriate for most citizens. However, my mission for more than fifteen years focused me like a laser on one issue, and it is just too late to try to change now.

CHAPTER 32

Texas Higher Education: Looking Back and Looking Ahead

As chancellor I was fortunate to work with a highly talented and dedicated team who helped the UT System make sustained progress in every aspect of its complex mission of teaching, research, health care, and public service. I believe institutions across the system strengthened their undergraduate education programs, providing better instruction, a higher-quality undergraduate educational experience, and stronger student retention programs. Similar advances were made in the graduate and research programs, as evidenced by a system-wide increase of 25 percent in research spending and by the presence of no fewer than seven Nobel laureates on the faculty of UT institutions. Advances were also recorded in providing excellent, affordable, and compassionate patient care through hospitals and clinics, with 60,000 hospital admissions and more than 3.7 million outpatient visits each year, as well as the provision of more than $824 million worth of indigent health care annually. And in their dedication to public service our faculty and staff continued to demonstrate an amazing commitment to the economic, social, and cultural welfare of their communities beyond the boundaries of the campuses.

Those four areas of achievement constitute the broad-based, fundamental elements of the mission of UT Austin and the UT System. When I announced in June 1999 that I planned to retire from the Chancellor's Office by the end of the following summer, I highlighted more specific areas in which I believed the UT System had made major progress under the team that I had led, and in succeeding months I reviewed most of those areas, along with progress that was made at UT Austin while I was in administration, with a variety of audiences around the state.[1] I recognize fully that I alone am not responsible for the achievements that I will enumerate below, and that I benefited at every step from a highly capable and dedicated team of staff members.

- Creation of the Executive MBA, the five-year integrated BBA/ MPA, and the Foundations of Business Program, along with building a significant endowment, all of which helped the UT Austin business school make a successful transition to the post-Kozmetsky era. (Chapter 2)
- The adoption of a modern registration system that permitted the university to effectively manage its limited faculty resources and course offerings. (Chapter 5)
- Resolution of the university's long-running dispute with the Blackland Neighborhood east of the UT Austin campus. (Chapter 8)
- Continued dedication to the principle of equal educational opportunity for all, while coping with the severe challenges presented by the *Hopwood* case. (Chapters 7 and 9)
- Successful development and funding of the Hobby-Eberly Spectroscopic Survey Telescope at McDonald Observatory. (Chapter 10)
- The expansion and funding of UT Austin's molecular biology program. (Chapter 10)
- Successful management of the crisis at the Performing Arts Center in the UT Austin College of Fine Arts. (Chapter 12)
- Naming and expansion of the Darrell K Royal–Texas Memorial Stadium. (Chapter 17)
- Assisting the state in its efforts to diversify its economy. (Chapter 18)
- Creation of a workable system of post-tenure review. (Chapter 29)
- Development of a distance education program throughout the UT System, including the establishment of a "virtual university" that helped our institutions meet the needs of students in a new age of technology. (Chapter 29)
- Creation of the Regional Academic Health Center in the Lower Rio Grande Valley, which ushered in a new era in medical education and health care in that region. (Chapter 28)
- Success in forging a highly efficient and effective governmental relations function for the UT System. One measure of this success is that from 1993 to 1999 state appropriations for universities increased by some 7.2 percent, adjusted for inflation. (Chapter 31)
- The establishment of the South Texas/Border Initiative, which

William H. Cunningham and George Kozmetsky in the Regents Room at the UT System in June 1999, where Cunningham announced he was resigning as chancellor. *AP Photo*/Austin American-Statesman, *David Kennedy*.

brought an extraordinary new level of educational opportunity to previously underserved parts of the state. (Chapter 26)

• The creation of the University of Texas Investment Management Co. and passage of the total-return constitutional amendment, which together modernized the management of the Permanent University Fund. (Chapter 27)

Also deserving of mention, at least in abbreviated form, are three other specific areas of achievement that have not been discussed in this book but that I remain proud of because of the progress that our team was able to record. These areas are financial management, public school partnerships, and the appointment of new component presidents.

Under the leadership of Executive Vice Chancellor Dan Burck, who later succeeded me as chancellor, and the outstanding staff of the Office of Business Affairs, the UT System developed what was without doubt one of the strongest programs of financial management in higher education anywhere in the nation. Evidence of that claim is easy to produce. In the mid- to late-1990s, for example, all three of the major independent agencies that assign ratings to corporate and government bonds gave their highest rating (triple-A or its equivalent) to UT System revenue bonds and Permanent University Fund bonds. This rating was critically important because it meant our bonds were worth more and we could therefore pay investors a lower rate of interest. No other public university in the nation had a triple-A bond rating during the years I was chancellor.

The UT System also implemented a highly successful program for cost savings, cost avoidance, and revenue enhancement—efforts that were a vital part of our successful management of the system during times of great economic and budgeting difficulties. Documented savings and revenue enhancement of approximately $624 million were realized from 1993 to 1999. Those savings made it possible for the system's institutions to enhance educational quality during years of relatively flat state appropriations.

I also took pride in our progress in contracting with Historically Underutilized Businesses (HUBs). This effort was led at the UT System with great skill and dedication by Associate Vice Chancellor Lewis W. Wright III. HUB purchases by the UT System increased from $59.8 million in FY 1993 to $162.6 million in FY 2000. Another success was the system-wide compliance program to provide continual monitoring of our responsibilities to comply with the myriad of laws and regulations affecting higher education. Our compliance program became a national model for universities.

We inaugurated programs designed to improve education at all levels, in keeping with the tradition of the UT System since its founding as a strong partner with the public schools of Texas. The system's commitment to a seamless continuum of education from pre-kindergarten to post-graduate studies is intense. In 1994 we commissioned a system-wide study to determine what

Dan Burck, former chancellor of the University of Texas System. *Courtesy of the UT System.*

we were doing to support the public schools and to make recommendations for new efforts. Regents Bernard Rapoport and Martha Smiley were particularly supportive of the initiative. We found that UT System institutions were spending more than $50 million each year from non-state-appropriated funds on dozens of programs to assist students and teachers in the public schools. Among our activities was strong support for the Governor's Reading Initiative, through activities related to advanced research, teacher education, and development of learning materials. We also began an Advanced Placement initiative and organized a K-16 Leadership Council. Executive Vice Chancellor Ed Sharpe, Associate Executive Vice Chancellor Francie Frederick, Associate Vice Chancellor Gwen Grigsby, and Associate Vice Chancellor Joe Stafford all deserve special thanks for the leadership roles they played in this critical initiative.

There were leadership changes at nine of the UT System's fifteen institutions while I was chancellor, and in each case the board of regents made appointments of extraordinarily qualified individuals. This is one of the most critically important functions of the board, and Regent Lowell Lebermann made a great contribution when he recom-

William H. Cunningham being presented the Presidential Citation from UT Austin President Larry Faulkner, fall 2005. *Courtesy of William H. Cunningham.*

mended revisions to the board's procedures for conducting presidential searches. I always provided the regents with my candid counsel regarding each of these appointments. I was enormously pleased that we were able to attract outstanding academic leaders for these positions. The presidents appointed during my tenure as chancellor were Robert Witt at UT Arlington, Robert Berdahl and Larry Faulkner at UT Austin, Franklyn Jenifer at UT Dallas, Charles Sorber at UT Permian Basin, Ricardo Romo at UT San Antonio, Rodney Mabry at UT Tyler, John Stobo at the UT Medical Branch at Galveston, John Mendelsohn at M. D. Anderson Cancer Center in Houston, and Ronald Garvey at the UT Health Center at Tyler. I disagreed with the board on only one occasion when it selected a president—the choice of Robert Berdahl, who came to UT Austin from the University of Illinois in 1993. I did understand, however, that the selection of a component president was ultimately a board call, and I did everything I could to make Berdahl's presidential term a success.

In addition to looking back on the range of accomplishments during my fifteen years as president and chancellor, I have given some thought to the major challenges that will continue to face Texas higher education well into the twenty-first century. I understand that Texas is a land of extraordinary diversity—in its geography, natural resources, economy, demographics, and culture—and that consensus among its various regions and communities of interest can be difficult to obtain. There has generally been broad agreement, however, on the importance of education, from early childhood schooling through graduate school, as the key to the state's economic and social development and as the basis for individual advancement. Aspects of this commitment can be found at all periods in our history—from the writings of nineteenth-century pioneers to the political programs of the most visionary leaders in our own time. Unfortunately, this historic underlying faith in education and the commitment to use enlightened government policies to help people realize their educational aspirations have faced serious challenges in recent years. We have seen challenges to the elite role of our great top-tier research universities and even threats to the basic levels of public funding that are necessary for all types of institutions of higher education to carry out their missions. We have also seen signs of a retreat from the historic commitment of Texas to provide adequate funding for the public schools.

These antieducation policies have been advocated by a small—but very vocal—minority, who have latched onto the antigovernment, anti-tax, and seemingly populist rhetoric that has become, increasingly, a feature of our national politics. Despite the campaigns of such people, virtually everyone I have met during my career has wanted their children or grandchildren to go to college. They have understood that college is the basis for economic advancement for most people. When I was regularly meeting with young people who were thinking about going to college I always told them that they should do it because they would be better educated citizens and, as a result, be better prepared to participate in the major questions that society faced. However, if this was not persuasive, I told them they should go to college for the money. The average college graduate makes $2 million more over his or her lifetime than someone who does not go to college.

Some recent critics of research universities like UT Austin and Texas A&M seem to think the public's aspirations for educational opportunity can be met through institutions that offer primarily undergraduate degree programs and that do not make investments in research and scholarship. We even hear demands for universities to de-emphasize research, on the theory that the expansion of knowledge can best be entrusted to private-sector businesses, which, it is believed, know best about what areas of research have value, with "value" defined almost exclusively in economic terms.

Apart from failing completely to understand the role of basic research in the advancement of civilization, the people who advocate these views seem to have little appreciation for the historic contribution that university research and advanced educational programs have made to this country. Many who today oppose government's role in supporting strong public research universities call themselves "conservative," but there is nothing "conservative" about undermining public support for education, and it is certainly not a traditional Republican position. Strong government support for the expansion of education was one of the founding principles of the Republican Party in the 1850s, and we can thank those early Republicans for visionary legislation such as the Morrill Land-Grant College Act of 1862, which awarded federal lands to the states to support the establishment of institutions of higher education. Even at the height of the political and economic crisis of the Civil War, the nation's leaders pursued policies aimed at broadening educational opportunities for the public in the long term.[2]

The real question facing Texas today seems to be whether we only want universities where professors and students are content to read what other people have said about quantum physics or Thomas Jefferson, or do we want at least two of our state universities to be institutions that focus a portion of their attention on research—the discovery and development of facts, processes, and ideas that broaden human horizons and advance human understanding. Most elite graduate research universities are also dedicated to excellence in undergraduate education, but however much they value undergraduate teaching, their true distinction comes from the expansion of knowledge through research conducted primarily by faculty members and their graduate students.

The major criticisms of elite institutions such as UT Austin and Texas A&M fall into six categories. I use the term "elite" advisedly; a major research university benefits the entire society in numerous ways, but its commitment to excellence does not permit it to bend to every "populist" fad, and however broad its appeal to the population as a whole, it is not designed to serve the educational needs of each and every citizen. I will outline the main criticisms of these institutions along with my response.

1. Tenure is seen as an obsolete practice that serves mainly to protect the "dead wood" on the faculty. Critics believe that professors who have tenure are gaming the system. It is important to correct three common misunderstandings related to tenure. First, tenure within the UT System is not a lifetime guarantee of a job. While terminating a tenured faculty member is not easy, it can and has been done a number of times during UT's history, including during the period I was president and chancellor. Tenured UT System faculty members go through a rigorous post-tenure review every five years. As described in Chapter 29, if they do not receive a positive review, they may be subject to a process that could lead to their termination. Second, abuses by tenured faculty are actually extremely rare in a highly competitive institution such as UT Austin. Faculty members in the UT System are carefully reviewed before they receive tenure by departmental college committees and by the dean of the college and president of the university. This does not mean that all tenured faculty are the best teachers or that some people who have tenure should, in hindsight, not have been given tenure, but as a result of the long, careful process mistakes are relatively rare. Third, significantly less than half of the faculty mem-

bers in the UT System have tenure. Fourth, without the existence of tenure, first-class academics from other states would never accept job offers at Texas universities. Prospective faculty members would simply not understand what was happening in Texas. It is not that they would be afraid of having a job that did not have tenure as much as it would be a concern that Texas was somehow going down an anti-intellectual path. Our universities would no longer be competitive in hiring new faculty, and the best faculty members that they already have would begin migrating to other states.

2. Academic research is viewed as detracting from the real business of education, being inefficient and focusing on arcane subjects of little or no value to society at large. Critics of elite universities argue that society would be better off relying on corporations to conduct research through their laboratories, thus freeing faculty members to spend more time on teaching. This view has little to do with reality—either with the true role of university research in society or the importance of research as a basis for sound teaching. There has been an informal compact in the United States for more than fifty years among major corporations, the federal government, and graduate research universities that these select universities will be primarily responsible for conducting the nation's basic research and that corporate America will concentrate mainly on applied research. There have been notable exceptions on both sides. For example, there was a time when Bell Labs was doing important basic research, but with the breakup of AT&T, that basic research commitment has diminished. Universities do engage in some applied research—often under contract to companies or the federal government. In addition, universities have patented intellectual property that has led directly to new products and significant royalties for faculty members and their institutions.

The much more typical example finds university scientists doing basic research, such as fundamental work in metallurgy, which might then be adapted by a company such as General Electric to develop lighter and stronger turbine blades for the next generation of jet engines. I would urge critics of university research to speak to a few of the millions of people who take statins every day to control cholesterol. Statins were developed by Professors Mike Brown and Joe Goldstein of the UT Southwestern Medical Center. Brown and Goldstein discovered the pathway in the liver that produced cholesterol and the receptors that triggered this development. A private pharmaceutical company (Merck) developed a statin that would block the liver receptors and thus reduce cholesterol production. Brown and Goldstein carried out the experiments and proved the statin did block cholesterol production in humans. They received the Nobel Prize for this accomplishment. The private for-profit pharmaceutical firms have refined and marketed Brown and Goldstein's research, but the basic research that made possible the applied research was done at an academic institution. Critics can dismiss this model as obsolete, but they do so at the peril of being proved wrong time and time again—and of having no viable model to replace it with. The true believers in the historical compact are the CEOs and directors of research at major U.S. companies. They testify regularly in Congress and in statehouses about their companies' ties to a select group of major universities, which they depend on as the life-blood of basic knowledge that they can then turn into the next generation of products and services that permit their companies and our country to be competitive.

Some critics of university research may acknowledge that studies of metallurgy or biochemistry may be okay, but they want to draw the line at much of the scholarship in the arts and humanities—where they see no practical application in society. The criticism starts by expecting all publicly funded research to have some immediate economic value, and it can quickly descend to the grossest level of anti-intellectualism. We have all known narrowly educated people whose first question to a young person studying literature or philosophy is, "What are you going to do with it?" Such critics seem to be blind to the limitless horizons that are opened by the humanities. It is no secret that the best-educated scientists and engineers often have passionate interests in literature, art, or music; the problem arises with people who themselves have mediocre educations and expect no more than that for other people. The good news for the critics of scholars in the arts and humanities who receive public research grants is that their work typically requires little money, at least compared to work in chemistry or physics. It is unfortunate that the critics do not understand the vital role of such studies in broadening our understanding of ourselves and our forebears, in cultivating humane and enlightened values, in making life worth living, and in producing thoughtful, informed citizens. There may already be hundreds of books in the library about Thomas Jefferson, but one never really comes to the end in exploring his life and work, no more than one can ever come to the end of studying molecular biology.

3. UT Austin is seen as inefficient and unproductive. Unfortunately for the critics who make this claim, the data are very clear that UT Austin is one of the most efficient and productive major research universities in the country. This has been verified by examining taxpayer expenditures per graduate, administrative cost per student, administrative cost as a percentage of the budget, and any number of other measures. There is no question that it is cheaper to teach accounting, philosophy, or even music in junior colleges or through private professors in a college-in-a-box organization such as the University of Phoenix. Such low-cost competitors often meet real needs of society and can offer certain students an educational opportunity they would not otherwise have, but they are not a model for all of higher education—certainly not for a state that wishes to offer programs of the highest quality across all academic disciplines and to develop a highly educated population that can meet the competitive challenges of the new century.

It is also important to understand that UT Austin is a highly complex type of educational institution, offering an experience that goes well beyond that of its low-cost competitors. Eighteen-year-old students come to Austin to spend four to five years in a relatively safe and secure environment. At the end of that time, they have become adults, their parents are perceived as much smarter than they were previously, they have investigated many realms ranging from politics, to great art, to the sailing club—and the good news is that they also received a magnificent education. The life-changing and life-enhancing experience of attending an institution like UT Austin cannot be adequately captured by any set of metrics. The numbers do, indeed, tell a great story about UT Austin, as I have made clear throughout this book; but numbers alone never tell the whole story.

4. Undergraduates, it is claimed, do not benefit from attending a graduate research university. This criticism is also out of touch with reality, and it is sad that some of the critics actually hold degrees from such institutions. These people apparently never understood the ways that their undergraduate experience was being enhanced by the type of institution they were attending. One of the great ironies of higher education is that the most academically talented entering

freshmen are often attracted to institutions whose academic prestige is largely a result of the quality of their graduate and research programs, not their undergraduate offerings. However, undergraduates benefit enormously from the facilities and qualities associated with a research university, such as great libraries, expanded cultural opportunities, sophisticated research laboratories, contact with people from all over the world, notable guest lecturers, and in many cases, world-renowned senior faculty who enjoy interacting with bright students at all levels and can be found teaching undergraduate courses in addition to conducting their research and supervising graduate students.

5. The critics assert that faculty members should be evaluated primarily, if not exclusively, on the basis of their classroom instruction. I believe student evaluations are important, and when I was president I told the deans that I would not consider any faculty member for promotion who did not have a history of using student evaluations that were available to the college promotion committee, the dean, and ultimately me. Today, every faculty member at UT Austin is required to use student evaluations in all of their classes.

Informed people realize there are several important problems with student evaluations when they are used as the sole method of assessing a faculty member's performance. First, faculty members do more than teach. They are involved with research and service. If we eliminate the last two responsibilities, then the problem might go away. It is important to realize that service is more than just sitting on a faculty senate committee. It consists of department committees that review the curriculum; advising individual students about courses they should take, degrees they should pursue, and graduate education opportunities that may be available to them; and assisting students in making career choices upon graduation. Of course, if none of this is important, and it would appear not to be to those individuals who want 100 percent of a professor's compensation to be based on classroom performance, then that system of evaluation might work.

The other problem with student evaluations is that most sophisticated people know they can be manipulated. While some teachers are truly more gifted in the classroom than others and they are rewarded and should be rewarded for this gift, others find themselves at a disadvantage because they teach very large classes (sometimes with more than 400 students) where it is hard to establish a personal relationship between the student and the faculty member. This leads to lower course evaluations. In the same manner, people who teach required courses such as English, history, mathematics, or statistics often find that many of their students are there only because they must take the course to graduate, not because it is inherently of interest to them. This, of course, tends to lead to lower evaluations.

6. Critics say that more courses should be offered through distance education. I am a strong supporter of distance education. As I discussed in Chapter 29, an innovative distance education program was established at the UT System during my tenure as chancellor. I do not believe, however, that distance education can be done on the cheap or that it is appropriate for all courses and all students in all situations. Some of the critics of elite campuses have said they feel the state's public universities should be able to deliver online the four most popular degrees the universities grant, for a total cost to the student of $10,000, which would include all fees and textbooks. This would not be $10,000 a year, but $10,000 for a four-year degree. This is patently absurd.

I am making the assumption that online education means well-done interactive instruction that is constantly updated to reflect the current thinking in a discipline. This is not the same as making a series of tapes available to students, updating these every five years, and sending out a multiple-choice exam for students to take at their pleasure. This type of educational program could certainly be much cheaper, but it would deliver an inferior product—and a product that would leave the student ill-prepared for a productive career or advanced degree program. A university education provides many more growth opportunities for students than merely taking classes, and these extracurricular activities are hard to duplicate in a distance education format. Once again, distance education, if it is done properly, can enhance a student's educational experience, but it is not a panacea for all students in all situations.

7. Critics want funding to be a function of outcomes. Some of the critics of elite universities say they should be funded as a function of quantifiable outcomes such as graduation rates, the percentage of students who do not change majors, and the ranks of graduating students' scores on standardized exams such as the GMAT, GRE, LSAT, and MCAT. This criticism meshes with the general emphasis on incentive-based compensation. The critics do not understand that this approach to state funding would just push more money into the elite

campuses and away from institutions that focus almost exclusively on teaching. Given an opportunity, most of the state's best undergraduate students would choose to attend one of the two current elite research institutions. I hope it is no surprise that these students will generally do better in college than their counterparts in high school who did not perform so well academically. As a group these students will tend to graduate sooner and will score higher on standardized exit exams— and the university they attended would then receive more incentive funding. While this system would make it much more difficult for some of the state's neediest students to attend local colleges, it would greatly benefit the flagship universities. The unintended consequences of this approach to state funding would be quite significant.

The criticisms of higher education lead some people to the conclusion that elitism in higher education is misguided and that while the state may need more universities, it does not need to support world-class powerhouse institutions that are the equal of the nation's most elite schools. Rather, the critics say, what the state really needs is more seats in institutions that focus most of their efforts on teaching undergraduate and master's level students. Such schools do meet the educational needs of many people, and they need to be cherished and nurtured. If the state's investment in higher education were limited to such institutions, one immediate result would be that an honors high school student from Houston who wants to study state-of-the-art quantum physics would have to leave the state to do so. A mid-term effect would be that this student's father, if he is diagnosed with liver cancer, would need to seek treatment outside the state because M. D. Anderson would no longer be the best place in the world to treat that disease. The long-term effect would be that Texas-based corporations would lose their competitive edge since the state's universities would not be providing highly educated graduates for a diversified economy.

Many people realize that a significant portion of the Texas economy for the foreseeable future will be information-based and will be built on intellectual property that has not even been created yet. In addition, Texas will continue to face competition from states such as New York and California that are willing to invest significant resources in their university research programs. Texas can decide to participate in this high-tech research endeavor or it can sit on the sidelines and hope that some other state's efforts just come our way. I have found that most Texans do not like depending on luck or the efforts of someone else to create their wealth. Finally, the young man who left Texas to seek his physics education would all too often not return to Texas. Rather than leveraging other states' resources by attracting the very best and brightest high school graduates, we would be exporting our own talent. Multiplied by the thousands of Texans who would leave the state to seek educational opportunity or would stay here to face diminished educational, social, and economic prospects, it is not a very pretty picture.

Local political and business leaders recognize that a research university brings more status and prestige to a community, as well as many economic and cultural benefits. They understand that flagship universities attract large amounts of federal and state research funds, and that this money can be multiplied throughout the local and state economy many times over. When a university brings in $100 million in research grants from outside the state, the overall economic impact for the state is likely to be in excess of $400 million. While a significant portion of this will be spent in a university's local community, the benefits can be felt throughout Texas. Community leaders also understand that flagship schools play a major role in attracting new employers. Companies often seek to locate in communities with a research university because they want access to state-of-the-art research, interactions with faculty members and graduate students, and a reliable supply of highly qualified undergraduate and graduate students. Companies are also attracted by the cultural and entertainment opportunities that a flagship university often provides, from athletic events to Broadway shows and art museums.

In addition to the need to satisfy the personal and economic needs of local community leaders, the graduate students and advanced undergraduates who get degrees from flagship institutions will play important roles in science, engineering, and business in the community. Without an advanced, highly educated population, Texas will not be able to compete in the long-term with states that invest in higher education. Some portion of the research that comes out of laboratories can be commercialized and can lead to new areas of science and business that can solve problems for society in a way that generates a significant profit for the state's entrepreneurial community.

The population of Texas has grown so dramatically that thousands of excellent Texas students are being turned away every year from

UT Austin and Texas A&M. As a result, I have spoken often about the need for Texas to develop more elite universities.[3] However, any attempt to develop new research universities must not be undertaken at the expense of UT Austin and Texas A&M. I have been surprised and greatly disappointed from time to time by proposals to do just that—divert existing funds from the state's only elite public universities in order to try to bring other schools up to their level. The necessity of protecting and even strengthening UT Austin and Texas A&M has meant that new research universities could be developed only through an investment of new state funds, not simply a reallocation of existing funds.

It is likely that Texas will be debating, well into the twenty-first century, the question of whether and how to develop new research universities. This is unfortunate, but it fits the pattern of the way Texas has been dealing with a host of other issues in higher education, not to mention other policy areas such as public school funding and social services for the economically disadvantaged. Within higher education, we continue to face numerous other serious questions such as how to make higher education accessible to all, regardless of economic status; how to increase the enrollment and success rates of all students, including the rapidly growing number of students from ethnic minority groups; and how to develop and support a range of health science institutions that meet the needs of all regions of the state in the twenty-first century.

We would probably be naïve to hold out hope for a golden age in which our state's elected leaders unite to pursue enlightened policies of sustained and unswerving support for higher education. In every era we have had a few leaders with that kind of vision, but not enough of them. We will be fortunate if our leaders implement policies of incremental change that bring areas of improvement, and if they manage to withstand the most serious threats from those who have little true understanding of the importance of higher education and even less vision of how an enlightened state government can take vigorous action to improve the lives of current and future generations. I believe UT Austin and the UT System contributed to that kind of enlightened government during the 1980s and 1990s, and I am grateful and truly honored that I had an opportunity to provide leadership to those institutions during that exciting era.

Notes

Note on Sources

Two main collections of documents were the basis for the research for this book. The first is the university archives and other collections housed at the Briscoe Center for American History at UT Austin. The collection from the Briscoe Center that we have relied on the most is identified in the endnotes as the UT President's Office Papers. It is impossible to overestimate the value of the Briscoe Center's collections in any project that seeks to elucidate the history of the University of Texas.

The second collection, identified as the William H. Cunningham Papers, consists of news clippings, photographs, press releases, correspondence, and other documents. This collection remains in my and Isabella's possession. These papers will eventually be made available to researchers as part of the collections of the Briscoe Center.

We have relied on many other sources that are commonly available through libraries and the Internet, including newspapers and magazines and reports of Texas state agencies such as the Legislative Budget Board. Various offices of the UT System also greatly facilitated our research by making available copies of documents in their files.

Perceptive readers may notice a sparseness of references to correspondence and other documents from the time that I served as chancellor. This is a result of a woefully short-sighted decision to destroy all but a few of the files from the chancellor's office after I left in 2000. I could not believe this apparently cavalier decision when I learned of it, and it remains inexplicable to me. It is my fervent wish that all public servants who are entrusted with the historical record will do everything in their power to preserve it for the benefit of posterity. In the case of the record of my years as chancellor, we are fortunate that it has been possible, largely through my personal papers and my conversations with colleagues, to recapture much of the record of key events from this period.

Chapter 2: Life with George—and Beyond

[1] As president of UT Austin I named Witt dean of the business school and I later supported his appointment as president of UT Arlington. After success in those roles he became president of the University of Alabama and chancellor of the University of Alabama System.

[2] Papers of William H. Cunningham.

[3] In May 2000, San Antonio businessman Billy Joe "Red" McCombs made a $50 million cash donation to the University of Texas business school. In recognition, the university board of regents merged the College of Business Administration and the Graduate School of Business, creating the Red McCombs School of Business in his honor. UT History Central: A Comprehensive Guide to University of Texas History, http://www.texasexes.org/uthistory/campus-tour.aspx?tourstop=18.

Chapter 3: Appointment as President and First Steps

[1] "Strong prospects vie for presidency at UT," *Austin American-Statesman*, May 31, 1985.

[2] "Dean of business college named president of UT," ibid., August 9, 1985.

[3] Transcript of interview of John Silber by the *Washington Post* and *Third Coast* magazine, UT President's Office Records, UT Files 1985–1986, Box 93-082/2.

[4] "Hopes high for UT successor; Cunningham viewed as tough, effective leader," ibid., August 10, 1985.

[5] Letter from Robert D. King to *Texas Monthly*, April 29, 1986, UT President's Office, UT Files, 1985–1986, Box 93-082/5.

[6] Note to Mike Levy from Peter Elkind, April 1, 1986, ibid.

[7] "New president sets agenda for UT-Austin," *The Dallas Morning News*, September 1, 1985.

[8] "A sign of the times; new University of Texas president has credentials to attract funds," *Houston Chronicle*, October 27, 1985.

[9] "Former business school dean viewed as a scholar and a manager," *The Dallas Morning News*, October 12, 1985.

Chapter 4: Hazing

[1] UT President's Office, General Files, 1984–1986, Box 93-082/37.

[2] Ibid.

[3] Ibid.

[4] "An archaic ritual," *The Dallas Morning News*, July 13, 1986.

[5] "Letter to Student Organization Presidents from WHC," November 13, 1985. UT President's Office, General Files, 1984–1986, Box 93-082/37.

[6] UT President's Office, General Files, 1984–1986, Box 93-082/37.

[7] Ibid.

[8] *The Daily Texan*, August 20, 1986.

[9] Sororities at UT had decided in the 1970s to withdraw from status as campus organizations rather than sign pledges against racial discrimination. These groups returned to campus status, with adherence to nondiscrimination policies, in January 1988.

[10] Report of the Commission on the Role of Fraternal Organizations, UT President's Office Records, UT Files, 1989–1990, Box 94-190/54.

Chapter 5: Enrollment Management

[1] "Enrollment Management at the University of Texas at Austin," a report to members of the UT Board of Regents, July 1987, UT President's Office General Files, 1986–1988, Box 94-16/5.

[2] The actual number was 213,000 in 2000. "The Texas Educational Pipeline," UT Austin Office of Admissions, July 2004. Papers of William H. Cunningham.

[3] Memo from Ronald M. Brown to William H. Cunningham re Enrollment Management at UT Austin, August 14, 1987, UT President's Office, General Files, 1986–1988, Box 94-16/5.

[4] UT Austin Strategic Plan, November 1985, UT President's Office, UT Files, 1985–1986, Box 93-082/2.

[5] "UT braces for growth in summer program," *Austin American-Statesman*, February 26, 1989.

[6] Letter from William H. Cunningham to James P. Duncan, May 15, 1990, UT President's Office, UT Files 1989–1990, Box 94-190/63.

[7] "UT to launch registration by phone," *The Dallas Morning News*, August 3, 1989.

[8] "Crowded out students get foot in president's door," *The Daily Texan*, September 7, 1989.

[9] "UT Austin Enrollment Management/Reduction Policies," May 1990, UT President's Office, UT Files, 1989–1990, Box 94-190/63.

Chapter 6: Apartheid and Divestment Protests

[1] The voluntary code of conduct known as the Sullivan Principles was developed in 1977 by the Rev. Leon Sullivan, an Episcopalian bishop who was a member of the board of directors of General Motors. The goal of the Sullivan Principles was to improve working conditions of blacks and to enhance their quality of life off the job.

[2] "Riot on UC Campus—91 Arrested/Apartheid Protest Roughest Since '60s," *San Francisco Chronicle*, April 4, 1986.

[3] Numerous student organizations in the United States and other countries were named for Steve Biko, a leader in South Africa's antiapartheid movement who was beaten to death by government interrogators in 1977 at age twenty.

[4] UT President's Office, General Files, 1984–1986, Box 93-082/37.

[5] A summary of Pifer's views was published as an op-ed article just a few days after the regents' meeting. See "Divestment Is a Political, Not a Moral Act," *The Wall Street Journal*, June 23, 1986.

[6] This is just one more example of my lifelong good luck. Flip a coin, and I can win the bet. Plan to take over my office early one morning, and I get a flat tire.

[7] "UT president meets with apartheid foes," *Austin American-Statesman*, November 23, 1986.

[8] "UT protesters tell why they barricaded office," *The Dallas Morning News*, September 16, 1987.

[9] "UT's S. African–related investments cut by more than 50%," *Austin American-Statesman*, June 26, 1989.

Chapter 7: Minority Student and Faculty Recruitment and Retention

[1] Executive Order 11246, September, 24, 1965, www.archives.gov/federal-register/codification/executive-order/11246.html.

[2] "UT urges Valley youths to climb college ladder," *Austin American-Statesman*, May 29, 1986.

[3] Memo from Shannon Janes to Ronald M. Brown regarding Minority Recruitment and Retention Programs, February 21, 1986, UT President's Office, UT Files, 1985–1986, Box 93-082/2.

[4] "IBM helps education college by supplying staffer's salary," *Austin American-Statesman*, July 11, 1987.

[5] "Cunningham Defends Current Racial Policies," *The Daily Texan*, April 9, 1986.

[6] Davis, who later taught at the University of California at Santa Cruz, left the Communist Party after the attempted coup against Mikhail Gorbachev in 1991.

[7] "Civil rights activist stirs UT crowd," *Austin American-Statesman*, January 16, 1990.

[8] Letter from Brett Campbell, Darrick Eugene, Kevin Williams, and Barron Wallace to William H. Cunningham, January 27, 1986, UT President's Office, UT Files, 1985–1986, Box 93-082/30.

[9] "Minorities to get head start in UT summer session," *Austin American-Statesman,* March 9, 1986.

[10] "Outreach centers to help young minorities aim for college," ibid., October 13, 1987.

[11] "Cunningham travels to sell UT," ibid., October 6, 1987.

[12] For example, the Education Department plan applied only to African Americans and Hispanics, while the Labor Department plan also applied to Asian Americans, Native Americans, and women.

[13] Memo from G. J. Fonken to Academic Deans on Affirmative Action Plans—Faculty Recruiting, November 2, 1984, UT President's Office Records, General Files, 1984–1986, Box 93-082/12.

[14] Memo from William H. Cunningham to Academic Deans regarding Minority Faculty Recruitment and Retention, October 7, 1987, UT President's Office, General Files, 1986–1988, Box 94-16/23.

[15] "UT aims to hire more minority faculty members," *The Dallas Morning News,* October 20, 1987.

Chapter 8: The Blackland Neighborhood

[1] "Town and gown clash over housing," *The New York Times,* April 9, 1989.

[2] "UT land plan breaks truce; East Austin group charges foul play," *Austin American-Statesman,* October 17, 1985.

[3] Letter from Katherine Poole to William H. Cunningham, October 22, 1985, UT President's Office, UT Files, 1985–1986, Box 93-082/38.

[4] UT President's Office Records, UT Files, 1985–1986, Box 93-082/9.

[5] *The Blackland Miracle,* Vol. 5, No. 5, May 1988. UT President's Office Records, General Files, 1988–1990, Box AR 94-16/79.

[6] "Meeting Regarding Blacklands," April 4, 1988, UT President's Office, General Files, 1988–1990, Box AR 94-16/79.

[7] Letter from Veon McReynolds to William H. Cunningham, UT President's Office, General Files, 1988–1990, Box AR 94-16/79.

[8] "UT has new deal for Blackland," *Austin American-Statesman,* June 16, 1988.

[9] "UT razes contested vacant cottages," ibid., July 26, 1988.

[10] Letter from L. Charles Merrill to Edwin R. Sharpe, UT President's Office, Box 94-16/37.

[11] "UT to limit land purchases in Blackland neighborhood," *Austin American-Statesman,* December 23, 1988.

[12] Letter from James Wilson to Charles Smith, UT President's Office, General Files, 1990–1992, Box 94-190/112.

Chapter 9: The *Hopwood* Case

[1] The Tarlton Law Library at the UT School of Law maintains a comprehensive collection of documents from the *Cheryl J. Hopwood v. the State of Texas* case, as well as background information, analysis by legal scholars, a timeline, and many other materials. Much of the material was prepared by Professor Douglas Laycock. The material is online at: http://tarltonguides.law.utexas.edu.

[2] *Adams v. Richardson,* 356 F. Supp. 92 (D.D.C.), *modified and aff'd,* 480 F.2d 1159 (D.C. Cir. 1973).

[3] "Tex. may appeal ruling on affirmative action," *Chronicle of Higher Education,* May 1, 2000.

[4] *Grutter v. Bollinger*, 539 U.S. 306 (2003).

[5] "Elite law firm on a mission in Hopwood case," *Austin American-Statesman*, July 6, 1998.

[6] http://tarltonguides.law.utexas.edu/content.php?pid=98968&sid=772247 (accessed December 21, 2011).

[7] Press release, Office of Public Affairs, UT Austin, August 20, 1994.

[8] "UT officials praise ruling in law applicants' suit," Associated Press story in *The Dallas Morning News*, August 21, 1994.

[9] "How Affirmative Action Worked at The University of Texas Law School." *Hopwood* documents compiled by Douglas Laycock, Tarlton Law Library, UT Austin.

[10] Hopwood documents, Tarlton Law Library, UT Austin.

[11] "UT regents decide to appeal Hopwood," *San Antonio Express-News*, May 14, 1998.

[12] "Morales snubs UT in Hopwood fight," ibid., April 29, 1998.

[13] "UT regents vote to appeal Hopwood," *Austin American-Statesman*, May 14, 1998.

[14] "UT to appeal decision against affirmative action," *The Dallas Morning News*, May 14, 1998.

[15] "Morales' beliefs: a moot point?" *Austin American-Statesman*, April 19, 1998.

Chapter 10: Progress in the Natural Sciences

[1] "Report of the External Review Committee on Molecular Biology," UT President's Office, UT Files, 1985–1986, Box 93-082/6.

[2] "Chair Recruitment and Program Development in Molecular Biology," ibid.

[3] Memo from William H. Cunningham to Gerhard J. Fonken, January 15, 1988. UT President's Office, UT Files, 1986–1988, Box AR 94-190/28.

[4] "External Advisory Committee Report," October 1988, UT President's Office, General Files, 1988–1989, Box AR 94-16/55.

[5] Letter from Robert E. Boyer to William H. Cunningham, November 30, 1988, UT President's Office, UT Files, 1988–1989, Box 94-190/46.

[6] Letter from William H. Cunningham to Robert E. Boyer, December 21, 1988, ibid.

[7] Draft of letter from William H. Cunningham to Ron Matthews, associate professor of mechanical engineering, June 25, 1991, UT President's Office, UT Files, 1990–1991, Box 94-190/75.

[8] Letter from Barbara Jordan to members of the Board of Regents, November 29, 1989, UT President's Office, General Files, 1988–1990, Box AR 94-16/49.

[9] Letter from Louis Beecherl to Barbara Jordan, December 28, 1989, ibid.

[10] "$3 million will support capital project, endowment," *On Campus*, April 23–29, 1990.

[11] Alkek's passionate loyalty to the Republicans may have been reinforced when President Reagan pardoned him after he had pleaded guilty to withholding information from federal officials in a scandal in 1979 involving oil regulations. He paid the government $3.2 million in restitution in that case, according to newspaper accounts.

[12] "Astronomy Review with President Cunningham," October 22, 1985, UT President's Office, UT Files, 1985–1986, Box 93-082/8.

[13] Memorial resolution for Harlan J. Smith, UT Austin Faculty Council, www.utexas.edu/faculty/council/2000-2001/memorials/Smith/smith.htm (accessed March 15, 2008).

[14] Thomas A. Sebring, et al., *West Texas Time Machine: Creating the Hobby-Eberly Telescope* (McDonald Observatory, 1998).

[15] Letter from G. David Gearhart to Shirley Bird Perry, January 9, 1989, UT President's Office, UT Files, 1988–1989, Box 94-190/48.

[16] Eberly, who died in 2004, was Penn State's largest donor, contributing with his wife more than $40 million to the university. Press release from Penn State University, May 19, 2004.

[17] Memo from G. J. Fonken to William H. Cunningham re McDonald Observatory—Spectroscopic Survey Telescope, August 21, 1989, UT President's Office, UT Files, 1988–1989, Box 94-190/48.

[18] Draft letter addressed to "Dear Team," probably written by Harlan Smith, August 22, 1989, ibid.

[19] Memo from G. J. Fonken to William H. Cunningham re McDonald Observatory —Spectroscopic Survey Telescope, August 28, 1989, ibid

[20] Memo from G. J. Fonken to William H. Cunningham re McDonald Observatory—Spectroscopic Survey Telescope Project—Funding Request, December 29, 1989, ibid.

[21] William H. Cunningham, handwritten notes, January 15, 1990, ibid.

[22] Sebring, et al., *West Texas Time Machine: Creating the Hobby-Eberly Telescope*, 21.

[23] Sebring, et al., *West Texas Time Machine: Creating the Hobby-Eberly Telescope*.

[24] "The Hobby-Eberly Telescope Completion Project," by John A. Booth, et al. *Proceedings of the SPIE* (International Society for Optical Engineering), Volume 4837, pp. 919–933 (2003). Other ways of figuring the capital costs have produced estimates as low as $18 million—still three times the original budget.

Chapter 11: Teaching English and Political Correctness

[1] "Multiculturalism sparks UT debate; classes' purpose, approach split campus," *Austin American-Statesman*, April 24, 1990.

[2] "UT saves itself from sociological indoctrination," op-ed article by William Murchison, *The Dallas Morning News*, July 28, 1990.

[3] "UT liberal arts dean resigns post to teach, write," *Austin American-Statesman*, January 9, 1991.

[4] "Members quit UT cultural diversity panel," ibid., February 6, 1991.

[5] Paul Kelly, "University Council approves multicultural proposals," *On Campus*, October 28, 1991.

Chapter 12: Crisis and Progress in the Fine Arts

[1] William H. Cunningham, remarks to faculty and staff of the College of Fine Arts, February 16, 1988. UT President's Office Records, General Files, 1986–1988, Box 94-16/5.

[2] "UT plans endowment for PAC concert series," *Austin American-Statesman*, February 17, 1988.

[3] William H. Cunningham, remarks to faculty and staff of the College of Fine Arts, February 16, 1988, UT President's Office Records, General Files, 1986–1988, Box 94-16/5.

[4] "UT plans endowment for PAC concert series," *Austin American-Statesman*, February 17, 1988.

[5] "A chance to start anew," ibid., July 13, 1988.

[6] "UT fine arts dean resigns to become Tacoma provost," ibid., December 1, 1988.

[7] "Gift to UT viewed as seed of excellence in fine arts," ibid., June 10, 1988.

Chapter 13: Fund-Raising at UT Austin

[1] Council for Aid to Education, Survey of Voluntary Aid to Education (CFAE Report), 1986–1987.

[2] "Rare Pforzheimer books bought for U. of Texas," *The New York Times*, January 22, 1986.

Chapter 14: Intercollegiate Athletics—Let the Games Begin

[1] In December 1988, the NCAA placed the OU football team on suspension for three years because of recruiting violations, and Switzer resigned. Among the charges was that Switzer had written personal checks to pay for players' rental cars and that a recruit had been given an envelope containing $1,000 in cash.

[2] The subsidies were totally eliminated by 2004. Today there is only one budget for both men's and women's athletics.

[3] This, by the way, was the first of two visits that I made to the Oval Office. The second came when I accompanied Bernard Rapoport on a visit to Bill and Hillary Clinton to talk about health care.

Chapter 15: Intercollegiate Athletics—Playing by the Rules

[1] "NCAA accuses UT of breaking rules," *Houston Post,* March 24, 1987.

[2] "Discussion of preliminary report from the NCAA concerning investigation of the football program," Statement to the University Council by William H. Cunningham, March 23, 1987, UT President's Office, General Files, 1986–1988, Box 94-16/32.

[3] Ibid.

[4] Charles Alan Wright, "Responding to an NCAA Investigation, or, What to Do When an Official Inquiry Comes," *Entertainment & Sports Law Journal*, vol 1: 1984, pp. 19–35.

[5] "UT settles women's sports lawsuit," *The Dallas Morning News,* July 17, 1993.

[6] "Legislator targeting college athletics," *Austin American-Statesman*, March 6, 1997.

[7] HB 2010, Texas Legislature Online, www.legis.state.tx.us/tlodocs/75R/billtext/html/HB02010E.htm.

[8] "Statement on final passage of SB 1419," UT System press release, May 30, 1997, Papers of William H. Cunningham.

[9] "Keep the athletic playing field level," *The Dallas Morning News,* May 24, 1997.

[10] Texas House of Representatives, House Journal, pages 4717–4732, June 1, 1997, http://www.journals.house.state.tx.us/hjrnl/75r/pdf/75RDay89.pdf. And excerpts from the weekly legislative newsletter of the Texas Council of Public University Presidents and Chancellors.

Chapter 16: The Demise of the Southwest Conference and the Birth of the Big 12

[1] "Adding four to eight divided Baylor, TCU," *The Dallas Morning News,* August 30, 2006.

[2] Reynolds's administrative tenure at Baylor paralleled much of mine at UT. He was president from 1981 to 1995 and chancellor from 1995 to 2000. We always got along well, and working with him was a true pleasure.

Chapter 17: Royal-Memorial Stadium

[1] "Berdahl to quit as UT president to lead Berkeley," *The Dallas Morning News*, March 7, 1997.

[2] "Berdahl voices hopes, worries for UT's future," *Austin American-Statesman*, April 22, 1997.

[3] Subsequent expansion projects, including expansion of the south and north end zones, brought the stadium's official seating capacity to 100,119.

[4] Title 109, Article 6145-13, Vernon's Texas Civil Statutes.

[5] "State law blocks stadium proposal," *Austin American-Statesman*, February 7, 1997.

[6] Ibid.

[7]Ibid.

Chapter 18: Economic Development and the Recruitment of Sematech

[1] Speech by Lt. Gov. Bill Hobby, Science and Technology Conference, Dallas, Texas, June 12, 1986, President's Office, General Files, 1984–1986, Box 93-082/40.

[2] "County authority expected to help finance Sematech," *Austin American-Statesman*, January 11, 1988.

[3] "Sematech expenses for UT estimated," ibid., February 12, 1988.

[4] Letter from Blanton to Clements, Hobby, and Lewis, January 8, 1988, President's Office, General Files, 1984–1986, Box 93-082/40.

[5] "The University of Texas at Austin and Sematech," ibid.

[6] "Sematech considers Texas," *The Dallas Morning News*, November 20, 1987.

[7] "Sematech Proposal Overview," October 19, 1987, President's Office, General Files, 1984–1986, Box 93-082/40.

[8] "Texas hopes of luring Sematech fade," *The Dallas Morning News*, December 12, 1987.

[9] "Texas lands high-tech venture," ibid., January 6, 1988.

[10] "Is Austin the next Silicon Valley?" *The New York Times*, January 13, 1988.

[11] "How Austin snared Sematech," *St. Petersburg Times*, June 26, 1988.

[12] See, for example, "Failed Sematech bid underscores Florida's education ills," *St. Petersburg Times*, January 10, 1988; "How Austin did it—twice: Texas city snared Sematech with political wiles, natural advantages," *The Boston Globe,* January 17, 1988; and "When Sematech, a consortium of American semiconductor manufacturers . . .," *St. Louis Post-Dispatch,* April 11, 1988.

[13] "Value of Sematech stressed," *The Dallas Morning News*, November 16, 1988.

[14] "Higher Education and the Economy of Texas," a slide presentation by William H. Cunningham to the Board of Directors of the Texas Chamber of Commerce, Austin, July 9, 1992, Papers of William H. Cunningham.

[15] "Investment in higher education pays off for Texas," UT System press release based on the report "The Economic Impact of the University of Texas System," January 9, 1995, Papers of William H. Cunningham.

[16] "Plan offered for Sematech renovations," *Austin American-Statesman*, January 12, 1988.

Chapter 19: Appointment as Chancellor

[1] "Cunningham to be new UT System chancellor," *The Dallas Morning News*, March 18, 1992.

² "State Secrets," *Texas Monthly,* March 1992.

³ "UT Chancellor: Dr. William Cunningham is the right man," *The Dallas Morning News,* March 21, 1992.

⁴ "Right choice for UT," *The Houston Post,* March 20, 1992.

⁵ "UT chief's business ties questioned," *Austin American-Statesman,* March 19, 1992.

Chapter 21: Early Interactions in State Politics

¹ "Report on future of Texas economy," Bureau of Business Research, 1985.

² "Bullock is scolded for claims," *Austin American-Statesman,* March 30, 1985.

³ UT President's Office, General Files, 1984–1986, Box 93-082/15.

⁴ "How the U. of Texas, Flexing Its Political Muscle, Foiled Budget Cutters," *The Chronicle of Higher Education,* June 19, 1985.

⁵ The Higher Education Assistance Fund was created by the voters in a constitutional amendment election in 1984 to provide capital support for institutions not covered by the Permanent University Fund.

⁶ In 1984, the legislature had replaced the state's basic $50 per semester tuition (for up to twelve hours) with a rate of $4 per hour regardless of how many hours a student took. The measure produced an estimated $11 million in new revenue statewide.

Chapter 22: The Budget Crisis of 1986

¹ Executive Order MW-36, Office of the Governor, February 18, 1986.

² Lieutenant Governor Bill Hobby, speech to the Texas Science and Technology Council, June 12, 1986, UT President's Office, General Files, 1984–1986, Box 93-082/40.

³ "Issues and Considerations," Texas Science and Technology Council, June 11, 1986, ibid.

⁴ This was actually the second special session of the 69th Legislature. The first was held May 28–30, 1986, and dealt mainly with indigent health care.

⁵ "UT leads rally for tax boost," *Austin American-Statesman,* August 5, 1986.

⁶ August 5, 1986, UT President's Office, General Files, 1984–1986, Box 93-082/15.

⁷ "Hobby budget plan seen as 'easiest to live with,'" *Austin American-Statesman,* August 9, 1986.

⁸ "Let's not jeopardize Texas' future," *Houston Chronicle,* August 17, 1986.

⁹ *The Dallas Morning News,* August 12, 1986; *Houston Chronicle,* August 13, 1986.

¹⁰ "UT exes begin barrage on Capitol to oppose endowment fund raid," *Austin American-Statesman,* August 14, 1986.

¹¹ "University fund shift called unconstitutional," ibid.

¹² Ibid.

¹³ "The method to Lewis' madness," *The Dallas Morning News,* September 8, 1986.

¹⁴ "A General Comment on the Growth of the State Budget Since 1976," UT President's Office, UT Files, 1985–1986, Box 94-16/5.

¹⁵ Legislative Budget Board, "Fiscal Size-up," 1988–1989 Biennium, p. 10.

¹⁶ "Statement by Jess Hay," October 9, 1986, UT President's Office, UT Files, 1985–1986, Box 94-16/5.

Chapter 23: The Budget Crisis Continues

¹ Legislative Budget Board, "Fiscal Size-up," 1988–1989 Biennium, p. 10.

² Ibid., p. 13.

³ Ibid., p. 14.

⁴ Legislative Budget Board, "Fiscal Size-up," 1990–1991 Biennium, pp. 4-20 and 4–22.

⁵ Ibid, p. 4–27.

Chapter 24: The New Grand Coalition

¹ "Population study projects troubling future for Texas," *The Dallas Morning News,* July 28, 1996.

² "Back to Basics—$1 billion program proposed in Texas to boost number of college graduates," *Houston Chronicle,* January 10, 1997.

³ "Texas higher education joining forces to get more funding," *Capital Markets Report,* December 9, 1996.

⁴ "State university chiefs push for more flagships—Chancellors to seek $1.2 billion for top-tier schools, scholarships, other needs," *Austin American-Statesman*, December 14, 1998.

⁵ "A commitment to higher education," ibid., June 29, 1999.

Chapter 25: Politics: The Great American Game

¹ "UT System educators help fill Bullock's coffers," *San Antonio Express-News*, February 9, 1997.

² "UT chiefs' link to Bullock money revealed," ibid., March 10, 1997.

³ "UT foundation's van rental called tax-law violation," ibid., March 13, 1997.

⁴ "UT's disturbing agenda," *Austin American-Statesman*, June 1, 1997.

⁵ "UT chancellor to enter the fray—Cunningham to judge whether university officials' political donations coerced," *San Antonio Express-News*, April 4, 1997.

⁶ "UT head disavows PAC gifts," ibid., July 24, 1997.

⁷ "Lieutenant governor defends Cunningham," Associated Press; published in the *San Antonio Express-News*, July 26, 1997.

Chapter 26: The South Texas/Border Initiative

¹ LULAC, the League of United Latin American Citizens, was the main named plaintiff in the lawsuit, but the San Antonio office of the Mexican American Legal Defense and Educational Fund (MALDEF) took the lead in litigating it. The UT System and other higher education institutions were among the defendants, and the state Attorney General's Office led the defense with a great deal of assistance from the UT System.

² Richardson did present the A&M regents with a plan for renaming the schools, and they approved the new names (Texas A&M International University, Texas A&M University at Corpus Christi, and Texas A&M University at Kingsville) in March 1993. This was after those names had already been included in the Senate version of the Appropriations Bill for the next biennium.

³ The excellence funds at UT Austin declined from $80 million in FY 1993 to $78 million in FY 1994 and $75 million in FY 1995.

⁴ "House nonsense: Lawmakers ought not set higher education policy," *Houston Chronicle*, May 20, 1993.

⁵ "Bordering the Future: Higher Education," a report by Susan Combs, State Comptroller of Public Accounts, July 1998, www.window.state.tx.us/border/border.html.

⁶ "Higher education system upheld," *Austin American-Statesman*, October 7, 1993.

Chapter 27: Asset Management

[1] "The legislative winners and losers of '95," *The Wall Street Journal*, May 31, 1995.

[2] "New management structure adopted for UT System investments," UT System press release, May 28, 1996.

[3] "Secrecy cloaks $1.7 billion in UT investments," *Houston Chronicle*, March 21, 1999.

[4] "UTIMCO changes policy on public disclosure," UT System press release, March 29, 1999, Papers of William H. Cunningham.

[5] "Open Meeting Policy Approved for UTIMCO," UT System press release, September 3, 1999, Papers of William H. Cunningham.

[6] "A Review of Controls over Investment Practices at Six Major State Investing Entities," Report No. 97-014, November 1996, Texas State Auditor's Offic , www.sao.state. tx.us/reports/main/97%2D014.html.

[7] The resolution authorizing the constitutional amendment is available at www.legis. state.tx.us/tlodocs/76R/billtext/html/HJ00058F.htm.

[8] "Prop. 17 would put our kids' educational future at risk," *Houston Chronicle*, October 28, 1999, and "Two sides of Prop. 17," *Odessa American*, October 31, 1999.

[9] See, for example, "For Prop, 17," *Houston Chronicle*, October 5, 1999; "Change would help investment strategy," *San Antonio Express-News*, October 15, 1999; and "Proposition 17: Texas will benefit by providing universities more funds," *The Dallas Morning News*, October 10, 1999.

[10] "Election results for Proposition 17," Memo from Michael D. Millsap to members of the Board of Regents and Chancellor William H. Cunningham, November 3, 1999, Papers of William H. Cunningham.

Chapter 28: Regional Academic Health Center

[1] "New teaching hospital has divided medical community in Valley," *Houston Chronicle*, August 2, 1998.

[2] "Doctors against the Rio Grande Valley teaching hospital," The Associated Press, March 24, 1998.

[3] "How McAllen missed the chance to snare a big health-care center," *The Wall Street Journal*, December 16, 1998.

[4] "Regents select 4 sites for Valley academic health center and increase its construction funds by $20 million," UT System press release, November 11, 1998, Papers of William H. Cunningham.

[5] "Some health centers to be ready in 2001," The Associated Press, November 16, 1999.

[6] "Valley doctors balk at UT medical branch in McAllen," ibid., April 29, 2000.

[7] "Regents approve gifts of land for Regional Academic Health Center," UT System press release, May 13, 1999, Papers of William H. Cunningham.

Chapter 29: UT System Academic and Health Issues

[1] "U.T. System Summary of Various Post-Tenure Review Policies," November 1996. Available under archived news releases on the UT System Web site: www.utsystem.edu/ news/1996/PostTenRev.htm (accessed March 15, 2009).

[2] "University of Texas, with an eye on the Legislature, starts a system of post-tenure reviews," *Chronicle of Higher Education,* December 12, 1996.

[3] "Cunningham 'debates' tenure review plan," *The Daily Texan,* October 9, 1996.

[4] A complete account of the discussion, as well as documents presented by the regents, is on pages 33–60 of the official minutes of the meeting. Meeting no. 897, November 13–14, 1986, www.utsystem.edu/board-of-regents/meetings/meeting-archive.

[5] Homer P. Rainey was president of UT Austin from 1939 to 1944. He was fired by the board of regents after he fought against actions by the board that included a weakening of tenure rules and other attempts to challenge the academic freedom of the faculty. The board's actions resulted in the university being censured for nine years by the American Association of University Professors. Rapoport supported Rainey's unsuccessful campaign for governor in 1946. When Rapoport became chairman of the regents he led a decision to name a campus building for Rainey.

[6] "UT System—Letter from Bernard Rapoport," November 15, 1996. www.utsystem.edu/news/1996/BRapoport-Ltr11-15-96.htm (accessed March 15, 2009).

[7] "TeleCampus growth leads to Phase II study," UT System press release, February 16, 1999, Papers of William H. Cunningham.

[8] "TeleCampus Web link for distance learning program," *The Daily Texan,* May 12, 1998.

[9] "UT TeleCampus: A Special Report Presented to the Executive Officers of the University of Texas System," October 1999, page 1, Files of the UT TeleCampus, the University of Texas System.

[10] "UT System offers seven online master's degrees for fall 2000," UT System press release, March 24, 2000, Papers of William H. Cunningham.

[11] "Online campus plan evaluated," *The Shorthorn,* March 4, 1999, and "Engineering online masters degree planned," ibid., September 8, 1999.

[12] "UT TeleCampus open a door to the future—Knowledge Management, including digital library services," UT System press release, October 29, 1997, Papers of William H. Cunningham.

Chapter 30: The Freeport-McMoRan Controversy

[1] "Cunningham has no conflict of interest," *The Daily Texan,* December 4, 1995.

[2] "A professor's resignation: Social conscience vs. corporate predation," *The Texas Observer,* September 29, 1995.

[3] "Cunningham exercises FM options, earns $650,000," *Austin American-Statesman,* April 4, 1996, and "Opportunism unseemly," ibid., April 8, 1996. A wire service version of the news story also appeared in *The Dallas Morning News* and the *San Antonio Express-News.*

[4] "The Howler's Commitment," Papers of William H. Cunningham.

[5] "Moffett building name spurs protests," *The Daily Texan,* November 30, 1994.

[6] "Gypsum mountains offering hope," *The Times-Picayune,* April 19, 1994.

[7] "Virtue of links to UT questioned," *Austin American-Statesman,* September 3, 1991.

[8] The Grasberg mine was the largest gold mine in the world and by 1996 was said to be producing one-eighth of the world's copper.

[9] In September 1992, Moffett offered Collier a job as head of the company's public relations office. Collier notified the *American-Statesman* about the offer at once and told the newspaper he could not write about the company again until he made a decision about the job offer. He accepted the job in November 1992.

[10] The main articles in the series are "Freeport taps global controversy," September 1, 1991; "Freeport consultants say all's well," September 2, 1991; and "Freeport record on rights scrutinized," September 3, 1991.

[11] Both letters are also available online at www.utwatch.org/corporations/freeport-files/feld-resignation.html.

[12] "Groups battle Freeport at Cunningham's house," *The Daily Texan*, October 3, 1995.

[13] "Moffett protestors perform 'The Wizard of Oz' parody," ibid., September 12, 1995.

[14] "Freeport settles dispute on mine's risk insurance," *Austin American-Statesman*, April 20, 1996.

[15] "UT regents stand by Cunningham, Moffett," ibid., November 11, 1995.

[16] "Bishop confirms abuses in Indonesia," ibid., November 19, 1995.

[17] "An Open Letter to the University Community by Robert M. Berdahl," November 16, 1995, Papers of William H. Cunningham.

[18] "UT president stands by building-naming promise," *Austin American-Statesman*, November 17, 1995.

[19] "Freeport threatens action over charges," ibid., December 14, 1995.

[20] "Cunningham quits Freeport board," ibid., December 15, 1995.

[21] Papers of William H. Cunningham.

[22] "Cunningham quits Freeport board,"*Austin American-Statesman*, December 15, 1995.

[23] "Academic doings in Texas and Colorado," *Fort Worth Star-Telegram*, April 9, 1996, and "The Ivory Tower," *Fort Worth Star-Telegram*, April 11, 1996.

[24] "Berdahl asks faculty to stop debate over building's name," *Austin American-Statesman*, January 30, 1996.

[25] "Faculty opposes naming building for Moffetts," ibid., February 20, 1996.

[26] "Group says UT should keep name of building," ibid., March 6, 1996.

[27] "UT Faculty Council behaved like kangaroo court, ignored need for evidence in fight over Moffett's gift," *The Daily Texan*, March 1, 1996.

[28] I hope the reader will forgive my sarcasm.

Chapter 31: The Numbers Tell the Story

[1] Fiscal years for Texas state agencies run from September 1 through the next August 31, roughly the same as an academic year at Texas colleges and universities.

[2] The accounting for "charity care" charged to hospital and clinic operations is carried as "indigent care"; while the term used for charges for physician services is "charity care."

Chapter 32: Texas Higher Education: Looking Back and Looking Ahead

[1] "Statement by UT System Chancellor Cunningham on his retirement," UT System press release, June 10, 1999, Papers of William H. Cunningham.

[2] Lewis Gould, *Grand Old Party: A History of the Republicans* (New York: Random House, 2003).

[3] Presentation to Chancellor's Council Annual Meeting, William H. Cunningham, April 28, 2000, Papers of William H. Cunningham.

Index

Guckian, James, 396–398, 400, 402, 420–421
gunman, 94–95
Gutenberg Bible, 183
Gutierrez, Roberto, 398–399, 401
gymnasiums, 74–75, 147–148
gypsum, 432

H

Hackerman, Norman, 324–325
handicap access, 148
Hansen, Thomas C., 231
Harbin, John, 351
Hardy, Darcy, 415
Hardy, G. P., *138*
Hargis, John, 106
Harkin, Tom, 292
Harlingen, 401–405, *405*
Harris, Chris, 319
Harris, Gerry, 172
Harry Ransom Humanities Research Center, 160
Hay, Jess, *189*; as board chairman, 287, 324; budget crisis, 298–299, 304, 308–309; Clements and, 321–324; coalition for higher education, 320–321; divestment presentation from students, 89; Fonken as executive vice president, 44–45; football, 206; Higher Education Legislative PAC, 350–351; letter to alumni, 309; molecular biology program, 143–144; Permanent University Fund raid, 311–312, 312–313; Pforzheimer Library, *185*, 187; as political mentor, 294; tax increases, 309, 320, 321–322; WHC, 43–44, 242
"Hay Ride." *See* coalition for higher education
Haywood, Norcell, 104
Haywood, Tom, 226
hazing: alumni and, 56–57, 61; anithazing legislation, 65; antihazing leaflet, *59*; antihazing pledge, 58, 60; Commission on the Role of Fraternal Organizations, 65–66; death of Mark Seeberger, 61–65; fraternities, 57–58, 60–65; hospitalization of pledges, 60; penalties for, 57, 60–61, 64–65; Phi Kappa Psi, 61–65; sororities, 66, 480; tolerance of, 58
Hazlewood, Mel, 398
Head, Hayden, 184, 185, 187
Headliners Club, 320, 336
health care legislation, 289–293

health education institutions: expansion in Lower Rio Grande Valley, 395–405; growing demand for, 477; noninstructional budget elements, 455; state appropriations, 452–453; tuition revenue, 454–455
Heath, Mavis, 10
Heath, William, 9
Heery International, 247
Heflin, Talmadge, 392
Heman Sweatt Symposium on Civil Rights, 103–104
Henderson, Don, 420
Herring, Charles, 295
Hewlett, Lan, 201
Hicks, Thomas O. "Tom," *382*; football conference change, 237–238; football suites, 251; hiring Mack Brown, 217; *Houston Chronicle,* 386; Permanent University Fund, 388; political action committee, 352; as regent, 279; Royal-Memorial Stadium, 239, 240, 246, 252; UTIMCO, 381–387
Hidalgo-Starr Counties Medical Society, 400–402, 404
hierarchy of UT System, 278
Higginbotham, A. Leon, Jr., 104
higher education: challenges facing, 467–477; changes in financing of, 300, 457–458; coalition for (*see* coalition for higher education); demand for, 476–477, 480; economic development, 254–255, 263–266, 306–307, 324; economic impact of, 253, 265; funding of, 446–460; governors, 337–338, 349; Hobby plan, 254–255; legislative attitude toward, 408; mission of, 27, 55, 71; outcome-based funding, 474–475; public support for, 304–305; review of, 461–477; state appropriations for, 326–327, 329, 343; Texas commitment to, 467–468; tuition financing, 448–449; value of, 468, 476. *See* coalition for higher education
Higher Education Assistance Fund, 487
"The High Finance of Higher Education," 296–298
high school students, 98–100, 108, 480
high tech companies, 170
Hill, Forest, 12–13
Hillman, Hal, 351
Hinojosa, Juan "Chuy," 395, 398, 401
Hispanic Americans: recruitment and retention, 111–112, 133, 459; scholarships

Medical Services, Research, and Develop-
ment Programs/Physicians Referral
Service (MSRDP), 456
Medicare, 401
Médici, Emilio, 9
Mendelsohn, John, *363, 467*
men's athletics program, 207, 208,
218–219. *See also* athletics program
mentors, 6–7, 23–24, 294
Meredith, James S., 104
Merrill, L. Charles, 128
Metts, Harold, 192–193
Mexican American League Defense and
Educational Fund (MALDEF), 488
Mexican Americans. *See* Hispanic Ameri-
cans
Meyer, Tom Montague, 193
Meyers, Mike, 242
Michener, James A., *191*; art museum, 192,
193; Jack Taylor Professor Emeritus,
189; Lady Longhorns basketball, 220;
Ransom, 188–189; relationship with
UT Austin, 188–192; writers programs,
189–191
Michener, Mari, 189–192, *191, 193*
Michigan courts, 133
Michigan State University, 2–3, 5–7, 91
Microeelectronics and Computer Technol-
ogy Corporation (MCC), 253–254,
262–263, 266, 309
Microelectronics Research Center, 261
Middleton, Harry, 243–244
Milburn, Beryl, 351
Miller, Charles, 386, 420
Miller, Herb, 101
Mills, Peter, 258, 262
Millsap, Mike, *397*; budget crisis, 326;
coalition for higher education, 334, 341,
344–345; football conference changes,
231; Junnel and, 288; Permanent University Fund, 313, 389; political action
committee, 350, 351–352, 353, 362;
Proposition 17 campaign, 390–394;
RAHC, 396–398; Royal-Memorial Stadium, 245; South Texas/Border Initiative,
370, 371–373, 376; UTIMCO, 382; in
Washington D.C., 290; WHC's appointment as chancellor, 274; Wilson bill, 224
minorities, faculty: affirmative action,
113–114, 482; candidate shortage,
112–113, 115–116; faculty recruitment
and retention, 112–116; Recruitment
and Retention Committee, 115; Target

of Opportunity hiring program, 101,
114–115
minorities, students: admissions quotas,
136; affirmative action, 97–98, 482; athletics scholarships legislation, 222; bridge
program for, 100–101; and coalition
for higher education, 342; enrollment
of, 111–112, 138–139, 459; graduate
degrees awarded, 113; graduate students,
116; graduation rates, 112; high school
visits, *109*; *Hopwood v. Texas,* 138–139;
IBM, 101; improving access to higher
education, 477; outreach centers, 100,
107–108, *335, 366*; Provisional Admissions Program, 70; quality of student
life, 116–117; recruitment and retention,
96–112, 132–133; review of applicants,
79; scholarships, 99–100; summer program for, 105; in UT Law School, 133;
Wilson bill, 225
Minority Faculty Recruitment and Retention Committee, 115
minority-majority state, 138–139
minority outreach centers, 100, 107–108,
335, 366
mirrors, telescope, 153, 154
misconceptions and myths: about donor
privileges, 180; about Permanent University Fund, 179; among high school
counselors, 108; combating among
minorities, 106–107; of institutional racism, 101–102
mission of university, 28, 55, 71
Mitchell, George, 292
Mobley, William "Bill": as chancellor of
Texas A&M, 336; football conference
change, 229, 230–232, 234; relationship
with WHC, 335; at University Outreach
Center, *335, 366*
Moffett, James R. "Jim Bob," *339, 425*;
Barton Creek development, 431; donation to molecular biology building,
150–151, 427–428, 451, 457–458;
hiring Collier, 490; on lawsuit threat to
protesters, 440; molecular biology building, 150–151, 358, 423–424, 427–428,
431–432, 451, 457–458; political action
committee, 352; WHC's Freeport-
McMoRan board service, 424–425, 441,
442
Moffett, Louise: donation to molecular
biology building, 150–151, 427–428,
451, 457–458; molecular biology build-

The Woodlands, 36
Woodruff, Paul, 409
Woodson, Herbert, 164
World Wide Web, 413–414, 415. *See also*
distance learning
Worley, Butch, 216–217
Wrather, George, 203
Wrather, Jack, 203–204
Wright, Charles Alan, *134*; committee on
free speech rules, 87; Faculty Senate,
12; *Hopwood v. Texas*, 134; NCAA
rules, 214, 215–216; support for WHC's
presidency, 50
Wright, George, 80–81, 104, *105*
Wright, Jim, 261–262
Wright III, Lewis: assistant dean for finance,
34; Historically Underutilized Business
(HUBs), 464; minorities, 106–107, 114,
115; photograph of, *121*; working with
WHC, 276

writing, teaching of, 161–167

Y

Yarborough, Ralph, 285
Yudof, Mark, *328*; committee on free
speech rules, 87; committee on tenure
review policy, 409; graduate tuition bill,
327; Royal-Memorial Stadium, 250–251
Yzaguirre, Mario, *335*

Z

Zaffirini, Judith, 226, 340–341, 371, 404
Zambrano Yepes, Eduviges "Kena," 20–21,
21
Zambrano Yepes, Maria Dolores "Lola,"
21
Zambrano Yepes, Teresa "Chata," 20–21,
21
Zander, Matthew, 60